The First Am...
Afri....

Expanded and Revised

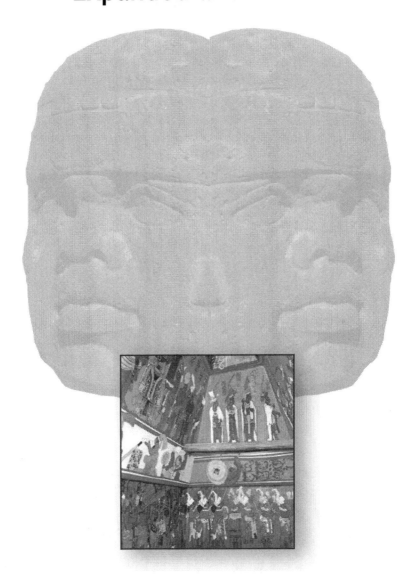

Second Edition
by David Imhotep, Ph.D.

© 2017, 2021 David Imhotep, Ph.D. All rights reserved.

Second Edition. This black-and-white edition is the newest published version of *The First Americans Were Africans: Expanded and Revised*; it is protected by the Intellectual Property Laws of the United States.

2021 Update: This book and the website(s) and social media sites associated with *The First Americans Were Africans: Revisited* contain copyrighted material, trademarks, and other proprietary information. You may not modify, publish, transmit, participate in the transfer or sale of, create derivative works of, or in any way exploit, in whole or in part, any proprietary or other material. No part of this document may be altered in any form whatsoever, electronic or mechanical—including photocopying, recording, or by any informational storage or retrieval system without express written, dated, and signed permission from the publisher.

ISBN: 978-1-7370745-0-2

Cover photo: The photo on the cover of this book comes from the Bonampak Murals, in a small building on top of a step pyramid in Chiapas, Mexico, next to Guatemala. The scenes inside it illustrate that the first Mayans were short statured, dark people. Interestingly enough, they wore African-styled, braided locks as seen on the back cover. They had some Black gods; for example, Ixtlilton, which in the Mayan language means, "The Little Black One." He was drawn a jet-black color and was the god of healing and medicine.

This book is printed on acid-free paper. More print information is available on the last page.

URLs: If any URL in this book does not work, Google the author's last name and title of the book or Google "archive.org," select the first entry, "Internet archive..." then type the URL into the window inside the block entitled, "Wayback Machine."

Because of the dynamic nature of the Internet, any Web addresses or links contained in this book may have changed since publication and may no longer be valid. The views expressed in this work are solely those of the author and do not necessarily reflect the views of the publisher, and the publisher hereby disclaims any responsibility for them.

Endorsements

"In *The First Americans Were Africans*, Dr. David Imhotep makes a passionate, *imaginative* and comprehensive case for a radical rewrite of orthodox history. I was provoked, entertained and intrigued by the book and many interesting possibilities that it opens up for consideration."

Graham Hancock
Author of *Fingerprints of the Gods*

"Dr. David Imhotep brings us the evidence that shows that Africans peopled the American continents before any other people. There are bound to be many people who will follow the lead of this pioneering scholar Dr. Imhotep. He puts into context much of the information that has been gathered over the years and makes it accessible to the ordinary reader, as well as to the scholarly reader. Imhotep's intent with this book is to burst onto the scene with a follow-up to the best of the works by Diop. Imhotep's work must be considered in the forefront of our new awareness of the great depth of African contributions to the world of science, art, and human beginnings on this very continent."

Molefi Asante, Ph.D.
Author of *The History of Africa*

"Dr. David Imhotep presents keen insight into the ancient history of America. You will discover the long antiquity of African people in the New World, and how they contributed to the rise of civilization in the West: the archaeological, linguistic and genetic evidence supports Dr. Imhotep's thesis of a pre-Columbus, African presence in America. It shows that David has opened a new path of scholarship relating to the peopling of the New World that is long overdue. Finally, we must conclude that multiple sources of evidence substantiate Dr. Imhotep's thesis that the first anatomically modern humans in the Americas may have come from Africa."

Clyde A. Winters, Ph.D.
Author of Afrocentrism: Myth or Science

"Imhotep's collection...the maps, photos, drawings and reports comparing the construction by Ohio Valley mound builders and New Mexican Pueblo cliff-dwellers to the Mandingo of Mali are thought-provoking. So are references drawn from Mexican Olmec legends of dark-skinned peoples arriving in bark-skin boats out of the sunrise. Imhotep's collection of evidence is not limited to comparing ruins. He delves into DNA links between peoples of Africa and the Americas and examines everything from pottery to plants to help prove his theory.

Are these and other points Imhotep makes enough to prove that Africans, and perhaps even Egyptians, explored, settled and traded across the South Atlantic? He presents a strong enough case to make the reader think it is packed with far too much evidence for the reader to ignore."

Clarion Review

GoodReads says: "Imhotep's evidence of African presence in America is simply overwhelming. Here is what the esteemed scholar, Molefi Asante says in the afterword: 'This book, *The First Americans Were Africans: Documented Evidence*, with its heavy references, is an answer that will allow others to read with confidence about the ancient record of African people in the Americas. It puts into context much of the information that has been gathered over the years, organizing it, ordering it in a manner that is accessible to the ordinary reader as well as to the scholarly reader.'

"We at Goodreads mostly agree with that assessment, and David Imhotep uses numerous methods to establish that the first Americans were indeed African people. Clearly, the 'Columbus "discovered" America' trope has been well debunked in numerous works, so the only mystery in mind, was who *were* the people who came to America first? Was it the so-called Indians or Native Americans? 'The American continent was inhabited by Asian and African blacks in very ancient times. The oldest skeletal remains found in the Americas are of blacks.'

"As Imhotep reminds us a few times in the book, science only requires eight coincidences to establish contact between two cultures. As you read the evidence of archaeology, linguistics, genetics, architecture and molecular science, there is only one conclusion reachable, the Americas were first peopled by Africans. As with all things of a historical nature it takes a bit of deductive and inductive reasoning to process the evidence into a logical conclusion. And that conclusion of African primacy, '*must therefore render any other possible conclusions to the contrary, as unscientific speculation or politically motivated at this point in time.*'"

Goodreads is the largest site for readers and book recommendations in the world.

Dedication

The Queens in *Stargate, The Mummy, 10,000 BC* and *Scorpion King*, are characters in fairy tales that paint negative and inaccurate pictures of ancient Nile Valley history and their people. The same is true of most of the movies of the American Wild West, where Native Americans are portrayed negatively. Despite all the evidence available, there are no accurate portrayals of the First Americans beyond depictions of slavery. *The First Americans Were Africans* paints a realistic picture of what actually took place during ancient times in the Western Hemisphere.

This is the second installment of the "Lifting the Veil Series" of books, with hopes that it will bring people together, rather than cause division. *The First Americans Were Africans* is dedicated to all souls searching for truth.

Acknowledgments

First and foremost, I would like to thank my wife, Teresa, my daughter, Laila and son, David, whose love and understanding made this book possible. I would like to thank Clyde A. Winters, Ph.D., for his masterful Foreword and extraordinary help with the contents of this book. I would like to thank Molefi K. Asante, Ph.D., for his profound and gracious "Afterword," and for introducing me to Dr. Winters. I would like to also thank Legrand Clegg Esq., for the help he gave. Thanks to Joanne Sprott for editing the new edition and Stephanie Abena Kaashe for her beautiful front cover design. Last, but not least, I would like to thank my very gifted artists, Marrwho Hasati, and Todd V. Williams.

Table of Contents

Chapter 7

Chapter 8

Illustrations

Foreword

Reflections

Did Africans Discover America? Yes, Indeed.

Dr. David Imhotep presents keen insight into the ancient history of America. In this book, he outlines the lost and stolen history of African people in ancient America. You will discover the long antiquity of African people in the New World and how they contributed to the rise of civilization in the West. "Most of us learned that people walked across a land bridge from Northeastern Asia to Alaska about 12,000 years ago."[1] Dr. Imhotep systemically destroys the notion that the Clovis culture represents the first American civilization.

Rather than begin his story of the African in America with the slave trade, Dr. Imhotep provides details about the first civilizations in the New World, which were created by Black and African people (Blacks are indirectly from Africa. Africans are directly from Africa). We know that the Beringia passage between Asia and North America was blocked by ice between 110,000–12,000 years ago. Archaeological evidence indicates that anatomically modern humans were living in South America between 30,000–15,000 years ago. We will learn that although the Ice Age was a barrier to man's overland migration to the New World, there were many Blacks here even before the ice melted.

Several peoples of African origin entered the Americas, including the San, Anu, or Negrito type and the Proto-Saharan variety of blacks. "Proto" means original or first and the Anu were the Pygmy people who, were hunter-gatherers in Africa.[2] Yet, it was they who founded the first civilization of Kush, Nubia and Egypt before the rise of the first Pharaoh, as well as the first civilization in Mesopotamia.

Today, archaeologists have found sites from Argentina to Chile that range in age between 45,000 and 50,000 years old. These sites are Pedra Furada (c. 45,000 B.C.) and Serra Da Capivara 50,000 years

1   Green, T. Can you dig it? (2005). Accessed: September 30, 2010 www.utexas.edu/features/2005/archeology/index.htm.

2   Winters, Clyde "Ancient African Writing Systems and Knowledge." (2010). Accessed: October 10, 2010 www.bafsudralam.blogspot.com/2010/03/paleo-africans-in-america.html.

ago. The fact that the earliest dates for habitation of the American continent occur below Canada, in South America, suggest that the earliest American settlers came from Africa before the ice melted at the Bering Strait and moved northward as the ice melted. This prehistoric African presence in the New World may explain the affinities between African languages and the Amerind family of languages.[3]

Yes, the American continent was inhabited by Asian and African Blacks in very ancient times. However, the oldest skeletal remains found in the Americas are of Blacks on the Eastern areas of the Americas. Marquez observed that, "it is good to report that long ago the youthful America was also a Negro continent... and, Lanning noted that "there was a possible movement of Negritos from Ecuador into the Piura Valley, North of Chicama and Viru' in early times."[4]

As stated above, these sites are Pedra Furada (c. 45,000 B.C.) and Serra Da Capivara, 50,000 years ago.[5] *Archaeologists originally dated the former from 48,000-10,000 years ago.*[6] *At Pedra Furada,*

3   Warwick, Bray. "The Paleoindian debate." Nature 332, March 10, 1988, p.107; "Man's New World Arrival Pushed Back," Chicago Tribune, May 9, 1991 Sec. 1A, p. 40; Allan Bryan, "Points of Order." Natural History Magazine, (June 1987) pp.7-11. http://hdl.handle. net/2246/6493.

4   Globe, Boston. "Man's New World Arrival Pushed Back" Chicago Tribune, May 9, 1991, Sec. 1A, p.40. Chicago, Ill. http://articles. chicagotribune. com/1991-05-09/news/9102110096_1_cave-of-numerous-stone-clay-fragment-south-america-show.

5   Marquez, C. (1956). "Estudios arqueologicas y ethnograficas." Mexico; Wiercinski, A. (1969). Affinidades raciales de algunas poblaiones antiquas de Mexico, Anales de INAH, 7a epoca, tomo II, 123-143; Wiercinski, A. (1972). An anthropological study on the origin of "Olmecs," Swiatowit, 33, 143-174; Wiercinski, A. (1972). "Inter- and Intrapopulational Racial Differentiation of Tlatilco, Cerro de."

6   Meltzer, David J., James M. Adovasio, and Tom D. Dillehay (1994) "On a Pleistocene human occupation at Pedra Furada, Brazil. *Antiquity* 68(261):695-714.; Parenti, Fabio, Michel Fontugue, and Claude Guerin. (1996) Pedra Furada in Brazil and its "presumed" evidence: limitations and potential of the available data. *Antiquity* 70:416-421; Santos, G. M. et al. (2003). A revised chronology of the lowest occupation layer of Pedra Furada Rockshelter, Piauí, Brazil: the Pleistocene peopling of the Americas. *Quaternary Science Reviews* 22 2303-2310.

Brazilian archaeologists have found cave paintings, hearths and deliberately flaked pebbles. Recent archaeological show evidence from...the Brazilian site of Boqueirao do Sitio da Pedra Furada with a long cultural sequence possibly extending as far back as 32,000 yr BP, and the Chilean site of Monte Verde. This latter site has one well-documented cultural episode radiocarbon dated at 13,000 yr BP and another possible one at 33,000 yr BP. There was mastodon hunting in Venezuela and Colombia (c. 13,000 years ago), and Dr. Walter Neves' discovery of a 12,000-year-old skeleton of an Africa.[7]

All of these are evidence of human occupation. Charcoal samples from the campsite age the site to 65,000 years ago.[8] The evidence shows the oldest skulls in the Americas do not add to the theory that the first peoples in the Americas entered from Asia in the west but from Africa in the east:

Several studies of craniofacial morphology showed that Paleoindians, who were the first settlers of the New World, clearly differ from modern Amerindians and East Asians, their supposed descendants and sister group, respectively.... These results give support to a model in which morphologically generalized groups of non-Northeast Asian descent (the so-called Paleoamericans) entered the continent first, and then dispersed from North to South America through Central America.[9]

The appearance of pebble tools at Monte Verde in Chile (c. 32,000 years ago), rock paintings at Pedra Furada in Brazil (c. 22,000 years ago), mastodon hunting in Venezuela and Colombia (c. 13,000 years ago), and Dr. Walter Neves' discovery of a 12,000-year-old skeleton of an African woman in Brazil, adds credence to the idea that the Americas were first settled from South America instead of from North America at Clovis. Archaeologist C. Vance Haynes noted:

If people have been in South America for over 30,000 years, or even 20,000 years, why are there so few sites? Perhaps inhabitants were so

---

7   Valladas, H., et al. (2003) "TL age-estimates of burnt quartz pebbles from the Toca do Boqueirão da Pedra Furada" (Piaui, Northeastern Brazil). *Quaternary Science Reviews* 22 (10-13): 1257-1263.

8   Parenti, and Tom D. Dillehay; Collins, Michael B. (2008). "Early Cultural Evidence from Monte Verde in Chile." Accessed March 2014 from http://adsabs.harvard.edu/abs/1988Natur.332.150D. p. 417.

9   Valladas, H. et al., burnt quartz pebbles.

few in number, or perhaps, South America was initially populated from directions other than north until Clovis appeared.[10]

P. S. Martin and R. G. Klein, after discussing the evidence of mastodon hunting in Venezuela 13,000 years ago, observed:

The thought that the fossil record of South America is much richer in evidence of early archaeological associations than many believed is indeed provocative. Have the earliest hunters been overlooked in North America? Or did the hunters somehow reach South America first?[11]

Colonel Alexander Braghine, White officer, said that Mr. Ernesto Franco in Quito Ecquador found a statuette—that, according to archaeologists, was at least 20,000 years or older—of a Negro. Franco went on to say that back then, "Negroes were numerous in the New World."

Dr. Imhotep also fills us in on the medieval African navigators who explored the Americas, especially the expedition of Abubakari II, Emperor of the ancient Mali Empire. He provides a detailed discussion of the watercraft, culture and intellectual gifts that they gave the various American Indian groups they encountered in the New World.

Dr. Imhotep also puts to rest the notion that Norsemen and Celtic mariners visited America before Columbus. He is especially wary of the data provided by Dr. Fell in his book *America BC*, offered in support of this hypothesis. Controversy surrounds the influence of ancient Europeans in the Americas. Some researchers claim that the Vikings and Celts settled America before Africans. The leading proponent of this theory was, again, Dr. Fell.

In his two books, *Saga America* and *America BC*, Dr. Fell argues this theory. He believes that these Europeans had colonies in the Northeast and Southwest part of the United States. In support of this theory Dr. Fell has published a number of inscriptions, which he claims were made by these early Europeans. The only problem with this theory is that the ancient Celts and first Vikings were Black people, and the inscriptions he claims

---

10   Gonzalez-Jose, R. et al. "Late Pleistocene/Holocene Craniofacial Morphology in Mesoamerican Paleoindians: Implications for the Peopling of the New World." *American Journal of Physical Anthropolgy* (2005) 128:772-780

11   Haynes, Jr. C. V. "Geofacts and Fancy." *Natural History Magazine*, (February 1988) pp.4-12:12. http://hdl.handle.net/2246/6494.

were written by Europeans were really written by Mande (A.K.A. Malinke or Mandingo)-speaking people from Mali who settled many parts of the Americas after 1300 A.D. Yes, the Celts were originally Black people too. In reviewing Winters' Foreword in this book, the ancient Greek historian, Ephorus (c. 405 B.C.), claimed that the Celts were Blacks or Ethiopians.[12] Tacitus, an ancient Roman historian, wrote about the Celts and the Picts being Black back in 80 A.D.

> *The Celts on the mainland of Europe were called Iberians or Silures. Iberia is the ancient name for Spain. Although the original Celts were Black, over time their name was stolen by Europeans. Father O'Growney has discussed the history of the Celts. He makes it clear that the original Celts were the Iberians. The Iberians were probably conquered by the Ligurians. Liguria was a coastal region of northwestern Italy. It is suggested that the Ligurians may be represented by the modern Basques of Spain.[13]*

The Ligurians took the name Celt. The Ligurians/Celts were conquered by the Gaulish-speaking people. Ancient Gaul was considered to be modern France, Belgium, the southern Netherlands, southwestern Germany, and northern Italy. The Gauls conquered the Ligurians and pushed them into Spain. It was these Gauls who imposed their language on the Iberian and Ligurian Celts.

The Gauls were Belgians, according to Father O'Growney. The Irish and Welsh are descendants of these Gauls. These Gauls spoke Gaulish or Gaelic.[14] The Germans conquered the Gaulish-Celts, and Gaulish disappeared around the 4th century A.D. All of the Black Celts in Britain were not erased by the Gauls, however. This is supported by evidence of the Ivory Lady of York, England. The reconstruction of the face of the Ivory Bangle Lady (c. 350 A.D.) indicates that she was African or Black. She was a wealthy woman whose features were indicative of the African type common to the British Isles at that time.

> *There is genetic and linguistic evidence that proves that the Celts were* ___*Black or African* *people. An examination of the language spoken by*

12   Ruhlen, M. "Voices from the Past." Natural History Magazine, March 1987, pp.6-10:10 http://hdl.handle.net/2246/6493; Joseph H. Greenberg, Language in the Americas. Stanford: Stanford University Press, 1987.

13   Haynes, Jr. C. V. "Geofacts and Fancy." pp. 4-12.

14   Ibid.

the Basque indicates a Niger-Congo substratum (underlying layer). Dr. C. J. K. Campbell-Dunn has found a Niger-Congo substratum in the Basque.[15]

He found Congo and Basque languages share personal pronouns, numerals and certain vocabulary.

There is also genetic evidence linking the Basque and Niger-Congo speakers.[A] (The super-script "A" means see Section Note "A" at the end of this chapter). The evidence suggests that both groups had this same genetic ancestry. This linguistic and genetic evidence supports the African origin of the Celts.

The original Danes or Vikings were Blacks.[16] This is made clear in the depiction of the Oseberg 8th-century Vikings on the Norway Sleigh carving of the Black seafarers that populated the region at this time. It is clear from this carving that the 8th-century Vikings were different from the blond, big-bodied folk of Viking legends. Given the fact that the first Celts and Vikings were Black, makes it clear that even if these people did reach the New World during the Middle Ages, they were not Europeans. But the proof that the first people to settle the Americas were Africans comes from surviving inscriptions.

The inscriptions deciphered by Dr. Fell in his work were not written in the Old Norse language as he claimed. These inscriptions were written by the followers of Abubakari the Great. He was a ruler of the ancient Mali Empire who made an expedition to the Americas in early 1300. Members of the Mali expedition left numerous inscriptions throughout the New World. Evidence shows that they wrote in the Manding writing system, which is understood by using the (African) Vai script to read the Mande inscriptions the Malians left in the Americas.[17]

I deciphered the Malian inscriptions in 1977. This article was published a year before Dr. Fell published America BC. In this article inscriptions were presented from the Americas including Brazil and the American Southwest. In 1979, I published additional inscriptions from the Southwestern part of the United States and Northeastern United States. These inscriptions came from the mound cultures,

15 Ibid.

16 Ibid.

17 Ibid.

Pueblo Culture, Nevada, Tennessee, New Mexico and the desert region.

There is additional ideographic evidence supporting the Malian presence the American Southwest. In Venezuela and the Adena culture we find mound cultures similar to the Mande mound cultures of ancient Mali, including a clay core and wooden house over the corpse.[18]

In the American Southwest, there are many signs related to the Malian expedition. These include the Kangaba sign, which indicates Mande settlement and the Vai symbol Nu, which represents "habitation" in the Mande languages. Mande habitation signs are prominent in the Anasazi region and the Painted Desert Petrified Forest National Park.

The most interesting Malian artifact from the Southwest is the Elephant Slabs. These remains, which came to the Arizona State Museum in 1950, were found at the Animas River near New Mexico. This Malian inscription depicts elephants and birds on the tablet in addition to Mande signs.

It now should be clear that the so-called epigraphic evidence of Vikings and Celts in the New World has nothing to do with a European colonization of the United States. The inscriptions deciphered by Fell relate to the Malian expedition to the Americas—not Celts or Vikings. Moreover, if there were Vikings and Celts in the Americas before Columbus, they were Black/African people, not European.

There is also genetic evidence that may allow us to recognize the possibility that Africans previously lived in the Americas before the Atlantic slave trade. Genomic evidence indicates that the Amerind genes[B] are descended from African females before they migrated out of Africa forty thousand years ago.[C&D]

We have been led to believe that Bantu mtDNA has been found among the Maya due to the slave trade. Although this is one view, the molecular evidence indicates that researchers have found L1, L2 & L3 clusters among many Mexicans, including the Cora, Mixtec and

---

18   Ibid.

Zapotecs.[19] Underhill et al., found African Y chromosomes among Mayan Indians. Many of these Native Americans (Amerinds) were isolated from African slaves.[20]

It appears that the Mayans inherited African chromosomes from earlier African immigrants. Amerinds and Europeans chromosomes are different. Amerind, European, and African chromosomes all differ from each other and can be separately identified by scientists. Amerind skeletons from Brazil dating between 400 and 7000 years ago have African chromosomes. This further suggests that Africans may have taken certain chromosomes to the Americas in ancient times.[E]

Guthrie found that the V-antigen of the Rhesus system is an indication of African ancestry. It has been found among Indians in Belize and Mexico, centers of Mayan civilization, thus, identifying their African ancestry. Dr. Guthrie also noted that A*28, common among Africans, has high frequencies among Eastern Maya.[21] In addition, Dr. Guthrie reported that six Mayan groups show the B Allele of the ABO system that is of African origin.

The Dafuna canoe found in Nigeria, dating before 12,000 years ago, indicates that Africans had the naval technology that would have allowed them to make a long-distance sea voyage. In addition, there are Negro skeletons found throughout the Americas dating before Columbus.[22] Amerind tribes, such as the Cora, were never in contact

---

19   Gonzalez-Oliver, Angelica et al. "Founding Amerindian Mitochondrial DNA lineages in ancient Maya from Xcaret,Quintana Roo." *American Journal of Physical Anthropology*, 116 (3) (2001):230-235. Accessed February 9, 2006. http://www3.interscience.wiley.com/cgibin/abstract/85515362/ABSTRACT?CRETRY=1; Green, L. D., "Mitochondrial DNA affinities of the people of North Central Mexico," *American Journal of Human Genetics*, (2000), 66:989-998.; Reidla, M. et al. "Origin and Diffusion of mtDNA Haplogroup X. *Am J Hum Genet*. 2003 November; 73(5): 1178-1190.

20   Underhill, P. A., L. Jin, R. Zemans, J. Oefner, J, and Luigi L. Cavalli-Sforza. "A Pre-Columbian Y Chromosome-Specific Transition and Its Implications for Human Evolutionary History." *Proceedings of the National Academy of Sciences of the United States of America* 93.1 (1996): 196–200. Print.

21   Underhill, P. A. et al., "Pre-Columbian Y Chromosome-Specific Transition." pp. 196-200.

22   Marquez, C. "Estudios arqueologicas y ethnograficas." pp. 123-143.

with Africans,[23] and a Mandekan substratum exists in the Mayan and Otomi languages, suggesting an African presence in the early Americas.[24]

In conclusion, the archaeological, linguistic and genetic evidence supports Dr. Imhotep's thesis of a pre-Columbus African presence in America. It shows that Dr. Imhotep has opened a new path of scholarship relating to the peopling of the New World that is long overdue. Finally, we must conclude that multiple sources of evidence, including molecular evidence,[F] linguistic evidence and naval technology of Africans 12–20,000 years ago, substantiate Dr. Imhotep's thesis *that the first anatomically modern humans in the Americas may have come from Africa.*

Clyde A. Winters, Ph.D.

Section Notes

A. There is also genetic evidence linking the Basque and Niger-Congo speakers. SRY10831.1, YAP, M2, M173(xR1a,R1b3), E3*-P2, E3b2-M81.[25]

B. Amerind Haplogroups (hg) are descendant from the L3(M, N, & X) macrohaplogroup): ABCDN and X. In other words, American Indians' genes are descended from Africans.

C. Amerindian Haplogroup L3 is recognized as one of the original haplogroups carried by females in Africa, before amh anatomical modern humans migrated out of Africa 40 thousand years ago (40kya).

D. The L3 (M,N,X) Macro=haplogroup converge at np 16223.[26] This is another gene that suggests that Africans may have taken and spread to the Americas in ancient times.

23   Lisker, R., Ramírez, E. Babinsky, V. (1996). "Genetic Structure of Autochthonous Populations of Meso-america: Mexico." *Am. J. Hum Biol* 68:395-404.

24   Winters, Clyde. (2008). "Malinke-Bambara Loan Words in the Mayan Languages." Accessed 11/13/2008.

25   Haynes, Jr. C. V. "Geofacts and Fancy." *Natural History Magazine,* (February 1988) pp.4-12:12. http://hdl.handle.net/2246/6494.

26   Haynes, Jr. C. V. "Geofacts and Fancy." *Natural History Magazine,* (February 1988) pp.4-12:12. http://hdl.handle.net/2246/6494.

E. Amerinds also carry the X hg. Amerinds and Europeans hg X are different.[27] Haplogroup X has been found throughout Africa.[28] Shim Shimada, et.al., believes that X(hX) is of African origin.[29] Although Amerind X is different from European hg X, skeletons from Br Fuegians dating between 400-7000 years ago have the transition np 16223. This suggest that Africans may have taken this hg to the Americas in ancient times. Guthrie found that the V antigen of the Rhesus system, considered an indication of African ancestry, among Indians in Belize and Mexico centers of Mayan civilization.[30]

F. Molecular evidence should include the np transition 16223 in hg X. This suggest that Africans may have taken the X hg to the Americas in ancient times. See more at: *http://www.exposingblacktruth.org/genetic-structure-blacks-in-ancient-mesoamerica/-sthash.hqDPzA7J.dpuf.*

27   Brooke Persons (2004). "Genetic Analysis and the Peopling of the New World" ANT 570, http://anthropology.ua.edu/bindon/ant570/ Papers/ Persons.pdf.

28   Makoto K. Shimada,* Karuna Panchapakesan, Sarah A. Tishkoff, Alejandro Q. Nato, Jr* and Jody Hey. (2007). "Divergent Haplotypes and Human History as Revealed in a Worldwide Survey of X-Linked DNA Sequence Variation, Molecular Biology and Evolution" 24(3):687-698.

29   Martinez-Cruzado, J. C., G. Toro-Labrador, V. Ho-Fung, M. A. Estevez-Montero et al. (2001). "Mitochondrial DNA analysis reveals substantial Native American ancestry in Puerto Rico, Human Biology"; and Ribeiro-Dos-Santos, A. K. C, S. E. B. Santos, and A. L. Machado et al. 1996. "Heterogeneity of mitochondrial DNA haplotypes in pre-Columbus natives of the Amazon region." *Am. J. Phys. Anthropol.* 101:29-37.

30   Guthrie, James L. "Human Lymphocyte Antigens: Apparent Afro-Asiatic, Southern Asian and European HLAs in Indigenous American Populations." Accessed March 3, 2006. http://www. neara.org/Guthrie/ lymphocyteantigens02.htm.

Introduction

The ancient Piri Re'is Map is probably the oldest map known to man. This map had to have been drawn before the last Ice Age ended. During that Ice Age, much more of the lands in the Northern and Southern latitudes were covered by ice, which means there was less water in the oceans. The water had been sucked up on to the North and South poles and the latitudes around then because of the extreme temperatures during the Ice Age. When the ice levels rose, the ocean and sea levels dropped. With less water in the oceans, more land there was exposed and visible for all eyes to see. One of those places was the ancient peninsula running between South America and connecting to, as shown on the Piri Re'is Map. This was also the exact same period that there was a glacial land bridge connecting Asia to modern-day Alaska.

So, people began to build on this newfound land. After 100,000 years or more, the planet took a turn for warmer temperatures—and just like what is happening to the world today—the ice began to melt and flooded the lower areas where they built. This cycle is happening today as one can see with global warming. This evidence can be found on ancient maps.

Many other old maps have also been found.

This is not the place to consider the implications of large numbers of ancient maps that have been found, drawn up before the eighteenth century and based on copies of even older maps, which display almost perfect longitudes. As has been shown elsewhere, such maps could be the legacy of a race of seafarers in remote prehistory—a lost advanced civilization that measured the globe and surrounded it with a net of geodetic co-ordinates more than 12,000 years ago.[31]

If the date of "*the net of geodetic coordinates more than 12,000 years ago,*" is correct, then these "*seafarers*" would have had to be Africans. Why is this? Because Africans were the only people on the planet Earth during that time period.

In his book, *Fingerprints of the Gods,* Graham Hancock used the ancient map as evidence for the possibility of:

---

31   Hancock, Graham, and Santha Faiia. Heaven's Mirror (New York, Three Rivers Press, 1998), p. 119.

A yet unidentified civilization of remote antiquity, but also startling evidence of its vast sophistication, technological advancement and evolved scientific knowledge.[32] There had indeed been an ancient lost super-civilization destroyed 12,000 years ago.[33]

In his *Maps of the Ancient Sea Kings*, Charles Hapgood produces concrete evidence of an advanced world-wide civilization many thousands of years before Egypt:

[It] looks as if these people had visited most of the Earth (p. 182). There is evidence that these people must have lived when the Ice Age had not yet ended in the Northern Hemisphere and when Alaska was still connected with Siberia Asia by the Pleistocene Ice Age "Land Bridge."[34]

And now, Dr. David Imhotep goes a little further and deeper, uncovering an intensified version of Hancock and Hapgood's vision; while adding...a little more, with a little less conversation:

Once upon a time, in the Golden Age of Zep Tepi, before the Ice Age there was a:

Peaceful/Ancient-African/Antediluvian/World-Wide/ Maritime/Megalithic/Mercantile/Super Civilization

This means that they were not a people prone to warfare, but a peaceful, ancient African civilization; one that existed long *before* the old catastrophic flood, that took place all over the world and ended Zep Tepi. They traveled the world by ship and built structures with very large blocks. When they reached a foreign land, they were peaceful; they partnered and traded with the indigenous people who were already there.

A perfect example would be the Olmecs, who began as three different peoples:

1. Unmixed indigenous Black Africans
2. Manding

---

32 Hancock, Graham. *Fingerprints of the Gods* (New York, Crown Trade Paperbacks, 1995), back cover.

33 Hancock, Graham. 2015. BBC Horizon: "Atlantis Uncovered and Atlantis Reborn, 28 October & 4 November 1999. www.graham-hancock.com/horizon_ script_2/.

34 Hapgood, Charles. *Maps of the Ancient Sea Kings* (Illinois, Adventures Unlimited, 1996), pp. 142, 182.

3. Africans who had mixed with the Asian-Mongolians, creating the "so-called" Native Americans

This new, three-group coalition, probably built "The Mother Civilization" in Central America, containing large temples and pyramids built with megalithic blocks.

Lastly, they built a mercantile international trading network with the distant Black folks across the Atlantic and Pacific Oceans, creating a connecting "Super-Civilization" around the globe. This pre-flood era is called the "Golden Age of Zep Tepi":

The Vedas of India identified it as the perfect time or the Golden Age of Humanity. Here we have the physical, archaeological and astro-ceremonial evidence to identify that the ancients themselves placed to identify that golden age in the epoch around 12,000 B.C.[35]

The Africans in the Americas were part of the "Primeval Nubian Techno-Complex of Zep Tepi." This Golden Age of the Nubian, Twa and Anu also has to be dated back:

Sometime between 21,000 B.C. and well before 4,000 B.C.... This is the first site to be carbon dated, and to a time long before the last Ice Age ended, strongly indicating that, contrary to standard academic theory, a highly developed pre-Ice Age culture once lived off the coast of the Bahamas and operated throughout the region.[36]

So, the age of Zep Tepi existed long before the Ice Age began. Why did it ever end? It was the Ice Age's catastrophic, devastating fire and flood that sadly ended this "Splendid Golden Age." Where did this Zep Tepi civilization begin? Let us narrow this area down somewhat and see which region of the world Zep Tepi most likely began.

It probably began where the first people and the first civilizations began, which would logically be somewhere in the Nile Valley. There are three pyramids on the sacred Egyptian Giza grounds, Khufu, Khafre and Menkaure. These pyramids are extremely ancient, and over the years have been known by different names. The most northern pyramid is the largest, the Great Pyramid. The third and smallest pyramid at the most southern

---

35   Bauval, Richard, and Thomas Brophy. *Black Genesis: The Prehistoric Origins of Ancient Egypt* (Vermont, Bear & Company, 2011), p. 299.

36   Little, Gregory. "Man-Made Bahamas Structure Dated To Before The Ice Age." *Atlantis Rising*, #90, 2011, p. 10.

point is that of Menkaure. The middle, or second pyramid is known as Khafre, Chefren, or Gebel Gibli. In this example we call the Second Pyramid Gebel Gibli.

An arc is part of a circle shaped like the letter "C." If an arc is drawn across the tops of the three Giza pyramids, a line can be drawn from the top of the middle pyramid to the center of the circle. "When the center of this circle is plotted on a map we find that it falls approximately 1.73 miles southeast of the Second Pyramid.... "[37] This is where the village of Kafr el-Gebel is located:

> Two-thirds of a mile south of the village of Kafr el-Gebel... is Gebel Gibli, which is a prominent rocky eminence located several hundred meters due south of the Great Sphinx. The Dream Stela of Thutmose IV between the paws of the Sphinx alludes to somewhere nearby called "the Splendid Place of the First Time (Zep Tepi)," and a good argument can be made to demonstrate that this is a reference to Gebel Gibli in its role as a primeval mound.... Indeed, one local name for Gebel Gibli is Tarfiye, which is interpreted as meaning the "first place," or the "place of beginning."[38]

Here, according to the example above, we have possibly located "the place of beginning" where Zep Tepi was located.

Let us take this a little bit further. We have now pinpointed the place where Zep Tepi probably occurred: "The Pyramid Texts place the dramatic event of creation and Zep Tepi at Heliopolis."[39] "Heliopolis is the Greek name for the Egyptian city of 'On.'"[40] Ezekiel made a play on the Hebrew word for Heliopolis at the time of Joseph, as the city of On. Today, this city of On is at the northeast boundary of Cairo close to the Giza plateau where the three pyramids now rest.

---

37   Collins, Andrew. 2017. "Giza's Cosmic Blueprint." http://www.andrew-collins.com/page/articles/cygnus_blueprint.htm.

38   Ibid.

39   Bauval, Robert. *The Egypt Code* (United Kingdom, Century, 2006), p. 182.

40   Tompsett, Daniel. (2014). "Heliopolis: A City of Two Tales." Last modified 2014. http://www.vision.org/visionmedia/history-ancient-egypt/77175.aspx.

According to Bauval and the Pyramid Texts, we now know where the Splendid Place of Zep Tepi occurred and when it ended, which was during the cataclysm causing the great flood which occurred around 11,000 B.C. During Zep Tepi we find:

An increasing number of historical and archaeological finds made around the world have been classified as "out-of-place artifacts" (ooparts). They have been called this because they appear unexpectedly among the ruins of the past with no evidence of a preceding period of development, their technological sophistication seems far beyond the capabilities of ancient peoples because they predated the civilizations that followed. Drawing on the literature and art of the Egyptians Chaldeans, Sumerians, Babylonians and others who actually were able to witness these ooparts, Rene Noorbergen's contention is that a superior race of man was responsible for these scientific marvels that bear testimony to a civilization with technology comparable to our own.[41]

One of the most solid ways to measure hard evidence is to use artifacts. The smaller ones are a little harder to measure. The larger and the more undisturbed they are the better evidence becomes. No pieces of evidence are larger than pyramids. Further, pyramids of stone fare far better when they are under water. Those artifacts that have been exposed to wind, rain, hot sun or snow wear and become weathered. The pyramids under water did not suffer the conditions just mentioned. They were wrapped and encased in water on all sides and always fared better than those that were exposed to the conditions just mentioned.

These monuments last as long as the mountains they are cut out of. Some of them have lasted since the time of Zep Tepi 100,000 or more years ago. As will be repeated in this work: No Asians, Caucasians, nor Red Indians built pyramids...only Black Africans. That is not to say they were any better...just first.

Let us now look at these extremely ancient sunken cities and pyramids. If they are under water, they were built before the Ice Age began 115,000 years ago, and whose ice subsequently melted and covered these areas:

---

41   Noorbergen, Rene. (2001). *Secrets of the Lost Races* (New York, TEACH Services Inc.), p. 206.

5 Cities Now Under Water:

(These http messages taken from the index and displayed throughout this document like the one below are meant for reader's convenience where necessary)

- Port Royal, Jamaica
- Yonaguni-Jima, and Step Japan Pyramid
- Dwarka, Gulf of Cambay
- Lion City of Quiandeo Lake, China
- Cleopatra's Palace, Alexandria, Egypt

http://earthporm.com/5-mind-blowing-underwater-cities/

Underwater Pyramids Around the World:

- Two are next to New Providence Island, Bahamas
  24°56'26.50"N 77°19'39.35"W
  https://www.ancient-code.com/a-set-of-mysterious-pyramids-have-been-spotted-on-the-ocean-floor/
- Azores of Portugal Pyramid (in the middle of the Atlantic Ocean
  https://www.azores-pyramid.org
- Pyramid City 3.5 miles off the Southwestern coast of Cuba
  http://www.andrewcollins.com/page/articles/lostcity.htm
- Bimini between Andros Island and the Berry Islands, approximately 100 miles from Bimini near the Tongue of the Ocean between Bimini and Andros, where they found and filmed a pyramid and building ruins with Egyptian-like fluted columns lying in the sand.
  https://www.trinfinity8.com/underwater-crystal-pyramids-of-the-world/
- Pyramid in the ocean off Cozumel, Mexico
  12°8'1.5"N, 119°35'26.4"W
  https://www.ancient-code.com/pyramid-discovered-off-coast-mexico/
- Underwater Chinese Pyramid 40 miles southwest of Xian, was constructed during the Hsia Dynasty between the years 2205 and 1767 B.C.
  http://kurnetshem.blogspot.com/2012/04/mysterious-underwater-pyramid.html

Chichen Itza was just named as one of the seven wonders of the world. Every visitor to the Yucatan should see this impressive site. Tulum is smaller, and is much closer (45 minutes vs. 2.5 hours) and has a breathtaking clifftop setting overlooking the Caribbean Sea. Coba is the largest site but is only partially restored. It is the only pyramid that you can still climb of the three there.

https://www.nationalgeographic.com/travel/world-heritage/chichen-itza/

Central and South America: Mexican pyramid of Cholula & Teotihuacan Caral Pyramid in Peru, Brazil, and one on the Nazca plain in Santa Catarina where most of the Brazilian pyramids have been discovered.

https://www.history.com/topics/ancient-history/pyramids-in-latin-america

Guatemala's two dozen Pyramids, including that of Takal.

https://www.livescience.com/23479-tikal-mayan-civilization.html

Mesopotamia had pyramids called Zigurats.

European pyramids in Bosnia.

https://www.smithsonianmag.com/history/the-mystery-of-bosnias-ancient-pyramids-148990462/

Pyramids in Italy, France, Egypt, Nubia, Mali.

https://eden-saga.com/en/pyramids-europe-africa-civilisation-of-pyramids.html

Recently, a 200,000-year-old city was found in South Africa.

https://sladisworld.wordpress.com/2016/05/11/the-remains-of-a-200000-year-old-advanced-civilization-found-in-africa/

China's Pyramids:

- Inner Mongolian pyramid (1 kilometer north of Sijiazi Town, Aohan County)
- Pyramid of Gathering (Tibet)
- Qin Shi Huang's Mausoleum Pyramid
- Zangkunchong Pyramid Step Pyramid (Ziban)
- Pyramid at Qin Chuan Plains in Shaanxi Province, Central China
  https://gbtimes.com/mystery-behind-chinas-giant-pyramid-hills
- The Pyramids of the Lizzie Ladder in Hong Kong 兹班階梯金字塔
- Pyramids in Asia in Ur & Iraq: A Google search on this phrase will bring up interesting results.
- Step pyramid found at bottom of China's Lake Fusyan (in the south-western Yunnan Province).
  http://kurnetshem.blogspot.com/2012/04/mysterious-underwater-pyramid.html

As you can see, pyramids have been built all over the world. Today some are on land, but most of the oldest of them are now under water. They are the most interesting because their ages cannot be fudged. Why? Because these structures could only have been built during the age of Zep Tepi which was before the last Ice Age melted and flooded all of these pyramid sites. Again, this period was well before the Caucasians, Asians or Red Indians existed; hence, these three groups could not have built these civilizations, for they did not exist yet as part of the human family. The only logical conclusion as to who built them, rests on people from "The Mother Land," that are now called Africans.

So, who were these people of Zep Tepi? The renowned British historian Godfrey Higgens, in 1836 wrote:

We have found the Black complexion or something relating close to it whenever we have approached the origin of nations.... In short, all the...deities were Black. They remained as they were first, in very ancient times.[42]

More clearly identified, John Denison Baldwin says, in his *Pre-Historic Nations*:

The Cushite race appeared first in the work of civilization. That this has not been distinctly perceived, is due chiefly to the fact that the first grand ages of that race are so distant from us in time, so far beyond the great nations of antiquity commonly mentioned in our histories, that their most indelible time to be really comprehended by superficial observation.[43]

To explain where these Cushites began, Baldwin says:

In Eastern Africa, the civilizers proceed from the south towards the Mediterranean, creating the countries in the Valley of the Nile. The traditions of inner Asia bring civilization from the south, and connect its origin with the shores of the Erythraean Sea, meaning the Arabian shores of the Indian Ocean and Persian Gulf; and these traditions are confirmed by the inscriptions found in the old ruins of Chaldea. These inscriptions reveal also the fact that these first civilizers were neither Semites nor Aryans, but a "third race," which ethnic and linguistic investigation have been slow to recognize.[44]

---

42   Higgens, Godfrey. (1883). *Anacalypsis: An Attempt to Draw Aside the Veil of The Saitic Isis*. Vol. 1 and 2. (London, Longman, Rees, Orme, Brown, Green, and Longman, Paternoster Row).

43   Baldwin, John. D. (1869). *Pre-Historic Nations: or Inquiries Concerning Some of the Great Peoples and Civilizations of Antiquity, and their Probable Relation to a still Older Civilization of the Ethiopian or Cushites of Arabia.* (New York, Harper & Brothers, 1869), p. 17.

44   Ibid.

It is curious to note that while Baldwin precisely identifies these "civilizers," who were "first in the work of civilization" in his earlier passage as Cushites, he does not mention them as the "third race." In Baldwin's defense, he was on the right track, but much more has been discovered since he wrote this piece in 1869. The knowledge about Zep Tepi is one great example of our history that is never mentioned in American history, and most other areas of the world.

There have been many others who have no excuse for deliberately ignoring or even changing the historic story. Writing the historic truth is a sacred task. Let us see what a Dogon priest had to say on this subject. Naba Lamoussa Morodenibig was a Dogon priest from a small African country directly south of Mali called Burkina Faso. He unequivocally states that much of history has been re-written or purposely not mentioned to support European cultural imperialism. In his book he states:

> *My intention in this book is not to rejuvenate the interracial polemic attack but only to bring a healing to all people while daring to attack those individuals really responsible for the lies the individuals who think they gain by pitting one group of people against another. One cannot build the future of humanity by denying some people's facts about their place in history. The truth frees us.*[45]

Similarly, the intentions for this work are exactly the same as Master Naba Lamoussa Morodenibig. My interest in this subject began when I was in primary school. We were taught that Columbus discovered America and came in contact with "Native Americans." Years later, school officials admitted that the Indians were really the first Americans not Columbus.

According to a Washington Post article by Peter Gibbon on October 12, 1998, "Columbus did not discover America."[46] Further, it is also the contention of this book that the people popularly portrayed as, "Native Americans"—The Red Man—were not the first Americans either! The

---

45 Morodenibig, Naba. (2008). *Philosophy Podium*. (Chicago, Firefly Productions), p. 97.

46 Gibbon, Peter. "Apologize for Columbus?" *The Washington Post*, October 12, 1998. www.washingtonpost.com/archive/opinions/1998/10/12/apologize-for-columbus/.

evidence presented in this book will change the way history is written about the Western Hemisphere and beyond, by emphasizing the facts derived by hard evidence.

The first item is that Columbus did not discover America:

During four separate trips that started with the one in 1492, Columbus landed on various Caribbean islands that are now the Bahamas as well as the island later known as Hispaniola. He also explored the Central and South American coasts. But he did not reach North America, which of course was already inhabited by Native Americans, and he never thought he had found a new continent.[47]

I remember beginning my study of the discovery of America when I was in primary school. Our teacher repeated over and over that Columbus discovered America in 1492. In our textbook, there was a picture of Christopher Columbus standing on the beach with the Spanish flag that he had just planted into the sand. His men stood around him, and their three ships, the Nina, the Pinta and the Santa Maria, were anchored just offshore in the blue waters of the Atlantic. The problem I had with this picture was that it contained Indians hiding in the background, behind the bushes, watching Columbus and his party come ashore.

That is when my troubles in school started. I immediately raised my hand and asked my teacher about the picture in the textbook: "Mrs. White, how could Columbus have discovered America if there were people, already there when he arrived? If Columbus discovered America, how could people already be living there?" The classroom fell silent. You could have heard a pin drop. My teacher turned red. She stumbled around for a few seconds trying to cover up the contradiction I had exposed to everyone. But the louder her voice became, the more unbelievable her story was. At the end, she asked me if I was now convinced that Columbus did, in fact, discover America? I do not remember, all these years later, exactly what I said.

Even as young as I was, I understood that Columbus discovering America did not make sense. I could have said, "How could Columbus discover America when the Indians were in the bushes when Columbus

---

47   Strauss, Valerie. "Christopher Columbus: 3 things you think he did that he didn't." *The Washington Post*, October 16, 2013. http://www. washingtonpost.com/blogs/answer-sheet/wp/2013/10/14/christopher-columbus-3-things-you-think-he-did-that-he-didnt/.

was discovering their land?" However, what I do vividly remember, is that she exploded at that point, grabbing and squeezing my hand, and took me to the principal's office where I had my first argument about folks distorting history.

Today, in the year 2020, 528 years after 1492, it is now known that Columbus did *not* discover America. Further, it is also now known that Columbus never set foot on the North American continent. Instead, he spent his time in the Caribbean Islands.

So now there is a new question to ask: "Were the Native Americans the first people in North America, before Columbus?" The evidence in this book will show that Native Americans were probably not the first people in the Americas. Quite unfortunately, the authors of history in the Western Hemisphere have not eliminated this "Columbus mis-education" from their textbooks. For example, as late as September 19, 2010, one writer wrote:

African-Americans have come to believe that their history began when the first slave ships docked in the mid-17th century...but our results suggest that it actually started far earlier. Two of Christopher Columbus' shipmates were the first Africans to set foot in the New World, a study has found...says Hannes Schroeder of the Centre for Geo-Genetics at the University of Copenhagen, Denmark, who did the analysis.[48]

This 2010 study now puts the first Africans in the "New World" in 1492. While clearing up one inaccuracy, it insinuates another. While the first Africans who entered the Americas were not slaves, they surely were not the first Africans in the "New World" of Columbus either. They were here long before 1492. The following article corroborates that 2010 study: (Stewart, T. D., April, 1939) "Negro Skeletal Remains from Indian sites in the West Indies. XXXIX, 52-62 Plate D. From Division of Physical Anthropology, United States National Museum, Washington D.C." In the fourth sentence on that plate, illustrated next to the number 52, the following post corroborates the 2010 study, saying:

...an undeformed Negro physical type inhabited the Virgin Islands in pre-Columbian times...Approved for publication by the Secretary

---

48   Barley, S. (9/16/2010). "Graveyard DNA rewrites African American history." *The Daily News,* September 19, 2010. www.newscientist.com/article/dn19455-graveyard-dna-rewrites-african-american-history.html.

of the Smithsonian Institution (Stewart, T. D., April 1939). Negro Skeletal Remains from Indian sites in the West Indies. XXXIX 52-62 Plate D. From Division of Physical Anthropology, United States National Museum, Washington D.C.[49]

Before this historical journey begins, one thing must be made perfectly clear about the views of the author. This must be understood so that the reader may see that racial prejudice has no place in this book, nor should it be practiced anywhere in this modern world. As a matter of fact, here is one fellow, Albert Einstein, who condemned racial prejudice:

In 1946, the Nobel Prize-winning physicist traveled to Lincoln University in Pennsylvania, the alma mater of Langston Hughes and Thurgood Marshall and the first school in America to grant college degrees to Blacks. At Lincoln, Einstein gave a speech in which he called racism "a disease of white people," and added, "I do not intend to be quiet about it."[50]

For the last three centuries, human beings have been cursed by the morbid idea of racism. G. L. Buffon was the first person to use the word "race," which began the conversation on "Race." Yes, for centuries humanity has been cursed with the idea that some people are "better" than others just because of the UV (ultraviolet) rays of our sun.

It was not until 1749 that Buffon introduced the word "race."[51] However, three years later…the first person to ever divide the "so-called" races into different categories was Blumenbach:

Blumenbach named whites after the Caucasus Mountains because he thought the purest white people originated there. He didn't seem to realize the following: Russians, Chechens, Armenians and other Southern Russians are considered to have Black origins…. The

49   Stewart, T. D. (April, 1939). Negro Skeletal Remains from Indian sites in the West Indies. XXXIX, 52-62 Plate D. From Division of Physical Anthropology, United States National Museum, Washington D.C.

50   Gerwertz, Ken. "Albert Einstein, Civil Rights activist." *The Harvard Gazette*, April 12, 2007. news.harvard.edu/gazette/story/2007/04/albert-einstein-civil-rights-activist/

51   Bailey, L. (10/30/2015). Ancient America Rising: AtlanABlack Continent. From: https://www.eurweb.com/2015/10/ ancient-america-rising-atlan-a-black-continent/

American Anthropological Association declares there is no such thing as race, which is merely a "social construct."[52]

There is, however, one part of the human family whose history has been ignored, and it is now being distorted and ignored more than the history of any other part of the human race. I am speaking of ancient African history and the descendants of Africans in the diaspora. Through DNA studies, science has now verified that there is only one race, and that is the human race, that originated in Africa. We are all one human family.

It is sad that even now, in the 21st century, the term "race" is still being used. It is on birth certificates, identification cards and even traffic tickets. But why? Think about it for a moment. This designation is being used despite DNA studies that have explained that there is no such thing as several human races. More on that as the narrative develops. Cavalli-Sforza, an Italian-born population geneticist, who has been a professor (now emeritus) at Stanford University:

> *...affirms his belief in interdisciplinary research and acknowledges his passion to make known that scientific data has established that the main differences among humans are between individuals, not between populations, 'or so-called races'.... Whatever differences exist, he argues, may be attributed to climate.*[53]

Similar damage has been done to the history of *my Native American relatives, the Navajo and Arapaho.* I have also felt the pain of that distortion of history. I remember the pain of watching stereotyped "Indians" on television Saturday mornings during my youth. Members of other parts of humanity have also suffered from similar distortions of their histories. A question that is often asked of me is: "How did you proceed to find the first Americans?"

Let me explain that by *analogy.* To find the animal that built a dam in a creek, I would investigate the creek and quickly eliminate the mountain lion because he is a great predator who hunts but does not build. I would also eliminate the old owl because he is the one to whom the other animals go to have their problems solved. We must study nature and begin in the

---

52   Blindon, Jim. "Buffon on Race." Accessed July 6, 2011. www.
anthropology.ua.edu/race/index.php?title=Buffon%20on%20 Race.

53   Birnbaum, L. C. (2001). *Dark Mother: African Origins & Godmothers.*
From Author's Choice Press, San Jose, New York.

most likely place—the creek—to find the dam builders. It would soon be evident that it is the beaver—with the wide, flat paddle-tail and large sharp teeth—who is the best equipped to builds dams. This line of reasoning led me to the conclusion that the first Americans were Africans.

To date, it has been 43 years since my spiritual father, the late, great Dr. Ivan Van Sertima wrote, *They Came Before Columbus* in 1976. As the reader shall soon see however, *The First Americans Were Africans: Revised and Expanded* is based on quite a longer list of pieces of evidence. The first piece is the strongest, and one of many that did not exist back in 1976. That fact is, that scientific DNA evidence has been shown to be correct almost 100% of the time. A short form of explanations of evidence that follows below is from our beloved, Dr. Ivan Van Sertima's publications (follow the page numbers for the books following). We shall now continue with evidence from his book, *They Came Before Columbus*, with his personal list):

Indians themselves, in Haiti, said Blacks came with **gold and copper spear tops** (p. 11). Later, Columbus landed in **South America** and saw a cotton handkerchief like those in **Guinea Africa** (p.14). Mexican King Montezuma witnessed in the first quarter of the 16th century a **Cortez Mexican mountain lion** skin (p. 102). There are many mounds in **Africa** and in the **Americas** (p. 102). **Americans** smoking pipes (p. 227) had the same totem animals as in **Africa** (p.227). The ritual practices and funerary customs are almost identical in **America** and **Africa** (p. 269). There is a King's double-crown in **Egypt** (p. 269) and the same found among the **Olmec** in Mexico (p. 269).[54]

From the book *African Presence in Early America*, we see:

Horizontal and vertical looms in **Egypt & Peru**
Peruvian bronze of the *same quality* as the **Egyptian**
Identical mummification formula in both **Egypt & Peru**
Identical Reed Boats of **Egypt & Peru**
Trepannation skull surgery in **Egypt & Peru**
Fitted megalithic masonry in **Egypt & Peru**
Identical reed boats in **Egypt & Peru**
Egyptian sun doors in a pyramid complex at **Tiahuanaco**

---

54   University Of South Carolina. "New Evidence Puts Man In North America 50,000 Years Ago." *Science Daily*. Accessed March 1, 2018. www.sciencedaily. com/releases/2004/11/041118104010.htm.

Egyptian dovetails or clamps to keep stone blocks to together at **Tiahuanaco**.[55]

There are **seven** similarities between **African** & **American** pyramids (p. 13)

There is a language link between **Mexico** & **America** (p. 17)

Identical mummification formulas between **Peru** & **Egypt** (pp. 16–17)

Also in **Egypt/Nubia** or with the **Olmecs** see:

Priestly dress
Emblems of power
The Royal flail
Sacred boat
Artificial beard
Feathered fans
Ceremonial umbrella
Hand-shaped incense spoons
Sculptures in which four figures hold up the sky
Human-headed bird
Mummification
Mummies with arms crossed with fingers open
Mummies with Egyptian-style wigs

Then from the book *Early America Revisited*, we see:

Ten pieces of evidence of Africans in Early America and crescent symbol formation on a rock wall in the **Virgin Lands** (verified as a Tifinag branch of **Libyan** script by Libyan Department of Antiquities)

Africans in the **Olmec** world started rituals that appeared nowhere else in the world except in the **Egypto-Nubian** civilization. (p. 52)

Among the "**Egypto-Nubian**," human-headed coffins found in Afgin, Nubia and Olmec Mexico (and in nowhere else in the world) (p. 54)

Tuxla **Mexico's** colossal, multi-ton carvings of "more than a dozen stone heads, indisputably **African** in physiognomy" (p. 73)

Olmec figurines representing Africans types with, distinctive **African** coiffures and earrings, ears, lips, noses, color of skin (p. 89–93)

---

55 Windsor, Rudolph. R. (1969). From Babylon to Timbuktu. *Philadelphia: A History of the Ancient Black Races Including the Black Hebrews.* (Pennsylvania, Windsor Golden Series), p. 2.

"A telltale dwindling in percentage in the foreign **Afrocoid** type found in the **Olmec** graveyards, dwindling from 13.5 to 4.5 in a few generations"

Africa's Pharaoh Ramses II's mummy had American nicotine residue, found in his stomach (pp. 134, 165)

Mummies in Munich tested positive for nicotine and cocaine. (p. 139)

Scores of skulls and skeletons of non-native type found by experts in the Olmec world (p. 120)

Embalming fluid in Peru *identical* with that used in ancient Egypt (p. 125)

Libyan & Malian language carved into a wall in the Virgin Islands pp. 52, 54, 61, 73, 89–93, 120, 125, 139, 155 (Note 26)

Adding all these pieces of evidence together, we have **66 pieces of evidence**. So, it looks as if we have nine (9) more pieces of evidence than **Heinz** has flavors of Ketchup at 57. (Pardon me, but after that hard read above, we all needed a little humor.) But seriously, this list has entries from five different academic fields, namely: anthropology, archeology, craniology, cartography and ethnography.

The evidence we have now speaks for itself and establishes that the Red Indians we see on television today do not look like the very first Americans. The message in this book is not meant to divide or disrespect anyone's culture, or cultural stories of any kind. As a matter of fact, some of them are very interesting and believable.

This next portion is a note about the sources that support the thesis of this work. In Part I, seven peer-reviewed articles support the major points relative to the thesis of this book. Incontrovertible evidence from an eighth article also supports this thesis. However, that article has not been peer reviewed (see Section Note "K") so far. The article in question studies one of the earliest dates that have been found for the evidence that Americans were Africans in a 51,000-year-old site in South Carolina found by Dr. Albert Goodyear. He has been a professor at the University of South Carolina since 1974. "The radiocarbon dates reported after tests by the University of California at Irvine Laboratory were widely viewed as 'unimpeachable' by a number of archaeologists."[56]

56　"New Evidence." https://www.sciencedaily.com/releases/2004/11/041118104010.htm.

When examining this book, all reviewers are to be advised that they are evaluating different degrees of certainty. For the reasons stated below, Chapters 1 and 2 have been separated from the rest of the book falling under the heading "Part I." The rest of the book falls under the heading "Part II." These sections have been separated because much of the evidence seen in "Part I" is derived from eight journal article sources. The sources from Chapters 3 to 8 are mostly not from journal articles, but from book, newspaper and magazine sources.

Peer-reviewed articles are constructed for authenticity, which allows for stronger conclusions, as any reader can see. Peer-reviewed articles would not support any data that was not evidence based. In "Part I" peer-reviewed journal articles were used to support the conclusions. Anyone who disagrees with peer-reviewed articles and the conclusions drawn from them are most likely not historians nor scholars, but they are those who have a hidden or political agenda.

To be thorough, "Part II" was added to cover relevant data and discoveries—peer-reviewed or not—just as a news reporter would. The methods used to investigate the data in "Part I" are not appropriate for "Part II" because "Part II" is more exploratory. The conclusions, inferences and judgments in "Part II" are only as strong as the evidence that is currently available for the researcher to find. "Part I" has more validity because the data needed for "Part II" to equal Part I does not yet exist. Therefore, language such as "most likely" is the best explanation for some items in "Part II."

In conclusion, the reader must be assured that the deficiencies and conclusions of the limited data in "Part II" should not be used for any evaluation of "Part I." Data is only as strong as the evidence that is currently available to study. The conclusions, therefore, are exactly as strong as the evidence presented.

The evidence from peer-reviewed articles in "Part I," however, are academically valid and confirm the thesis of this book: The First Americans were Africans.

PART I

Chapter 1

Christopher Columbus: Sinner or Saint?

In fourteen hundred and ninety-two Columbus sailed the ocean blue; he sailed, and sailed, and sailed, and sailed, to found this land for me and you.

Yes, in elementary school many of us learned this rhyme and were told that it was Columbus who discovered America. But why did the European native Columbus sail west, when all sailors knew, back then, that India is east of Europe?

Christopher Columbus and the Spice Trade of India

The reasons why Christopher Columbus ventured west towards the Americas are very complicated:

Like the Spanish and other Europeans, the chief desire of the Portuguese was to tap into the lucrative spice trade, including items such as cloves, pepper and ginger. The spice trade, Europeans knew, originated somewhere in Asia and made its way through India before entering the hands of Muslim traders, who brought the product to European markets. Trade with Asia in spices would not only enrich the nation that established contact, but also would weaken the Muslim world and strengthen the Christian world by diverting the overland spice trade to a European sea trade. This promise of great wealth and sense of religious completion drove the Portuguese to explore the coast of Africa in search of a route to India. The same ideas motivated Columbus to seek a route to Asia and the spice trade by sailing West.[57]

---

57 Locks, C., S. Megel, P. Roseman & T. Spike. *History in the making: a history of the people of the United States of America to 1877.* (Georgia, UNG Press Books, 2013) http://digitalcommons.northgeorgia.edu/books/1.

Sailing west to reach the east? Were we not all taught that during Columbus' time people thought the world was flat and that if a boat sailed too far west it would fall off the edge of the Earth? Could Columbus have heard that the Earth was not flat but, indeed, round?[G]

This story seems to be the logical reason Columbus sailed west across the Atlantic thinking he would reach Asia. It makes common sense. It would strengthen European trade, while weakening the Muslim world. The problem Columbus had, however, was that the Americas were in the way. At that time Europeans did not know of the existence of North, Central and South America.

How did the Paleoamericans (the first people in the Americas), come to be called, "Indians"? Were not the first people to be called Indians, the people from East India? How did that name jump all the way around the world from India to the other side of the planet in the Americas?

What people did Columbus see when he reached the Western Hemisphere? He saw Black people. Columbus named the people he saw in the Americas "Indians," because he thought he had reached India. Columbus thought that because they were Black like the people of India, they were "Indians" whom the British traded with for spices, in India.

What did Columbus do when he reached the Western Hemisphere? What did he feel about the people he found there? To set the tone, let us first read a letter actually written by Columbus, in his own words. He explains exactly what he thought of the people he found there:

I read from a letter Columbus wrote to Lord Raphael Sanchez, treasurer of Aragón and one of his patrons, dated March 14, 1493, following his return from the first voyage. He reports being enormously impressed by the indigenous people. "As soon...as they see that they are safe and have laid aside all fear, they are very simple and honest and exceedingly liberal with all they have; none of them refusing anything he may possess when he is asked for it, but, on the contrary, inviting us to ask them. They exhibit great love toward all others in preference to themselves. They also give objects of great value for trifles, and content themselves with very little or nothing in return.... I did not find, as some of us had expected, any cannibals among them, but, on the contrary, men of great deference and kindness." But on an ominous note, Columbus writes in his log, "Should your Majesties command it, all the inhabitants could be taken away to

Castile Spain, or made slaves on the island. With 50 men we could subjugate them all and make them do whatever we want."[58]

Columbus could not have wished for a better reception than that. Instead of fighting, the indigenous people gave him and his crew the "red carpet" treatment. But what happened during Columbus' second voyage from England to the same area?

This is a passage from Hans Koning's book, *Columbus His Enterprise:*

On the supply ships getting ready for the return to Spain. Columbus therefore turned it into a massive slave raid as a means for filling up these ships. The brothers of Columbus rounded up 1,500 Arawaks Taínos—men, women, and children—and imprisoned them in pens in Isabella, guarded by men and dogs. The ships had room for no more than 500, and thus only the best specimens were loaded aboard. The Admiral then told the Spaniards they could help themselves from the remainder to as many slaves as they wanted. Those whom no one wanted were simply kicked out of their pens. Such had been the terror of these prisoners that (in the description by Michele de Cuneo, one of the colonists) "they rushed in all directions like lunatics, women dropping and abandoning infants in the rush, running for miles without stopping, fleeing across mountains and rivers." Of the 500 slaves, 300 arrived alive in Spain. Only 60% survived the voyage where they were put up for sale in Seville by Don Juan de Fonseca, the archdeacon of the town. "As naked as the day they were born," the report of this excellent churchman says.[59]

In the piece just covered above, it can clearly be seen that while Columbus may have started off as a businessman, his ambition or greed began to get the best of him. Columbus opened the door to the west for the Europeans—the doorway led to the Americas. The following selected review originates in a book authored by an American historian and Professor of American Studies at the University of Hawaii, by the name of David Edward Stannard.

---

58   Bigelow, William. "Discovering Columbus Re-reading the Past." Accessed January 6, 2015. www.reimaginerpe.org/node/960.

59   Koning, Hans, and Bill Bigelow. Columbus: His Enterprise: Exploding the Myth. (NYU Press, 1991). http://www.jstor.org/ stable/j.ctt9qftv6. Quoted in A People's History for the Classroom, Rethinking Schools, Wisconsin. 2008.

Before the advent of Columbus, Stannard's Indians, as presented in the first section, lived an Edenic existence, from the Bering Strait to Tierra del Fuego. On Indian cultural achievement, the author wants it both ways: where they are civilized, he has them by far the superiors of the Spanish conquistadors; where they are simple hunters and gatherers, they have chosen an ideal life, in perfect harmony with the abundance of nature.... It is evident that Stannard leans strongly toward those researchers who see even the highest currently accepted estimates of the number of pre-Columbian Indians as too low (p. 268). Of the hypothetical 100-million-plus Indians of 1492 and their descendants, the author represents, again following the most extravagant estimates, that...population loss among native societies routinely reached and exceeded 95 percent.[60]

A loss of over 95% of the "hypothetical 100-million Indians" truly sounds like a Native American Holocaust began because of Columbus. As a matter of fact, if the reader wishes for more, they will find many books written that cover that topic. At this point the reader is probably wondering where all of those people whom the Spanish killed in the Americas came from.

This book contains the information needed to find where those "100-million souls," that Stannard covered, first originated. As I stated in the introduction, they were not brought to the Americas in slave ships. These hypothetical "100-million Indians" were already here in North, Central and South America when Columbus arrived.

Human Origins

From where did these first Americans begin? It all began in ancient Africa. Some sailed directly to the Americas. Others traveled to Europe, and Asia, and eventually ended up in the Americas. To understand exactly what happened, we must dig into the details. At a site in Olduvai Gorge, in Tanzania, Africa anthropologists have found a human habitation with

---

60   Stannard, David E. (1992). *American Holocaust: Columbus and the Conquest of the New World.* Oxford and New York: Oxford University Press. p. 268. Quoted in Theodore O'Keefe. "A Failed Look at Europe's Impact on America's Native Peoples" *The Journal of Historical Review*, May/June 1993 (Vol. 13, No. 3). Accessed: August 3, 2016. https://codoh.com/library/document/2427/?lang=en.

"sharp-edge stone tools" among its belongings. The humans were of short stature, only 4.5 to 5.5 feet tall.[61] Leakey and others theorized that it was, indeed, a short African race, which preceded a taller one. "The first Homo-sapien Europeans were Africans, more specifically, short-statured, sub-Saharan Khoisan Africans known by the haplogroup N DNAH they carried with them to ancient Europe 40,000 years ago."[62] This evidence has been scientifically documented in Dr. Imhotep's graduate school dissertation. This Khoisan or Aurignacian migration from Northwestern Africa to Europe was documented in *Nature Magazine* (2011):

The earliest anatomically modern humans in Europe are thought to have appeared around 43,000–42,000 years before the present, by association with Aurignacian sites and lithic assemblages with a collection of stone tools assumed to have been made by modern humans rather than Neanderthals.[63]

Additional facts are presented in the same article in *Nature Magazine*:

Using archaeological studying ancient artifacts, craniometry the scientific measurement of skulls, anthropological the physical and cultural study of humankind, and studying human genes using samples of ancient mtDNA we examined the possibility that there was a third exit from Africa, of anatomically modern humans (AMH) across the Straits of Gibraltar into Iberia North Africa into Spain and thence throughout Eurasia. The finding of ancient Sub-Saharan mtDNA and related evidences make it clear that the Aurignacian culture was taken into Eurasia from Africa by Cro-Magnon people crossing the Straits of Gibraltar.[64]

---

61   Ashley, Gail M. "Early human habitat, recreated for first time, shows life was no picnic". Accessed August 4, 2016. phys.org/ news/2016-03-early-human-habitat-recreated-life.html.

62   Jones, David C. (2007). *The Origin of Civilization: The Case of Egypt and Mesopotamia from Several Disciplines.* Union Institute & University.

63   Higham, Tom et al. "The earliest evidence for anatomically modern humans in northwestern Europe." *Nature* (2011) doi10.1038/ nature10484. Accessed November 10, 2011 http://www.nature.com/nature/journal/vaop/ncurrent/full/nature10484.html.

64   Ibid.

These sub-Saharan people who left Africa, crossing the Straits of Gibraltar into Europe—then heading north and east—are known by several names: Khoisan, Koi-Koi, Aurignacian, Cro-Magnon and later Grimaldi.

Until recently it was assumed that the earliest dates for hg N genes were in Eastern Eurasia. This view has changed recently as a result of the extraction and examination of ancient mtDNA from Cro-Magnon skeletons dating to the Aurignacian period. The archaeological evidence indicates that (AMH) anatomical modern humans replaced Neanderthal during the Aurignacian period in Europe between 32–35kya. The Khoisan Aurignacian civilization appears to have expanded from Africa's West to East. The founders of this culture came from Africa. Some researchers have argued that the Aurignacian culture was introduced to Europe from Africa. They based this conclusion on the fact that its tool kit was foreign to the Mousterian type, and the culture appears in a mature form throughout Europe from France to Central Europe. The "Classic Aurignacian" culture probably began in Africa, crossed the Straits of Gibraltar into Iberia, and expanded eastward across Europe.[65]

During the brief Ice Age, an interstitial warming period was experienced in Europe circa 40,000 years ago. The Khoisan entered many European landscapes from Africa during this period. Some of these areas were inevitably valleys. In one of these European valleys, one of the Khoisan's many groups—several thousands of years latter—was labeled the Yurok, an African subgroup. After leaving their valley, sailing west, and landing in the Americas, they were called Native Americans.

For reasons unknown, these people packed all that they had and began their journey west into the Americas, where they settled. Eventually some of them headed south. The Yurok specifically stated they ended their long journey at the "furthermost southern border" of South America. That area is none other than Tierra del Fuego.

There may have been some African Fuegians already there when the Yurok arrived, but there was no mention of this. No ancient mass graves or weapons have been found in Tierra del Fuego. The assumption is that

65   Winters, Clyde. "The Gibraltar Out of Africa Exit for Anatomically Modern Humans." Webmed Central BIOLOGY 2011;2(10):WMC002319 doi: 10.9754/journal.wmc.2011.002319. Accessed August 3, 2016.

there was no evidence of violence among these ancient African/Fuegians, nor against them from outsiders.

The first people in the southernmost region of South America were dubbed "Fuegians." The evidence established is that the Fuegians from South America are genetically connected to the Khoisan people of sub-Saharan Africa (illustrated by the man on the cover of the first edition of this book in 2011).

"The Fuegians were related to the Khoisans because of the Y chromosomes they carried. Fuegians 100–400 BP carried haplogroup A1. Hg A1 is an African haplogroup,"[66] We can now safely say that they were the same people. We can see the origin of the Khoisan people here:

We analyzed the literature on ancient DNA of Paleoamericans. It was found that the Paleoamericans carried mtDNA belonging to the M macrohaplogroup and Y chromosome R. The Paleoamericans were Khoisan. The Khoisan was the Cro-Magnon people who introduced the Solutrian cultures into Spain and the North America. These founding indigenous Americans came to America in boats from Africa, which was the only place Paleoamericans could sail from, to reach the Americas during the last Ice Age.[67]

To finish with the DNA evidence of the first people in the Americas, the Chinese must be mentioned. Why? The old "Clovis Theory" maintains the first Americans were Chinese. Well, here we will expose who the first Chinese really were. Chinese scientist, Professor Jin Li, agrees with other Chinese scientists, Wang and Li, that the first Chinese had their roots in and originated in Africa.

The current Y chromosome evidence suggests multiple early migrations of modern humans from Africa via Southeast Asia to East Asia. After the initial settlements, the northward migrations

66 García-Bour, Jaume. Pérez-Pérez, Alejandro. Álvarez, Sara. Fernández, Eva. López-Parra, Ana. M. Arroyo-Pardo, Eduardo, and Turbón, D. "Early population differentiation in extinct aborigines from Tierra del Fuego-Patagonia: Ancient mtDNA sequences and Y-Chromosome STR characterization." American Journal Physical Anthropology. (2004) 123: 361-370. doi:10.1002/ajpa.10337.

67 Winters, Clyde. "African origins Paleoamerican DNA." CIBTech Journal of Microbiology ISSN: 2319-3867 (Online) Accessed on August 3, 2016 from http://www.cibtech.org/J-Microbiology/PUBLICATIONS/2015/Vol-4-No-1/03-CJM-004-CLYDE-AFRICAN-DNA.pdf.

during the Paleolithic Age shaped the genetic structure in East Asia...Once it became generally accepted that modern humans evolved recently in Africa, the times and routes of migration to East Asia remained controversial. The migration history of haplogroup D-M174 is most mysterious. By now, we have known little about the origin and dispersal of this haplogroup. This haplogroup was derived from Africa haplogroup DE-M1 (YAP insertion) and is associated with a short black Asian physical style. Haplogroups E and D are brother haplogroups. While haplogroup E was carried westwards to Africa by the tall black people, haplogroup D might have been carried eastwards to East Asia by the short black people.[68]

Blood Type

We shall now deviate from chromosomes and haplogroups to blood types. First, we see a quote from the Smithsonian Institute:

The species that you and all other living beings on this planet belong to is Homo sapiens. During a time of dramatic climate change 200,000 years ago, Homo sapiens evolved in Africa.... Type O blood is said to be the oldest blood and shows a connection to the hunter-gatherer cultures. [The scholar also raises the question,] If the oldest Homo sapiens were the oldest cultures, would not Africans be the oldest hunter-gatherers as well? O Negative blood cells are called "universal" meaning they can be transfused to almost any patient in need.[69]

We see that even the Smithsonian Institute says Africans were the first Homo sapiens, the first people. Hence, would not the first people have the first blood type, and one that is universal? Additionally:

Coca and Diebert anticipated finding similar blood group distributions in the Asian and Indian populations, which would further support the widely held theory that Native Americans had

---

68   Wang, Chuan-Chao. Li, Hui. "Inferring human history in East Asia from Y chromosomes" Investigative Genetics. 2013; 4: 11. Published online 2013 Jun 3. doi: 10.1186/2041-2223-4-11, Accessed August 4, 2016. http://www.ncbi.nlm.nih.gov/pmc/articles/PMC 3687582/.

69   "What does it mean to be human?" Smithsonian National Museum of Natural History. Accessed August 3, 2016. http://humanorigins.si.edu/evidence/human-fossils/species/homo-sapiens.

immigrated to the Americas from northeastern Asia. They were surprised to find that, to the contrary, the blood group distributions of the East Asian and American Indian sample groups were quite different. The American Indians had a very high likelihood of being the universal red cell donor by having Type O negative blood type.[70]

Therefore, we see that type O blood is the "universal blood donor" because **it is "the oldest blood type."** This also means that this type can be transfused to almost any patient in need. Would not the "oldest blood type," logically belong to the "oldest peoples on Earth?"

If the oldest descendants are the "Universal Blood Donors with Type O blood," said Coca and Diebert, and "The American Indians had a very high likelihood of being the universal red cell donor." Would it then be logical to say that the American Indians have "a very high likelihood of being" of African descent?[71] Hence, we see that "type O blood is the 'universal blood donor' because it is "the oldest blood type." Would not the "oldest blood type" belong to the "oldest peoples on Earth," the Africans?

A Smithsonian National Museum of Natural History author wrote, "If the oldest Homo sapiens were the oldest cultures, would not the Africans be the oldest hunter-gatherers as well? O Negative blood cells are called 'universal' meaning they can be transfused to almost any patient in need ..."[72]

So, Africans, the most ancient people on Earth, have O Negative blood. See the following article to find out just exactly what that means.

---

70   Ewen, Alex. "Bering Strait Theory, Pt. 6: DNA, Blood Types and Stereotypes" Indian Country Today Media Network, July 19, 2014. Accessed August 3, 2016. http://www.geneticsandsociety.org/article.php?id=7919.

71   García-Bour, Jaume et al. "Early population differentiation...," pp. 361-370.

72   "What does it mean to be human?" Smithsonian National Museum of Natural History. Accessed August 3, 2016. http://humanorigins.si.edu/evidence/human-fossils/species/homo-sapiens.

What is a Universal Blood Donor?

People with type O negative blood are called universal donors because type O negative blood is compatible with any blood recipient's type.[73]

The Mystery of Human Blood Types

The human body naturally makes antibodies that will attack certain types of red-blood-cell antigens. For example, people with type A blood have A antigens on their red blood cells and make antibodies that attack B antigens; people with type B blood have B antigens on their red blood cells and make antibodies that attack A antigens. So, type A people can't donate their blood to type B people and vice versa. People who are type AB have both A and B antigens on their red blood cells and therefore don't make any A or B antibodies while people who are type O have no A or B antigens and make both A and B antibodies.[74]

So, briefly re-stating the above content from The Smithsonian, Lorne Laboratories and Erin Wayman, Africans were the first people on Earth; they had the oldest blood, "O Negative" that is the oldest blood; and believe it or not, Africans are the "universal blood donors."

Here is a poem, written by Dr. Imhotep:

Just because:
Just because you say one thing, but it's really another,
Doesn't make it true, I'm sorry my brother.
Aren't the first people Africans, the universal blood donors?
Update historic records and stop making boners.
Don't spit in the wind and tell me it's rainin'…MAN,
Stop changing history, but I don't think you can.
We're seeking truth, to us it's no obstacle.
We see through the lies, your theories ain't logical!

To end this discussion, disclosed later in this work, will be the study of the celebrated geneticist, Luca Cavelli-Sforza. He wrote in *History and*

---

73   "What is a universal blood donor?" Lorne Laboratories, Accessed March 16, 2015. https://www.lornelabs.com/news-events/blog/what-is-a-universal-blood-donor.

74   Wayman, E. "The Mystery of the Human Blood Types." Smithsonian Magazine. Accessed October 22, 2012. https://www.smithsonianmag.com/science-nature/themysteryofhumanbloodtypes86993838/#lxo6fzxrKKbdhvr7.99.

Geography of Human Genes that "genetically speaking, white skin was not in existence before 3000 B.C."[75] This is another "genetic nail in the coffin" concerning the blood type issue, as well as the Clovis theory. If you need to go further in this line of study and find out more about the biology of "skin color" and how the different peoples' skin colors came to be, just google the following: Gloger's Rule, Allen's Rule, and Bergman's Rule.

More Evidence of Africans in America

Moving back from biology to history, Clyde A. Winters, Ph.D. provides twelve points to consider about the first Americans in their journey from Africa to the Americas:

1. The Australians represent an Out of Africa (OOA) population that settled in Asia.

2. Ice separated much of South America east to west.

3. The first Americans appear in Brazil, Chile and then Argentina at least by 30,000 B.C.

4. Craniometric skull measurement evidence shows that the first Americans look like Africans not Amerinds.

5. Craniometric evidence also shows Asia was dominated by the Australian population until the rise of Sahulland when the Melanesian people appear in the area. Beringia was still under ice at this time.

6. The Melanesian type reached the East Asian mainland by 3000 B.C., long after Africans had settled Latin America.

7. Between 15,000 and 12,000 B.C., we see numerous Africans in the populations of Mexico and Brazil. Statues dating to this period have even been found off the Yucatan coast in the Caribbean.

8. The first Americans did not look like the Australians or modern Amerinds.

9. Iconography (symbols) of pre-classic people like the Cheria, Ocos and other groups of Negroes, not Amerinds like the Maya, occur.

---

75   Cavalli-Sforza Luigi L., Paolo Menozzi, and Alberto Piazza. (1994). *The History and Geography of Human Genes*. (New Jersey, Princeton University Press), p. 145.

10. Amerind groups not associated with African slaves carry African genes.

11. The Maya carry African Y chromosome.

12. The Maya carry African genes. Mexico's Negro Costa-Chicanos claim that they have never been slaves and are indigenous to Guerrero and Oaxaca on the Pacific coast. The first Americans came from Africa, not Siberia. These people probably came to the Americas by boat.

We have traced the Anu/Twa DNA coming to North America from two directions…take your pick: first from Africa by way of South America, or later north from Scandinavia by way of Canada. Their mode of transportation—when traveling over water—was the papyrus reed boat, which pre-dated all wooden boats.

Paleoamerican Phenotypes

The Paleoamericans are classified phenotypically as African, Australian or Melanesian based on multivariate methods and quantitative analysis. This grouping should only be Sub-Saharan African and Australian populations because the Melanesians and Sub-Saharan Africans share the same craniometric measurements. The craniometrics illustrate that Paleo-Indians belonged to the Black Variety, but they do not allow us to establish conclusively where the Paleoamericans originated. Some researchers believe the Paleoamericans came from East Asia across the Bering Strait or from Europe because of the Solutrean tools found throughout North America.

These points of origination are unlikely because the Ice shelf in the Northern Latitudes would have prevented passage from these destinations to South America where the oldest Paleoamerican sites have been excavated. The most likely place the Paleoamericans came from was Africa, which is closer to the Americas than either Europe or East Asia. Africa is also the location where the Solutrean culture originated and later expanded into Iberia.[76]

The evidence seems to say that the very earliest Americans came directly from Africa. Some did arrive from Africa by way of Western Europe, such as the Yurok; and yes, some Africans eventually may have

76   Winters, Clyde. (2015). *We Are Not Just Africans: The Black Native Americans* (Self-Published).

come from China, or ventured to the Americas by way of present-day Alaska. They were not, however, the first Americans.

They would have had to cross over from Asia before 115,000 YBP (years before present) when the Bering Sea froze to a point where one-to-two-mile-high glaciers eventually formed, which made it impossible to cross. Note: YBP is used instead of B.C. (before Christ) and CE (current era) instead of A.D. (after Christ's death) to avoid offending Christians.

In July of 2012, Journalist Simon Moya-Smith interviewed David Reich, Professor of Genetics at Harvard. Smith asked Reich:

"We all know the Bering Strait theory as just that—a theory," I said. "When did scientists elevate it to fact?...Is it a fact?"

"No," he said. "I don't think it is considered fact. I think that it's a hypothesis about history, but no, it's not fact."[77]

These diminutive peoples were the earliest form of modern Homo sapiens, going back in time over 350,000 years in Africa, and possibly 115,000 years in Europe in the form of the Grimaldi Man[78] who was also known as Aurignacian. Both early groups were diminutive (short) Africans,[79] ancestors of the Anu/Twa, who first migrated to Europe from Africa. Many books and articles discuss the Grimaldi and Aurignacian separately. The next section clears up any confusion about the relationship between those two groups.

Diop's research revealed, "The first Homo sapiens in Europe, as we have already seen, are the migratory Negroid who was responsible for the Aurignacian Industry,"[80] (This industry was a collection of Aurignacian tools, and essentials):

The Grimaldi Negroid was responsible for the Aurignacian industry, having been an invader into Europe from Africa, as Bordes himself

77 Moya-Smith, S. "Harvard Professor Confirms Bering Strait Theory Is Not Fact." *Indian Country Today.* July 31, 2012. https://indiancountrymedianetwork.com/news/opinions/harvard-professor-confirms-bering-strait-theory-is-not-fact/.

78 Van Sertima. (1985). *African Presence in Early Europe.* (Transaction Publishers), p. 230.

79 Ibid., p. 14.

80 Diop, Cheikh A. (1981). *Civilization or Barbarism: An Authentic Anthropology.* (Lawrence Hill Books), p. 40.

acknowledges. François Bordes was a French scientist, geologist, and archaeologist. The Aurignacian (industry) arrived in France fully developed.[81]

Therefore, the scientific case has been made. There is no difference between the Aurignacian race and the Grimaldi. They were both Black Africans and the first Homo sapiens in Europe. The Aurignacian were in Europe as early "as 40,000 years ago."[82] Knowing that both of these names refer to the same group, we can now probably say that if the Grimaldi were diminutive (of short stature), so were the Aurignacian.[83]

Is it not a strange coincidence that as the Homo sapiens arrived in Africa, it was the "Neanderthal who then suddenly disappears around 40,000 years ago...without leaving any descendants"? Consequently, "There is no other variety of Homo sapiens that precedes the Grimaldi and therefore Aurignacian in Europe or in Asia." By using the word "variety," Diop means no other color of Homo sapiens were in Europe—or Asia for that matter—except those of the dark hue. He then goes further to say, "Whites were absent from Egypt, and practically remained that way until 1300 B.C."[84]

Since the evidence shows that the shorter Africans were the first Homo sapiens in Africa, Europe and Asia, what about the Americas? It appears extremely likely that diminutive Blacks appeared in the New World as its first human occupants.[85] Their presence is suggested most strongly by the exceptionally short statures of the Yahgan and Alikuluf peoples who occupy the southernmost tip of South America on Tierra del Fuego. They all were descendants of the short Anu/Twa from Africa.

From what part of Africa did the Anu/Twa begin? Churchward, a British scholar, seems to answer that question. He wrote:

---

81   Ibid, pp. 40-41.

82   Gibbons, Ann. "Europeans Trace Ancestry to Paleolithic People." *Science*, November 10, 2000, Vol. No. 5494-1248, p. 1080.

83   Van Sertima Ivan. (1992). African Presence in Early America (New Jersey, Transaction Publishers), p. 217.

84   Diop, Cheikh A. *Civilization or Barbarism*, p. 29.

85   Van Sertima Ivan. *African Presence in Early America*, p. 216.

But, Gentlemen, it was in Africa that the little Pygmy was first evolved from the Pithecanthropus Erectus or an Anthropoid Ape—in the Nile Valley, and around the lakes at the head of the Nile. From here these little men spread all over the world, North, East, South and West, until not only Africa, but Europe, Asia, North and South America and Oceania were populated by them.[86]

Many historians before and after Churchward have joined in his unifying assessment, for one can plainly see—in ascending order—that:

According to many Eurocentric and Afrocentric scholars writing on the subject, the Anu were an aboriginal Black population of ancient times that occupied Africa, Asia and Europe. Those researchers and scholars espousing that view include: Rouge (1856), Amelineau (1897), Petrie (1897), Capart (1901), Massey (1910), Hewitt (1910), Dutt (1925), Houston (1926), Naville (1926), Banerji (1934), Heras (1953), Hall (1963), Bryant (1963), Diop (1974).[87]

One may add to that list Dr. Imhotep's (2007) work in his dissertation, "The Origin of Civilization: The Case of Egypt and Mesopotamia From Several Disciplines" that certainly plays a part in "espousing that view." For a bird's eye view of these human movements, see Fig. 1, the map covering the Nile valley as well as Asia and Europe below the 51st parallel.

Caucasians developed long after Black people, and before the Asians were in existence.When the first Caucasians from the steppe population reached:

Southwestern Eurasia.... These pale-skinned people would gradually have replaced the resident, Indigenous dark-skinned people, though pockets of dark-skinned African types survived well into the historic period. Little-Blacks—the Khoisan, were able to keep their dark skin color and could survive there during the Ice Age because they had access to vitamin D-laden northern salt-water fish and therefore escaped the selection pressure. Others lost their dark color which evolved into white skin as seen further inland.[88]

---

86 Churchward, Albert. (1912). *Origin and Evolution of Primitive Man* (Illinois Lushena Books Inc.), pp. 12-13.

87 Brunson, James E. (1991). *Predynastic Egypt: An Africa-centric View* (Illinois, Brunson), p. 41.

88 Finch, Charles S. (1991). *Echoes of the old Dark Land: Themes from the African Eden* (Georgia, Khenti Press), p. 33.

The indigenous dark-skinned people were landlocked and lived farther inland. They did not have access to vitamin D from fish, which before had chemically enabled the others to retain their dark skin. This whole process is scientifically documented and carefully explained by a medical doctor in his 1991 book.[89]

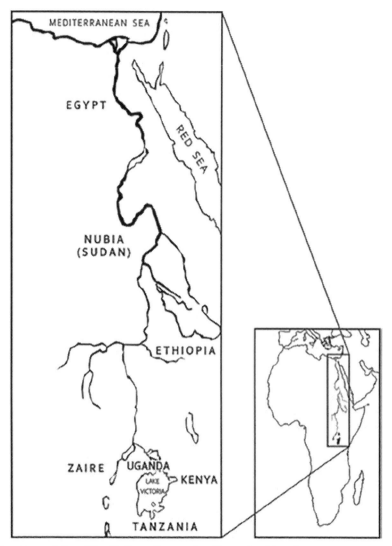

Fig. 1: Map of the Nile Valley. *Drawn by Marrwho Hasat.*

This process of losing their color, called "differentiation," came about because of a sudden return of the Ice Age in Europe. It is this process that

89   Ibid.

caused the loss of sunlight and lack of vitamin D, which changed these dark inland people to a lighter hue.

Complementing this analysis, in his book *The History and Geography of Human Genes*, world–renowned geneticist, Cavalli-Sforza, Ph.D. also explains the reason for the change in skin color. He clarifies that there is a clear connection between climate and physiological traits:

> *A classical physiological trait is skin color on which climate acts in many ways. By absorbing ultraviolet rays, a dark skin is advantageous in protecting against solar erythema and skin carcinomas, but it is a bar against the production of vitamin D in the lower skin layers. Especially when the diet produces little or no vitamin D, a white skin is very necessary in high latitudes.... If this is true, then the white skin color of northern Europeans evolved (and inversely changed during) the last 5000 years from a light-brown color characteristic of Caucasoids from West Asia and North Africa to a white skin color.[90]*

The individuals trapped in their frigid area, whose skin was unable to adapt to a white skin color, died. Their skin did not adapt and turn white because of their inability to absorb the vitamin D from the sun. Cut off from the rest of the human family, land-locked far from those who could consume fish, it was in relative isolation that dark-skinned people underwent adaptations in a frigid, relatively sunless environment. This resulted in the creation of a "so-called" new human race characterized by pale skin, lightened straight hair, varying shades of eye color, and narrowed angular nasal facial features.[91] Their bodies adapted to their environmental conditions.

Cro-Magnons are the presumed ancestors of modern Europeans and Cro-Magnons—are a recent immigrant from Africa.... We all emerged out of Africa.... Our genes betray this secret of common racial distinctions of modern humans that have unfortunately given rise to centuries of prejudice and inequality [but] are shown to be merely geographical variants.[92]

---

90   Cavalli-Sforza, Luigi et al. *The History and Geography of Human Genes*, p. 145.

91   Finch, Charles S. *Echoes of the old Dark Land*, p. 141.

92   Stringer, Chris. McKie, Robin. (1997). *African Exodus* (Oklahoma, Holt Paperbacks), pp. 162, 214, front cover flap.

A millennium after differentiation took place, members of the Caucasian part of the human family finally reached far northwestern Europe into Scandinavia:

The entry of Whites into Scandinavian countries and the Arctic circle began.... Mostly after the 5th century A.D....and used the services of men and even African indigenous women (by definition) to ferry them around and teach them about the region as much as was done in a painting that can be seen from Washington's site, which shows a boat full of White Vikings with a Black man guiding them.[93]

Africans, such as the Khoisan, predated the Caucasian Scandinavian people in Europe by hundreds of thousands of years. It was these Africans who eventually taught the White Vikings how to build ships and master seafaring skills when they arrived from the land-locked Russian steppes. They had to adapt or die. Is it not true that seafaring skills are found among people who live near bodies of water, and not land-locked people as those found in the Russian steppes?

In addition to the ships, the second transportation vehicles these short Black Vikings adapted and made were the first snow sleighs. Some of these original sleighs can be seen today at the Viking Ship Museum in Oslo, Norway. However, the famous Oseberg Sleigh (see Fig. 37 in Chapter 5) was found in a burial mound in Scandinavia. Those mounds were only built by Africans. The sleigh was built with iron runners on the bottom so it would slide across the snow like silk over skin. Iron runners lasted far longer than wooden runners.

The first sleighs, like the first boats, were not built with nails or metal rivets, as the White Vikings would later use. The oldest "sewn" boat found so far is Khufu's "Pyramid Boat," that was found in a gigantic pit, surrounded by a megalithic stone tomb, a few feet from the Great Pyramid of Giza in Egypt:

The earliest boats were sewn with animal guts...then, and thousands of years later were replaced with rivets as soon as iron gradually

---

93 Washington, Paul M. (2006). "The African-Egyptian Heritage of the Vikings: an African Prehistoric Europe, Parts I and II." Accessed August 30, 2011. www.beforebc.de/Related.Subjects/Ships.Seafaring/02-17-800-36-01.html.

became accessible for the boat builders.[94] The oldest complete boat in the world is known as the boat that was found in a megalithic stone enclosure, buried next to the Great Pyramid of Giza. It is a wooden sewn "Solar Boat," tied together in the interior hull of the boat with ropes. Kamal el Mallakh finished telling me the tale of how he had found Cheops' Solar Boat in its air-tight pit.[95]

A sewn boat is a type of wooden boat that is clinker built and held together with tendons or flexible wood, such as roots and willow branches. Sewn boat construction techniques were used in many parts of the world prior to the development of metal fasteners and continued to be used long after that time for small boats to reduce construction costs where metal fasteners were too expensive.[96]

The sleighs were sewn and contained iron runners. How did these first smiths in Europe learn how to make metal? Were they first to do so? In Chapter 5, under "Metallurgy," we will cover how the Dwarves' ancestors, the Khoisan, entered Europe 40,000–45,000 years ago and brought their metallurgical skills with them from Africa. These fellows were not called a "Smith" (a worker in metal) but were called "Blacksmiths," by the first Caucasians and obviously the name stuck. Some of their descendants were most likely the diminutive mound builders who constructed the iron smelting furnaces inside mounds, whose ruins can be seen today along the Ohio River.

In Fig. 2, we see that the bed of the sleigh was made of wood. There is a "wood-carving cut into the Oseberg sleigh."[97] An enlargement of one of the carvings on the sleigh is most interesting (see Fig. 38 in Chapter 5).

94   Loset, Jorn O. "How to build a Viking ship." (2004). Accessed November 2, 2015. www.vikingskip.com/norse-shipbuilding.htm.

95   Dunn, Jimmy. (n.d) "Egypt: Discovery of Cheops' Solar Boat by Kamal el Mallakh, Egypt Antiquity News." Accessed November 2, 2015. http://www.touregypt.net/featurestories/solar.htm.

96   "2012 BC: Recreating The Oldest Boat Found In Western Europe." Before It's News. Jan. 15, 2012. Accessed May, 9, 2016. http://beforeitsnews.com/2012/2012/01/2012-bc-recreating-the-oldest-boat-found-in-western-europe-1628050.html.

97   "Wood carving on Sleigh Oseberg Iron Age Norway." Flickr (2001). Accessed September 14, 2011. http://www.flickr.com/photos/28772513@N07/3568314744/.

There are three short people in the scene. One man and two women on either side of him, with one woman on a horse. All of these short people have classic prognathism (forwardly jutting jaws, an African trait).

Fig. 2: Khufu's Pyramid Sewn Boat. *Permission from Jim Henderson/ Crooktree.com.*

If an average Black person puts his/her hand up as if to cough, the lips and nose touch the hand. If an average White person does this, only the nose would touch the hand. This is especially true with the lady on the horse. Obviously, this lady has very full lips. The lady to the left of the man is wearing a cornrow hairstyle that is still worn by Black women today; the man is wearing his hair in the same style. There are four distinct African features here: short people, prognathous jaws, full lips and an African circular cornrow hairstyle. It would be logical to say that these people (featured on the sleigh) were most likely the builders of the sleigh, just as the Africans built the first boats in Scandinavia.

The Bull-horned helmet (see Fig. 3) is another article that was copied by the White Vikings from Africans. Just about every time a picture of a Viking is displayed, he is wearing this most noticeable icon. Even the "so-called" Viking horn helmet was not invented by the Vikings, according to Washington.

The earliest horned crowns worn in history harken back to 7000 B.C. in the Sudan and are worn by women. Then from 2254 to 2218 B.C.

during the first Dynasty of Akkad is the African...Naram Sin wearing a bullhorn crown.[98] *Akkad was one of the first two African cities in early Mesopotamia. Naram Sin was the king of Akkad, the second oldest civilization in Mesopotamia after Sumer. A carving of this African wearing his bullhorn crown can be seen on an African victory stele from the 23rd century B.C. This stele can be seen today in the Louvre Museum in Paris, France.*[99]

Fig. 3: Bull-horned Helmet Images. *Courtesy of Dreamstime & Vector.*

These bull-horned helmets were found in Africa thousands of years before Caucasian Vikings wore them. Notice the African's helmet, with pointed horns, so like the Viking on the left. The African also has a beard and a weapon in his hand.

There is another practice that may also have begun with the Black Vikings; the filing of their teeth. After studying a mass grave in Scandinavia, archaeologists have concluded the Vikings filed their teeth, according to National Geographic news.

98   Washington, Paul M. (2006). "The African-Egyptian Heritage of the Vikings: an African Prehistoric Europe, Parts I and II." Accessed August 30, 2011. www.beforebc.de/Related.Subjects/Ships.Seafaring/02-17-800-36-01. html.

99   Mark, Joshua J. "Naram-Sin." *Ancient History Encyclopedia.* August 7, 2014 https://www.ancient.eu/Naram-Sin/.

Researchers say the Vikings may have learned the practice of filing their teeth from a foreign culture. Some of the oldest cases of tooth modification come from Mexico, dating as far back as 1400 B.C.[100] It would be scientifically correct for us to conclude that it would be impossible for Caucasian Vikings to have been in Mexico in 1400 B.C. when evidence shows us they first entered America in 1000 A.D., 2400 years later.

In his search for Aztec God Ixlilton, "The Little Black One," Cartier explored the St. Lawerence region in the middle of the 16th century, and he found no evidence of Vikings or Celts; he saw no traces of their culture.[101] Cartier looked again all around that area and still found no traces.

More evidence of tooth filing has been found as far north as "the Chesapeak Bay.[102] Evidence shows us that Africans all across their continent have a history of filing or modifying their teeth: "Tooth mutilation existed in sub-Saharan Africa"[103] In Angola, West Africa, "Tooth modification was a fairly common practice among pre-colonial West African societies." and "Several African countries" filed their teeth.[104]

Evidence suggests that tooth modification existed in most parts of Africa. It then spread to others when Africans began to leave the continent 100,000 years ago and migrate to the Americas and 40,000 years ago to Europe. After taking into account the earlier notes on DNA, the evidence says that the White Vikings copied tooth decorating from the Black Vikings. We see that the first Eurasians began with a dark complexion. They lost their skin color during the Ice Age. It was these two groups who accounted for the western and eastern steppe populations.

---

100 Oleson, Tryggvi J. (1963). *Early Voyages and Northern Approaches 1000-1632* (Toronto, McClelland and Stewart Limited), p. 6.

101 Mallery, Arlington H. (1951). *Lost America: The Story of Iron-Age Civilization Prior to Columbus.* (The Overlook Company).

102 "Cranium of a woman with filed teeth." Smithsonian National Museum of Natural History. (n.d.). "Accessed on September 12, 2011. http://anthropology.si.edu/writteninbone/tooth_notching. html.

103 Handler, Jerome S. (1994). "Determining African Birth from Skeletal Remains: A Note on Tooth Mutilation." Accessed on September 12, 2011. http://jeromehandler.org/wpcontent/uploads/ToothMut_AfBirth94.pdf.

104 Jones, A. Tooth mutilation in Angola. *Br Dent J* 173, 177-179 (1992). https://doi.org/10.1038/sj.bdj.4807989.

The list of evidence for Africans in Scandinavia consists of seven items:

1. Boats
2. Sleighs
3. The late entry of Caucasians into Scandinavia
4. Carvings
5. Bull-horned helmet
6. Filed teeth
7. DNA

The evidence is overwhelming. It can be clearly seen now, from the mountain of evidence collected, that the first Vikings were also Africans.

Where do the Asians fit into this story? After many centuries in frozen Ice Age Europe, the ancient Black Cro-Magnon evolved into the White Cro-Magnon to survive the savage cold of the north. The black Grimaldi (also known as Aurignacian) and the new White Cro-Magnon most likely mixed their bloods and created the "Chandalade Man who would be the prototype original people of the Yellow Race."[105]

Note: For more on the "Yellow Race," see Section Note "C" in Dr. Winters' Reflections prior to the Introduction.

The Asians are said to be the offspring of Blacks and Whites from "a mongrel, born in cold climate, from both stocks of the last Grimaldi and the new Cro-Magnon in Europe."[106] Do you see what logical conclusion this is all leading to? We are all one large family and just one race—the human race. In the end (or in the beginning) if you go back far enough, we come from archaeologist Johanson's or should we say, from Africa's "Lucy"—the oldest, best preserved skeleton of any erect walking human skeleton ever found.[107]

There is DNA evidence that shows that the early Eurasians were dark people, not White:

Mark Stoneking and co-authors from the Max Planck Institute for Evolutionary Anthropology in Germany have a new paper on human

---

105 Diop, Cheikh A. *Civilization or Barbarism*. Lawrence Hill Books, p. 16.

106 Ibid.

107 Johanson, Donald, and Maitland Edey. (1981). *Lucy: The Beginnings of Human Kind*. Simon & Schuster, New York. back cover.

pigmentation genes in Human Genetics. From the paper it points out that.... These DNA results probably suggest that early Eurasians were dark, and evolved their light skin pigmentation separately, with different genes contributing to the depigmentation of Caucasoids and Mongoloids.[108]

Another piece of evidence comes from an international team headed by Professor Jin Li.

An international study has found that the Chinese people originated not from Peking Man in northern China, but from early humans in East Africa who moved through South Asia to China some 100,000 years ago. Hong Kong's Ming Pao daily reported a finding that confirms the single origin theory in anthropology. Based on DNA analyses of 100,000 samples gathered from around the world, a number of human families evolved in East Africa some 150,000 years ago, says Li Hui, a member of Jin's team. Also collected were samples from 160 ethnic groups in China. About 100,000 years ago, some of those humans began to leave Africa, with some people moving to China via South and Southeast Asia, Li said.[109]

Therefore, a German as well as a Chinese professor together say that the first Chinese person evolved from dark to light skin.

Section Notes

G. Flat vs. Round Earth

In 1513 A.D., Admiral Piri Re'is made copies of a source map that took in account for the curvature of the Earth. The curvature in the source map was not due to an error in scale.

In the early days of mapmaking we accumulated more and more evidence of the ancient existence of spherical trigonometry applied

108 Stoneking, Mark. "Human pigmentation genes in Africans, Europeans, and Chinese." (2006). Accessed August 30, 2010. http://www.dienekes.blogspot.com/2006/09/human-pigmentation-genes-in-africans.html.

109 Li, Jin. (2004). "The First Chinese were Black." Accessed January 15, 2015. http://www.trinicenter.com/FirstChinese.htm.

to mapmaking. This mathematical technique, and its application to map making was known in an era long before Greece.[110]

Spherical trigonometry was known before the Greeks, and so was the map Piri Re'is copied that his name has been attributed to. Spherical trigonometry was used in making those pre-Greek maps. A "sphere from Greek L. σφαῖρα-Gr. sphaira, is any round body or figure having the surface equally distant from the center at all points; a globe; a ball."[111]

A sphere, as the Greeks defined it, is the shape of a globe or a ball. One cannot precisely measure points on a globe, or draw a global map with linear measurement, using a ruler. In this case, to draw and measure points on a globe in map making, one must use trigonometry for the curvature of the globe.

Our cartographic friends in the U.S. Air Force had suggested such a projection. Precise evidence reveals that Piri Re'is map predates Greek cartography. It is unthinkable to think it was drawn without spherical trigonometry.

Evidence reveals that Piri Re'is map predates the Greeks *except that it is unthinkable to think it had been drawn without spherical trigonometry.*[112]

In this case, if one is using spherical trigonometry, one is most likely measuring a globe, or as the Greeks defined it, a sphere. By extension, if spherical trigonometry had to be used to draw the original map that the Piri Re'is map was based on; then it must have been the map of a "globe" or a "ball" shaped object. Logic demands that if they were not drawing a map of a "globe" or a "ball" shaped object, then why would the use of spherical trigonometry be employed?

Therefore, the people who drew the map that Piri Re'is map was based on, most likely knew the world was round. The drawing of the original map "was presented by the apparent use of plane trigonometry at a time, according to the historical record, spherical trigonometry was known"[113] to

---

110 Hapgood, Charles H. *Maps of the Ancient Sea Kings*, p. 182.

111 Webster's New Universal Unabridged Dictionary (Baber and Dorset, 1983), p. 1746.

112 Hapgood, Charles H. *Maps of the Ancient Sea Kings*, p. 183.

113 Ibid.

the pre-Greeks. According to the original map taken from the Alexandria Library in Egypt, someone before the Greeks knew the world was round. How was it Columbus knew the world was round but his European associates did not know?

Where Did the Moors Originate?

The Moors had conquered Spain in 711 and ruled until 1492. "Salamanca University, dating back to 1218, is the oldest and one of the most prestigious universities in Spain." Salamanca University was actually "Chartered in 1218 A.D. by King Alfonso IX of Leon" (although teaching began as early as 1130 A.D.). Years later, would the Moorish professors in that university not know that the Earth was round by 1492?[114] Therefore, why would the fact that the Earth was round not be a logical conclusion, at least for the elite? If someone wanted to know where the Moors originated, the smartest way to answer that question would be, "How far back do you wish to start? Let us take a trip all the way back to the Moors, who were Africans from Mauritania. That is about as simple as asking, "Where was the Brooklyn Bridge built?"

Going back further, we are told that the Moors were Berbers. Let us look at the Berbers first. They lived in North Africa, west of the Nile Valley.

The original Berbers, who were called Moors, were the North African ancestors of the present day dark brown/black people of the Sahara and Sahel, mainly those called Fulani, Tuareg, Sanhaja, Kunta, as well as the Trarza of Mauritania and Senegal, and various tribes presently living in Chad, Morocco and Algeria.[115]

Now, let us turn our attention to the Arabs. Who were the original Arabs?

J. D. Baldwin wrote an authoritative book in 1869, *Prehistoric Nations*. He was a member of the House of Representatives from Massachusetts from 1863–1869. His research revealed the **original Arabians were Cushites from Ethiopia**.

---

114 Salamanca University. (n.d.) "Salamanca University Spanish Courses." Accessed December 2, 2014. http://www.salamanca-university.org.

115 "The Berbers...original MOORS of Spain." America: Losing the Empire,1/15/13. Accessed December 4, 2014. https://tetrahedron.wordpress.com/?s=The+Berbers...original+MOORS+of+Spain&searchbutton=go%21.

The word *Ethiopia* is derived from the Greek word Aethiop and means, "The land of burnt faces." The first people to be called Ethiopians were the people of Meroe in the sixth century B.C. Meroe lies at the confluence of the White Nile and the Blue Nile. The modern nation of Ethiopia is a direct descendant of the Kingdom of Axum.[116] "From the Cushite race belongs the oldest and purest Arabian blood, and also the great and very ancient civilization.[117] Cush was the African name of Ethiopia before the Greeks named it. No matter how you twist it, the Moors were Black Africans, mostly originating from East Central Africa, where all human life began.

Now, back to Columbus. The myth below shows the theory that the Earth was flat was "discredited by Columbus' time."[118] Why is this data not taught in the schools of today?

The #1 Myth: Columbus wanted to prove the world was round

The theory that the earth was flat and that it was therefore possible to sail off the edge of it was common in the Middle Ages but had been discredited by Columbus' time. His first New World journey did help fix one common mistake, however: it proved that the earth was much larger than people had previously thought. Columbus, basing his calculations on incorrect assumptions about the size of the Earth, assumed that it would be possible to reach the rich markets of eastern Asia by sailing west. Had he succeeded in finding a new trade route, it would have made him a very wealthy man. Instead he found the Caribbean, which was then inhabited by cultures with little in the way of gold, silver or trade goods. Unwilling to completely abandon his calculations, Columbus made a laughingstock of himself back in Europe by claiming that the Earth was not round but shaped like a

---

116 "The land of burnt faces." December 21, 2009. Accessed December 9, 2015. https://meliponula.wordpress.com/2009/12/21/the-land-of-burnt-faces/.

117 Baldwin, John D. (1874). *Pre-historic Nations* (New York, Harper & Brothers), p. 74.

118 Minster, Christopher. "The Truth About Christopher Columbus." (2017). http://latinamericanhistory.about.com/od/thevoyagesofco-lumbus/a/09columbustruth.htm.

pear. He had not found Asia, he said, because of the bulging part of the pear near the stalk.[119]

We now see that Columbus was aware that the Earth was not flat. Columbus probably wanted to travel west instead of traveling the ancient path to the east to reach India for her spices.

The Piri Re'is Map

In 1929, in the Imperial Palace in Constantinople, a map was found. It was signed with the name of Piri Ibn Haji Memmed, an admiral of the Turkish navy known to us as Piri Re'is. Examination of the map showed that this map differed significantly from all other maps of America drawn in the 16th century because it showed South America and Africa in correct relative longitudes. This was most remarkable, for the navigators of the 16th century had no means of finding longitude except by guesswork.[120]

Antarctica was mapped when its coasts were free of ice. There is evidence that the people who had drawn the original map must have lived when the Ice Age had not yet ended in the Northern Hemisphere.[121]

The last Ice Age ended at least 8,000 years ago.[122] This means that the original map had to be drawn on or before 8,000 years ago. There is an exciting coincidence here. Unless they built it under water, this date was the most recent date that the Bimini Breakwater and Pier and Andros Platform could have been built. So, these structures should have existed at the same time.

In the first sentence in the preface of Hapgood's book, *Maps of the Ancient Sea Kings*, it states that, "This book contains the story of the discovery of the first hard evidence that advanced peoples preceded all people known in history."[123]

There were other maps in ancient Egypt's Library of Alexander:

119 Ibid.

120 Hapgood, Charles H. *Maps of the Ancient Sea Kings*, p. 182.

121 Ibid. back cover.

122 Creative Obsessions (n.a.). "Ice Age." Accessed June 10, 2009. http://donlehmanjr.com/Mountain/07%20Ice%20Ages.htm.

123 Hapgood, Charles H. *Maps of the Ancient Sea Kings*, p. 182.

We had strong support for the conclusion that the Piri Re'is source map was of ancient vintage. It appeared to reflect an unexpected level of scientific achievement in Alexandrian science—that is, it suggested that the geographers of the great "Museum" or "Academy" attached to the Library of Alexandria. The Mysteries might have solved the problem of applying mathematics to mapmaking— something that all known geographers from Eratosthenes to Ptolemy in the 2nd Century A.D. knew ought to be done but were unable to accomplish....

The only era of brilliance in science between the days of Ptolemy and the modern period of the Renaissance was the great era of Arab science from the 10th and 13th centuries, but even then the Arab maps reflect no application of trigonometry to map making.... In Greek times mathematics was in advance of mathematical instrumentation. There was no instrument for easily determining the longitude of places.... However, the Piri Re'is map and other maps we went on to study, seemed to suggest that such an instrument or instruments had once existed.

By default of any alternative, we seem forced to ascribe the origin of this part of the map to a pre-Hellenic people—not to Renaissance or medieval cartographers, and not to the Arabs, who were just as badly off as everybody else with respect to longitude, and not to the Greeks either.

The trigonometry of the projection (or rather its information on the size of the Earth) suggests the work of Alexandrian geographers, but the evident knowledge of longitude implies a people unknown to us, a nation of seafarers, with instruments in finding longitude undreamed of by the Greeks and, so far as we know, not possessed by the Phoenicians either.[124]

Repeatedly, we see that neither the ancient Greeks nor the Arabs had the knowledge or instruments of how to make such a map as the mapmakers in Africa's Nile Valley were able to make for centuries, probably even before the Ice Age ended. How else could we see the ocean so shallow that it connected to Antarctica before the flood? Impossible:

The Piri Re'is Map found in Istanbul in 1929, copied by Admiral Piri Re'is, is part of a world map said to have been copied from a Greek

---

124 Ibid., preface.

original in the Library of Alexandria. Among other features, the Piri Re' is map shows detailed features of Antarctica, evidently drawn several thousand years before Antarctica was "discovered," as well as the true shape of Antarctica without the ice covering.... Other features indicate an advanced knowledge of astronomy, trigonometry and the ability to determine longitude, were not known to our culture until the reign of George III of England who died in 1820.[125]

Many books and magazines have echoed such ideas. Again, as late as 1995, in his book, *Finger Print of the Gods*, Graham Hancock used the Piri Re'is map as evidence for the possibility of a prehistoric super-civilization. He said:

The true enigma of this 1513 map is not so much its inclusion of a continent of Antarctica not discovered until 1818 but its portrayal of part of the coastline of that continent under ice free conditions which came to an end 6,000 years ago and have not since recurred.[126]

Hence, how would the actual coastline of Antarctica be known if it has always been covered in modern times? "The Piri Re'is Map was redrawn in 300 B.C. from maps taken from the Library of Alexander in Africa."[127] A search to find the people who drew this map has been done. The first thing to do was to find the center of the map, which would be the most likely place for the people who drew the map to be found. In a letter from Lorenzo W. Burroughs—Captain USAF and Chief of the Cartographical (map-making) Section—wrote a letter to Charles H. Hapgood from Keene Teachers College. The letter stated that Richard W. Stratchan of MIT wrote, "there is remarkably close agreement Piri Re'is' use of the portolano projection (centered on Syene, Egypt) was an excellent choice."[128]

Syene is in southern Egypt very close to Nubia. Did the knowledge of a "round Earth" eventually reach Spain and the Moors from Egypt? Syene

---

125 The Antarctic and Piri Reis Map. (n.d.). Accessed January 7, 2015. https://www.bibliotecapleyades.net/mapas_pirireis/esp_mapaspirireis04.htm.

126 Hancock, Graham. *Fingerprints of The Gods*, p. 70.

127 Van Sertima, Ivan. (1998). *Early America Revisited* (Transaction Publishers), p. 121.

128 Hapgood, Charles H. *Maps of the Ancient Sea Kings*, p. 244.

is in southern Egypt very close to Nubia. Did the knowledge of a "round Earth" eventually reach Spain and the Moors from Egypt?

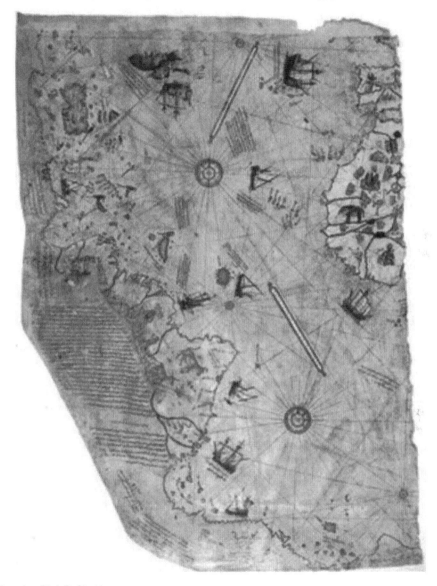

Fig. 4: Piri Re'is Map

Over time, Europe lost the ability to read or write, which brought on a Dark Age of ignorance. Also, because of the Moors' translation of Greek writings, literacy was restored back to Europe (p. 149)…. Additionally, the Moors kept contact with Mother Egypt, for they had established caliphates not only in Bagdad and Cordova but also at Cairo in Egypt. Moors provided a vital link between ancient and modern civilization. The light of knowledge, which illuminated the Moorish lands of Spain and Sicily, was instrumental in dispelling the gloom of ignorance that enveloped medieval Europe.[129]

Could the news of a round Earth, over time reach Spain from Syene, Egypt? The answer is yes, since there were no time limitations put on this question. Most of these maps were of the Mediterranean and the Black Sea. But maps of other areas survived. These included maps of the Americas, as well as maps of the Arctic and Antarctic Seas. It becomes clear that the ancient voyagers traveled from pole to pole.[130]

H. Did the First Americans Come from Asia or Africa?

There are reports that the First Americans were from Asia and Australia. DNA evidence indicates, however, that the First Americans came from Africa.

They were short-statured Anu/Twa who eventually became the Fuegians of Tierra del Fuego—the southernmost area in South America—and populated most of South America at one time. Previously found all over the Americas, they were eventually pushed down to the southernmost tip of South America.

> *The results obtained using morphological and molecular data find that Fuegian populations are distinct from the rest of the Amerindians.*[131] *Researchers believe the Fuegians are the remnants of the earliest settlers of the New World.... The Fuegians have a different genetic makeup than others. South America's Fuegians and the African Khoisan carry the same M174 gene related to the D haploid group.*[132]

Again, from scientific evidence we see that "The Fuegians were related to the Khoisan because of the Y chromosomes they carried. Fuegians in

---

129 Moore, Keith. (2008). *Freemasonry, Greek Philosophy, the Prince Hall Fraternity and the Egyptian (African) World Connection* (Indiana, Author House), p. 149-150.

130 Hapgood, Charles H. *Maps of the Ancient Sea Kings*, p. 244.

131 Perez, S. Ivan, Valerie Bernal, and Paula N. Gonzalez. "Morphological Differences Aboriginal Human Populations from Tierra del Fuego." *American Journal of Physical Anthropology*. (2007) 133:1067-1079.

132 Winters, Clyde. "30,000 BC The First African Americans" video presentation. Accessed February 5, 2009.

100–400 BP carried haplogroup A1. Hg A1 is an African haplogroup."[133] Here, we have concrete evidence that the African Khoisan and the Fuegians at the most southern tip of South America were related. Yes, the people of Tierra del Fuego were definitely "distinct from," and definitely arrived in an **earlier** migration wave than other Native Americans. They were short Africans who arrived tens of thousands of years before the Asians in the Americas.[134]

Therefore, all the claims that the original Americans came from Asia, Australia, Melanesia, or anywhere else but Africa first, are not backed by hard evidence. Besides that, scientists have stated:

They first came to America in a period very remote. The autochthonous black races in America either gradually mixed with the Indian ones, or became extinct, but in a very remote time Negroes, or Negroids were numerous to the New World.[135]

(The definition of *autochthonous* is indigenous rather than descended from migrants or colonists.)

This passage seems to be saying it was the "indigenous black races" who entered the Americas "in a period very remote" and became the first Americans. So, it was them—the "black races"— who "were either gradually mixed with the Indians or became extinct" by mixing with the Indians who this passage says were not autochthonous.

The more numerous Asian/Red Indians crossing over the Bering Strait by the thousands bred out the "autochthonous black races" and took on the modern Indian genotype look. But then, after the Vikings and after Columbus' Caucasians began to flood America, their color changed yet again. Since then, some of these "Native Americans" have become so light-skinned they look like pure "Caucasians."

I have been told that these are the folks, with just a couple percent of "original native blood," who are the ones that "The Powers That Be," are making it easy to build casinos on Indian reservations. They used to be

---

133 García-Bour, Jaume et al. "Early population differentiation...," pp. 361-70.

134 Ibid., pp. 361-370.

135 Braghine, Alexander. (2004). *The Shadow of Atlantis 1940* (Montana, Kessinger Publishing), pp. 40-41.

called "$5 Indians." However, a new name for these so-called "Indians" has been coined. They are being referred to now are "Pretendians." This is humorous, but at the same time it is very true.

It is a shame that the little land left to the "real Natives" is now being used by a people who have very little "Native" blood left in their bodies. So, we see that David Reich, professor of genetics at Harvard, was correct when he stated, "We all know the Bering Strait theory as just theory, but no, it's not fact."

Chapter 2

They Came Before Clovis

When discussing ancient American history, one very interesting question that invariably emerges is, "Who were the first Americans and from where did they originate?" Was the first American, "The Red Man" who we saw on television every Saturday morning—with long hair blowing in the wind as he masterfully rode his horse bareback—fighting the U.S. Calvary? In the last several years new evidence has been surfacing that will undeniably alter, and quite possibly completely change the story we have seen on television and been taught in school. Also, the most widely accepted discovery in North America concerning the first Americans has been the Clovis discovery.

What is Clovis, its significance, and ramifications? This question will be answered in three steps:

1. What is Clovis and what is the prevailing theory about Clovis?

2. What evidence is there to confirm this new analysis?

3. Who were the first people at Clovis?

For years ancient American history has been anchored by the Clovis story. Clovis is an archaeological site in New Mexico that was first excavated in the 1930s. The "Holy Grail" for the "Clovis First" theory—claimed to be the site that contained evidence for the first Americans arriving in 9400 B.C., who walked from Asia across the Bering Strait[136] to Alaska. Until recently, this claim was widely taught across America for many years. New findings should have caused the story of the route of entry into the Americas to change drastically. However, the basic story is still in place today with two small updates to keep the textbook theories alive. This original theory is that the first American people could have taken the northern route from Asia to Clovis. But during the last Ice Age, in some areas, the glacier was a mile or two high, blocking the inland route.

The dates the ice covered the Bering Strait and its extent of coverage differs depending upon which glaciologists are referenced. The path from Asia to Alaska and Canada was blocked by ice from 115,000 until 10,000

136 Smith, Chuck R. "Paleo-Indian Period and Tradition Making a Living in the Early Americas." (2000). Accessed June 10, 2009. https://www.cabrillo.edu/~crsmith/noamer_paleo.html.

years ago,[137] when the Ice Age ended. During that period, colder weather must have rolled in, producing even larger ice barriers: "The time period in question, 35,000 to 10,000 years ago, saw a growth and expansion of huge ice sheets that covered vast regions of the two continents"[138] (the two continents being Asia and North America). Therefore, migration across this glacier is extremely doubtful.

If Clovis was dated 9400 B.C., and the passage was blocked 10,000 years ago (10,000 years ago is the same as 8000 B.C.), then the Clovis people would have had to cross one- or two-mile-high glaciers, 1400 years before they melted, and passage to Clovis would have been open. This theory logically has been shot down. So, two "updated" theories were invented to save this postulation.

Instead of walking overland through the middle of the Alaskan glacier, one updated theory speculates that the first Americans left Asia by walking around the glacier in far eastern Asia where the Pacific Ocean meets land by hugging the shore of far eastern Asia. They would continue east to Alaska and Canada, then south along the shore to modern Washington State, until the glaciers ended. They would then walk inland away from the shore. This way they could have "theoretically" avoided the big glaciers, as they walked along the sandy beaches of the Pacific Ocean from far eastern Asia to Alaska's beaches, and down to Washington State's beaches.

Even today, cruise ship tourists sailing to Alaska during the spring have witnessed large chunks of ice falling from the top of an iceberg, all the way down into the ocean. Therefore, no shore was available for the ice to fall on. In some areas, the shore was completely covered by a glacier. However, during the Ice Age, the glacier was much larger and extended out far beyond the beach landmass into the ocean. There was no shore for hundreds, and possibly thousands of miles. If there was no shore on which to walk, the Clovis theory does not work. There was no shore in the far north back then because Alaska was among the other areas experiencing the Ice Age.

---

137 Adams, Jonathon. (n.d.). "NORTH AMERICA DURING THE LAST 150,000 YEARS. Accessed June 10, 2009. https://www.esd.ornl. gov/projects/gen/adams2.html.

138 Soffer, Olga., and N. D. Praslov. (1993). *From Kostenki to Clovis* (New York, Kluwer Academic/Plenum Press), p. 4.

Even today, Alaska is north of the freezing zone of the 51st parallel. Therefore, this logically means that during the Ice Age when it was even colder, Alaska was freezing and covered by a glacier, including the beaches.

In "1824 Russia and USA signed a treaty accepting 54 degrees, 4 minutes latitude as the southern boundary of Russian America." Disregarding the 1824 date and the treaty with Russia statements, we focus on the southern part of Alaska that is a distance of 2 degrees 4 minutes latitude. That area is north of the 51st parallel. Therefore, that area of 2 degrees 4 minutes latitude, in the "Distance (as the crow flies) is 211.42 miles—spherical earth.[139]

That area, farther north, is colder since it is 211.42 miles north of the 51st parallel. Translated into simple terms, *the shores of southern Alaska were completely frozen even more solid during the Ice Age.* The freeze line is more than 211 miles south of the Alaskan shores. This would rule out any "shore hugging" trips that we were told were a possible way the Asians reached Alaska and eventually North America during the last Ice Age. Another problem with this theory is that there is no evidence found of ancient boats—or even pieces of ancient boats—that could have been used to make this ancient Pacific Coast journey 10,000 years ago. With that being said, there are some archaeologists who still hold on to this unfounded theory "although they have yet to find any preserved boats in early, Pacific Coastal, American sites."[140]

The second updated theory is that the first Americans could have sailed from Australia or Melanesia to South America, which would take many months to reach. By the way, Melanesia is located just north of Australia and stretches southwest to the island of Fiji. It is common knowledge that the islands from Australia down to Fiji, were first inhabited by Brown people. The suffix of Melanesia, Polynesia and Micronesia is "nesia."

The suffix "nesia" is a derivative of "nesos." Furthermore, "nesos" is from the Greek language meaning "island." Melanesia, Polynesia and Micronesia are all islands. Melanin is a "dark brown pigment." Pigment means "natural coloring." Melanesia means either "Dark Brown Island," or "Island of Dark Brown People." The reason all of this is mentioned is due to the secondary theory above, that the first Americans could have

---

139 Morse, Stephen P. "Computing Distances between Latitudes/Longitudes in One Step" (2008). http://www.stevemorse.org/nearest/distance.php.

140 Pringle, Heather. "THE 1st AMERICANS." *Scientific American* 305, no. 5 (2011): 36-45. http://www.jstor.org/stable/26002874.

sailed from Australia or Melanesia to South America. What this secondary theory is telling us is that if the first Americans came from an island that was inhabited by dark brown people would they, or their ancestors, not also have been Africans?

Leaving aside the traditional way of thinking, are there other possible routes the first Americans could have chosen to reach the "New World" (the Americas) from the "Old World?" The answer is, "Yes, indeed." The western route would be the one the Vikings took, island hopping from northwestern Europe west to Canada. However, this route would not be practical either, because northwestern Europe had experienced the Ice Age as well. The reason for this is, as you will soon see, the Vikings' Scandinavian home is well over 1000 miles farther north than southern Alaska. This means there was even more ice to travel on—as mentioned earlier, from the other example of southern Alaska's latitude being 54 degrees, 4 minutes latitude. Greenland is even farther north and colder than Alaska at a chilling 72 degrees latitude. The distance (as the crow flies) is 1194.97 miles further north—spherical earth from Alaska's latitude.

The 1194.97-mile marker did not begin from the freezing line and continue north to Greenland's most southern point. It began at Alaska's latitude, 211.42 degrees south of Greenland. By adding 211.42 to 1194.97, we see that Greenland is 1406.39 miles above the freezing point area. That would rule out the island hopping in exchange for an oceanic voyage from one continent to another.

Finally, we see that the two theories are now "dated." Let us now look at how the Europeans may have tried to travel to the Americas from the northern part of Europe. Even though the northern route has been ruled out because of the glaciers, let us look at how far it would be to travel to the New World from Northern Europe after the Ice Age ended.

Island hopping required covering a distance from Norway west to Iceland, to Greenland and on to Canada, which was 1240 miles (1077 nautical miles). They would experience very cold weather and have to navigate icebergs even larger than the one that sunk the Titanic. Why?

Because these icebergs would have been formed in far colder weather in the Ice Age, than those of the warmer times of the Titanic. All the islands above, including Canada on the mainland, would have been buried under glaciers as well. By the time they reached the closest, most eastern part of Canada, with snow or ice covering Baffin Island, they would have had to travel as far south as New York to find land not covered by the Ice Age snow.[141] To find the most conservative estimate, we will measure from the southern point of Baffin Island at the capital city of Iqaluit to New York City. That distance is another 1400 nautical miles.[142] The total distance would have been 1400 + 1077 = 2477 nautical miles. For your information, 2477 nautical miles would be equal to 2850 land miles from Norway to Canada to New York where the Ice Age ice ended.

What then is the shortest distance from the Old World to the New? The answer is that from the bulge in the African continent west to Brazil in South America is the shortest route (see Fig. 5). This direct route across the Atlantic from Africa to South America is nearly six times closer than a trip from Australia, east to South America. That route is 1300 miles further than from Africa, west to South America.

How long would the Africa-to-South America trip take by boat? To answer this question, we shall draw from an experiment conducted by Dr. Allen Bombard, M.D., in 1964. He was a physician from Liberia. Bombard was aware of the ocean currents off the African coast that run like conveyor belts to the Americas and back. He rented a boat without an oar, sail or rudder, and drifted in the current from Africa to the Americas in a documented 52 days.[143] He had a supply ship for food and water but they never touched the boat to propel it.

Hence, the first Americans may not have come from Asia. New evidence has surfaced from several different areas that made it necessary to take another look at all these theories. The first Americans are referred to as Paleoamericans. That is a term that describes the people who lived in the Americas during the Paleolithic period, which extends from two million to 11,000 years ago.[144] Also, the terms Paleolithic and Pleistocene are synonyms and refer to the same time period. However, both must be used, not to confuse the reader but to be able to correctly and directly

141 Edmonds, Molly. "How the Ice Age Worked" May 13, 2008. HowStuffWorks.com. https://history. howstuffworks.com/historical-events/ ice-age.htm. February 19, 2018. https://history.howstuffworks.com/ historical-events/ice-age.htm/printable.

142 "Bali & Indonesia on the Net." (n.d.). Accessed October 8, 2010. http:// www.indo.com/cgi-bin/dist?place1=new+york+city&place2=iqaluit.

143 Van Sertima, Ivan. *African Presence in Early America*, p. 71.

144 Klein, Richard G., and Anne Pike-Tay. (2014). "Paleolithic,"*Access Science* (McGraw-Hill Education), https://doi.org/10.1036/1097-8542.483950.

quote necessary evidence from different sources that use different terms. Regardless of the term used—the Paleolithic and Pleistocene predate the Holocene. Unfortunately, despite overwhelming evidence to the contrary, many sources still ignore the Paleolithic finds in the Americas but cite the late Pleistocene and early Holocene discoveries. Where is the hard evidence for the claim that the first Americans walked over from Asia? There is only one archaeological site of note in the Bering corridor between Canada and Asia:

> *The Old Crow site in the Yukon region of Canada also was long thought to be evidence of the pre-projectile point horizon on the basis of a single radiocarbon date of 26,000 to 29,000 B.P. on bone speculated to have been used by humans when fresh before the bone had begun to decay. However, follow-up dating showed that the undoubted materials at the site were not even Pleistocene in age.*[145]

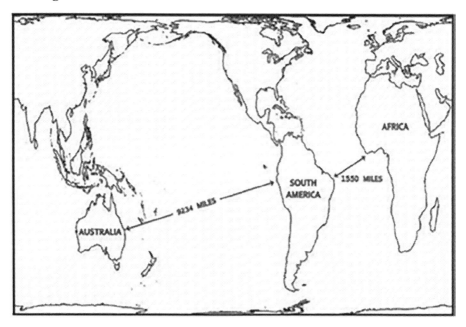

Fig. 5: Map of the World. *Drawn by Marrwho Hasati.*

In this case the public was deliberately misled; sloppy scholarship was detected. Either way, the Old Crow site was bogus. The Pleistocene Epoch

---

145 Jablonski, Nina G. (2002). *The First Americans: The Pleistocene Colonization of the New World* (California, University of California Press), p. 174.

was the period dating from 1.8 million years ago to 8000 B.C.[146] This means the Old Crow site would have had to be later than 8000 B.C. not earlier. Thus, the site was *not* in the Pleistocene but in the Holocene Epoch. Now that the Old Crow site has been eliminated, 85% of the five oldest sites of the earliest occupants are now closer to the Atlantic Ocean side of the American continent than the Pacific side.

The Fig. 5 map of Central and South America displays the evidence, which supports the thesis that the first Americans probably did not migrate here from Asia because of the prohibitive mileage. The second nail in the coffin is that, by extension, it is now accepted that the first humans and the oldest civilizations existed in Africa. With Asia out of the picture, where is the most likely origin of departure for the first Americans? Is it from Africa or Southern Europe? Southern Europe is only mentioned because northern Europe is out of the question for it was covered with large glaciers during the last Ice Age.[147]

Therefore, there is no evidence and no trail that can be followed from the fluted, Late Pleistocene, points from Asia to the Americas. It is now clear that the "big-game-hunting cultures" of the Pleistocene did not follow fictitious herds of animals crossing the frozen tundra, migrating to the Americas from Asia. (Note: The definition of "fluted points" mentioned in the quote are spearheads shaped mostly from flint. They have grooves on them from their creators chipping away the flakes making the points sharp.) In 1993 scholars found patterns of genetics in non-Amerinds. Then, in 1996 Haydenblet and Sutter found dental variations in South America.[148]

We have extensively studied the exodus of the first humans from Africa to arrive in Southern Europe 40,000 to 45,000 years ago. That is far more recent than the most conservative peer-reviewed date for the arrival of the first Americans from Africa about 250,000 to 350,000 years ago. Many

---

146 "Pleistocene." (2010). Accessed January 16, 2010. http://www.answers.com/topic/pleistocene.

147 Powell, Joseph F., and Walter A. Neves. "Craniofacial Morphology of the First Americans: Pattern and Process in the Peopling of the New World." *American Journal of Physical Anthropology* 110, no. S29 (1999): 153-88.

148 "Pleistocene." (2010). Accessed January 16, 2010. http://www.answers.com/topic/pleistocene.

scientists ignore the Paleolithic finds in the Americas. Let us see if the following evidence exposes the flaws in that theory.

Nina Jablonski is an author, professor and head of the Department of Anthropology at Pennsylvania State University. She agrees that the evidence shows that the first Americans did not enter the Americas from Asia into Alaska. Jablonski's studies led her to write:

> *The current archeological and biological evidence does not support the assumptions of the Clovis migration theory about Paleo-Indian Paleoamerican migration routes. For example, there are no instances of Late Pleistocene, pre-Clovis fluted points at the entry-point to the Americas, Alaska.... Despite intensive efforts, research also has produced no Clovis-like, big-game-hunting cultures in the interior of northeast Asia.*[149]

Fig. 6: Map of Central and South America. *Drawn by Marrwho Hasati.*

---

149 Jablonski, Nina. G. *The First Americans,* p. 170.

Mongolians' First Entry into the Americas

Note: Before beginning this section, there will be a change of terms. The scientific community—i.e., Gonzalez-Jose et al. 2005—have labeled the modern Native Americans of today, as Amerinds (i.e. American + Indians).

It is appropriate, at this point, to give the background of one of the most important of the Amerind documents (their Bible), called the "Walam Olum," (meaning "The Red Record").

It was written by Mongolian Amerinds. In their records, the Mongolians did not reach the Americas until 2600 B.C. This is the date that the Walam Olum gives their own ancestors, who first arrived in the Americas and began mixing their blood with the resident African/Proto-Americans. That would be the first time some of the American Africans' skin would lighten.

After the Vikings and Columbus opened the doors to North America, some of their skin colors lightened yet again. As a matter of fact, a few of these, "Amerinds" have become so light-skinned that they look like what the their descendants would call "pale faces." I have been told that these folks—with just a couple percent of "original native blood"—are the ones who, "The Powers That Be," are courting to build casinos on Indian reservations. The name of these Amerinds, who used to be called the so-called "$5-dollar Indians," has been buried. Their new name is the "Pretendians." They are pretending they are Indians so they can receive the benefits of having majority native blood. It is a shame that the little land that is left to the real Amerinds is now being used by a people who have very little or no "Native" blood left in their bodies.

Today, Mongolia is a country in East and Central Asia. When did the first Mongolians enter the Americas? Another date that we are told they first entered is around 3000 B.C. This 3000 B.C. date was not chosen at random. It is based on scientific analysis carried out by the following sources: Lahr, Neves, et al. (1996). Support for Laher, Neves et al. comes from Jantz and Owsley (1997), Steele and Powell (1992, 1993, 1994), as well as Powell and Steele (1993).

Sources for non-Amerind craniofacial morphology skull or facial bones not belonging to Amerinds among early North Americans: Cann, Fox, 1996, and Horai, et al. In summary, all the scientists above studied skulls, genetic patterns and dental variations to verify the first entry of Mongolians into the Americas that only began after 3000 B.C.

As mentioned earlier, the natives themselves —in the Walam Olum— give us their date of 2600 B.C. Either way, their dates are dwarfed by the arrival of Africans by 250,000 years or more in Central America.

Now, to better understand the journal containing the article that states where the Holocene Epoch emanates from. The *Yearbook of Physical Anthropology* is an "annual journal of review articles that summarize and evaluate recent literature in topics of current interest to biological anthropologists."[150] It stated: "Further, if the Mongolians did not come during the Late Pleistocene Epoch, then when did they reach the Americas? As mentioned before, the Mongolians did not enter the Americas until the Middle Holocene."[151]

Where did this "they came in 3000 B.C." conclusion come from? Let us take a closer look at this issue. The Holocene Epoch began 10,000 years ago and continues to the present day, according to the University of California's Museum of Paleontology and the United States Department of Agriculture.[152] That would make the middle of the Holocene Epoch 5,000 years ago, which is equal to about 3000 B.C. This means that after diligent scientific study of ancient American skulls, "only during the Middle Holocene or later did the 'Mongoloid' populations enter the Americas."[153]

150 American Association of Physical Anthropologists. (2009). *The Yearbook of Physical Anthropology.* Accessed June 5, 2011. http://www.physanth.org/publications/yearbook-of-physical-anthropology.

151 Follin, Sven, M. B. Stephens, M. Laaksoharju, A.-C. Nilsson, John Smellie, and Eva-Lena Tullborg. "Modelling the evolution of hydrochemical conditions in the Fennoscandian Shield during Holocene time using multidisciplinary information." *Journal of the International Association of GeoChemistry* 23 (2008) 2004-2020.

152 "The Holocene: The Last ~10,000 years." (n.d.). University of California Museum of Paleontology. Accessed February 26, 2010. http://www.ucmp. berkeley.edu/quaternary/hol.html; "The Holocene Epoch (10,000 Yr BP To Present)." (n.d.). United States Department of Agriculture. Accessed February 26, 2010. http://www.srs.fs.usda.gov/sustain/draft/history/histry-14.htm

153 Powell, Joseph F., and Walter A. Neves. "Craniofacial Morphology of the First Americans," pp. 153-88.

It has therfore been scientifically determined that there was no Paleolithic Asian Clovis migration during the Pleistocene times (that ended in 8000 B.C.), as we have always been mistakenly taught by American textbooks. In "History 110," Dr. Olson-Raymer of Humboldt State University, California humbly admitted: "The myths about the indigenous peoples of North America have persisted largely because of the desire by the conquering Europeans to justify and rationalize the consequences of their actions."[154]

When the Mongolians finally did enter North America from Asia across the Bering Strait in 2600 B.C.,[155] their sheer numbers slowly diluted the blood of the first Americans who were already there, and whose numbers had plummeted after surviving a cosmic catastrophe—which will later be explained in detail. The mixing of blood with the Mongolians influenced the Proto-Americans; their physical appearance began to change.

Since most of the Mongolians probably came on foot rather than by boat (as the Proto-Americans had to do), many more of them were able to enter North America at one time. They were also able to come more often because of the convenience of walking as opposed to building a boat and sailing. This eventually allowed them to physically outnumber the Paleoamericans. The Walam Olum corroborates this crossing:

> [F]rom Asia into the New World, and of the encounters of the people who were already living there.... Historically, the Delaware Indian elder Winnie Poolaw of Anadarko, Oklahoma, further declared, "The Walam Olum is like our Bible."[156]

Why Did the Asians Migrate to the Americas?

The Walam Olum states that the Hiung-nu people were at war with the Yellow Emperor of China (whose name was Huang Di and his followers the Huang-ti). "In ancient times the Yellow Emperor was known to have been a child prodigy. As he grew he showed himself to be sincere, wise,

---

154 Olson-Raymer, Gayle. "History 110 - The Original Inhabitants - What They Lost and What They Retained." Accessed June 2, 2015. http://users.humboldt.edu/ogayle/hist110/na.html.

155 McCutchen, David. *The Red Record* (New York, Avery Publishing Group Inc., 1998), p. 4.

156 Ibid.

honest, and compassionate."[157] Without knowing the details, on the surface it looks as though the Yellow Emperor and his Huang-ti followers were the "good guys" and the Huang-nu were the "bad guys. The Huang-ti people (of the Yellow Emperor) drove away the Hiung-nu people. They escaped from the Huang-ti in Asia, then traveled east across the Bering Strait into the Americas around 2600 B.C., "ten thousand strong."[158]

How does this affect the so-called sacred theory of the first Amerinds coming from Asia? The Walam Olum states that the Mongolian-Hiung-nu people arrived in the Americas around 2600 B.C., which is 6800 years after the Clovis artifacts were found. If the first Mongolians arrived in 2600 B.C., then who were the people at the Clovis site in 9400 B.C.? Since the Mongolians from Asia arrived too late to create Clovis, does this not further debunk the credibility of the "Clovis First" theory?

When the Hiung-nu people left Mongolia in 2600 B.C. and began to migrate to the Americas, they came in wave after wave at different time periods. After their initial entry from Asia in 2600 B.C., another large wave of Mongolians entered America in 1250 A.D.[159] That is almost 4000 years after the Hiung-nu entered America back in 2600 B.C.

As mentioned earlier, when these Mongols entered the Americas, they came in greater numbers than the Africans had earlier. The Africans had walked or had come to the Americas in small boats for the Ice Age was in full swing back then. The shores from Asia to Alaska were almost completely, or even totally covered with Ice. In this later migration, 20,000 Mongolians are said to have entered across Beringa from Asia at one time. J. D. Baldwin (1871) agrees with the combative foreigners and wrote, "Perhaps the Proto-Americans found the country mostly unoccupied and saw there but little of any other people until an eruption of warlike barbarians came upon them from the Northwest."[160]

---

157 Ni, M. *The Yellow Emperor's Classic of Medicine* (Massachusetts, Shambhala Publications Inc., 1995), p. 1.

158 Ibid., p. 4.

159 Childress, David H. (1992). *Lost Cities of North & Central America* (Illinois, Adventures Unlimited Press), p. 366.

160 Baldwin, John D. (1871, 2009) *Ancient America: in Notes on American Archaeology* (Pennsylvania, Kissinger Publishing, LLC), p. 27.

What follows is an example that illustrates that politics has no business in academia or scientific discoveries. As late as 1989, a report stated that five archaeologists from South America had held back new data they found on older pre-Clovis discoveries. It was reported that the reason these archaeologists did not make their older finds public was that they feared their funding would be cut by colleagues in North America who "endorse the short chronology"[161] of Clovis—the 9400 B.C. date.

This new data showed there were people in the Americas long before Clovis, which is an example of the long chronology. This data was most likely held back because it supported the theory that the first Americans were not the people of Clovis, and their culture was far older than had been reported.

Another relevant story that portrays how politics pollutes history happened when Firestone (one of the authors of *The Cycle of Cosmic Catastrophes*, 2006) was conducting fieldwork for his book on the catastrophe that ended the last Ice Age. Firestone found concrete evidence of pre-Clovis people living in Canada. When he took this evidence to the local museum (which he declined to name) to be displayed, however, "They declined as it was too controversial for them."[162] Again, what a shame it is, when politics becomes a factor in the field of history.

Here is the last nail in the Clovis-First coffin. The Clovis points that were found 9,400 years ago do not match the points found in Asia, the land where they were said to have originated.

Later, Firestone also found that: "the American Clovis points are very unlike flint points from Asia, their supposed land of origin."[163] Considering this evidence, how could the Clovis people have been the same people from the same culture but with different flint points?

Another serious falsehood some people should be ashamed of, that has been going on for centuries, is how the First Americans' land has been and is still being stolen. "There are 493 Indian gaming operations in the United

161 Marder, William. (2005). *Indians in the Americas* (California, Book Tree), p. 8.

162 Firestone, Richard, Allen West, and Simon Warwick-Smith. (2006). *The Cycle of Cosmic Catastrophes: How a Stone-Age Comet Changed the Course of World Culture* (Vermont, Bear & Company), p. 81.

163 Ibid., p. 239.

States."[164] These operations are controlled and operated not by the Natives on their reservations, but by organized gambling syndicates. Black Indians (Black Birds) are losing their land on reservations today. Surprisingly, they are not losing land to the "Red Birds" (Red Indians).

One may be surprised to know that it is not the Red Birds but some White birds (White folks), many of whom have very little so-called "Indian blood"—and sometimes none at all—who are moving to reservations these days. They are building casinos to take advantage of certain tax advantages. These casinos are not owned by Black Birds, or even Red Birds. Dr. Clyde Winters makes it crystal clear that:

> To ensure that Black Native Americans BNA would never be able to get their land back, White Americans created the myth that the Native Americans were descendants of Mongoloid people from East Asia. This myth was solidified in the minds of people around the world through the export of American cowboy movies, that always depicted Apache or Mongoloid Indians as the authentic Native Americans or Indians (p. 16). Today there are few Afro-Americans recognized by Native Americans by the United States government. This is due to the fact that BNA were forced to declare on government records and Census forms that they were "Colored" Americans or "Freedmen," the same connotation that was applied to the former African slaves (p. 156).[165]

This myth and the Clovis myth are still not only still perpetuated on television and in the movies, but even in most schools in the United States today. Black Indians are still being discriminated against as Black Americans are today. In another form of discrimination, in 2016 Chief War Horse put Dr. Imhotep on the phone with a Black Indian in Oklahoma who told him that if anyone in Oklahoma, who is of a dark complexion, dresses in Amerind attire, and goes out in public—they will be **immediately arrested!**

> In this last example, Dr. Ivan Van Sertima (1991) mentioned an example of political absurdity that occurred at the 1974 Cairo Conference—which was held to determine once and for all just who the Ancient Egyptians were. Of the twenty-two scholars invited to the

164 "500 Nations." (n.d.). *500 Nations Indian Casinos SuperSite*. Accessed September 16, 2015. http://500nations.com/Indian_Casinos.asp.

165 Winters, Clyde. *We Are Not Just Africans*, pp. 16, 156.

conference only two were Black, Dr. Cheikh Anta Diop of Senegal and Dr. Theophile Obenga of the Congo. At the end of the conference all agreed, however, that the Ancient Egyptians were Black. The record shows that Dr. Van Sertima reported that just after the agreement was made, however, one of the White scholars still yelled out, "Even though they were Black they were White."[166]

The example above is similar to one that occurred when Stefan Anitei wrote an article in 2007, entitled "The First Americans were Black!" The article is written very similarly to other Australian-American migration articles. After Anitei wrote and admitted, "The first inhabitants of the Americas belonged to the Negro type (Blacks)....However, you do not have to think they were of the African type. They belong to a racial group called the Black Asians."[167]

What does that mean? If Anitei mentioned that Black Asians do belong to the Negro type, but at the same time says you do not have to think they were Africans? What message was he really trying to convey?

Cowboys and Indians or Cowboys and Africans? Evidence of pre-Clovis African Occupation

There is peer-reviewed evidence of Africans in South America 100,000 years ago and in North America (in the state of South Carolina) 51,700 years ago.[168] These first people in the Americas are labeled Paleoamericans. Earlier we saw evidence that illustrates that the first Americans who entered during the Paleolithic period before Clovis were Africans, and it is most probable that the Paleolithic Africans sailed here directly from Africa.

Let us now look at these oldest sites in the Americas. The antiquity of evidence for a western entry from Asia through Alaska to Canada does

166 Van Sertima, Ivan. (7/27/91). "Lecture given at the National Medical Association Convention," Indianapolis, Indiana.

167 Anitei, Stefan. (2007). "The First Americans Were Black!" Accessed July 6, 2009. http://news.softpedia.com/news/The-First-Inhabitants-of-the-Americas-Were-Black-64307.shtml.

168 Santos, G. M., M. I. Bird, F. Parenti, Guidon N. Fifield, and P. A. Hausiaden. (2003). "A revised chronology of the lowest occupation layer of Pedra Furada Shelter Piaui, Brazil: the Pleistocene peopling of the Americas." *Quaternary Science Review*, Vol.22, Issues 21-22, Nov-Dec 2003, pp. 2303-2310.

not come close to the age of evidence in eastern America. The 56,000-year date emanates from rock solid evidence in a peer-reviewed journal (and it is the conservative date to be used for the thesis of this book claiming the first Americans were from Africa). A new, much older date just found in 2008, replaces the old possible dates of Africans in the Americas. The new date is based on tests conducted by French anthropologist Niede Guidon, Director of the American Man Foundation. Her group is the same that gave us the 56,000-year date.

However, there is now, an even older date, based on tests of stone tools using the luminescence dating method. It suggests a new date of 100,000 years ago for people in the Americas that Guidon posted in 2014. Guidon also says, "Our data to date suggests that the first humans came to northeastern Brazil and the Caribbean from Africa."[169] This South American site at Pedra Furada also contains evidence of human occupation in a cave in northeastern Brazil. Later, a skeleton was found along with rock engravings and rock paintings, which were also found in the cave.

In North America, a South Carolina University Professor Dr. Albert says, "humans lived along the east bank of the Savannah River circa 50,000 years ago."[170] The 51,700 years-old North American site found in Allendale County, South Carolina, by the Savannah River is less than thirty miles from the Atlantic Ocean. (Fig. 7 shows Dr. Albert Goodyear, holding the flint worked by human hands at the 51,700 years level.) As seen in the introduction of this book, the evidence for the ancient African migrations comes in multiple forms. This data exposes the false premise that the first Americans came from Asia once and for all.

Evidence has been presented here to cement the fact that Africans were the first in South, Central and then in North America. Moving on to Central America, "early Mexican skulls show no clear resemblance to Amerinds or East Asians. This was found after a thorough study of ancient Mexicans skulls done by Gonzalez-Jose et al. (2005)."[171] These skulls were from the Late Pleistocene, which ends after 8000 B.C., as the title of the

---

169 Thomson, Sheila. "Interview with Niède Guidon." (2013) www. maria-brazil.org/niede_guidon.htm.

170 Santos, G. M. et al., revised chronology of the lowest occupation layer, pp. 2303-2310.

171 Gonzalez-Jose et al., "Late Pleistocene/Holocene Craniofacial Morphology, pp. 772-80.

2005 article suggests.[172] The people of whom these skulls belong are undoubtedly African as well. Central America's first American evidence can be added to the South and North American evidence.

Fig. 7: Dr. Albert Goodyear. *Courtesy of SCIAA, Daryl P. Miller.*

In Fig. 7, you can see Dr. Albert Goodyear measuring extremely old artifacts that were found deep in the lowest occupation layer. This professor is not afraid to get his hands dirty on old objects that some other professors would not do.

Did Egyptians Sail Beyond the "Pillars of Hercules"?

There may be some readers who will say, "You do have evidence of Africans in the Americas 100,000 years ago, but they must have walked there because there is no evidence of humans sailing that early. Hence, we do not believe this theory is correct." Yes, there have been articles concerning Africans, especially Egyptians, that doubt they ever sailed. Here are just a few of a long list of statements that have been inaccurately stated about Egyptian ships and navigation. They say that Late Pleistocene,

172 "Pleistocene." (2010). Accessed January 16, 2010. http://www.answers.com/topic/pleistocene.

which ends after 8000 B.C., as the title of the 2005 article suggests.[173] The people whom these skulls belong to are undoubtedly African as well. So, Central America's "First American" evidence can be added to the South and North American evidence. In addition:

> *The ancient Egyptians were no great travelers. Unlike the Phoenicians and Greeks who spread out all over the ancient Mediterranean, the Egyptians stayed home and left the foreign lands to the foreigners, much of the time at least.*[174]

What? "From earliest times Egyptians built boats for transportation, fishing and enjoyment."[175] Does this mean that they built ships for nothing else? They also say that: "Egyptian seagoing ships were inferior to those used by other peoples."[176] Though the ancient Egyptians had seaworthy boats,—e.g., the funerary boat in the boat pit on the Gizeh plateau—the tradition is that they never sailed the Mediterranean Seas to Greece.[177]

On the other hand, *we have evidence to the contrary. The February 2011 edition of* The New York Times *reported that Greek and American archaeologists and geologists have found new evidence on the island of Crete, in the Mediterranean Sea. That is the startling implication of discoveries made the last two summers on the Greek island of Crete. Stone tools found there, archaeologists say, are at least* **130,000 years old**, *which is considered strong evidence for*

---

173 Ibid.

174 Frankfort, Henri. (2000). *Ancient Egyptian Religion: An Interpretation* (Courier Dover Publications), p.106.

175 "Ancient Egyptian Boat-Building." Max Energy Limited, 2012. http://www.solarnavigator.net/ancient_egyptian_boat_building.htm.

176 Dolinger, Andrew. "Ships and Boats." (2000). Accessed August 4, 2016. http://www.reshafim.org.il/ad/egypt/timelines/topics/navigation.htm; Usai, D., and S. Salvatori, "The oldest representation of a Nile boat," *Antiquity* Vol 81 issue 314 December 2007.

177 Coppen, Philip. "Egypt: Origin of the Greek Culture" *Frontier Magazine* 5.3 (May-June 1999). http://www. philipcoppens.com/egyptgreece.html.

the earliest known seafaring in the Mediterranean and cause for rethinking the maritime capabilities of pre-human cultures.[178]

The very first sailors and peoples were from the Nile Valley. At first, they thought that these early sailors were limited to just using rafts.

But archaeologists and experts on early nautical history said the discovery appeared to show that these ancient mariners had craft sturdier and more reliable than rafts. They also must have had the cognitive ability to conceive and carry out repeated water crossings over great distances in order to establish sustainable populations producing an abundance of stone artifacts.[179]

To clarify, these people traveled repeatedly back and forth in sailboats to the island of Crete from the Nile Valley. This enabled them to enjoy an uninterrupted, long-lasting civilization, producing many stone artifacts. Even if the earliest date of 100,000 years is used for Africans in the Americas, that is 30,000 years after they began voyages to Crete 130,000 years ago. 30,000 years is more than enough time for them to have ventured out of the Mediterranean and to find America. The very fact that there is:

An ancient harbor on the Red Sea proves ancient Egyptians mastered oceangoing technology and launched a series of ambitious expeditions to far-off lands. Did the ancient Egyptians ever cross the ocean and reach South America? The Ancient Egyptians weren't very inclined towards travel. I have no idea where you would have heard this, but it wouldn't have been very possible for Ancient Egyptians to travel to South America.[180]

Again, we see an author who writes that the Egyptians never sailed to the Americas? That conclusion *may not necessarily be true*:

One of the first documented instances of Africans sailing and settling in the Americas were black Egyptians led by King Ramses III, during

178 Wilford, John N. "On Crete, New Evidence of Very Ancient Mariners." *New York Times*, Science: Online. February 15, 2010. Accessed January 20, 2017. http://www.nytimes.com/2010/02/16/science/16archeo.html.

179 Ibid.

180 Curry, Andrew. "Egypt's Ancient Fleet: Lost for Thousands of Years, Discovered in a Desolate Cave." *Discover Magazine Online*. September 6, 2011. Accessed June 9, 2015. http://discovermagazine.com/2011/jun/02-egypts-lost-fleet-its-been-found.

the 19th dynasty in 1292 B.C. In fact, in 445 B.C., the Greek historian Herodotus wrote of the Ancient Egyptian pharaohs' great seafaring and navigational skills.[181] The discovery of American narcotics in Egyptian mummies has left some historians amazed. Recently, archaeologists discovered the presence of narcotics only known to be derived from American plants in ancient Egyptian mummies. These substances included South American cocaine from Erythroxylon *and nicotine from* Nicotianatabacum. *German toxicologist Svetla Balabanova reported the findings, which suggest that such compounds made their way to Africa through trans-Atlantic trade that would predate Columbus' arrival by thousands of years.[182]*

The Egyptians even had sailing myths way back, 4,000 years ago: "When Pharaoh Amen-em-het ruled Egypt in about the year 2000 B.C.... He sailed down the Red Sea and out into the ocean beyond."[183]

The evidence speaks for itself. The ancient Egyptians sailed to the Americas. Africans have been in the Americas for at the very least, 250,000 years. The Mongolians do follow, but not until around 197,400 years later! But how do the Mongolians evolve and change into Amerinds, otherwise known as Native Americans?

The Native Americans seen on television are a mixture of African and Mongolian bloods. What? Some people may ask, "The Indians I see today have straight hair. How could they be part African?" That is simple to answer. A perfect example is found in the aboriginal Australians, or the dark-skinned peoples of Southern India. Both groups have dark skin; yet most have straight hair and not the pepper-corn hair of many Africans.

Furthermore, some of the dark-skinned Australians even have blue eyes. How can this be? It is explained by genetics. A counter argument

181 Chengu, Garikai. "Before Columbus: How Africans Brought Civilization to America." *Global Research*, October 12, 2014. http://www. globalresearch. ca/before-columbus-how-africans-brought-civilization-to-america/5407584.

182 Gordon, Taylor. "10 Pieces of Evidence That Prove Black People Sailed to the Americas Long Before Columbus." *Atlanta Black Star* January 23, 2015. Accessed May 22, 2015. http://atlantablackstar. com/2015/01/23/10-pieces-of-evidence-that-prove-black-people-sailed-to-the-americas-long-before-columbus/2/.

183 Parkinson, Richard B. (1997). *The Tale of Sinuhe and Other Ancient Egyptian Poems, 1940-1640 BC.* (New York, Oxford University Press).

could be posed that the first documented African slaves (brought by the Spanish) did not arrive in the Americas until 1520 A.D. These slaves were imported because the Amerind slave population was decimated by disease[184] after Columbus arrived in the Americas.

As mentioned earlier, the Paleoamerican Black Africans have been in the Americas for 250,000 to 350,000 years. This book reveals that the only Paleoamericans were Africans. As explained earlier, the Black part of the human family was the first to exist.[185] This does not make Africans inferior or superior, just first.

This next account is based on an Algonquin oral tradition and not tangible evidence. The picture in Fig. 8 was taken on June 6, 1924 in Providence, Rhode Island. The picture is one of the Nipmuc and Narragansett Indians—they both are parts of the Algonquin family. A Black Indian, Konkontu Peauwe, told Dr. Imhotep that his mentor is in the picture standing in the second row, the second man from the right wearing a chief's headdress. Konkontu's mentor's name was Chief Sunset, whose English name was Ed Michaels. These people have an oral historic tradition. Konkontu agrees with the history written on their website. This website details through oral tradition the following facts:

> New England was settled over 10,000 years ago by the Paleo-Indians coming from the southwest...with other cultural groups who came later; these settlers became the Algonquins which includes the Nipmunks.[186]

"The Hopi Indians, who live in the arid highlands of northern Arizona, have inhabited the same place for a millennium, far longer than any other people in North America."[187] The Hopi, one of the Pueblo tribes, say their ancestors came from the South and did not cross the Bering Strait.

184 National Park Service. (2009). "North American Slavery Timeline: Lesson Plan Two." Accessed August 5, 2009. https://www.nps.gov/abli/learn/education/upload/LessonPlanTwoResourceFileJuly21.pdf.

185 Finch III, Charles S. (1991). *Echoes of the Old Dark Land*. (Georgia, Khenti Press), p. 5.; Cavalli-Sforza, Luigi et al. *The History and Geography of Human Genes*, p. 145.

186 "Nipmuck Indians of Chaubunagungamaug" (n.d.). Accessed on May 3, 2010. https://www.nipmuck.org/history.html.

187 "Restoration," (2008). Accessed August, 24, 2014. https://extension.arizona.edu/sites/extension.arizona.edu/files/pubs/az1465.pdf.; Turner, J. "Arizona: A Celebration of the Grand Canyon State." Utah.

The Hopi people trace their history in Arizona to more than 2,000 years, but their history as a people goes back many more thousands of years. According to their legends, the Hopi migrated north to Arizona from the south, up from what are now South America, Central America and Mexico. The tribe's teachings relate stories of a great flood and other events dating to ancient times, marking the Hopi as one of the oldest living cultures in documented history.[188]

The Hopi remember the great flood of 13,000 years ago, and they were here long before 2000 years ago. It is curious to hear that the Algonquin also say they came from the southwest. This takes us back to the Proto-American period. That was long before the first slaves were brought here to North America in 1520 A.D.

Fig. 8: Algonquin Indian Council Early 1920s. *Courtesy of the Haffeneffer Museum of Anthropology, Brown University.*

---

188 Hopi Tribe, from the Inter Tribal Council of Arizona. ITCA Online, 2011; Four Corners, by Dorothy Nobis, Globe Pequot Press, 2001, p. 157.

Referring back to Konkontu, he also told Dr. Imhotep that no one in the Fig. 8 photo had ever been a slave or had their ancestors been slaves. Also, in the picture, notice the Black Indian standing third from the right—next to Chief Sunset—wearing a suit and tie. His name is Chief James Cisco, who was a Senior Chief. The Senior Chief and other Black Indians lived in a redwood house that can be seen today just behind the road sign in Fig. 9 marking the "Indian Reservation" that had been there since the beginning of White occupation. It is a state sign erected by state officials. Interestingly, the road sign in question stands on the curb in front of the Indian Reservation in Grafton, in which the first two lines say, "THESE FOUR AND ONE-HALF ACRES HAVE NEVER BELONGED TO THE WHITE MAN!" This is a significant statement! It is equaled only in the United States by the Chahta Black Indians in Louisiana. The entry to their I-95 highway—the Mississippi River—is possibly where some of the earliest First Americans entered North America.

Fig. 9: Indian Reservation Sign & Dr. Imhotep. *Photography by Teresa Gray-Jones.*

Back to Fig. 8. Study Chief Cisco's face for a moment. His genealogy is no doubt very interesting. Another interesting item that is behind the "Four and One-Half Acre" sign is that there is an Algonquin Burial Ground at the rear of this four and one-half acre reservation property. In another eastern Algonquin Burial Ground, it was found that the "skulls found in old burial grounds show...their faces not so broad as the brachycephalic

Asians, the heads are much more elongated, dolichocephalic like Africans and remarkably high, resembling the Eskimo."[189]

The **Algonquian** are one of the most populous, and widespread <u>North American</u> <u>native</u> language groups. Today, thousands of individuals identify with various Algonquian peoples. Historically, the peoples were prominent along the Atlantic Coast and into the interior along the <u>Saint Lawrence River</u> and around the <u>Great Lakes</u>. This grouping consists of the peoples who speak <u>Algonquian languages.</u>

Where Were the Algonquins Located?

The Algonquin Family (adapted from the name of the Algonquin tribe):

> *A linguistic stock, which formerly occupied a more extended area than any other in North America. territory reached from the east shore of Newfoundland to the Rocky Mountains.... The Eastern tribes from Maine to Carolina. The Algonquin are also known as the Lenape.[190]*

The Algonquin, however, should not be referred to as Lenape until after 2600 B.C., when the Mongolian-Hiung-nu people entered the Americas from Asia and mixed their blood with the Proto-American Algonquin people. Before the Algonquin began to mix with the Mongolian-Hiung-nu people, the Algonquin were Proto-American Africans. Once they mixed, they were called Lenape, or as Gonzalez-Jose et al. (2005) refers to them, Amerinds. We are using data from the Walam Olum's date of entry into the Americas as 2600 B.C. instead of using the Powell et al. date of after 3000 B.C. (McCutchen 1998) out of respect for the traditions of the ancient ones.

According to the Walam Olum, when the Mongolian-Hiuang-nu entered the Americas fighting and mixing their blood with the Proto-Americans (after 2600 B.C.), they eventually arrived in Delaware on the

---

189 Hodge, F. W. Algonquin Indian Genealogy, from the *Handbook of American Indians North of Mexico,* by Frederick W. Hodge, House of Representatives 59th Congress, 1st session. House Document No. 926, part 1, (Serial Set 5001), Washington, DC: Government Printing Office, 1906, p. 40.

190 Ibid.

East Coast in 1396 A.D. By the time the Mongolian-Hiuang-nu reached Delaware, they had been mixing their blood for 1204 years.

This point is made, so the reader will not be confused, and understand the following: When the Walam Olum tells of a war in the Midwest between the Algonquin and the Mound Builders, it must be understood that these are not the same people fighting each other. Also, the first Mound Builders were from Africa just as the first Algonquin originally were before they mixed. As mentioned earlier, the Mongolian-Hiuang-nu migrated or expanded across North America from Asia and headed east. They had mixed their blood for more than a millennium and were not the same people by 1386 A.D. It is not known if it was either a migration or an expansion, or both. At this point, the Mongolian-Hiuang-nu were no longer just Mongolian or African. The exact migratory route the Mongolian-Hiuang-nu supposedly traveled was across the northern part of the North America continent. According to the Walam Olum, they traveled from Washington State, east, across the Rocky Mountains once they left Alaska. After descending out of the mountains, they loosely followed the Missouri River east, and then southeast, until it joined the Mississippi River. When they reached the Mississippi River region, they clashed with a large group of Mound Builders called the Adena or Talegas, depending on whom you ask.

The Walam Olum, originally written by Amerinds, called the Mound Builders the Talegas. This reminded Dr. Imhotep of a trip to Egypt when a Nubian Elder in Aswan was asked, what is the African name for Lake Victoria? Lake Victoria is close to 255 miles long and 155 miles wide. This is a huge lake, therefore, we find many different groups of people who have lived around the lake for tens of thousands of years. Not surprisingly, each group living there has a different name for the lake. Similarly, it is safe to say that there are probably more than just two names for the people who built the mounds, since they are found all over eastern North America, Canada, Europe and Africa. W. E. B. Du Bois said they were a riverine people:

> *The mounds in the United States are usually found near rivers. In the Ohio Valley 10,000 mounds have been discovered. In the north, the mound zone begins in western New York and extended along the southern shore of Lake Erie into what is now Michigan, Wisconsin and on to the states of Iowa and Nebraska. In the southern United States the mounds lined the Gulf of Mexico from Florida to eastern*

Texas, and extended up through the Carolinas and across to the state of Oklahoma.... The mounds of the "Mound Builders" were probably replicas of Negro forts in Africa. That this tendency to build forts and stockades proceeded from the Antilles, whence the Arawaks had come in the beginning of the sixteenth century, is proved by the presence of similar works in Cuba. These are found in the most abandoned and least-explored part of the island and there can be little doubt that they were locations of fugitive Negro and Indian stockades, precisely such as were in use in Africa.... The results indicate that the African and American mounds have statues built in the same style with many of the same features. They support Wiener's theory that the Mande speaking people built some of the Mississippian mounds. We find many similarities between the art styles of the inhabitants of the mounds found in the area that encompassed ancient Mali, and the mounds built in the United States and South America.[191]

It seems that war-like Lenape clashed with the Mound Builders and the Mound Builders did not fare so well. That may have turned out different if the Lenape had to go up against the Iroquois.

The area where the Lenape clashed with the Mound Builders of Cahokia is just north of where St. Louis is today. It was there that the Lenape joined forces with the Iroquois and began "the Talegas Wars that were among the largest battles ever fought in ancient America."[192]

By the way, the Black Iroquois Indians were also from Africa. It was the Iroquois Confederacy who gave the American colonists the items that made up their Constitution.

Congress, on the occasion of the 200th anniversary of the signing of the United States Constitution, "acknowledged the historical debt which this Republic of the United States of America owes to the Iroquois Confederacy and other Indian Nations for their demonstration of enlightened, democratic principles of government and their example of a free association of independent Indian Nations."[193]

191 Du Bois, W. E. B. (2009). *The Gift of Black Folk: The Negroes in The Making of America.* (Square One Publishers).

192 Ibid.

193 Message, Kylie. (2014). *Museums and Social Activism* (London* New York, Routledge, Taylor & Francis Group), p. 192.

In a similar fashion, the Africans taught those who would listen, the first "scientific method" with all of its components available today including the first translation that is in *Mdu Ntr called hieroglyphics*. The mound-building Talegas were defeated and fled south never to return. From there the Lenape loosely followed the Ohio River east to the Allegheny River heading north to just below Lake Ontario. Leaving the Great Lakes area, they traveled east-southeast, finally crossing into Delaware. They then turned and headed northeast to middle Connecticut. In Connecticut, the Lenape turned northwest, finally ending their long journey around twenty miles into the State of Ontario, Canada. When they reached Ontario in 1396 A.D., they were in an area surrounded by Proto-Americans who were most probably Skraelings (the so-called "Pygmy"). The Walam Olum does not record another battle. So, they probably settled there, blending in and mixing even more with the Proto-Americans. This is where their Walam Olum migration story from Asia ended. For clarification, identity is important:

"Mound Builders" were not the native Americans we call "Indians." They were a pre-historic culture or cultures that inhabited much of the area we know as the United States.[194]

However, logically speaking, before the Europeans began to enter the Americas, Africans were there first. Then the Asians entered, but there were only two groups before they began to mix. Therefore, if the Mound Builders were not the Asians, logically they would have to belong to the other group, the Africans.

There may have been confusion between the Adena and Talegas, but none between the Adena and the Hopewell. However, there is a dispute as to who the Hopewell people were, i.e. those who built the Hopewell mounds. Some believe they were a separate people from the Adena, and others believe they were related. An example in Ohio may show you who the Hopewell people were and how they may have been related to the Adena:

Textbooks sometimes say that the Adena were succeeded by the Hopewell, but the relation is unclear; the Hopewell may simply have been a later stage of the same culture...("Hopewell" only refers to the farmer on whose property an early site was discovered.).... The

194 Bond, L. (n.d.). "The Mounds and Mound Builders of Union County." Union County Public Library. Accessed September 13, 2010. http://www. union-county.lib.in.us/mound_builders.htm.

Hopewell, too, built mounds, and like the Adena seem to have spoken an Algonquian language.[195]

The mound-building Hopewell were probably just a "later stage" of the Algonquin-speaking Adena people. "The 'Mound Builders' can be divided into three consecutive groups. The first two are classified as woodland."

They are the "Adena, Hopewell and Mississippi...of the 'Woodland Period.' These people lived over a wide area from the Atlantic to the Mississippi Valley."[196] The Mississippi group of Mound Builders obviously lived up and down the Mississippi River. But they are found over a much vaster area. The Americas had mound monuments as large as the pyramids of Egypt as seen in the Cahokia, Illinois mound, just a few miles from St. Louis, Missouri.

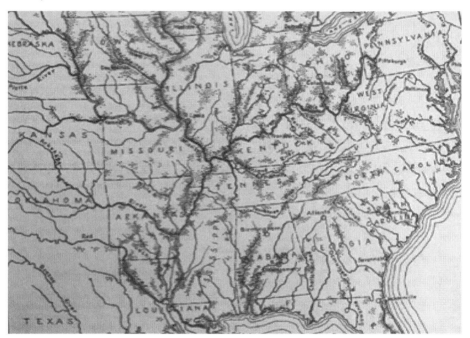

Fig. 10: Map of North American Mounds. *Courtesy of Dr. Gregory Little.*

195 Mann, Charles C. (2005). *1491: New Revelations of the Americas Before Columbus.* (Random House Publishing), p. 290.

196 Ibid, p. 294.

Southern Algonquin

The VDHR (Virginia Department of Historic Resources) has revealed in their literature that the "American Indians were in Virginia at least 16,000 years ago."[197] That is 14,508 years before Columbus' arrival. Even though this 16,000-year-old discovery is far more recent than the 51,700-year-old South Carolina find, the VDHR's mention of the 16,000-year discovery is still 4000 years before the Bering Strait glaciers first began to melt around 12,000 years ago. Relating this find to Clovis, Paleoindians are documented—by the State of Virginia—to have been in North America 6600 years before the Clovis people in 9400 B.C.

So, since this group of Paleoindians was in North America for four thousand years before Clovis, who is the most likely group to have been in Virginia 16,000 years ago? Here again, a familiar name resurfaces; the best guess is that it was the African/Algonquin.

Maps tracking the Algonquin show that their first concentration was in Southeastern Canada and the Northeastern United States, not the Northwestern states.[198]

Another note that sets the Algonquin apart from other Amerinds, is the fact that several different tribes were asked where they originated. The most popular answer was something to the effect that they have always been here on Turtle Island (North America) and did not migrate from anywhere. The Americas, were also known as "Abya Yala" by the South American indigenous tribes of the equatorial regions, "Ixachitlan" and by the Mexican tribes, and more recently, Turtle Island by the Canadian First Nation tribes of the lower lands.[199]

Our creation story says we came from the Heavens, we came from the stars, we came from beneath the earth, we came from the lakes, we came from the valleys, we came from the hills, we came from

197 Home, J., (n.d.). "Settling the James River: Colonization." Accessed June 12, 2009. https://www.nps.gov/articles/settlejames.htm.

198 Campbell, L. et al. (2004). "North American Indian Cultures (map)." Washington D.C: National Geographic Society. http://maps.nationalgeographic.com/maps/print-collection/north-american-indian-cultures.html

199 Inejnema, Bikbaye. (2007). In Search of the Gods: Exploring the Kemet/MesoAmerican Connection Part II. *The Rising Firefly, Journal of Kemetic Culture, Philosophy and Spirituality*, Vol. 62, pp. 52-54.

the mountains, we came from the canyons and islands. These are our creation stories, which have to be accepted as faith, much as Christianity has to be accepted by faith, and it is no less valuable. This is what we have been passed down from generation to generation of where we believe we were created.[200]

Origin Stories versus Evidence

To clarify the origin issue, a curious event took place in The Smithsonian's National Museum of the American Indian, in Washington, D.C.). On the afternoon of September 4, 2010, a Native American, Dennis Zotigh, gave a general admission lecture in the Potomac Room. Mr. Zotigh says he is a mixture of three tribes: the Khoisan, the Santee Dakota, and the Ohkay Oweengeh. Inside the rotunda of The National Museum of the American Indian, he gave a basic speech about the so-called "Native Americans" followed by a question-and-answer period. Dr. Imhotep asked Zotigh from where did the Native Americans originate? Mr. Zotigh's answer was a little longer than the standard answer we had always been given. Dr. Imhotep has the "live taping" of Mr. Zotigh's answer; he said: **"Four tribes and Columbus tell us Africans were here first."**

Fig. 11: Native American, Dennis Zotigh, speaks. *Photo taken by Dr. Imhotep in The Smithsonian's National Museum of the American Indian, in Washington, D.C.*

---

200 Zotigh, Dennis. "The National Museum of the American Indian," *The Smithsonian Institute*, September 4, 2010.

Many origin stories have been handed down from generation to generation. Who is to say if they are true or untrue? Are we to judge these stories? Absolutely not. However, just where do the truth and facts begin to fade? A real scholar does not rely on cultural truths or just passed-down stories alone, for you will lose a debate every time.

A scholar relies on evidence gathered and analyzed using the scientific method. Why? Here is an example: The truth is it rained yesterday, and that is also a fact. Today the fact is, it is not raining, and that is the truth. Here we see there is a weakness in using those words in an argument. The weakness is, as we saw above, that truth and facts can change. A better word to use that never changes what actually happened is "evidence," as in a crime scene. Evidence trumps truth or simple observed facts every time because **evidence does not change**.

Why was all of that necessary? The reason is that Mr. Zotigh, the Indian in Fig. 11, based his opinion on a "story," but not on evidence. Please understand that this does not mean all stories handed down from generation to generation are not sometimes true and to be respected. The only point to be made here is the origin of the first Americans, in this book is based on evidence, hard evidence.

Hitler's Nazi Minister of propaganda, Joseph Goebbels said:

"If you tell a lie big enough and keep repeating it, people will eventually come to believe it."[201] Have you ever heard an Amerind repeating one of their old sayings as many other groups do? The following Amerind saying may actually be a fabrication that has been repeated so many times, for so long, it is believed to be the truth: **"We have always been here."** Unfortunately, they have no evidence backing up that statement. It is an unfortunate myth, repeated by so many Amerinds over the years, that its source is no longer known, so it cannot be backed by evidence. On the other hand, let us now look at some actual hard evidence that shows us that Amerinds may not have always been here.

---

201 "The Nazis in Power: Propaganda and Conformity" https://www.facinghistory.org/resource-library/decision-making-times-injustice/nazis-in-power-propaganda-conformity. Accessed 21 September 2015; "Joseph Goebbels: On the 'Big Lie,'" Jewish Virtual Library website, www.jewishvirtuallibrary.org/joseph-goebbels-on-the-quot-big-lie-quot. Accessed 13 January 2009.

"If you repeat a lie long enough, it becomes truth,"[202] but does it? On the other hard evidence withstands the sands of time! Remember earlier in this work, we counted 66 pieces of evidence for the first Americans? Here is an in-depth look at the first four:

1. DNA evidence: How often is it correct? 99.8% of the time.

Let us study the making of this myth. Firstly, according to DNA, the Black Indians came to the Americas either directly from Africa; or indirectly, beginning in Africa—then temporarily lived in Europe—but finally sailed to the Americas. Below, please find the genetic evidence that the so-called "Native Americans," were not the first people in Americas. Their direct ancestors, the Africans, were the first people in the Americas a.k.a. the Amerindians, Amerinds, or Proto-Americans. With all due respect, the Native American ancient saying: "We have always been here" (in the Americas) is not supported by science.

The most predominate Y chromosome of Native Americans in North America is **R-M173. R-M173 is found in the northeastern and southwestern parts of the United States** along with mtDNA haplogroup X(25%). **Both haplogroups are found in Africa but are absent in Siberia.**[203]

What this means is that Native Americans and Africans are directly related by their R1 Y-chromosome linage because of their African forefathers. But interestingly, Mongolians (Siberians) from Eastern Asia, do not have the R-M173 with mtDNA haplogroup X markers. Also, tracing the DNA coming in from the northeastern United States; it probably exhibits the influx of the Anu/Twa Africans by boat from Scandinavia to Greenland, and then to Canada. Then of course, turning south, into the northeastern United States, we see that they were preceded by the Anu/Twa Africans who entered South America by boat into Brazil and migrated north through Mexico. This possible migration could have continued into the southwestern United States. These migrations occurred—of course—tens of thousands of years before the Clovis event.

---

202 Stille, Alexander. (2006). *The Sack of Rome by Alexander.* (Penguin Books), p. 14. Quoted in Moore, M. (2003). *A World Without Walls: Freedom, Development, Free Trade and Global Governance* (Cambridge University Press), p. 63.

203 Winters, Clyde. *We Are Not Just Africans*, pp. 17, 21.

2. Common sense backed by anthropological evidence: The study of bones.

Fig. 12: Neanderthal from John Anthony Gurche. *Wikipedia*

The first Neanderthals were Africans (discussed later but see her now in Fig. 12). In all three of the Americas—North, Central and South—no one has ever discovered any human (ancient) archaic bones older than Homo sapiens. They have never found bones relating to Australopithecus, Homo-habilis, Homo-erectus, Neanderthal, or Homo-floresiensis. Therefore, can "red-skinned" Native Americans still say, "We have always been here?" Are we not all part of the same family, from the same place? Africa?

3. Four different, actual migrations African-Indians made themselves across the Atlantic.

The four groups are the Shawnee, Saulk, Yuchi and Yurok Indians. The first two tribes were part of the Algonquin Nation, and each had a migration story of originally coming from across the Ocean. The Algonquin Indians are Indians groups today who claim that they originated somewhere other than in the Americas. The following data is not based on a story, but is an *actual part of documented* history. The first origin story is from the early 1800s A.D. Shawnee Indian agent, John Johnson, reported in a letter that the Algonquin Indians told him that they came from across the sea (the Atlantic Ocean):

[This report was] later still reprinted by Schoolcraft in 1851 in his Archaeologia Americana page 273, Johnson wrote: "The people of this nation have a tradition that their ancestors crossed the sea to get to the Americas. They are the only tribe with which I am acquainted who admits to a foreign origin. Lately (i.e., 1819) they kept yearly

sacrifices for their safe arrival in this country. From where they came, or at what time period they do not know.[204]

These people not only passed the story of their origin down from generation to generation, they held yearly sacrifices to commemorate their journey to the Americas. The Algonquin, whose name means, "they are our relatives," can be traced to an early people—the Proto-Algonquins—who moved into and populated much of eastern Canada shortly after the retreat of the East Glacier around 15,000 years ago. Based on their own history, these are the only North American Indian people to have originated somewhere in the Atlantic, then moved westward up the St. Lawrence and into the Great Lakes area. A second separate origin story of the Sauk Indians, comes from yet another tribe in the Algonquin linguistic family. It concerns the Indians of Sauk County, which is near Baraboo, Wisconsin:

When French immigrants were settling in the town of Baraboo during the early 1800s, resident Sauk Indians still revered...a giant who saved their ancestors by leading them to safety on the shores of Turtle Island—the Sauk name for North America—after a Great Deluge drowned their original lodge place in the Sunrise Sea (Atlantic Ocean).[205]

What body of water sits towards the sunrise in North America? Would that not be the Atlantic Ocean? If it were the Sunset Sea, it would be the Pacific. Logically, the Salk Indians indicated they came from the direction of the morning sun, in the east. They also mentioned that a "Great Deluge" had drowned their land. That would probably be one of the many flood stories that have been recorded by peoples all over the world. The recollection of this flood would make their tribe older than the last Ice Age melt.

The Sauk Indians themselves were also known by their Algonquin tribal name—the Osakiwug, or "People of the Outlet," a reference

204 Fell, Barry. (1982). *America B.C.: Ancient Settlers in the New World.* Revised Edition, p. 279.

205 Joseph, Frank. (2009). *Advanced Civilizations of Prehistoric America: The lost Kingdoms of the Adena, Hopewell, Mississippians, and Anasazi.* Bear and Company), p. 114.

to people landing on the eastern shores of North America after the Great Flood.[206]

The third example was the Yuchi tribe from the Gulf Coast of Alabama. Yet they claim that their original homeland lay far across the Sea. In a fourth example, Proto-Americans have indicated that they originated in an area across the Atlantic Ocean.

A brilliant anthropologist by the name of, Alan H. Kelso de Montigny wrote an article in the *International Anthroplolgical Review* in 2010. The title of the article was, "Did a Gigantic Meteroite (i.e, an Asteroid) fall into the Caribbean, and create the Lesser Antilles 6000 years ago?" He arrived at his dating theory after collating native traditions in the region. Was this the, "Great Deluge" the elders told them about?

The impact may be connected with the creation of the Carolina Bays and/or the other impact sites as noted by Otto Muck. Muck earned an engineering degree from, the Munich College of Advanced Technology. He held patents for around 2000 inventions by the time he died in 1956. Because of the evidence, he believed in the story of Atlantis located on the Mid-Atlantic Ridge and that it was destroyed by an asteroidal impact in the Caribbean. He calculated that the disaster occurred in 8498 B.C.[207]

(Atlantipedia.ie/samples/otto-muck-amended: Otto Heinrich Muck (1892–1956) was born in Vienna, which is adjacent to Germany)

With circumstantial evidence from old stories that the natives from the Caribbean, Central America, and South America have kept for centuries, there must be something to their historic stories saying, "the Old Moon Broke"; coupled with the physical evidence. By the Moon breaking, "they meant an extraterrestrial object, a comet fragment perhaps, that fell into the ocean causing mass destruction. It was on a scale of the type expressed in the various myths and legends preserved by the indigenous peoples of the Caribbean."

After moving from Africa to the Caribbean, to Alabama and then Florida, some descendants of the Yurok people still live in California

---

206 Joseph, Frank. (2011). Mysteries of the Effigy Mounds, *Atlantis Rising* Vol. 90. www.atlantisrisingmagazine.com/article/ mysteries-of-the-effigy-mounds/.

207 O'Connell, Tony. "Muck, Otto." Atlantipedia. January 4, 2010. http://atlantipedia.ie/samples/otto-muck-amended/.

today. In 1916, Lucy Thompson (a.k.a Che-Na-Wah Weitch-Ah-Wah, a Klamath River Yurok woman—see Fig. 13) wrote a very interesting story.

Before introducing this lady, the book does not give a description of her. There is, however, a photograph of her on the cover of her book as seen above. She is a darker-complected person, wearing a beautiful Amerind skirt and top. Her hair is worn in two bushy pony-tails. She does not have a long thin nose, but has a slightly wide-flat nose, and a prognathic, non-European look. Her lips are between full and thin. The covering on her head is not a bonnet. Surprisingly, she is not wearing feathers; instead she wears a typical African skullcap. This is the most interesting and surprising item that she wears. This is not an anomaly.

One of Dr. Imhotep's favorite books is *The Cycle of Cosmic Catastrophes* by a nuclear physicist and has been part of the Isotopes Project at Lawrence Berkeley National laboratory; he is joined by the owner and CEO of an international scientific consulting company and a field exploration and mining geologist in Australia.

One of his source books explained in detail what cataclysmic phenomenon caused the last Ice Age to end. The reason we bring this book to your attention is that this book has a picture of a "Native American Princess" who is not wearing a traditional Plains Indian bonnet, or even one feather in her hair; instead, she wears a West-African skullcap (also called a Kufi Cap)! But seeing the same kind of cap as that of the Yurok woman is not the only coincidence. Why would a darker-skinned Native American be wearing a traditional African hat? Many different cultures wear skullcaps, from the Jews and the Islamic peoples to the Pope. Where did they copy this style from and who were the first to wear them? There is other evidence:

> *Actually, a skullcaps appear in the oldest Egyptian tomb paintings. They are also seen in the hieroglyphs.... Actually, many shapes and sizes of caped skullcaps were once the norm in ancient Egypt. Muslims and old fashioned Asians also wear skullcaps, but the American Indian seems to have no skullcap traditions at all.*[208]

The evidence, however, points to Africa. But if the Amerinds that we know of today do not wear skullcaps, then why does Che-Na-Wah Weitch-

---

208 Hernandez, Rev. A. (1968). *My Kingdom for a Crown: An Around-the-World History of the Skullcap and its Modern Socio-Political Significance*, pp. 28-29. Accessed June 1, 2013. http://www.dieter-philippi.de/files/literature/1968_antonio_hernandez_-_history_of_ the_skullcap.pdf.

Ah-Wah wear a skullcap? In some pictures in her book, she looks like a typical African-American lady, and in others she looks like a darker brown Amerind. Here is the evidence drawn from the cover and inside her book: She looks to be a mixture of both Amerind and African heritage. Her religious affiliations are deeply rooted with her tribe, which rules out Islam, Judaism, or any other Western religion. Logically, the cap most likely comes from her African heritage.

Fig. 13: A Yurok Woman. *From http//www.yuroktribe.org/contactus.htm.*

It is important to note that there seem to be no skullcap traditions for a certain small number of nations, such as the Native Americans, Polynesian, Micronesian, Islander and Aborigine.[209]

After introducing herself, she says that her people have a historic tradition of migration across the Atlantic Ocean to the Americas. Then, she begins to tell the historic trip her people made:

---

209 Ibid.

In our recollections of the past, we left the land of our birth (Cheek-cheek-alth) many thousands of years ago.... For years we wandered down a European land, always moving south having our origin in the far north...as it might have been for centuries until we reached the rolling waves of the ocean. Upon reaching this saltwater, we made boats or canoes, and paddled west over the waves until we reached the opposite shore, having crossed the straits safely. Having reached this opposite shore upon this new continent...we continued...always going south as before.[210]

She remembers:

We carried the memory...of the far north, the huge icebergs.... The splendors of the aurora borealis flickered across the snowy fields.... In this land of the frozen north some of our people were left, the Esquimau Eskimo; they were given a different language as they were separated from our sturdy band across the snowy fields and have long since from this time on inhabited the land of the perpetual snow.

Tho I am a pure, full-blooded Klamath River woman...a member of...the exclusive priestly society known as Talth...I can understand every word, every nod and gesture made in our language. Therefore, I feel that I am in a better position than any other person to tell the true facts of the religion and the meaning of the many things that we use to commemorate the events of the past.[211]

In Fig. 13, notice the intricate beadwork and Yurok clothing that Che-Na-Wah Weitch-Ah-Wah wears. Also, notice the African cap on her head, along with native hair wrappings on her pony tails.

We finally find the fourth group, the Yuroks. The first hint that the Yuroks were originally Africans is that one of their splinter groups was the Esquimau, which linguistically changed over time to Eskimo. You may read about "The First Eskimos" in Section Note W, where you shall learn that the Eskimo people's heritage began in Africa. They lived in the bitter Arctic cold before the White man came…but even today, they do not have a White a skin color.

Once the Yurok reached the shores of "this new continent," they continued their historic trek and story in the Americas:

210 Thompson, Lucy. (1916). *To The American Indian: Reminiscences of a Yurok Woman* (California, Hayday Books), pp. 76, 77, 78.

211 Ibid., p. 76.

72

Thus we traveled down a great continent, leaving behind at our stopping places a portion of our people, which were given different languages...and our tribes became numerous.... We traveled over the continent of North America to the equator and regions of perpetual sunshine; and beyond the equator, over the continent of South America to its furthermost southern borders, where we merge into the regions of ice and snow again...at Tierra del Fuego.[212]

This is the story of the Yurok people, who spoke of their beginnings in their treasured Cheek-cheek-alth Valley in Northern Europe. How did the Proto-Yurok come to be in Northern Europe in the first place? This leads us to the second hint that the Yurok were probably African. The third hint was covered earlier, in that the Fuegians and the Khoisan had the same DNA, i.e., the M174 coupled with the D haploid groups.

Leakey and other scientists have shown us that the first Homo sapiens began in Africa. We know the first Europeans were Africans. The Yurok's possible ancestors—the Khoisan/Aurignacian—migrated from northwestern Africa to Europe in the north. Other Africans migrated east to India or China, while some migrated to West Africa and on to the Americas. To make a long story short, that was just one more hint of the Yurok's African heritage. If all of these are but coincidences, they are most assuredly remarkable coincidences.

The other Africans mentioned to have sailed to the Americas are a major African population called the Mande from Sub-Saharan African, and the Paleoamericans.

4. Architectural evidence

In a couple of places in the American Midwest there are ancient Pueblo cliff dwellings. The most well-known structure is the Pueblo Cliff Dwellings. Curiously, there is an identical structure in Mali, Africa. What do they have in common?

A. They are both high up on the side of a cliff.
B. The cliff has a concave shape.
C. They both sit back inside that concave aperture.
D. They have identical Pueblo mud dwelling architecture.

There is more cliff above where they stand, and if you are on top of that mountain and look down you cannot see the dwellings for they are packed

---

212 Ibid., pp. 76, 77.

back in the cave. All you see is the bottom of the cliff. The probability that they were built by different people, and there being two identical cliff dwellings— halfway around the world from one another—is astronomical!

We have now witnessed several separate sacred traditions from four entirely different native groups: the Shawnee, Saulk, Yuchi, Yurok, Mande or Manding. The Mandinka, Khoisan, Anu, Twa—a variety of Proto-Saharan Blacks—and much later, Mansa Abubakari from Mali brought between 25,000 and 80,000 African warriors to the Americas by boat! The evidence shows that Black Africans have been coming to the Americas for 250,000 to 350,000 years, and possibly for even longer.

The Yurok were the only group always moving south, eventually ending at the tip of South America. These stories of originating across the ocean to the east, handed down from generation to generation indicate that their people did not originate in the Americas. More of these stories will probably surface as time goes on.

The evidence continues here, beginning with skulls and skeletons, footprints in lava, ancient campsites, genetic M-174 and D haploid groups, linguistics, ancient cave paintings, ancient tools, architecture, Egyptian script, artifacts, and ancient structures above and below the ocean waves. Let us go back to the first group whose tradition says they did not originate in the Americas. From a study of the word *Algonquin*, we see the area where they most likely first appeared:

The word Algonquin *means "At the place of spearing fishes and eels," and is also used in reference to a geographical area, which lies in the upper northeastern corner of the United States and across the border into Canada.*[213]

That is the territory the short, dark-complected Skraelings inhabited. Again, as mentioned earlier, we see further evidence that the Algonquin were first concentrated in the northeastern United States and southeastern Canada. There is no mention of a western origin or migration. Therefore, they either sailed straight across the Atlantic (as the Yurok contend) or skipped from island to island in the far north as the Vikings would later do. This is the same time period and area that the Skraelings occupied. Speaking of the Algonquins, a genealogical article says, "in Labrador

---

213 "What can you tell me about the Algonquain Indians?" (1999-2009). Accessed 12 September 12 2009. https://www.aaanativearts.com/what-can-you-tell-me-about-the-the-algonquain-indians.

just north of New England we see that they came into contact with the Eskimo."[214] And "The Skraelings were also the very first Eskimos."[215]

Could the Skraelings have also been the first Algonquin Indians, just as the Skraelings were the first Eskimos? The Skraelings were short. Ancient, so-called "Pygmy" skulls have been found as far south as Holliston Mills, in eastern Tennessee. Looking back, the Yurok woman remembered:

We carried the memory...of the far north, the huge icebergs.... The splendors of the aurora borealis flickered across the snowy fields.... In this land of the frozen north some of our people were left, the Esquimau [Eskimo]; they were given a different language as they were separated from our sturdy band across the snowy fields, and have long since from this time on inhabited the land of the perpetual snow.[216]

"Also inhabiting parts of North America in the Bronze Age were Pygmy types (see Fig. 14); though still living in east Tennessee as late as the first millennium B.C., range back in time to at least 40,000 years ago, as shown by carbon dating (Fell, 1982)."[217] As can be plainly seen in the next figure, the jaws are projected forward in an identical style to an African *dolichocephalic* (long-headed) skull, not an Asian (round-headed) skull trait. The *brachycephalic* skull trait with the short jaw appeared on this planet only more recently than 10,000 years ago.[218] These short African Khoisan (with dolichocephalic skulls) predated the Algonquin in the Americas. The Algonquin later spread out and became the most heavily populated and widespread of all the North American Paleoindians, but originated in only a few tribes. The Algonquin speakers covered an extremely large area ranging from Quebec, Canada, and the Carolinas of

214 Hodge, F.W. (1906). "Algonquin Indian Genealogy." Accessed 17 February 2010. http://www.accessgenealogy.com/native/tribes/algonquian/algonhist1.htm.

215 Oleson, Tryggvi J. *Early Voyages and Northern Approaches*, p. 9.

216 Thompson, Lucy. *To The American Indian*. pp. 76-78.

217 "European Bronze Age Visitors in America." (n.d.). Accessed December 10, 2016. http://www.faculty.ucr.edu/~legneref/bronze/ bronze1.htm.

218 Diop, Cheikh A. *Civilization or barbarism*, p. 16.

U.S., west to the Rocky Mountains.[219] The wide linguistic distribution of Algonquin speakers suggests a very ancient past.[220] It seems that after spreading out and settling down for good, it was most likely that, "The Algonquian tribes were mainly sedentary and agricultural, probably the only exceptions being those of the cold regions of Canada and the Siksika of the plains."[221] There is however no direct evidence of the first Algoinquin speakers being natives in the Virginias 16,000 years ago as mentioned earlier.

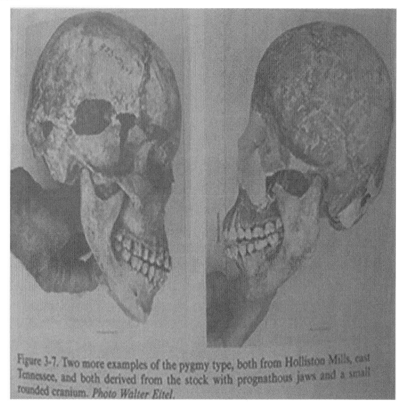

Figure 3-7. Two more examples of the pygmy type, both from Holliston Mills, east Tennessee, and both derived from the stock with prognathous jaws and a small rounded cranium. *Photo Walter Eitel.*

Fig. 14: Tennessee Skulls. Notice how the jawbone projects forward. A common sign of an African prognostic jawbone. *Courtesy of Walter T. Eitel.*

219 "Algonquin" Dictionary.com Unabridged, Based on the Random House Dictionary, Random House, (2016). Accessed December 10, 2016. http://www.dictionary.com/browse/algonquian?s=t.

220 Thompson, Irene. "Algic Language Family" About World Languages. (2016). Last Modified October 1, 2016.

221 "Algonquin Indian Genealogy." (n.d.). Accessed October 2, 2010. http://www.accessgenealogy.com/native/tribes/algonquian/algonhist1.htm.

Having said that, there is evidence that 12,393 years later in 1607, Captain John Smith (who built the first permanent settlement in Virginia) reported being captured by "Black" Indians.[M]

Kanentiio, an Amerind, has another full story also disagreeing with the standard story. In his story, the glacier in the Bering Strait was one-to-two miles high, and the trip across the glaciers was 1,500 miles long through a part of the world that, "is swept by hurricane force storms which drive the temperatures so low skin turns to ice wherever it is in contact with the air."[222]

The VDHR's report is evidence that natives in Virginia most likely did not migrate across the Bering Strait from Asia. Hence, the natives in Virginia 16,000 years ago could not have been Mongolian. Why not? They did not cross the Bering Strait from Asia that early, nor is there any skeletal evidence to show that the Mongolians entered the Americas until the Middle Holocene,[223] a period roughly from 7,000 to 5,000 years ago, which was warmer than the present day.[224]

It is therefore highly probable that the VDHR's Algonquin in Virginia 16,000 years ago came from the east not the west and were most likely Africans. The details about 1607, when Captain John Smith reported that, he was captured by "Black Indians," were interesting. Just seventy-four years later, another interesting remark was made about the color of the Indians, this time in New England. William Penn, the founder of Pennsylvania, made an interesting remark about the native population:

> In 1681, the Indians of New England, or "Moors" as they were also styled by the settlers, were pronounced by William Penn to be "as Black as Gypsies"...*See Mr. Eggleston's article in The Century Magazine of May 1883. This statement of Penn's may even mean

222 George-Kanentiio, D. "Bering Strait Migration Theory A Big Lie." February 4, 2015. Accessed March 1,2016. http://www.indianz. com/ News/2015/016340.asp.

223 Powell, Joseph F., and Walter A. Neves. "Craniofacial Morphology of the First Americans: Pattern and Process in the Peopling of the New World." *American Journal of Physical Anthropology* 110, no. S29 (1999): 153-88.

224 Follin, S. et al. "Modelling the evolution of hydrochemical conditions in the Finnoscandian Shield during Holocene time using multidisciplinary information," p. 2004; NOAA. "Mid-Holocene Warm Period – About 6,000 Years Ago." (2011). https://www.ncdc.noaa.gov/global-warming/mid-holocene-warm-period.

that the British Gypsies of 1681 were quite black. Penn was not alone; other Englishmen who had colonized the western shore of the Atlantic spoke of the Indians there as being "as black as Gypsies."[225]

Just to be sure that the color of the "Gypsies" Penn was referring to in New England were Black and of African heritage, here is more evidence to make his meaning crystal clear. The so-called "savages," the Galloway Gipsy and the Irish rebels, were all described by Derrick as *ciuthachs*; or men with platted hair, and the last two are known as men of **swarthy skin.** So, here we have dark-skinned men with **plaited hair**.[226] How could they be anything but of African descent?

Scientists believe the migrations into the Americas consisted of two distinctly different peoples: the Paleoamericans in pre-glacial times, and then much later, the Mongoloids in the post-glacial times. The Paleo-American African skulls were long, narrow, dolichocephalic, and had delicate features. In contrast, the Mongolian skulls were round, brachycephalic and had rugged features.[227]

The small number of early American specimens discovered so far, have smaller and shorter faces and longer and narrower skulls than later Native Americans, more closely resembling the modern people of Africa, Australia, and the South Pacific. This has led to speculation that perhaps the first Americans and Native Americans came from different homelands.[228]

Paleoamerican Skraelings with protruding, prognathous jaws from 40,000 years ago, identical to African jaws, can be seen in Fig. 14.[229]

---

225 Mac Ritchie, David. *Ancient and Modern Britons Volume 1* (Freeman, S. Dk: Pine Hill Press, 1884/1991), pp. 357, 374.

226 Ibid., p. 138.

227 Powell, Joseph F., and Walter A. Neves. "Craniofacial Morphology of the First Americans," pp. 153-88.

228 Kumar, Mohi. "DNA From 12,000-Year-Old Skeleton Helps Answer the Question: Who Were the First Americans?" *Smithsonian Magazine*. May 15, 2014 https://www.smithsonianmag.com/ science-nature/dna-12000-year-old-skeleton-helps-answer-question-who-were-first-americans-180951469/#56pyb8MfE-wR15ies.99.

229 "European Bronze Age Visitors in America." Accessed February 24, 2010. http://www.faculty.ucr.edu/~legneref/bronze/doc/bron58. htm.

If Amerinds migrated to the Americas from Asia as we are taught in school, and were unmixed since their arrival, would they not look just like their Asian relatives of today? The "so-called" full-blooded Amerinds are said to have a reddish-brown skin tone, darker than the Mongolian Asians. They were referred to pejoratively as "redskins" until very recently. They were not referred to as "Yellow-skins," as with Mongolian Asians who are of a lighter complexion. They also do not have the round brachycephalic heads of their Asian ancestors, whose heads are long and narrow—dolichocephalic as Africans. This is because they are of a mixed heritage of African and Mongolian.

From Christopher Columbus we have an eyewitness account of what the natives looked like when he arrived in 1492, southeast of North America:

They all go naked as their mothers bore them.... They were very well built, with very handsome bodies and very good faces. Their hair is coarse almost like the hairs of a horse's tail and short; they wear their hair down over their eyebrows, except for a few strands behind, which they wear long and never cut. Some of them are painted black, and they are the color of the people in the Canaries, neither black nor white, and some of them are painted white and some red and some in any color (sic) they can find.[230]

The strongest evidence of African presence in America before Columbus comes from the pen of Columbus himself. In 1920, a renowned American historian and linguist, Leo Wiener of Harvard University, in his book, *Africa and the Discovery of America,* explained how Columbus noted in his journal that Native Americans had confirmed that they had seen and knew that "black-skinned people had come from the south-east in boats, trading in gold-tipped spears."[231]

When he first arrived in the Western Hemisphere, Columbus probably thought that he had discovered India because the people were brown-skinned, the color of carob. However, something is not right here. The educational system has taught us that the first Americans came from Asia

230 Mayfield, Marlys. *Thinking for Yourself* (Massachusetts, Thomson-Wadsworth, 2007), p. 34.

231 Chengu, Garikai. "Before Columbus: How Africans Brought Civilization to America. "Global Research Center." October 7, 2015. Accessed November, 6, 2015. http://www.globalresearch.ca/before-coum-bus-how-africans-brought-civilization-to-america/5407584.

(specifically Mongolia, which is north of China), and currently they most certainly do not have brown or black skin. If Columbus landed in the West Indies and saw yellowish-red skinned people as we see the Amerinds today on television, would he not have thought he landed in Mongolia or China? Instead he saw brown-skinned people and thought he was in India.

Another clue as to the color of these natives when the Spanish came is the "Carib" name of the Carib Indians (also referred to as the Tahinos). Carob powder has a dark brown color. Does it not make sense that when the Spanish first saw these people, they called them the color of their skin? This was probably how the Caribbean Sea was named.

Columbus encountered the Carob people on his voyages to the Americas. Some of them "had canoes, complete with masts [and sails] that held 25 to 70 people."[232] He also had another encounter with them while in Britain. He noticed that:

> *a powerful current reaches the British Isles all the way from the Gulf of Mexico [where he first ran into brown-skinned men in canoes in a very strong current. While in that current he noticed] two "brown-skinned, flat faced individuals" (with long black hair) whom Columbus assumed were Indians, that is, from India. [This group of Indians were the Micmac, who] "were a sea going tribe...part of the tribe was not the taller Algonquin stock, but a shorter, darker people. When they [the Micmac] landed in Scotland, the taller Celtic peoples called them "Pixies," a name that still exists in the folklore of the British Isles. The Romans called them Picts. The Micmac/Picts" stayed apart from the Celts, living in the Highlands and keeping their own customs and language. In 1534 when the French were fighting the Algonquin Indians, one branch of the large tribe were the Micmac near a branch of the St. Lawrence River.*

> *In 81 C.E. war broke out between the Picts and Celts. The Picts won and conquered one-third of England. [They were later absorbed by the larger Caucasian population.] On both sides of the Atlantic it appears that the inhabitants were very small people. In Scotland, the Duncan Clan received its name originally from Donnacaidh, their high chief. The word itself was a title meaning "Brown Warrior." The reality of pre-Columbian ocean crossings would one day be discounted by nationalism and the attempt to legitimize land grabbing by the*

232 Kenyon, J. Douglas. (2016). *Missing Connections: Challenging the Consensus* (Massachusetts, Atlantis Rising), p. 223.

Europeans. Clearly the evidence of the voyages of discovery made in both directions presents a different picture.[233]

These people are direct descendants of the Twa and Anu, the first Homo sapiens. When they crossed over into Canada they were later labeled "Skraelings." After reading the last few paragraphs, considering the evidence and applying inductive reasoning, one would have to say that the color of the first people Columbus saw had brown (Carob-colored) East Indian skin tones, not yellowish-red skin tones. To close this issue, the evidence of the pre-Clovis (before 9,400 B.C.) occupation of the Americas by non-Mongolian Paleoamerican Africans is overwhelming.

It is agreed that the Vikings came to the Americas before Columbus. However, when the Vikings first reached the Americas, they met a people who had already been in the Americas nearly 100,000 years according to a *New York Times* article. They met a group of short Africans whom the Vikings called Skraelings. The Vikings themselves said the Skraelings looked like African pygmies.[234]

The Africans who had already been in the Americas carried mtDNA haplogroups X and R-M173 that are absent in Siberia according to Dr. Clyde Winters.[235] They met a group of short Africans whom the Vikings called Skraelings. The Vikings later commented that they were very surprised at the Skraelings short stature.

According to Tryggvi J. Oleson, "It is the central thesis of this book that the [short] Dorset antedate the [tall] Tunnit; that they were the Skraelings of the sagas, of the [African] pigmy primitive people..."[236] The evidence points to the Skraelings being in Canada and New England even before the time period of the Lenape. The idea that the first Americans were Africans from the east and not Asians from the west was a surprise. Obviously, there are no Skraeling pictures in existence today in Canada, nor in North America. However, they can be seen in Mexico and all over South America. Therefore, it is safe to say they looked similar to the diminutive Africans of

---

233 Ibid., pp. 223-227.

234 The Black History Basement and Attic (11/26/16) https://www.facebook.com/232897930456823/posts/fig-7-on-the-border-between-uganda-congo-now-zaire-courtesy-of-david-mendozather/235213403558609.

235 Winters, Clyde. *We Are Not Just Africans.*, pp. 17, 21.

236 Oleson, Tryggvi J. *Early Voyages and Northern Approaches.* p. 9.

today depicted in Fig. 15. In the photograph, David Mendoza is seen with a group of diminutive Africans in the Ruwenzori Mountains on the border between Uganda and the Congo in 1967. Where did these "Skraelings," as the Vikings would have called them, originate? To answer that question, we must backtrack a bit to finding the origin of the Eskimo and thereby also find the Skraelings.

Note: W. I. Morton is Head of the Department of History and Provost of the University College, University of Manitoba in Winnipeg, Canada. He is the Executive Editor of The Canadian Centenary Series, that is an enormous seventeen volumes-long study.[237]

In the first of the seventeen volumes, Tryggvi J. Oleson details the origin of the Eskimo:

> *It is the central thesis of this book that the Dorset people precede the Tunnit Caucasian Icelanders, and; that the Dorset people were the Skraelings of the Sagas, the pygmy...and that the present-day Eskimos are the result of an intermixture between the Dorset people and the Tunnit, that is the Icelanders.*[238]

Fig. 15: On the border between Uganda & Congo (now Zaire). *Courtesy David Mendoza.*

---

237 Ibid.

238 Ibid., pp. 9, 175.

In other words, the short African Skraelings—a.k.a. Dorset people—and the Tunnit Caucasian from Iceland intermixed, and gave birth to the Eskimos. The Eskimo people did not migrate to Canada from Asia in the west, as we have been incorrectly taught. They were born and originated in Iceland and Greenland in the east. The Skraelings, like the Eskimo, did not come from the west; they also came from the east (of Canada).

> *Their ancestors were from Africa by way of Western Europe. In the northern extremities of the Americas, short Africans most likely entered eastern Canada in boats from Europe by island hopping as the Vikings did much later. In Northwestern Europe we see that "the extreme north of Norway was also inhabited by a race of 'Skraelings;' and that these people were the same as the African 'pygmies' of classical writers."[239] In Greenland they lived, "just 450 miles from the pole."[240]*

In Canada, it was found that in "the territories either side of the Gulf of St. Lawrence, and as far south as Massachusetts, were Skraelings... but these people are called Lapps in some books."[241] The Skraelings stretched from Canada east to "the extreme north of Norway...[to the] extreme north of Asia."[242] One point that must be made perfectly clear, however, is that these small Blacks were not confined to, nor were they found only in Canada or the northern extremities before the Vikings came. They were found all over the Americas down to the southernmost extremities of South America in Tierra del Fuego (see South American Map Fig. 6) and west to Hawaii where these diminutive people were called the Menehune. Then we have the short Black Negritoes of Philippines, and short Black Australians. Towards India, we also find dwarves on the Andaman Island in the middle of the Bay of Bengal, just east of India. These short people are literally found all over this planet!

Unfortunately, in South America, these short Africans were pushed down from Northern Brazil to Tierra del Fuego by the Mongoloids from

---

239 Branigan, Tania. "Solo walk into dangers of the Arctic." *The Guardian* April 13, 2001. https://www.theguardian.com/uk/2001/apr/14/arctic.

240 MacRitchie, David. *The Testimony of Tradition*, p. 190.

241 Ibid.
242 Darwin, Charles. *The Voyage of the Beagle* (New York, Penguin Classics, 1909), pp. 210-211.

Asia or Amerinds until they were eventually exterminated, genetically absorbed, or a combination of the two.

Linguistic Evidence:
Africans Were in the Americas First

In the 18th century, on one of his voyages, Captain Cook stopped at the tip of South America. Cook said the language of the "little people" sounded like "so many guttural and clicking sounds."[243] This is further evidence of a South American–Proto-American linguistic link. What more do we need to show the connection? The short Africans of South Africa today speak with clicking sounds. The click language "was part of the ancestral human mother tongue."[244] Delving just a little deeper into that ancestral mother tongue, we can see the work of Quentin D. Atkinson, a biologist at the University of Auckland in New Zealand:

[Atkinson] is one of several biologists who have started applying to historical linguistics the sophisticated statistical methods developed for constructing genetic trees based on DNA sequences.... Dr. Atkinson's finding fits with other evidence about the origins of language. The Bushmen of the Kalahari Desert belong to one of the earliest branches of the genetic tree based on human mitochondrial DNA. Their languages belong to a family known as Khoisan and include many clicking sounds, which seem to be a very ancient feature of language. And they live in Southern Africa, which Dr. Atkinson's calculations point to as the origin of language.[245]

Note: The "click language" can still be heard today from Africa to the Americas to Australia, where aborigines make "a clicking noise with his/

243 Wade, Nicholas. "In Click Languages, an Echo of the Tongues of the Ancients." *The New York Times*. March 18, 2003. Accessed August 25, 2009. http://www.nytimes.com/2003/03/18/science/in-click-languages-an-echo-of-the-tongues-of-the-ancients.html.

244 Wade, Nicholas. "Phonetic Clues Hint Language Is Africa-Born." *The New York Times*. 2011. Accessed July 30, 2011. http://www. nytimes. com/2011/04/15/science/15language.html.

245 Kickett-Tucker, Cheryl. "Research and Urban Aboriginal School Children: Considerations and Implications." (1998). Accessed August 2, 2010. http:// www.aare.edu.au/publications-database.php/2212/research-and-urban-aboriginal-school-children-considerations-and-implications.

her voices."[246] This language can be heard in the movie, *The Gods Must Be Crazy*, being spoken by Black Africans. African-Americans today, who have never been exposed to the click language in any way, can click as well. A case in point is when in 2004, Mr. Broadus the rapper, A.K.A. Snoop Dogg, made the clicking sounds in his record, "Drop it like it's hot!" Is this called, "genetic memory" or is it just a coincidence?

In the 17th century, when the Dutch settlers first landed in South Africa, they also described the Bushmen and the Hottentots as short and speaking with a clicking sound.[247]

> *Since the oldest mtDNA in Assistant Professor of Genetics at the University of Hawaii Cann's sample came from a short Bushman or San individual from the Kalahari Desert, we can say that these people are representative of the oldest living branch of the human race—they spoke with clicks.*[248]

Moving on to Northwest Europe, Greenland and Canada where "Other researchers more specifically point out that the Twa, Picts, Lapp, Ainu, and Eskimo are all members of the *same original African stock...*"[249] MacRitchie says these short mound-dwelling people "must be Twas or Twa mixtures due to the *telltale presence of 'clicks'* some of their observed speech patterns"[250] contained.

In review: "The Fuegians were related to the Khoisan because of the Y chromosomes they carried. Fuegians 100-400 BP carried haplogroup A1. Hg A1 is an African haplogroup."[251]

---

246 Walker, Eric, Newton, A. P., and E. A. Benians (eds.). (1963). *The Cambridge History of the British Empire* (Cambridge, Cambridge University Press), p. 20.

247 Ibid., p. 227.

248 Van Sertima, Ivan. *African Presence in Early Europe*, p. 230.

249 Ibid., p. 227.

250 García-Bour J. "Early population differentiation in extinct aborigines from Tierra del Fuego-Patagonia: ancient mtDNA sequences and Y chromosome STR characterization." *Am. J. Phys. Anthropol.* 123, 361-370. (doi:10.1002/ajpa.10337); Finch, C. S. *Echoes of the old Dark Land*, p. 27.

251 Finch, Charles S. *Echoes of the Old Dark Land*, p.27.

According to Finch and Walker, the Khoisan are short "Bushman or San individuals from the Kalahari Desert."[252] The original Fuegians also had dark skin and peppercorn hair similar to some Southern Africans today, as seen in the photograph of an original Fuegian. As to how long the Fuegians have been in the Americas, see the paintings, artifacts, and charcoal residue found in Brazilian hearths, which date back to at least 56,000 years, and stone tools dating back to 100,000 years ago. Were the Fuegians the same people as the Amerinds? This question was scientifically answered by Perez, Bernal and Gonzalez (2007) when they wrote, "In summary, the results obtained using morphological and molecular data find that Fuegian populations are distinct from the rest of Amerindians,"[253] who entered the Americas (2600 B.C.) much later than the short Proto-American Africans (of at least 100,000 B.C.).

This means that the Fuegians are genetically different and apart from the Amerinds. The Fuegians appear to have preceded Amerinds in the Americas by tens of thousands of years. It can, therefore, be scientifically stated that the Fuegians are genetic brothers and sisters of the Khoisan in South Africa where the evidence above directly points to their precedence. These Khoisan, at the very tip of South America were, indeed, "distinct from" the other Amerinds. Why? Because most of the Amerinds of the Americas lived farther away. Tierra del Fuego is pretty isolated.

Because of their isolation and genetic relations to the Khoisan, the Fuegians were darker than the Amerinds. The Khoisan were featured in Eric Walker's book, *The Cambridge History of the British Empire* (1936). Walker wrote that Schultze supposedly coined the Khoisan name to identify a people from the same ethnic group. They were the Bushmen and Hottentots who both share the feature of short stature.[254] Shetlandic folklore says, "The first folks that ever were in our British Isles were the Picts or another way to spell Pechts.... They were very small [African] people.... The Finns were of the same race as the historic Pechts.... The Lapp, Finn, Samoyed and Eskimos were all related.... In the 18th Century they were described, "as black and wild in their appearance as any Americans

252 Perez, I.I., et al. "Morphological Differences of Aboriginal Human Populations from Tierra del Fuego," pp. 1067-1079.

253 Walker, Eric, A. P. Newton, and E. A. Benians (eds.). *The Cambridge History of the British Empire*, p. 20.

254 MacRitchie, David. *The Testimony of Tradition*, p. 104.

whatever."[255] The Pechts, Lapps and Finns were descendants of the Anu and Twa.[256]

There is a logical progression here following the evidence that the Eskimos came from the East, as did their fathers, the Anu and Twa. For those who want to know which group is older, the Twa or Anu, we shall yield to an expert. Dr. Rosland Jeffries, the wife of Dr. Leonard Jeffries, says they are the same people: "The earliest of our human ancestors were called the Twa, San and Anu.... The people called the Twa are known by many names and because of their primacy.... Anu is yet another name for the Twa."[257] According to García-Bour, Stix, MacRitchie, Walker, Finch and Jeffries, they were the same short people the Khoisan were, and related to the Anu, Twa, Pechts, San, Skraelings, Bushmen, Hottentot and Fuegians. MacRitchie, Walker and Fince reported that they all spoke with clicks. Right or wrong, different names were given to all these short Africans who spoke with a clicking sound.[258]

These people had brilliant architectural skills. Later in the history of Europe, we shall find that the Pechts built round towers, castles, churches, stupendous bridges and the Cotes-du-Nord chapel, which, "is said to have been built in one night by the fairies."[259] We also see that "According to myth, a dwarf god built the Pyramid of the Magician, in a single night"[260] as well. This pyramid can be seen today in Mexico. Their local tradition says "pygmies" built that pyramid. We now have two architectural structures short Africans are said to have built in one night, but do not end the count there. A third example would be the **Black dwarfs, called the Menehune**

255 Van Sertima, Ivan. *African Presence in Early* Europe, p. 230.

256 Jeffries, Rosalind. "Saharan Cave Art to Nile Valley and Diffusion." Presentation at ASCAC 28th Annual Ancient Kemetic Studies Conference, Temple University, Pennsylvania, October 21, 2016.

257 Winters, Clyde. E-mail message to author February 5, 2009. video, "New Movie: 30,000 BC The First Americans" on YouTube.

258 MacRitchie, David. *The Testimony of Tradition*, pp. 65, 85, 152.

259 Dermott, A. "The Spectacular Ancient Maya City of Uxmal." September 6, 2015. Accessed May 2, 2015. http://www.ancient-origins.net/ancient-places-americasy/spectacular-ancient-maya-city-uxmal-003768.

260 Luomala, Katherine. (1951). *The Menehune of Polynesia and Other Mythical Little People of Oceania* (New York, Kraus Reprint), p. 17.

in Hawaii, who also built great structures in a single night.[261] Would this be magic, or advanced architectural skills developed over tens of thousands of years?

Fig. 16: Uxmal Pyramid of the Magician in the Yucatan Peninsula, Mexico. *Public Domain.*

> *Uxmal (pronounced "oosh-mal"), means either "built three times" or "what is to come, the future," (now known as the Pyramid of the Magician). Legend says that the first king of the city was bested by a magical dwarf named Itzamna, who won Uxmal and the position as king by building the tallest monument in the city in one night. Here we have a fourth example of a dwarf building a structure in one night.[262]*

The Anu/Twa have been traced from the Nile Valley to Mali (where they are called the "Tellem"); across the narrow Straits of Gibraltar (separating Africa from Europe) to Portugal; to Germany and England (where they are called Picts, and Lapps); to Scandinavia where they are called Finns; to Greenland; to Canada (where they are called Skraelings); to North America (where they are called the Mound Builders); to the tip of South America where they are called the Fuegians. In the Philippine Islands back in the 1540s, navigator Ruy Lopesde Villalobos and his Spanish shipmates dubbed them as "Negritos" (Little Blacks). In Indonesia, on the Island of Flores, several diminutive skeletons were discovered in a cave and named "hobbits," as in J. R. R. Tolkien's trilogy, *The Lord of the Rings*.

---

261 Dermott, A. "The Spectacular Ancient Maya City of Uxmal."

262 MacRitchie, David. *The Testimony of Tradition*, pp. 14, 53, 64, 80, 91, 92, 107, 114, 123, 127, 144, 159, 144, 169.

These diminutive Africans have been given many names. In MacRichie's book they were called: dwarfs (p. 64); Leprechauns (p. 107); Elves and Pixies (p. 127); the names Pix or Picts and Fairies (p. 114); Brownies (pp. 80, 159); Musicians (p. 123); Goblins (p. 144); Enchanters (p. 169); Sorcerers and Great Magicians (p. 53); Wizards and Witches (p. 14); who had magical powers exceeding Gypsies (p. 92); Supernatural powers (p. 169); and the female dwarfs had the gift of prophecy: "she stood 'on a sort of elevated stage, a dolmen when delivering her prophecy'...is very suggested of a cromlech" (p. 91).[263]

The physical appearance of Briton's Finns or Skraelings suggest that they were Pygmies who were originally Black—later, almost Black to White[264] after mixing with the Caucasian Britons their appearance was still of a race of **"flat-noses" with flowing locks** and a **race of pygmies**.[265] (See Dr. Imhotep's editorial on "King Arthur" and how his famous Queen Guinevere was an African Pecht woman [from Scotland], as found in *Atlantis Rising Magazine*,[266] also found on Dr. Imhotep's website: HistoricalTruth.Info).

Depending on the source, these small Africans in the British Isles are depicted as savages on one hand, and very intelligent on the other hand. "The dwarf races appear as possessed of a higher culture than the race or races who were physically their superiors,"[267] i.e. their Caucasian neighbors.

Another group of ancient South Americans worth mentioning here are the Southern Patagonians. They resided in what is the southern part of modern-day Argentina that joins with the northern part of Tierra del Fuego. The Patagonian and Fuegian skulls were different from all the rest of the Amerind skulls, "based on their robusticity and dolichocephaly,"[268] meaning, they were strong, with large and long skulls.

263 Ibid., p.175.

264 Ibid., pp.13, 31, 38, 42, 60.

265 Imhotep, David. "Reader Forum," *Atlantis Rising* #80, p. 6. (2010).

266 Luomala, Katherine. *The Menehune of* Polynesia, p. 115.

267 Perez, S.I. et al. (2007). "Morphological Differentiation of Aboriginal Human Populations From Tierra del Fuego," pp. 1067-1079.

268 Anitei, Stefan. (2008). "The Enigma of the Natives of Tierra del Fuego: Are Alacaluf and Yahgan the last Native Black Americans?" Accessed August 11, 2009. http://news.softpedia.com/news/The-Enigma-of-the-Native-of-Tierra-delFuego80693.shtml.

In modern times, of the three unrelated groups in Tierra del Fuego, two are short Blacks:

The Onas were very distinct from other Fuegians. They were tall, men's height varying between 1.7 and 1.8 m (5.6 to 6 ft.), with massive bodies, wide faces, large prominent noses and straight hair.... Instead, the Yahgans and Alacalufs were very short (male average height was of 1.55 m or 5 ft 2 in), with feeble bodies. The head had a receding forehead, a very wide nose and wavy hair. Today, Fuegian languages are extinct or on the verge of extinction, and few people of pure blood remained.[269]

There is a trail of evidence that connects the short Africans from the Nile Valley to the Americas, like pieces of a puzzle. To reach the Americas, some sailed directly from Africa, landing in South and Central America. Others took the northern route, from Africa through Western Europe, to Scandinavia sailing to Greenland, and finally the Americas. Along the way, some of these short Africans made a detour west to the British Isles. How did these first Britons reach the British Isles? Some probably sailed, but others could have walked.

It must be understood that these first Britons made their way to Britain during the last Ice Age. During that age the world's water levels were down far lower than today, and "it was possible to walk from England to France."[270]

The oldest human settlement ever found in the British Isles was in Scotland dating back 14,000 years ago. Later, in the section on artifacts and structures, this 14,000-year date will come up again linked to Stonehenge. In a nearby small town just a couple of miles away called Amesbury, in Southwestern England, a 4300 years-old corpse has been found that the press dubbed, "The King of Stonehenge."[271] Archaeologists were excavating a gravesite and found two skeletons whose "legs were curled in

269 White, I. "Quaternary Landscape Development I The Nature of The Quaternary." (2002). Accessed April 3, 2008. http://www.staffs.ac.uk/schools/sciences/geography/staff/harrist/landev/lect13notes.htm.

270 Stone, R., (2005). "Mystery Man of Stonehenge." Accessed December 15, 2005. http://www.smithsonianmag.com/travel/mystery-man-stonehenge.html.

271 Ibid., p.1.

a fetal position."[272] Fetal position burials were a common practice in the pre-dynastic Nile Valley. At one of the burial schemes, archaeologist W. F. Petrie found "at Nagada and Ballas in Upper Egypt which is Southern Egypt...an almost invariant never changing burial scheme...the body was contracted into a fetal position...which evokes the idea of rebirth."[273]

More evidence points to the fact that these two corpses were not Celtic nor were they buried by the Celts. The Celts did not bury, but cremated their dead.[274] "It was cremation, and not grave burials, that had been the general practice of the wandering Teutonic peoples of the North.... Later burial practices...were not the only cultural components introduced to Nordic Europe by the Africans. In support of Van Sertima, Dr. Imhotep states the Caucasian Celts were a part of the greater Indo-European group who did not bury their dead but cremated them."[275]

At this point the reader is directed to the Foreword (Reflections) in this book that convincingly presents evidence of an African/Celtic origin.

The King of Stonehenge could not have been, nor could his undertakers have been Celts, because these Caucasian Celts did not arrive in the British Isles for another 2300 years.[276] Here is what some people have said about the Celts:

We don't know the name of the builders of Stonehenge, but we're pretty sure it wasn't the Celts or "Druids."...Druids were a class of learned men and women in Celtic society, but when Stonehenge was built, the Celts were probably not in Britain. Some historians of the British Isles point out that the original inhabitants of these isles

272 Van Sertima, Ivan.(1994). *Egypt Child of Africa* (New Jersey, Transaction Publishers), p. 39.

273 Álvarez-Sanchís, J. R. (2000). "Oppida and Celtic society in western Spain." *Journal of Interdisciplinary Studies*, Vol. 6. Accessed December 7, 2009. http://www4.uwm.edu/celtic/ekeltoi/volumes/ vol6/6_5/alvarez_sanchis65.html.

274 Van Sertima, Ivan. *African Presence in Early* Europe, p. 76.

275 Imhotep, (Jones) David. (2007). *The Origin of Civilization: The Case of Egypt and Mesopotamia from Several Disciplines.* Union Institute and University, Cincinnati, Ohio, Dissertation Proquest.

276 Pyatt, E. J. (2007). "Bad Celtic Page." Accessed on November 24, 2009. http://www.personal.psu.edu/ejp10/lingland/faqbadcelt.html-henge.

were "not only non-Celtic, but also non-Teutonic and philologically allied with people who spoke a non-Aryan language," therefore they were not Aryans.... A study of the original Celts by Squire goes even further, describing these people as short, dark-skinned, dark-eyed and haired, and boldly stating that their language belonged to a class called Hamitic and that they came originally from Africa.[277]

Squire made it very plain who these original Celts were. Prolific writer and archaeologist Godfrey Higgins in *Anacalypsis*, also wrote that originally the "Celtic Druids...of whom the Druids were priests...who were but early individuals of the black nation..." Cushites are from Cush or Kush, modern Ethiopia, i.e. African Celts, who built the great temples in India and Britain.'"[278] Higgins also said, "the Celts were Cushites Africans and he wasn't the only one to hold that opinion."[279]

The very first archaeological stage identified as "Celtic" is the Hallstat culture (800–400 B.C.), which is generally confined to the Alps to the north and east of Italy, nowhere near Britain.[280] The Celts entered the British Isles later on their trek to the west. Even at the Celts' earliest date given in the Hallstat culture of 800 B.C., a serious question must be asked: Who were the people in the British Isles 14,000 years ago if they were not Caucasian Celts? Do not forget it was the short Africans who walked across the land bridge during the last Ice Age from Europe to England. Greece began in 1200 B.C.[281] and was the very first documented Caucasian civilization with evidence of having megalithic structures. But were those stones not left by the "African Pelasgian civilization" that preceded the Greeks? That is 500 years before Berry Fell's mythological Scandinavian King's voyage to America to build the megalithic chambers. Rome began

277 Van Sertima, Ivan. *African Presence in Early Europe*, p. 14.

278 Higgins, Godfrey. (1836). *Anacalypsis*. (London: Longman, Rees, Orme, Brown, Green, and Longman, Paternoster Roe), p. 59.

279 Ibid., p. 14.

280 Martin, T. R. (1999). "An Overview of Classical Greek History from Mycenae to Alexander." Accessed December 14, 2009 http://old.perseus.tufts.edu/cgibin/ptext?doc=1999.04.0009.

281 Mark, Joshua. "Rome Founded" *Ancient History Encyclopedia* (2009). Accessed July 2, 2009. http://www.ancient.eu/Rome/.

in 753 B.C.[282] The Romans were the first documented Caucasians to sail out of the Mediterranean Sea into the Atlantic Ocean. They were said to have been sailing to the British Isles looking for tin. The Romans, however, did not reach Britain until approximately 700 years later in 55 B.C.[283]

The Phoenicians and the Egyptians had been voyagers for tin before the Britons. The Bronze Age in the British Isles was from 2200 to 700 B.C. Therefore, the Caucasian Celts entered the scene long after all these groups. But as far as the Western Hemisphere is concerned, as Robert E. Funk, chief archaeologist for the New York State Museum from 1971 to 1993 said, "There are **no Celtic ruins in the New World to be found whatsoever.**"[284]

Evidence shows that the Vikings were the first documented Caucasians to visit the Americas, not the Celts, and that was not until 1000 A.D.[285] which was 2700 years after Fell's Scandinavian King made his mythical voyage during the Bronze Age in 1700 B.C.

Proto-Viking ships were found in Scandinavia. There is a connection between the Proto-Viking ships and those of the Nile Valley. "The excavation of a 5000-year-old wooden boat at Abydos in southern Egypt" was done in the 1990s followed by the excavation of 13 other boats. "The excavated ship is a '**sewn boat**,' its thick wooden planks lashed together with rope running through mortises. It is about 75 feet long, seven to ten feet wide, has a draft of two feet, and a narrow prow and stern."[286] The two curved extensions, on the other hand, northern Europe's first boat:

The Scandinavian Hjortspring Boat is northern Europe's oldest plank-built vessel. The boat is almost 20 meters long...and could

282 Nichols, K. L. (2009). "A Simplified Medieval Britain Timeline." Accessed December 1, 2009. http://faculty.pittstate.edu/~knichols time.html.

283 "From the beginning of man to the Bronze Age." (n.d.). Accessed December 7, 2009. http://www.stedmundsburychronicle.co.uk/Chronicle/5mbp-700bc.htm.

284 Kilgannon, Corey. "Putnam's Mysterious Chambers of Stone." Accessed December 22, 2013. http://www.nytimes.com/2001/04/22/nyregion/putnams-mysterious-chambers-of-stone.html.

285 Oleson, Tryggvi J. *Early Voyages and Northern Approaches*, p. 19.

286 Schuster, A. "This Old Boat." Archaeology. (December 11, 2000) Accessed September 11, 2011. http://www.archaeology.org/ online/news/Abydos.html

carry 24 men with weapons as well as other gear. The boat consists of a bottom plank and two wide planks on each side, sewn together with bast. At both ends the boat is furnished with two curving extensions. The Hjortspring Boat is evidence of shipbuilding with roots dating back to the Bronze Age.[287]

Here is a later Scandinavian ship with iron rivets:

It represents a linked chain of evidence about shipbuilding design, before, during, and after the Viking Age. The planked Hjortspring boat... is about fifty feet long and formed of five broad thin, slightly overlapping boards which are stitched sewn together with hide thongs. like that of the Hjortspring boat, the later Nydam ship has a true curved prow joined to the bottom plank. Instead of being sewn, the planking is held together by iron rivets.[288]

As mentioned above, the Hjortspring boat was built "before the Viking Age." This means the Caucasian Vikings most likely did not build it, and it was probably built by the Blacks or Khoisan. The Hjortspring boat was built around 1500–500 B.C., because the quote above dates it to the Bronze Age.[289] This means that the Egyptian boats are even 1900–2900 years older than the Hjortspring boat, which is northern Europe's oldest plank-built vessel. The Nydam ship was made later with iron rivets probably made by Caucasian Vikings.

The first Caucasians did not enter Scandinavia until 600 A.D.[290] Therefore, they could not have built the later Hjortspring boat of 1500–500 B.C. Even at the later date of 500 B.C., that would be 1100 years later.

---

287 Jernalder, A. (n.d.) "The Hjortspting Boat." The National Museum, Frederiksholms Kanal 12, DK-1220 Copenhagen K. tel: 33 13 44 11. Accessed September 11, 2011. https://en.natmus. dk/historical-knowledge/denmark/prehistoric-period-until-1050-ad/the-early-iron-age/the-army-from-hjortspring-bog/ the-hjortspring-boat/

288 Tryckare, Tre. *The Viking* (Sweeden, Cagner & Co., 1066), p. 248.

289 World Heritage Convention." (n,d.) Bronze Age Burial Site of Sammallahdenmäki. Accessed September 11, 2011. http://whc.unesco.org/en/list/57.

290 Washington, P. M. "The African-Egyptian Heritage of the Vikings: and African Prehistoric Europe, Parts I and II." 2006. Accessed August 30, 2011. http://www.beforebc.de/Related.Subjects/Ships. Sea-faring/92-10-825.html.

The sewn plank Hjortspring boat is a double-prow boat as were the boats in Egypt. The people who probably built the first sewn boats in Scandinavia would most probably be the Sami. The Sami are also called the Lapp people: "Lapp" refers to the indigenous people of Lapland (northern Scandinavia), but it's a name used by outsiders.

On the Kola Peninsula adjacent to Finland in Scandinavia, they call themselves Saami, Saam or Sami.[291] The Tmi, also known as Lapps, were the first inhabitants of vast timberlands and tundra above the Arctic Circle in the area known as Lapland. They were originally Khoisan or Anu (or Ainu) because "the Sámi were living in their current region during the last Ice Age (20,000–16,000 B.C.), continuing their way of life even through the time of the last glacial coverage of Scandinavia."[292] They could not have started out with white skin then because, according to genetics, there was no white skin that long ago. **Do not forget that these cousins of the "Twa, Lapp, Ainu, and Eskimo are all members of the same original African stock,"**[293] namely the Khoisan, who entered Europe at the very least, 40,000 years ago.[294]

A *Discover Magazine* article gives us further evidence of an African background for the Sami, who, along "with the Basque are the only living non-Indo-European languages whose origins are prehistoric."[295] So, if the Sami are also called the Lapp people, and the Lapp and Anu were African people, then the original Sami were, and began as (African) Khoisan people who entered Europe 40,000 years ago. As quoted above the first Lapps, or Sami were diminutive Africans: "the Sami were considered 'sub-

291 Madorsky, Rachel. (n.d.). "The Most Written Indigenous People on the World-Sami-Saami-Lapps." Accessed on September 9, 2011 from http://ezinearticles.com/?The-Most-Written-Indigenous-People-on-the-World-Sami-Saami-Lapps&id=2009014.

292 Merin, Jennifer. "Sami Artisans of Scandinavia Use Traditional Techniques in Crafts." June 21, 1990. Accessed September 9, 2011. http://articles.latimes.com/1990-06-24/travel/tr-926_1_herd-reindeer.

293 Stroud, M. (n.d.). "The Origin and Genetic Background of the Sámi." Accessed September 9, 2011. http://www.utexas.edu/courses/ sami/dieda/hist/genetic.htm.

294 Van Sertima, Ivan. *African Presence in Early Europe*, p. 230.

295 Winters, Clyde. "Origin and Spread of Haplogroup H." Bioresearch Bulletin (2010) 3: 116-122.

humans,' and were treated as such by the Germans because many of them were short with dark features instead of having the blond hair and blue eyes that the Germans considered superior."[296]

Thousands of years later, history books stated: "We first hear of them the Sami in the year 98 A.D. from the Roman historian Tacitus in his book, *Germania*. At that time, they were called 'Fenni' or Fin, for whom Finland was probably named. Tacitus described them as a primitive hunting tribe who roamed the forests near northern Germany."[297]

These Proto-Viking-Sami were the people who most probably taught the Caucasian Vikings how to make the first boats in Scandinavia. These were "Sami sewn boats,"[298] but even that era was well after the Naqada II boat's existence before 3400 B.C. "The Caucasian or 'steppe population' largely entered the Near East probably from the Western Steppe, Kazakhstan and the Ukraine, as well as the Mediterranean, and Europe after 2100 B.C. and continued migrating there until the Middle Ages"[299] The definition of the "steppe" is "one of the great plains of southeastern Europe and Asia, having few or no trees."[300]

If you look on a map, find India, and then look north between the Indian and Tibetan boundaries, you will find where the Asian great plain ends (at the eastern part of the Pamir Mountains), and the Tarim Basin begins.

Section Notes

I. Distances

The distance from "Australia to Peru in South America is 9234 miles" (Air miles), whereas the distance from the Northern African coast is a

296 Khan, R. "The men of the north: the Sami." *Discover Magazine* December 8, 2010.

297 Johnson, J. (2001). The Sami and World War II. Accessed September 14, 2011. http://www.utexas.edu/courses/sami/dieda/hist/wwii. htm.

298 Ibid.

299 Woodard, K. (n.d.) "The Sami vs. Outsiders." Accessed September 9, 2011. http://www.utexas.edu/courses/sami/dieda/hist/sami-west. htm#early.

300 Washington, P. M. "The African-Egyptian Heritage of the Vikings."

"1500 to 1600-mile trip to the Americas."[301] A trip from Australia to South America is well over six times farther than from Africa to South America. At most, the distance of 9234 miles is 7634 more miles to make the trip from Australia to South America, than from Africa to South America.

J. 20,000 Mongolian invaders

Author David H. Childress talks about a possible pyramid in Aztalan, Wisconsin, that is now covered by a lake. Aztalan is northwest of Chicago. This is supposedly the site of an ancient city built by Proto-Americans. The largest pyramid under the lake is a smaller version of the Teotihuacao, Mexico's "pyramid of the Sun."[302] Kingsley Craig, a historical researcher, worked for the Epigraphic Society. He informed Childress about Aztalan (an ancient city in the Mississippi Valley). He claims that around 1250 A.D., 20,000 Mongols left Asia for North America, escaping the clutches of Genghis Khan. Craig says they traveled east to the Mississippi Valley. At that time, there were many African mound communities all along the Mississippi River. He says these Mongols attacked and completely destroyed Aztalan, and then headed south, destroying the cities and temples areas as they went. Craig says the Mongols settled down in northern New Mexico near the Gallina River. Archaeologist Frank C. Hibben says that:

> It seems obvious that the Gallina people were not the ordinary Pueblo Indians, most likely Proto-Americans. The physical makeup of these skeletons in the towers they built was slightly different. Many of their utensils and weapons were radically different...absolutely un-Pueblo like.[303]

Craig's research of a massacre of Proto-Americans by people from Asia.

The BBC article stated: "Other evidence suggests that these first Americans were later massacred by invaders from Asia." This data that originated from a BBC article and television special: "Ancient Voices: The Hunt for the First Americans" was shown on BBC Two at 2130 BST

301 *Webster's New Universal Unabridged Dictionary* (1983). Steppes, p. 1784.

302 Flight Distance between Australia and Peru." Accessed January 3, 2010 http://www.convertunits.com/distance/from/Australia/to/Peru.

303 Childress, David. H. *Lost Cities of North & Central America*, p. 362.

on Wednesday 1 September 1999.[304] The first Americans were different people from the invading Asians. Craig wrote that, "The physical makeup of the skeletons in the defensive towers they built was slightly different."[305] The skeletal evidence shows they were not "invaders from Asia" but Paleoamerican Pueblo. In reaction to this terrible slaughter:

> [T]he Pueblo Indians, in a remarkable mobilization of all the various tribes, finally sieged them at Gallina, and killed the Mongolian warriors to the last man and woman, leaving not even one alive... he also found evidence of a mass slaughter in the valley from a fierce battle.[306]

In addition to the last two pieces, there is a third item that fits into this story. Childress claims there is a book that corroborates these stories called *The Dene and Na-Dene Indian Migration 1233 A.D.—Escape from Genghis Kahn to America*, by Ethel G. Stewart.[307] There is a 17-year difference from the first report of 1250 A.D. In September of 2010, a fourth and more up-to-date report on this event was published. It seems that this event has been precisely dated by the latest dating technique. This report says that 14,882 people were killed in 800 A.D. in Durango, Colorado.[308]

Durango is just northwest of Gallina, across the New Mexico state line in Colorado. The differences between the two major reports of this mass killing in southwestern North America are minor. The number killed differs by a few hundred. The dates differ by a little more than 600 years. The areas where it is said to have taken place are only around 100 miles away from each other. The probability that all these data were from the same event is very good. We know that the event took place, and now we also have an updated report on the probable number of people killed and the probable site where it took place.

---

304 Ibid., p. 366, 367.

305 "First Americans were Australian." (1999). Accessed August 26, 2006. http://news.bbc.co.uk/2/hi/sci/tech/430944.stm.

306 Childress, David. H. *Lost Cities of North & Central America*, p. 376.

307 Ibid., p. 362.

308 Stewart, Ethel G. (1991). *The Dene and Na-Dene Indian Migration 1233 A.D.-Escape From Genghis Khan to America* (NY, Isac Press), p. 386.

Unlike the industrious mound builders, who lost out to the first large wave of the Huang-nu from Mongolia, the Proto-Americans won the war against a second large group from Mongolia fleeing Genghis Khan. Is there an in-depth account of how the first Americans came to the Americas? This subject is very deep and involved, and to give the reader the full story is beyond the scope of this work. You can find more details in Dr. Imhotep's dissertation.[309] But here is a brief explanation. The Aurignacian Africans were the first Homo sapiens to enter Europe in approximately 40,000 B.C.[310]

Before the last Ice Age, there were only Negritic (Black) peoples on this planet. This migration to Europe occurred during a brief warming event during the Ice Age, which began 115,000 years ago. After a few years the warming period came to a close and the full force of the Ice Age returned. During that colder period the color of the Aurignacians' skin began to lighten. It was not until thousands of years later that the mesocephalic trait appeared during the Mesolithic period (around 10,000 years ago), and the brachycephalic so-called "Yellow race" first appeared much later.[311]

With the color of the Yellow race described, the source used for the picture of the small "pygmy" brachycephalic (round) skulls with projecting jaws that were found in the reference shall be addressed.

In this source, Fell (1982) wrote that the skulls "were pygmy types, some having a brain capacity equal to that of a 7-year-old child (950 cc), although their teeth pointed to middle-aged individuals."[312] It seems that by comparing the skull to a "7-year-old-child," Fell was writing about the skull size and not the cognitive ability of the people. Then he said the skulls were round with projecting jaws, and that this type dates back to 40,000 years ago. With most of the above, there is no problem. The part that may be confusing, and leading the reader comes next.

---

309 Viegas, Jennifer. "How genocide wiped out a Native American population." September 20, 2010. Accessed on, September 21, 2010. http://www.msnbc.msn.com/id/39268873/ns/technology_and_science-science/?gt1=43001.

310 Imhotep, (Jones) D. *The Origin of Civilization.*

311 Jones, D. C. *The Origin of* Civilization, p. 49.

312 "European Bronze Age Visitors in America." (n.d.). Accessed February 10, 2010. http://www.faculty.ucr.edu/~legneref/bronze/doc/bron58.htm.

Fell wrote, "These traits link them with the pygmies of Malaya and the Philippines, who are believed to have originated in southern Mongolia."[313] When people hear the name Mongolia they think of yellow-skinned Asian people. This leads the reader to think that these skulls belonged to yellow-skinned Asian/Mongolians. As Diop explained previously, there were no Yellow or Asian people in existence 40,000 years ago.

Furthermore, to have traveled from Malaya and the Philippines to the Americas, which are literally halfway around the world, was not probable back then. As seen in "Section Note I," traveling from Asia to the Americas is at least five times farther than from Africa to the Americas. These short Africans more likely originated in Africa. It is much more reasonable to assume that they sailed to the Americas from Africa, and/or island hopped, as the Vikings would later do, from Northern Europe to the Americans. By bringing them to Tennessee from Malaya and the Philippines rather than from Africa (where they originated) is not very probable.

K. Pre-Clovis Evidence: All 9 are peer-reviewed journal articles

Note: These nine articles verify this author's thesis that the first Americans were indeed Africans.

1. **250,000 years ago**. Just visit Micah Hanks' work at the 250,000-year-old **Hueyatlaco archaeological site**,[314] where they excavated in the Valsequillo Basin that is near the city of Puebla, Mexico in 1962. This excavation was carried out by Cynthia Irwin-Williams, who co-discovered this site with Juan Armania Camacho. This excavation was carried out in association with the U.S. Geological Survey. They recovered several ancient stone tools that were found "in situ" next to animal remains.

---

313   Ibid.

314   Hanks, Micah. "Controversial Hueyatlaco Site Suggests Humans Were in the Americas 250,000 Years Ago." Mysterious Universe. 8th Kind Pty Ltd, May 25, 2017. https://mysteriousuniverse.org/2017/05/controversial-hueyatlaco-site-suggests-humans-were-in-the-americas-250,000-years-ago/.

Dating the stone tools by using thermoluminescence or absolute dating has its weaknesses. "Weaknesses of these stylistic paradigms (for example in Pettitt & Pike 2007) were pointed out."[315]

A *more universal method* is C-14 radiocarbon dating. This method measures the decay of that unstable isotope carbon-14, which all living organisms absorb. Therefore, using the animal remains found next to the stone tools was a better fit to date the tools.

Several other "sophisticated independent tests were made namely: uranium-thorium dating, fission track dating, tephra hydration dating, and the study of mineral weathering to determine the date of the artifacts."[316] That comes from the 1981 journal, Quarternary Research paper.

Interestingly, the biostratigraphic researcher, Sam Van Landingham, has published **two peer-reviewed analyses that confirm the earlier findings of circa 250,000 years ago** for the tool-bearing strata at Hueyatlaco.

So, the 250,000 year date for the stone tools seems to be a solid find.

2. **130,000 years ago**. From *Science Magazine* we have a date of humans in the Americas of 100,000 years ago. A controversial study in *Nature* claims humans reached the Americas 130,000 years ago. This jaw-dropping claim is based on broken rocks and mastodon bones found in California that a team of researchers say point to human activity.

See https://www.nature.com/news/controversial-study-claims-humans-reached-americas-100-000-years-earlier-than-thought-1.21886 also see: https://www.livescience.com/58851-humans-occupied-north-america-earlier-than-thought.html

3. **100,000 years ago.** Dr. Nieda Guidon wrote that, "I think it's wrong that everyone came running across the Bering chasing mammoths—that's infantile. I think they also came along the seas."[317] Now in her eighties

---

315   Ruiz, Juan F., and Marvin W. Rowe. (2018). "Dating Methods (Absolute and Relative) in Archaeology of Art." Centre De Recherche Et D'Etudes Pour L'Art Préhistorique. www.creap.fr/pdfs/Dating-Methods-Springer2014.pdf, p.2036.

316 Steen-McIntyre, V., R. Fryxell, and H. Malde. (1981). "Geologic Evidence for Age Deposits at Hueyatlaco Archaeological Site Valsequillo Mexico" (PDF). *Quaternary Research*. 16: 1-17. doi:10.1016/0033-5894(81)90124-1. Archived (PDF) from the original on July 6, 2013.

317 Guidon, N., A. Pessis, F. Parenti, C. Guerin, E. Peyre, G. M. dos Santos. (2002). "Pedra Furada, Brazil: Paleo-Indians, Paintings, and Paradoxes." *Athena Review*, Vol.3, no.2. Accessed March 4, 2010. http://www.athenapub.com/10pfurad.htm.

and mostly retired, Guidon hasn't softened her tone at all. She currently maintains that people first arrived in Brazil from West Africa, perhaps as far back as 100,000 years ago. Her evidence comes from the presence of ancient fire and tools of human craftsmanship at habitation sites.

4. **56,000 years ago**. Pedra Furada in northeastern Brazil represents the oldest known human occupation site in the Americas. The radiocarbon laboratory "returned samples of greater than 56 ka 56,000 BP"[318] as reported in the 2003 *Quaternary Science Review*. They found Paleoamericans' charcoal residue from campfires. After the first article an even earlier date was documented, which stated that, "Hence, it appears that humans were already at this site about 60,000 years ago, and possibly even earlier."[319]

The 60,000-year figure stirred up a hornet's nest of controversy. New improved tests in 2003 retested the charcoal samples from the previously dated charcoal using a different dating technique. "Measurements on five of the samples were greater than 56 ka BP."[320] When this discovery was made, it was the most ancient find for the peopling of the Americas in the history of archaeology.

5. **51,700 years ago**. A South Carolina professor and archaeologist, Dr. Albert Goodyear III, found an ancient campsite dated 51,700 years ago. This surprise was found close to the Savannah River less than 30 miles from the Atlantic Ocean. Four meters below the surface, Goodyear found artifacts and burnt plant remains from an ancient campfire. He also found a chunk of flint that was being used to make micro blades for knives and spear tips. "The two 50,000 dates indicate that they are at least 50,300 years."[321] Goodyear said, "This is the oldest radiocarbon-dated site of human activity in North America."[322] (This is the only one of eight articles that was not peer-reviewed at this time but Dr. Goodyear says he is working on it and will have the peer-reviewed status soon.)

---

318 Santos, G. M. et al. "The Pleistocene Peopling of the Americas," pp. 2303-2310.

319 Ibid., pp. 2303-2310.

320 Guidon, N. et al. "Paleo-Indians, Paintings, and Paradoxes."

321 Santos, G. M. et al. "Pleistocene peopling of the Americas," pp. 21-22.

322 "New Evidence" https://www.sciencedaily.com/releases/2004/11/041118104010.htm.

6. **48,500 years ago**. Serra da Capivara National Park, in Sao Raimundo Nonato PI, Brazil, contains 1000 wall paintings. Radiocarbon dating of charcoals collected from several different layers at the rock shelters called Toca da Pedra Furada, Guidon and Delibrias and Parenti found ages ranging from 6200 to 48,500 years.[323]

7. **40,000 years ago.** Very hard evidence—in volcanic stone—shows the presence of modern humans in Mexico as early as 40,000 years ago. A report of "human footprints preserved in 40,000-year-old volcanic ash near Puebla, Mexico" has been confirmed.[324]

8. **33,000 years ago**. Mt. Verde, Chile, some of the artifacts recovered showing human occupation were burnt wood, charcoal and flaked pebbles to cut and scrape; they were found after "they also examined the material from the deeper, 33,000-year-old layer.... These are real human artifacts.... There is no doubt the age—it's 33,000 years old."[325] This is the only Paleoamerican site that is not on the Atlantic side of the Americas; but it is still less than 400 miles from the Atlantic Ocean.

9. **17,650 to 15,200 years ago**. Meadowcroft Rockshelter in Pennsylvania is the location where "They state that man was using the rockshelter by at least 14,255 ± 975 B.C. and maybe as early as 17,650 ± 2400 B.C. during a Wisconsin full glacial occupation by man in the shelter."[326]

10. **5000 years ago?** The first Asians (Mongolians), entered the Americas 4600–5000 years ago (2600–3000 B.C.). This assessment was based on "craniofacial morphology among early skeletons in North America... lowland Paleoindians or Paleoamericans from Brazil were

323 Watanabe, S. et al. (2003). "Some Evidence of Date of First Humans to Arrive in Brazil." *Journal of Archaeological Science* 30, 351-354 doi:10.1006/jasc.2002.0846

324 Rennie, P. R. (2005). "Geochronolgy: Age of Mexican ash with alleged 'footprints.'" *Nature* 438, E7-E8 (1 December 2005). doi:10.1038/nature04425.

325 Dillehay, T. D., and M. B. Collins. "Early cultural evidence from Monte Verde in Chile." *Nature* 332, 150-152 (March 10, 1988); doi:10.1038/332150a0.

326 Mead, J. I. "Is It Really That Old? A Comment About The Meadowcroft Rockshelter Overview." *American Antiquity*, vol. 45, no. 3 (Jul., 1980), p. 57.

morphologically distinct from Northeast Asians, and morphologically similar to populations from Australia and Africa."[327]

> *Paleoamerican skulls clearly differ from the East Asian and Amerindian skulls. Although the first Paleoamericans were from Africa, "all those groups probably formed part of a first dispersal route out of Africa."*[328]

Then there are also some reports of a boulder in Haiti with claims to have legible symbols carved into it, possibly dating back one million years or more. This book, however, wishes to keep the integrity of the first edition which has the subtitle which reads, "documented evidence."

There are several more sites that claim to be even older, but they are all said to be too controversial. This book is concerned with sites and dates that can be relied upon. We want to keep an "open mind" but not go too far and have a "hole in our head" where common sense and solid evidence turns to liquid and drains out of that hole.

L. John Smith and Black Indians?

In 1607, the Englishman, Captain John Smith, built the first permanent Caucasian settlement in North America in Jamestown, Virginia. While building the settlement, Smith made contact with the Powhatan tribe. In 1607 A.D., Smith described the Chief of the Powhatans by writing, "Powhatan more like a devil (sic) than a man with some two hundred more as black (sic) as himself."[329] When Smith described the Powhatans as devils and black, he was referring to skin tone and not war paint. Also, historically speaking, were the Amerinds not referred to as, "The Red Man?" So, if Winters' agrees saying "early Americans would certainly be able to tell the difference between paint and complexion."[330]

Whether the Powhatans were Black at that late date or not, does not change the fact that the first Americans were Africans. The Powhatans were part of the Algonquian speakers, who were the largest group of Indians in

327 Powell, Joseph F., and Walter A. Neves. "Craniofacial Morphology of the First Americans," p. 162.

328 Gonzalez-Jose, Rolando., et al. "Late Pleistocene Craniofacial Morphology," pp. 772-780.

329 "Native Peoples in Early Colonial Virginia," (n.d.). Accessed April 6, 2009

330 Winters,Clyde. *We Are Not Just Africans*, pp. 17, 21.

Virginia as late as the time Smith arrived. There were more than 10,000 Algonquins in Virginia alone before the colonists arrived.[331] John Smith's description of "Black Powhatans" occurs between the time Africans entered the Western Hemisphere 100,000 years ago and in modern times when some White Americans created the myth that Native Americans were descendants of Mongolian people from East Asia.

M. 100,000 years ago, John Smith's yell, the myth

Let us study the making of this myth. Firstly, according to DNA, the Black Indians came to the Americas either directly from Africa or indirectly after migrating to Europe first, and finally sailing to the Americas.

First, genetic evidence that the so-called Native Americans were not the first people in the Americas:

The most predominate Y chromosome of Native Americans in North America is the African R-M173. R-M173 is found in the northeastern and southwestern parts of the United States along with the mtDNA haplogroup X (25%). The Mongoloids are indirectly related to the Black Indians and Africans because of the climate in ancient Asia; another mix between the two occurred in more recent years in the Americas after their arrival across the Bering Strait. African haplogroups are found in Africa but are absent in Siberia. The Mongoloids are not now, nor were they ever Black Indians. The mixture of both Mongolians and Africans produced Native Americans or Amerinds (also called Amerindians). On the other hand, Black Indians are also called Paleoamericans, and they come from Africa; but they are not mixed with Mongolians:

> *The African specific R-M173 yDNA form a Sub-Saharan African (SSA) Subclade (subclass), which in association with the SSA R-M269 subclade in Africa, reveal that there was a gene flow from SSA toward mongoloid people in North America.*[332]

The statement above makes sure that we understand that African DNA was carried by Africans to the Americas at the latest, 100,000 years ago. Dr. Winters in his Academia.edu paper:

---

331 Ibid., p. 19.

332 Ibid., p. 25.

Shimada et. al (2007) believes that XhX is of African origin...and Amerinds carry the X haplogroup as well. The pristine form of R1*M173 is found only in Africa.[333]

This also means that Amerinds had to come from Africa because the gene XhX is of African origin, and only in Africa can pristine R1*M173 be found. All of this is extremely important. On the opposite eastern side of the Americas, "Spanish explorers found Sub-Saharan Africans already in the New World."[334]

There is a preponderance of different kinds of scientific, genetic and archaeological evidence which again suggests that, "Indians" have not always been here. This is stated by Dr. Imhotep who has absolutely no axe to grind, for he has two so-called Native American bloods. On his mother's side he has Navaho, on his father's side he has Arapaho; and he is very proud of it! Yes, Africans arrived first, but after 100,000 years or more, cultures change. In this case, the African culture gradually changed to that of the Black Native American Indian.

But wait, if that 51,000-year-old yell for the First Americans made you flinch, this next date will make you faint. *National Geographic* has reported that evidence of humans has been found in California that is 130,000 years old:

...researchers say they've found signs of ancient humans in California between 120,000 and 140,000 years ago....[A] paleontologist at the San Diego Natural History Museum, whose team describes their analysis today in Nature*...[As] Deméré and their colleagues tell it, their evidence is a mastodon skeleton, bone flakes, and several large stones...that appear to be rudimentary tools are far heavier than the surrounding particles.[335]*

In the same article, another researcher involved, Michael Haslam—an Oxford archaeologist who studies tool use in non-human primates agrees:

I think that the evidence presented in this paper backs up the author's claim that a mastodon has been broken apart using stone tools.

---

333 Ibid., p. 20.

334 Ibid., p. 20.

335 Ibid.., p. 20.

Overall, I think that we need to consider humans as the starting hypothesis for this site and go from there.[336]

Also, in Hueyatlaco, Mexico:

...an archeological site in the Valsequillo Basin near the city of Puebla, Mexico. After excavations in the 1960s, the site became notorious due to geochronologists' analyses that indicated human habitation at Hueyatlaco was dated to ca. 250,000 years before the present....The excavation was associated with the U.S. Geological Survey.... The stone tools were discovered in situ in a stratum that also contained animal remains. Radiocarbon dating of the animal remains produced an age of over 35,000 ybp. Uranium dating produced an age of 260,000 ybp, ± 60,000 years. In 1981, the journal Quaternary Research *published a paper by Steen-McIntyre, Fryxell and Malde that defended an anomalously distant age of human habitation at Hueyatlaco. The paper reported the results of four sophisticated, independent tests: uranium-thorium dating, fission track dating, tephra hydration dating and the studying of mineral weathering to determine the date of the artifacts. These tests, among other data, validated a date of 250,000 ypb for the Hueyatlaco artifacts....Using the zircon Fission track dating method, geochemist C.W. Naeser dated samples of ash from Hueyatlaco's tool-bearing strata to 370,000 ybp +/- 240,000 years. We usually do not use Wikipedia, but in this case their story and especially their references were impeccable.*[337]

References

Note: All of these references and numbers pertain to the one article above.

1. Irwin-Williams, C., et al. Comments on the Associations of Archaeological Materials and Extinct Fauna in the Valsequillo Region Puebla Mexico, American *Antiquity*, Volume 34, Number 1, Pages 82-83, Jan 1969.

---

336 Greshko, M. 2017 "Humans in California 130,000 Years Ago?" *National Geographic Magazine.*

337 Steen-Mcintyre, Fryxell, & Malde. "Geologic evidence for age of deposits at Hueyatlaco archeological site, Vasequillo, Mexico." pp.1-17.

2. Szabo, B. J., H. E. Malde, and C. Irwin-Williams. Dilemma Posed By Uranium-Series Dates On Archaeologically Significant Bones From Valsequillo Puebla Mexico, *Earth and Planetary Science Letters*, Volume 6, Pages 237-244, Jul 1969.

3. Gonzalez, Silvia, David Huddart, and Matthew Bennett. (2006) Valsequillo Pleistocene archaeology and dating: ongoing controversy in Central Mexico. *World Archaeology*, 2006, vol. 38, no4, pp. 611-627.

4. Irwin-Williams, C., et al., Comments on the Associations of Archaeological Materials and Extinct Fauna in the Valsequillo Region Puebla Mexico, *American Antiquity*, Volume 34, Number 1, Pages 82-83, Jan 1969; Irwin-Williams, Cynthia. (1978) Summary of Archeological Evidence from the Valsequillo Region, Puebla, Mexico. *In Cultural Continuity in Mesoamerica*, David L. Browman, ed. The Hague: Mouton Publishers.

5. Steen-McIntyre, V. R. Fryxell, and H. Malde. (1981). "Geologic Evidence for Age Deposits at Hueyatlaco Archaeological Site Valsequillo Mexico" (PDF). *Quaternary Research*. 16: 1-17. doi:10.1016/0033-5894(81)90124-1. Archived (PDF) from the original on July 6, 2013.

6. Webb, Mark Owen, and Suzanne Clark. (1999). "Anatomy of an Anomaly." *Disputatio*, 6.

7. Frison, George C., and Danny N. Walker. "New World palaeoecology at the Last Glacial Maximum and the implications for New World prehistory." Chapter 17 in *The World At 18000 BP: Volume 1, High Latitudes*. Olga Soffer and Clive Gamble, eds. London: Unwin Hyman (1990).

8. http://www.xmission.com/~tlacy/mom.txt

9. VanLandingham, S. L. Corroboration of Sangamonian Age of Artifacts from the Valsequillo Region Puebla Mexico by Means of Diatom Biostratigraphy. *Micropaleontology*, Volume 50, Number 4, Pages 313-342, 2004.

10. VanLandingham, S. L., Diatom Evidence for Autochthonous Artifact Deposition in the Valsequillo Region Puebla Mexico During Sangamonian (sensu lato = 80,0000 to ca. 220,000 yr BP and Illinoian (220,000 to 430,000 yr BP), *Journal of Paleolimnology*, Volume 36, Number 1, Pages 101-116, Jul 2006.

11. Liddicoat, Joseph C. (2008). Paleomagnetism of the Hueyatlaco Ashat Valsequillo, Mexico, Geological Society of America Abstracts with Programs, Vol. 40, No. 6, p. 241 (Greshko. 2017).

If the last article made you flinch and faint, the next one will make you scream. Here again—more evidence—this time from the 250,000-year site in Mexico, and it seems to be piled up, but also is now being ignored:

Based on this information, the study's authors (archaeologists Cynthia Irwin-Williams et.al) concluded the following: Fission-track ages on zircon phenocrysts from two of the younger tephra layers (370,000 ± 200,000 and 600,000 ± 340,000 yr) agree with concordant uranium-series dates for a camel pelvis that was found associated with bifacial tools at Hueyatlaco. These dates are compatible with the depth of burial and subsequent dissection of the Hueyatlaco deposits, as well as with the degree of hydration of volcanic glass shards and with the extent of etching of heavy-mined mineral phenpcrysts from within the tephra layers.[338]

---

338 Steen-Mcintyre *et al.*, "Geologic evidence," pp.1-17.

PART 2

Chapter 3

How are the Groups
and Their Artifacts Related?

Africans traveled to South America before landing in North or Central America.[339] Genetic evidence has confirmed that fact.[340] Scientists have found that the small-statured Khoisan from the Kalahari Desert in South Africa are blood relatives of the first Americans found at the tip of South America.

> *DNA furnishes an ever-clearer picture of the multi-millennial trek from Africa all the way to the tip of South America...A genetic family tree that begins with the San Khoisan of Africa at its root ends with South American Indians.... Scientists trace the path of human migrations by using bones, artifacts and DNA...from contemporary humans and can be compared to determine how long an indigenous population has lived in a region.*[341]

The Proto-Mandingoes, Egyptians, and Algonquins/Skraelings entered the Americas thousands of years after the first Americans began arriving from Africa around 100,000 B.C. The Proto-Saharans and the Proto-Mandingoes come from the same area where "Researchers discovered fossils recently in Eastern and Central Africa that show formerly unknown

---

339 Santos, G. M. et al. "A revised chronology of the lowest occupation layer of the Pedra Furada Rock Shelter, Piaui, Brazil: The Pleistocene People of the Americas." *Quarterly Science Review* 22 (2003) 2303-2310).

340 Winters, Clyde. "Genetic Evidence of Early African Migration into America." May 19, 2011. Accessed 11/1//14 from http://www.plosone.org/annotation/listThread.action?root=18395.

341 Stix, G. "Traces of a Distant Past" 2008. Accessed January 8, 2011. http://www.iitk.ac.in/dord/research_news/stix_SciAmerican.pdf; Winters, Clyde. E-mail to author February 5, 2009, video, "New Movie: 30,000 BC The First Americans" Americans" on YouTube.

human species living between 3.3 and 3.5 million years ago,"[342] which the Egyptians called "placentaland."[343]

Note: For simplicity sake, both the Proto-Saharans and the Proto-Manding shall be referred to as Proto-Manding.

Who were the ancestors of today's Native Americans who built these mounds? Whatever the Mound Builders were called, they were part of the Algonquin family called the Adena. "The Adena seem to have spoken an Algonquian language."[344] They are yet another Algonquin tribe. The first Algonquin were most likely short statured before mixing with other taller groups. There have been skeletons of regular-sized people found in burial mounds, but there have been signs of dwarfs in the mounds too.

During 1901, Ohio Historic Society archaeologists excavating Chillicothe's Burial Mound Number 21 found an extraordinary effigy pipe carved from local pipestone that had been quarried around the hills of Portsmouth, Ohio. The 10-inch-high figure is the realistic representation of a man dressed in what must be a faithful reproduction of Adena attire. The figure depicts a remarkable kind of...dwarfism.[345]

The average person's arms and legs are longer than their torsos. We have all heard someone tell a taller person that they are "all legs." Well, a dwarf does not have that blessing. Their legs are mostly shorter than their torsos.

In March of 1942, Charles Snow, a Harvard-trained physical anthropologist at the University of Kentucky, sent a letter to Richard Morgan, then the Ohio Historical Society's Curator of Archaeology, asking permission to reproduce an image of the Adena Pipe for a paper he was writing about two "Indian Dwarfs from Moundville."

---

342 Durando, J. "Fossils of new early human species found in Africa" USA Today Network. 3/28/15.

343 Finch, Charles S. *The Star of Deep Beginnings* (Georgia, Khenti Press, 1998), p. 4.

344 Mann, Charles C. *1491: New revelations of the Americas before Columbus*, p. 290.

345 Joseph, Frank. *Advanced Civilizations of Prehistoric America*, p. 36.

He expressed his opinion that " in its realistic treatment the figurine appears to be that of an achondroplastic dwarf."[346]

The pipestone is a carving of an Adena man, who is also a dwarf. Evidently dwarfs were held in high regard back then, at least in Ohio. In this next example, a full-sized body of a dwarf was found buried in a mound. "How such a person became to be portrayed is unknown. Another mound in Waverly, Ohio, did contain a skeleton of a dwarf, suggesting a particularly high honored status."[347]

Waverly, Ohio, is in Southern Ohio near the Ohio River only 17 miles from Chillicothe, Ohio. These two mounds containing dwarfs were relatively close together. This could mean that dwarfs either built one or both of those mounds or were living among the people who built them. Adena, Ohio was close to the Ohio River area where many iron-smelting furnaces inside mounds were found. Dwarfs were known for smelting iron in Africa and Europe. The ancient Adena people were known as:

public works engineers, astronomers, and metalsmiths, (or smithies) the land's first farmers and potters. The Adena, therefore, exhibited the same skills as the dwarves who were the first to bring civilization to ancient Egypt. Were they the same people? It is true they had talents in many disciplines, but they are better remembered by the name inextricably linked with their most visible achievement: The Mound Builders.[348]

First, in 1881, John W. Powell appointed Cyrus Thomas to be the Director of the Eastern Mound Division of the Smithsonian Institute's Bureau of Ethnology.

When Thomas came to the Bureau of Ethnology, he was a "pronounced believer in the existence of a race of Mound Builders, **distinct from**

346 Lepper, Brad. "Is the Man on the Adena Pipe a Dwarf?" March 14, 13. Accessed January 12, 2017. https://www.ohiohistory.org/ learn/collections/ archaeology/archaeology-blog/2013/may-2013/is-the-man-on-the-adena-pipe-a-dwarf.

347 Childress, David H. "Archaeological Coverups." *Nexus Magazine*, Volume 2, #13 (1992). Mapelton Qld: Australia: Nexus from http:// www.geocities. com/saqatchr/page45.html.

348 Wicke, C. R. (1965). "Pyramids and Temple Mounds: Mesoamerican Ceremonial Architecture in Eastern North America." *American Antiquity* Vo. 30 No. 4 p. 409, April, 1965.

the American Indians.".…*So The Smithsonian began to promote the idea that Native Indians, at the time being exterminated in the Indian Wars, were descended from advanced civilizations and were worthy of protection.*[349]

"Distinct from" literally means different than. Those Indians were correct. They were descended from advanced, older civilizations.

Second, part of the "Red Indian's *distinct* ancestors," were the Mound Builders in Northern North America, namely: Cahokia in Missouri; the Iron Smelting Mound Builders along the Ohio River; the Mound Building Civilization along the Mississippi River; Poverty Point Mounds in Louisiana; and the Egyptians who had catacombs of caves off the Colorado River in Springville, Arizona.

Then in Central America there were the Olmecs, who begin sometime before 10,000 B.C. They arrived thousands of years before they morphed into the Mayans. They were pyramid builders in Central America, with accomplishments such as the Pyramids of the Sun and the Moon complex; temple and pyramid builders in South America, as in Tiahuanaco and Peru; and the civilization in the Bahamas and Caribbean before the Ice age-ending cataclysmic melt/flood wiped them out.

Among the others whom the flood wiped out in the Caribbean were the Egyptians, who had built the Bimini Road long before the Ice Age melt. Do you think these people should be called "advanced civilizations" as well? Bond backs what Thomas wrote more by saying that, *"'Mound Builders' were NOT the Native Americans we call 'Indians.' They were a pre-historic culture or cultures that inhabited much of the area we know as the United States."*[350] They were African.

A third scholar to agree with Thomas and Bond about the mounds is Wicke. He wrote an article in *The Journal of American Antiquity* stating that: "Chard…in his 'Invention Versus Diffusion: The Burial Mound Complex of the Eastern United States' has refuted the hypothesis of Asiatic

---

349 Eisen, J. (1999). *Suppressed Inventions*. (Berkley Pub. Group: N.Y.), p. 216.

350 Bond, L. (n.d.). The Mounds and Mound Builders of Union County. Union County Public Library. Accessed on September 13, 2010. http://www.union-county.lib.in.us/mound_builders.htm.

origin for burial mounds."[351] That means these Indians' ancestors were also "distinct from the Asians" as well. The Amerinds probably were not the people who built the so-called "Indian Mounds" in America, as Thomas and Bond agreed. This is not meant to demean or discredit Asiatic or Amerind peoples for their talents and aptitudes, but to alert the world of the true origin of the Mound Builders.

So, neither the Asians nor the Amerinds built the American mounds. The third group does not seem a likely candidate either. That group should include European settlers, simply because, **"...post-Columbian white settlers not only do not build mounds, they systematically destroy them!"**[352] It, therefore, seems logical that through the process of elimination, the only group left who could have built the mounds were the short Black Africans.

> *That monumental work (Ancient monuments of the Mississippi Valley, Squier, & Davis) concluded that* **the ancestors** *of the Native Americans constructed the mounds. The Bureau of Ethnology, a branch of the Smithsonian continued to sponsor fieldwork and publications on mounds. In 1894 Cyrus Thomas' massive 742-page report on the "Mound Explorations of the Bureau of Ethnology" was issued. It also stated that the mounds were the work of the ancestors of Native Americans...Fueling those speculations was the fact that the native tribes occupying the eastern portion of the New Word often couldn't explain who built mounds or what their purpose was.*[353]

There is another historian who had witnessed that the so-called "Native American" Indians were "distinct from," and not the same people who built the mounds. In mentioning the people who built the mounds, he was referring to Africans instead of Red Indians. This was Carlos Cuervo Marquez (1858–1930), an anthropologist, ethnologist, botanist, journalist, military general, diplomat, historian, politician, as well as president of the National Academy of History in Mexico. He also wrote several archaeological and ethnographic studies.

---

351 Wicke, C. R. *Pyramids and Temple Mounds*, p. 409.

352 Conner, William D. (2009). *Iron Age America Before Columbus* (Illinois, Coachwhip Publications), p. 48.

353 Thomas, C. "Report on the Mound Explorations of the Bureau of Explorations." Washington D.C., Government Printing Office, 1894).

Marquez conjures up the same feeling about those ancient ones who built the mounds by using Mr. Thomas' phrase of "distinct from." He comes a little closer to truly describing those folks who created "the most ancient Mexican sculpture":

The Negro type is seen in the most ancient Mexican sculpture. The Negroes figure frequently in the most remote traditions of some American Pueblos. It is to this race, doubtlessly belongs the most ancient skeletons, distinct from the Red American Race which have been found in various places from Bolivia to Mexico. It is likely that, we repeat, "America was a Negro Continent."[354]

The previous page should "seal the deal," in that the short, dark Africans in the Americas were a completely different people—short and very dark—compared to the half-Asian and half-Caucasian, taller and of a lighter complexion—"Red" hue—so-called "Indians." This is by no means meant to speak ill of the lighter-skinned Indians, but to just *differentiate* so the public will know once and for all that the dark-skinned "Indians," predated those of a lighter complexion.

When the first Mongolians from Asia and Caucasians from Europe finally did reach North America, to north they found:

*Earthen mounds, cones, terraced platforms, animal effigy shapes, and mound dwellings dotting the landscape west of the Appalachian Mountains. The people the Mongolians ran into **were not primitives, but builders of well-established civilizations.**[355]*

Speaking of well-established civilizations, **Egyptian artifacts** have been found across North America from the Micmac/Algonquin writings on the East Coast, to the artifacts and Egyptian place/names in the Grand Canyon. Scattered among related data ahead are eleven archaeological finds that are related to ancient Egypt.

Most of these artifacts were found inside mounds. Some of these finds are controversial and have been branded unauthentic by some. On the other hand, could the people who labeled these artifacts as fakes have hidden political agendas? Whether the item is or is not genuine is not the point. This study is just reporting interesting artifacts that deserve further

354 Marquez, E. A., "America was a Negro Continent." *Archaeological and Ethnographic Studies* Vol. 1. Pub. Madrid, Spain, (1920).

355 Pastore, Ronald J. "The Mound Matrix Mystery," *Atlantis Rising* #28, (2001), p. 28.

study. They are too important to skip over, but on the other hand, may be too controversial to use as a piece of evidence for the thesis of this work. These items will be briefly covered and we shall let the public judge their authenticity for themselves.

If the giant Cahokia mounds are not enough proof of civilization, let us look at an outline of the eleven other artifacts that make their case. Many of them were excavated from mounds:

1. Cylindrical seals

Cylindrical seals like those of the Pharaohs of ancient Egypt have been found in Ohio."[356] A cylinder seal communicates with words or symbols that are engraved into the seal. To have a language, and some sort of writing symbolic communication, are signs of civilization, not hunter-gatherers. Cylinder seals were mostly made of baked clay. Hunter-gatherers are mobile and do not usually stay in one place long enough to build kilns for making clay molds. A sedentary people with the ability to communicate in writing and build kilns must indicate a civilized people.

2. Plate ornament

A copper plate ornament that was found in one of the Hopewell burial mounds has a profile of what looks like a Hopewell man. His hair looks distinctly like a typical "Afro-hairstyle." He also has something in his ear that looks identical to typical African earlobe stretching as seen in another example. This example can be seen on "Plate 30 Olmec Negroid stone head (Tres Zapotes II)"[357] in the pictorial section of Dr. Van Sertima's *They Came Before Columbus*. Another Olmec stone head (the first of a colossal head was found near the Mexican Village of Treszapotes in 1858 A.D.) has an example of earlobe-stretching, as well as corn-rolled braids.[358] The Afro-hairstyle and earlobe stretching are both signs of an African culture.

3. Bust of a Nubian's head

The most glaring artifact found in Seip Mound in Ohio is the bust of an African's head carved into a rock that Fell, author of *America B.C.*

---

356 Ibid., p. 2.

357 Van Sertima, Ivan. *They Came Before Columbus*, Plate 30. (New York, Random House, 1975).

358 Ibid.

says "exemplifies the Nubian stock."[359] This illustrated that its builders were most likely Africans.

4. Copper scrolls

A group of copper scrolls were found buried in mounds. One example was a thin sheet of copper with words etched into the scroll much like the famous Roman scrolls. Another interesting fact is that copper etching (engraving) samples were found in mound ruins. The etching process requires temperatures of six hundred degrees. Amerinds did not have that type of technology. It seems that Dr. Eller L. Henderson was probably at Spiro Mounds, Oklahoma, Walkerton, Indiana, and Fall River, Massachusetts.[360]

5. Skeletons wearing copper armor

Next, we see that "A few other 'Skeletons in Armor' have been found. Two were in Maine and one at Fall River, Massachusetts."[361] Copper armor is certainly not as hard or effective as iron, but it is better than no protection at all.

6. Davenport stele

The Davenport Stele contains a carving of "Opening of the Mouth Ceremony," which is of Nubian/Egyptian origin. This is either an Egyptian artifact, or one that could have been carved by non-Egyptians who had detailed data on one of the Egyptian religious ceremonies. This artifact is also called the "Djed Festival Tablet." It was discovered in a burial mound in 1874 in Iowa.[362] The religious similarities here are numerous and sometimes are not only similar, but identical to the Djed Festival of ancient Egypt. Because of the complexity of the Djed Festival, it shall not be discussed in any detail. This ceremony traces back, however, before Egypt to Nubia because the Egyptian God Osiris is part of the ceremony. This means that the Djed Festival predates even Egypt. Osiris was an Anu

---

359 Fell, Barry. *America B.C.: Ancient Settlers in the New World* (New York, Pocket Books, 1976), p. 189.

360 Childress, D. H. (1992). *Lost Cities of North & Central America*, p.376.

361 Stapler, W. M. (1998). "Ancient Pemaquid and the Skeleton in Armor," *NEARA Journal*, Volume XXXII, No. 1, Summer 1998.

362 Ibid.

from Nubia. The stele contains carvings of Egyptian writing and a carving of a picture of the festival on one side of the stele. On the other side is a picture of two Egyptian Obelisks, a pyramid and African animals.[363]

7. Pontotoc stele

The next find is in the same category as the Davenport Stele. In Oklahoma, an Egyptian artifact was found that would be difficult to be explained away or claimed to be vaguely Egyptian. It is called the Pontotoc Stele, and it looks as if Pharaoh Akhenaten drew it himself. This stele, carved into a rock slab is a typical picture of the straight lines of sunrays in a triangulation drawing shining down on the earth. Two of the panels have Egyptian inscriptions translated as, "When Baal-Ra rises in the East, the beasts are content." These identify the inscriptions as an extract from the Hymn to the Aton by Pharaoh Akhenaten.[364] This is more than just a trace of evidence of Egyptians in America, and this time, it is literally written in stone.

8. Mega-tons of copper

Proto-Americans made use of copper but not enough to get anywhere near disposing millions of tons of it. The amount of copper mined was reported to be between one hundred million to five million tons. The evidence can be seen today on the island of Isle Royale in Lake Superior, Michigan, where there is an empty five-mile ditch. There is also ancient evidence of other copper mining in Wisconsin.[365] "On Isle Royale alone, over 2000 ancient mining pits can be seen today,"[366] which supports the tremendous amount of copper excavated. (To where did all of this copper disappear? See the map in Fig. 17 to trace the route of the *St. Lawrence River* from the Atlantic Ocean to Lake Superior where Isle Royale is found.) This copper mining is verified by four journal articles.

An Olmec wall painting was found in a cave at Juxlahuaca, Mexico, that depicts a priest performing the Egyptian "Opening of the Mouth Ceremony" for a subject. This painting is extremely similar to an actual

363 Fell, Barry. *America B.C.: Ancient Settlers in the New World*, pp. 261-267.

364 Childress, David. H. *Lost Cities of North & Central America*, pp. 241-242.

365 Fell, Barry. *America B.C.: Ancient Settlers in the New World*, p. 159.

366 Ibid., p. 376.

Egyptian picture from the Egyptian Book of the Dead of the same ceremony occurring in Egypt.[367] This ceremony is only one in a list of complex rituals performed in ancient Mexico that are unique and distinctly African not appearing anywhere else on the planet.

(A list and examples of these ceremonies is beyond the scope of this book.)

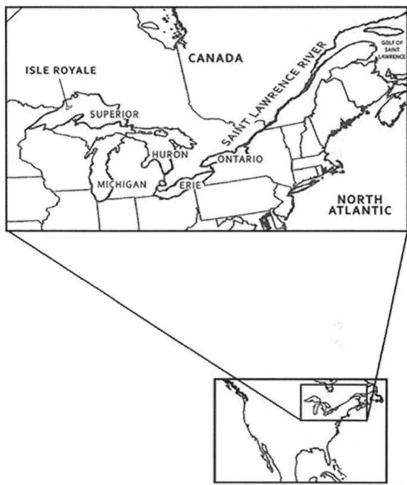

Fig. 17: Map of St. Lawrence River. *Drawn by Marrwho Hasati.*

This contact with the Egyptians is possibly seen once more in Arizona. Again, the Algonquin covered an extremely large area: "Their territory

---

367 Little, Gregory. L., John Van Auken, and Lora Little. *Mound Builders: Edgar Cayce's Forgotten Record of Ancient America* (Tennessee, Eagle Wing Books, 2001), p. 73.

reached from the east shore of Newfoundland to the Rocky Mountains... The Eastern tribes from Maine to Carolina."[368]

9. Egyptian wall painting

When the first White men moved into Colorado and Arizona, they found that some parts of it had Egyptian names along the Colorado River that cuts through the Grand Canyon in the Rocky Mountains. "The area around Ninety-four Mile Creek and Trinity Creek had areas (of rock formations, apparently) with names like Tower of Set, Tower of Ra, Horus Temple, and Isis Temple."[369] Next, a newspaper article appeared in the Phoenix Gazette—Monday evening, April 5, 1909—that serves as evidence to confirm the discovery of a cave with Egyptian artifacts.

This issue is clouded with controversy, however. More on this subject is found at the end of the chapter, but it cannot be corroborated by the Smithsonian Institution.

10. Caves containing artifacts

At Harvard's Widener Library, Dr. Thompson located copies of 300-year-old papers composed by a Jesuit missionary in Canada's eastern provinces. The priest had apparently put together a teaching aid for his Micmac Indian students who copied out the Lord's Prayer in hieroglyphics.

11. Micmac hieroglyphic writing

On close re-examination, about half were recognizable as hieratic, a simplified form of Egyptian hieroglyphics. More surprisingly, the Micmac characters corresponded to the meaning of the Egyptian glyphs.[370]

We have just covered eleven items that strongly look as if they have a connection between ancient Egypt and the Americas. The belief that Egyptians were in the Americas before Columbus is seconded by "Rafique

---

368 Child, Hampton. (1886). *Gazetteer of Grafton County*, N.H. 1709-1886 (New York, The Syracuse Journal Company), p. 112.; Hodge, F. W. (1906). Algonquin Indian Genealogy. Accessed February 17, 2010; Van Sertima, Ivan. "Nile Valley Civilizations" (New Jersey, Journal of African Civilizations, 1985), p. 241.

369 Childress, David. H. *Lost Cities of North & Central America*, p. 324.

370 Joseph, Frank. (2014). *Archaeological Discoveries of Ancient America* (New York, Rosen Publishing Group), p. 22.

Jairazbhoy, who dates the coming of the Egyptians to America during the reign of Pharaoh Ramses II."[371]

> *Who were these ancient copper miners, and where did they go? It has been suggested that the estimated 100 million to 500 million tons of copper that came out of Wisconsin and Michigan circa 3000 B.C. went to the Mediterranean to fuel the blossoming Copper Age that was happening there at that time. Even the low figure of 100 million tons of copper represents a far greater quantity than primitive America could, in all probability, have absorbed. There are only a few instances of copper artifacts found in the United States and Canada. Copper scrolls have been found in some mounds and skeletons found wearing copper armor, such as those found in Spiro Mounds, Oklahoma, Walkerton, Indiana and Fall River Massachusetts.[372]*

If mining was being done in 3000 B.C., these miners had to be Africans mining this copper. Geneticist Cavelli-Sfortza wrote that genetically speaking, white skin was not around before 3000 B.C. This data can be found on page 145 of his *The History and Geography of Human Genes*.

Before we go too deeply into Michigan copper, we must explain that in 1911, anthropologist Grafton Elliot "asserted that copper-working spread from Egypt to the rest of the world"[373] and not the reverse. When their original source ran low many years later, the Egyptians probably looked all over for another great source for Copper. They surely found one in Lake Superior's Isle Royale.

When Did This American Copper Boom Begin?

Records and actual sites of copper mines have been studied in the Lake Superior region. From what we know, there were no large copper extractions in the Americas before 6000 B.C.:

> *Then, around 5556 B.C. an ambitious mining enterprise of truly industrial proportions opened with great suddenness around the Lake Superior shores of northeastern Wisconsin, thereafter spreading throughout the region, where the world's purest high-grade*

---

371 Van Sertima, Ivan. *African Presence in Early America*, p. 14.

372 Childress, David. H. *Lost Cities of North & Central America*, p. 376.

373 Gaillard, G. *The Routledge Dictionary of Anthropologists*, p.48.

copper may be found. To William P. F. Ferguson, an early and still-respected authority on North America's ancient mining, "the work is of a colossal nature, and amounted to the turning over of the whole formation to its depth and moving many cubic acres—it would not be seriously extravagant to say—cubic miles of rock. The diggings extended over 150 miles on Lake Superior coast, and through three Michigan counties. Some 5000 ancient mines have been identified at the Great Lakes."[374]

Would that type of enterprise take decades if not centuries to mine? These statistics are just amazing. Since we have established that Africans have been traveling to the Americas for at least 100,000 years, is it probable much of the ancient Eastern Hemisphere's copper could have easily originated from the Western Hemisphere? Why is it that most of the copper probably did not come from European mines?

Indeed, though it is undoubtedly the case that Europe had a "Bronze Age," archaeologists have accepted that much more copper was used than what they have been able to attribute to European mines. So where did an extremely large part of the copper come from? The answer, as bizarre as it may sound, could be America. This happened because...Europe's economy between 2000 and 1000 BC stood and fell with copper, used for the creation of bronze. At the same time, large quantities of copper were mined in America, though no one seems to know who was using it. A question of a world economy, and supply and demand?...Would it be impossible to assume that a world economy of copper and tin existed in 3000 B.C.? For those who believe that the answer is that this is impossible—note how dangerous it might be to expel such a possibility out of hand.[375]

The Ancient Koster Site, Located South of Eldred, Illinois

American Indians used this copper site in the lower Illinois River valley with relatively few interruptions from 8700 years ago until

374 Joseph, Frank. "Copper Mining in Ancient America." *Atlantis Rising*, No. 110. March/April. (2015). Accessed February 2, 2015 from http://atlantisrisingmagazine.com/article/copper-mining-in-ancient-america/.

375 Coppens, Philip. (1999). "Copper: A World Trade in 3000 BC?" Accessed February 2, 2015. http://www.philipcoppens.com/copper.html.

around 800 years ago...Northwestern University excavated an extraordinary site on Theodore and Mary Koster's farm. Evidence spanning 300 or more generations of American life was documented at the site through years of archaeological fieldwork and study in the 1970s.[376]

With what we now know about who these "American Indians," it is likely that they were not Amerinds. The logic behind this is that Mongolians did not enter the Americas before 2600 B.C.—according to the Walam Olum or the "Red Record"...in their own words. The 8700-year old date would still be back 4100 years before the Mongolians crossed over into the Americas.

One must first put this time of 8700 years in context. Those people in the lower Illinois River Valley, were most probably Africans, for they had been in the Americans' millennia before any other group. The Asians entered the Americans from Asia around 1400 years after mining began in the Great Lakes area and 400 years before it was in full swing. The Vikings entered the Americas from Greenland around 1000 A.D., 4000 years after mining began in the Great Lakes area and 3000 years after it was in full swing. It was therefore, more likely Africans who began mining the copper in the Great Lakes area from the beginning. William P. F. Ferguson, an early and still respected authority on North America's ancient mining said:

[T]he work is of a colossal nature, and amounted to the turning over the whole formation to its depth and moving many cubic acres—it would not be seriously extravagant to say cubic miles of rock. Indians, called the "Old Copper Indians" by archaeologists, maintained copper mines in the Keweenaw Peninsula and Isle Royale. Here they dug thousands of mining pits...Extracting as much as half a million tons of copper; this required a force of tens of thousands of men.[377]

Yes, the Great Lakes were rich with places in which to mine copper. They also extracted copper for many cubic miles in many locations:

376 "Archaic Archaeological Site." (2000). Illinois State Museum. Accessed on February 23, 2015 from http://www.museum.state. il.us/muslink/nat_amer/pre/htmls/a_sites.html; Joseph, Frank. (2015). "Copper Mining in Ancient America." *Atlantis Rising*, No. 110. March/April.

377 "Native American Netroots" (March 31, 2012), Accessed February 23, 2015. http://nativeamericannetroots.net/diary/1313.

The number of railway cars required to haul the prehistoric excavations would have been a quarter-of-a-million tons per car, equaling five thousand railroad cars filled with copper nuggets...end-to-end, their combined length would be twenty-five miles of railroad cars with each car carrying about fifty tons of nuggets. If the Michigan copper was removed over a two thousand-year period, then in each year, on the average, there had to have been the equivalent of two railroad cars freighting one hundred tons of copper each summer... Who could have been responsible for such a tremendous enterprise so much in technological contrast to a few Paleo-Indians concerned with only several pounds of floating copper? Their settlements—were utterly unlike anything associated with local Native Americans—twenty—six multi-room stone foundations spread over 300 feet.[378]

It would seem that natives carrying just a few pounds of copper, in canoes or on their backs—as the article mentions—could never have moved one hundred tons of copper all year long for two thousand years. So, it would be illogical to believe they were only using canoes to transport the copper. They must have been using mega-ships like those seen carved into the front wall of Queen/Pharaoh Hatshepsut's tomb in Egypt. Further, and even worse, they could only have moved it during the summer months when the snow from the vicious Michigan winters could not interfere with their travel. This book has given several examples of how much communication and trade was important to the early Americans:

If these Native Americans did mine one hundred tons of copper, it should still be here in the Western Hemisphere. But where is it now? As mentioned earlier, "no-one is able to answer as to what became of the copper that was mined" in the Americas. There is no mention of such an amount of copper, or even bronze in ancient America that has shown up today. So where did it go? [The answer is:] It was probably used to make bronze in the earliest civilizations in descending order of their existence, namely: Egypt, Mesopotamia, and then heading east and west to Greece Rome, India, China, and lastly Europe—after the Moors entered Spain and ended the Dark Ages bringing the Renaissance (e.g., first universities —the University of Salamanca) into Europe.[379]

---

378 Frank, Joseph. *Copper Mining in Ancient America*, p. 46.

379 Coppens, Philip. Copper: A World Trade in 3000 B.C.? (n.d.). Accessed on February 23, 2015. https://www.eyeofthepsychic.com/copper/.

Which of these civilizations—8700 years ago—could have begun to move such amounts of copper from the Great Lakes area of North America? It was most probably the first people to make watercraft that were sailing back and forth to the island of Crete.

Modern humans have existed for around 200,000 years on the Greek island of Crete. Stone tools found there, archaeologists say, are at least 130,000 years old.[380]

This gives them 192,444 years to make it to Michigan! That gives them much more time than they needed.

What is particularly interesting is that the style of the tools closely resembles artifacts from the stone technology known as Acheulean, which originated with pre-Homo sapien populations in Africa.[381] The evidence shows that Africans had been sailing to Crete since the first modern people and civilizations developed along the Nile. Evidence shows that the first civilization in existence that later built the first mega-ships, were the Egyptians. Mention must be made again, of the carving of such a mega-barge/ship that can be seen today on the ancient funerary temple belonging to the female Queen/Pharaoh Hatshepsut. This phenomenally large cargo ship is carrying not one but two giant obelisks weighing 750 tons each, which is 1500 tons in total.

This is the size of the cargo ship the 600-yard-long pier and breakwater at Bimini in the Bahamas was built for docking before the Ice Age ended. We know this because this structure lies under 25–30 feet of water today. As explained earlier, there was no Phoenicia until 1450 B.C.[382] If these mines were being worked in 3000 B.C., before Phoenicia existed, it seems that only the people from the Nile Valley are left to have worked the mines. Why? Because they were the only people before the Phoenicians with the capability to move that type of load in large ships across vast distances.

The illustration shows a reconstruction of an obelisk ship barge, with two obelisks (weighing well over two thousand tons secured

380 Zorich, Zach. (2011). "Paleolithic Tools-Plakias Crete." *Archaeology* Vol. 64, No. 1, Jan-Feb 2011. Accessed May 10, 2011. http://www. archaeology. org/1101/topten/crete.html.

381 "Humans Have Been At Sea For A Very Long Time," *Atlantis Rising* #81 (2010), p. 71.

382 Diop, Cheikh A. *The African Origin of Civilization* (Connecticut, Lawrence Hill, 1974), p. 109.

on deck.[383] [In another account], "According to Roman Historian Diodorus, the largest ship in the fleet of Senwosret (Sesostris) of 1900 B.C. measured 480 feet in length (more than four times the size of Columbus' Santa Maria).[384]

Which people of prehistoric times would have been able to use five hundred million tons of copper, and who had the ability to then ship it? Egypt. Do not forget that this time period totally predates Rome, Greece, or even Phoenicia.

The Egyptian coppersmith must have been a man of importance since he had to make saws, chisels, knives, hoes, adzes, dishes and trays, all out of copper or bronze, for artisans of the many trades. There still exist very serviceable early Egyptian bronze strainers and ladles; like tongs, some of which had their ends fashioned into the shape of human hands. Thebes has yielded beautifully preserved bronze sickle blades with very business-like serrated edges. The author once handled a copper knife, shaped like a large penknife and almost as sharp, although it was Pre-Dynastic, i.e. about 5,000 years old. The Egyptians even possessed bronze model bags, which were carried by servants at important funerals.[385] They seem to have been the most industrious of people.

Manding/Egyptian/Olmec Connection

Studies show that the Mande travelled widely beyond their homeland:

A major ethnic group among the ancient Egyptian/Nubians were the Manding people...the archaeological data suggests that the original homeland of the Mande was more than likely the Saharan highlands area, and the southern Sahara 800 years ago.[386]

---

383 Partridge, Robert. *Transport in Ancient Egypt* (London, The Rubicon Press, 1996), p. 65.

384 Finch, Charles. *The Star of Deep Beginnings*, p. 210.

385 "The Early Egyptians." Copper Development Association Inc. (2015). Accessed February 4, 2015 m http://www.copper.org/education/history/60centuries/ancient/theearly.html.

386 Winters, Clyde. (2005). *Atlantis in Mexico: The Mande Discovery of America* (LuLu.com), p. 102.

It has also been stated that, "The Proto-Manding migrated over Africa by an ancient river system. This Proto-Manding migration had to have taken place during the "African Aqualithic Period."[387]

Why would they leave their homes if all was well? They most likely left because their beautiful land was turning into desert. Before the dry pattern began, there "was a wet period in Africa that lasted thousands of years at a time when the Sahara was still fertile and had great lakes.[388] The Nile flowed west across the Sahara and emptied into the Atlantic Ocean"[389] during very ancient times.

These facts are never discussed in history classes. This route would have enabled East Africans direct access to the Atlantic Ocean…thus the Americas. The longer route would be to sail up the Nile River many miles north to the Mediterranean Sea. They would then have to head many more miles west to the Atlantic Ocean in order to sail to the Americas. Their boats were ready for the task at hand:

In the riverine cultures of the Proto-Saharans, each community had marine architects, ship builders and expert sailors. The presence of an elevated bow and stern in many boats depicted in Saharan rock art and the peculiar "bow string."[390]

This one brilliant attachment allowed the bow of the boat to be raised to an upright position. This bowstring was made so that when a wave would break on the bow of the boat, it would "ride" the wave instead of being swamped by the wave.

These were the "magical ingredients" that transformed these ships from river craft to oceangoing vessels. It was the "'bowstring,' a string for the front of the boat and a 'fuse' for the rudder oar in the rear to steer the boat that indicate these ancient ships were used for navigation on the open seas." These oceangoing vessels traveled for weeks and sometimes months. They would navigate with the sun by day and the stars by night.

---

387 Ibid., p. 88, 97.

388 Jones, David C. *The Origin of Civilization*, p. 114.

389 "Satellite imaging and other evidence of a "Green Sahara" and an old Nile River" (2013) Accessed January 12, 2017. http://www. abovetopsecret. com/forum/thread939148/pg1.

390 Winters, Clyde. *Atlantis in Mexico*, p. 73.

"To navigate these boats the Proto-Saharans used celestial navigation."[391] Yes, **they used the stars as road maps** after the sun set in the evenings.

When Did This "African Aqualithic" Wet Period Begin?

Brooks and Smith (1987) revising Sutton's (1974) date for the "African Aqualithic Period" have produced relatively new evidence that has the promise of culture pushed from 9000 B.C.,[392] further back in history to 23,000 B.C.[393] Later West African civilizations were a continuation of the African Aqualithic civilizations 20,000 to 10,000 B.C.[394]

According to Barton, "[In] the ancient Zingh Empire which existed as early as 15,000 B.C., the civilizations of the Western Sahara and the forest kingdoms flourished."[395] These Africans traveled from the Nile and East Africa to Central and West Africa by the now extinct river networks of this very wet African period. Their rivers were used as highways across the land. Regressing back to the Mande, what other connection do the Manding people have to the Americas? The Olmec/Manding and America's Algonquin have several things in common. The first commonality is that they both claim to have come to the Americas from across the sea from the east, towards the rising sun (as the Shawnee, the Sauk, and the Yurok said they did). It was the Spanish who recorded this:

Friar Diego de Landa (1978:8, 28) in Yucatan before and after the Conquest, wrote that "a certain race who came from the EAST, who

391 Winters, Clyde. *Atlantis in Mexico*, pp. 19, 73.

392 Sutton, J. E. G. "The Aquatic Civilization of Middle Africa." *Journal of African History* (1974), XV, 4, pp. 527-546. Great Britain.

393 Brooks, Alison S., and Catherine C. Smith. "Ishango revisited: new age determinations and cultural determinations." *The African Archeological Review*, 5, (1987), pp. 65-78.

394 Barton, Paul A. (1998). *A History of the African Olmecs* (California, 1st Books Publishing), p. 50.

395 Winters, Clyde. (1998). "Evidence of the African Migration to America and Olmec Religion." Accessed January 30, 2017. http://olmec98.net nama2. htm.

God delivered by opening for them twelve roads through the sea." Tradition probably refers to the twelve migrations of the Olmec people. This view is supported by the stone reliefs from Izapa, Chiapas, Mexico, published by the New World Foundation. In Stela 5, from Izapawe, we see a group of men on a boat riding the waves. (Wuthenau, 1980; Smith, 1984; Norman, 1976).... This stela also confirms the tradition recorded by the famous Mayan historian Ixtlixochitl, that the Olmecs came to Mexico in "ships of bark" and landed at Pontochan, which they commenced to populate (Winters, 1984: 16).[396]

But who were the different groups, and from where did they originate?

This was probably the ancient homeland of the Dravidians, Egyptians, Sumerians, Niger-Kordofanian-Mande and Elamite speakers. We call this part of Africa the Fertile African Crescent.[397] There is a wealth of archaeological evidence that over eight thousand years ago, the great culture bearers of civilization in Egypt, the Indus Valley and Mesopotamia formally lived in the Saharan region of Africa before it became a desert. These people lived in the highland areas of the Sahara. These mountain regions formed a Crescent shaped area. We call this region the Fertile African Crescent. In the Archaeological literature these people were called Capsians, Negroid, Brown Race, Mediterraneans, Dravidians, or Kushites. We call these people Proto-Saharans...the Proto-Saharans began as a single linguistic community, which shared cultural traits that were fashioned in their Saharan homeland.[398]

From their own writings, let us turn back the clock and listen to what the Egyptians said about their beginnings:

---

396 Winters, Clyde. "Ancient Writing In Middle Africa." (1981). Accessed January 30, 2017. http://www.academia.edu/3036834/An_Unofficial_History_of_Dravidian_Writing.

397 Winters, Clyde. (2012). "The Proto-Saharan Precursor of Ancient Civilization." Accessed January 20, 2017. https://www.scribd.com/document/113687462/Proto-Saharan-Precursor-of-Ancient-Civilizations.

398 Finch, Charles. (1998). The Star of Deep Beginnings (Georgia, Khenti Press), p. 4.; Winters, Clyde. Atlantis in Mexico, p. 45-6.

The Nile River seems to have functioned as an "umbilical" to link the northern tier of the continent to its East African Placentaland."[399] *In the last report presented by the late Dr. Leakey at the Seventh Pan-African Congress of Pre-History, Leakey stated that he was in.... general acceptance that the whole human race had its origin at the foot of the Mountain of the Moon.*[400]

From the Mountain of the Moon area, humans moved south and north following the Nile River from Kenya to Ethiopia—originally called Kush—home of the Kushites. The original Manding lived in the southern Saharan highlands (Winters 1986 b)....The evidence we have regarding the spread of the Proto-Mande from the Saharan highlands in the east to the shores of the Atlantic Ocean in the west.[401]

The southern Saharan Highlands are located near: "The Ethiopian Highlands...form a rugged mass of mountains in Ethiopia, Eritrea and northern Somalia in northeastern Africa."[402] These Proto-Saharans came to **Mexico in papyrus boats**. A stone stela from Izapa, Chiapas in southern Mexico shows the boats these Proto-Saharans used to sail to America. The voyagers manning these boats probably sailed down to Lake Chad and then down the Lower Niger River, which emptied into the Atlantic. This provided the Mande a river route from the Sahara to the coast.

These rivers, long dried up today, once emptied into the Atlantic. Once in the Atlantic Ocean, Africans could sail to Mexico and then Brazil by the North Equatorial Current, which meets the Canaries Current off the Senegambian coast.[403] Can you imagine how many miles they saved using these ancient Niger and Nile river system short cuts? This made their

399 Diop, C. A. (1986c). Origin of the Ancient Egyptians quoted in Ivan Van Sertima and L. Williams (Eds.), *Great African Thinkers* p. 35. New Brunswick, NJ: Journal of African Civilizations Ltd., Inc.

400 Winters, Clyde. (2013). "African Empires of Ancient America." Accessed June 10, 2015. http://olmec98.net/olmec2.htm.

401 Winters, Clyde. (1986). "The Migration Routes of the Proto-Mande." *The Mankind Quarterly*, 27(1):77-96.

402 Pape, Thomas., Daniel Bickel, and Rudolf Meier. (eds). (2009). *Diptera Diversity: Status, Challenges and Tools* (The Netherlands, Hotei Publishing), p. 165.

403 Winters, Clyde. (n.d.). "African Empires of Ancient America."

ancient trading networks far more accessible. Just think, today's Nile is over 4000 miles long. During the ancient African Aqualithic period, maps show us that length was several times that, not to mention combining with the expanded Niger River systems. It was over these ancient river systems that the Mande expanded across Africa.

Changing gears…what about the Olmecs? Believe it or not, there is still an Olmec bloodline. The next picture is one of the residents of the Yucatan Peninsula who says his ancestors were Olmec. During our conversation, we ended up discussing the Olmec Heads in Central America. He then got a little excited and said, "Look at my head, it is shaped like the Olmec stone heads." These heads were carved out of a single, giant piece of stone weighing 2–3 tons. The faces are obviously African, with large, wide fleshy noses, thick lips and small rolls of pepper-corn hair. In the same vein, there is also a Colossal Nubian head of Tarharqa from Karnak (Egypt) that is now a part of an exhibit at the Nubian Museum in Aswan in southern Egypt. There is no doubt they are both from African artists…and possibly from the same region in Africa. Remember, Abubakari II assembled 2000 ships and sailed to the Americas in 1311 and did not return to Africa later.

Fig. 18: Dr. Imhotep with a relative of the ancient Olmec territory in the Yucatan Peninsula (notice his native facial appearance). *Photography by Teresa Gray-Jones.*

But that is not all. Olmec Heads and megalithic carvings were also found as far south as Lamanai and Lubaantum in Belize; Guatamala; Hunduras; Cerros; and many other sites throughout Mexico and Central America. Then in 1920 the Harvard archaeologist, Leo Warner, traveled to Tuxla, Mexico where they found Mande symbols from West Africa;

carvings, steles and scripts that are—believe it or not—similar to the Cherokee language, which is very strange and lifts eyebrows—does it not?

Arguments continue until today: "The Olmec civilization appears to have suddenly appeared in Mexico without any evidence of a preceding culture"[404] How could that be? The Olmecs were always called the "Mother Civilization, copied and adopted by all the others."[405] But they did not magically appear out of nowhere. It took thousands of years to develop a culture that could invent, and then build, such items on a massive scale. They were obviously not an "in situ" civilization. They came in ships of bark says "The Olmec Stela":

> *The oral traditions of the Maya and the Aztec people, recorded by Spanish chroniclers Friar Diego Landa and Father Bernardino de Shogun...and the* Popal Vah *which is a historical text by the Quiche Mayan Indians. All of these traditions claim that the Olmec people arrived in Mexico from a land across the sea. The Olmec, according to Michael D. Coe (1989) and Jacques Soustelle (1984), introduced the calendar, government, religious traditions, and architectural styles to Meso-America.... Most people in Mexico only knew the Olmec people as "the people who live in the direction of the rising sun"...arrived in Mexico from a land across the sea…the term Olmec means "dwellers in the land of rubber.".... They are accomplished artists, engineers and scientists. The Manding people, who formed the base of the Olmec people, and the Kushites were both ancient Ethiopians, who founded the 25th Dynasty.... They were accomplished artists, engineers and scientists. They constructed elaborate pyramids and large sculptured monuments weighing tons.*[406]

Remember, Egypt (Kemet) was once a colony of ancient Kush (Ethiopia).

The sun rises across the sea in the east. This means the Mayans **and** the Aztecs said the Olmecs came from across the Atlantic Ocean. Moving on from Central America, where did they land in North America? In Chapter 1, we covered archaeological evidence that shows, "the Africans in South

---

404 Ibid.

405 Winters, Clyde. *We Are Not Just Africans*, pp. 5, 6.

406 Ibid.

Carolina landed on her eastern shores at least 51,700 years ago in Allendale County."[407] Then they slowly drifted to the west. For example:

The vanguard of Algonquian-speaking peoples, the Blackfeet, emerged from the eastern mountain woodlands to the grasslands; they came to rest early in the eighteenth century on the Northern Great Plains at the eastern base of the Rocky Mountains.[408]

Another significant, earlier population of Africans landed in South America long before the Manding people. When the Manding reached Central America and began mixing with the local population, they were labeled Olmecs. The Olmecs called themselves the Xi, or the plural Xiu. It is also interesting that "the term Olmec is derived from the word olli" (rubber).[409] To be precise, the Olmecs were supposedly a mixture of Manding and Amerinds. Do not forget that the Manding made up the base of the Olmecs. The Egyptians, the Manding, and the base of the Olmecs are related to each other. When the Manding reached Central America, they were joined by natives already in that area…referred to as "The Grandmother culture." In his book, *Africa and the Discovery of America*:

Leo Wiener presented evidence that the high civilizations of Mexico (Maya and Aztecs) had acquired many of the cultural and religious traditions of the Malinke-Bambara (Manding people) of West Africa…. Wiener discussed the analogy between the glyphs on the Tuxtula Mexican statuette and the Manding glyphs engraved on the rocks in Mandeland Africa.[410]

The trip from the Africa to America is not as difficult as one would imagine. The waters of the world's oceans are not static, they move. The part we are concerned with is the movement of the medial Atlantic Ocean. It is well-known that if someone in Western Africa seals a bottle with a note in it and throws it into the Atlantic, it will eventually reach the Americas because the currents in the ocean move like conveyor belts between the

---

407 University of South Carolina. "New Evidence Puts Man in North America 50,000 Years Ago." *Science Daily*. November 18, 2004. Accessed June 17, 2009. http://www.sciencedaily.com/releases/2004/11/041118104010. htm

408 Utley, Robert. *The Indian Frontier 1846-1890* (New Mexico, University of New Mexico Press, 2003), p. 20.

409 Winters, Clyde. "Evidence of the African Migration."

410 Winters, Clyde. *Atlantis in Mexico*, pp. 10, 130.

two continents. This is explained in print, as well as in two illustrations, in Van Sertima's book (1992).[411]

There was so much traffic on the Atlantic in the 17th century that when the first few European explorers saw so many African sailors in their ships passing them by; they gave the Atlantic Ocean the name the "Ethiopic Ocean." Further, the Indian Ocean was once called the Eastern Ethiopian, or Ethiopic Ocean by ancient mapmakers[412] and others. The "Persian Gulf of Sumer"[413] in Columbus' day was called the Ethiopian Sea in classical Greece. Yes, under a picture of this map the caption reads, "As late as 1650 the South Atlantic was called the Ethiopic, or Ethiopian Ocean, and most of Africa as far as South Africa was called Ethiopia."[414]

According to Dogon Priest, Naba Lamoussa Morodenibig, the continent of North America, was known as "Melanesia, which means 'land of the people of Melanin,' simply because the America of that day was the country of the Black man."[415] No one but Black people populated all three Americas before the Ice Age ended. It was like another Africa before other people began to move there. Note: Please do not confuse this ancient name for North America with the Melanesian islands of the Pacific Ocean. Morodenibig says that Melanesia was the first ancient name for North America.

The Grandmother civilization of short Africans arrived in the Americas 250,000–350,000 years ago. The Mother civilization of Olmec Civilization arrived many tens of thousands of years afterward and was multiracial. We are told the Olmecs came to the Americas around 1500 B.C., which may not be accurate. They were made up of African-Proto-Americans. Either way the Asians came around 2600 B.C., and mixed with Native American-Amerinds who had African and Asian bloodlines combined. All three groups together formed the Olmec people. However, it was the "Manding

411 Van Sertima, Ivan. *African Presence in Early America*, pp. 67, 172-173.

412 Rogers, J. A. *Africa's gift to America* (New York, Helga M. Rogers, 1961), p. 16.

413 Brunson, James. (1991). *Predynastic Egypt: An African-centric view* (Illinois, James Brunson II).

414 Van Sertima, Ivan. *African Presence in Early America*, pp. 67, 172-173.

415 Morodenibig, Naba (2008). *Philosophy Podium* Vol. I (Illinois, Firefly Productions), p. 98.

people who formed the base of the Olmec people, and the Kushites that founded the 25th Egyptian Dynasty."[416] They were both from the Nile Valley. They mixed with the Proto-Americans and Amerinds.

> *Von Wuthenau (1980) and Wiercinski (1972b) highlight the numerous art pieces depicting the African or Black variety who made up the Olmec people. This re-analysis of the Olmec skeletal material from Tlatilco and Cerro, which correctly identifies Armenoid, Dongolan and Loponoid as euphemisms for 'Negro' make it clear that a substantial number of the Olmecs were Blacks, support the art evidence and writing which point to an* **African origin for Olmec civilization.**[417]

The present data on the Proto-Olmecs (the Manding) originating and first arriving from across the Atlantic in the east, is evidence based! Is there any other relevant information that would solidify the ancient Americas; more precisely, the Western Hemisphere's connection with Africa?

Yes, there is…gold! Columbus' son, Ferdinand, also wrote that these Black men carried spears whose tips were made of *guanan*, which was the natives' word for gold. Thirteen West African countries use guanin for gold.[418] (This is the first linguistic connection in existence between the people in the Western Hemisphere and Western Africa.) Columbus then sent a sample of the gold spear tips back to Spain to be evaluated. The gold on the spear tips was not solid gold, but a metal alloy. An alloy is a collection of several metals melted together. The formula they used to make their spear-tip alloy was "of 32 parts, 18 were of gold, 6 of silver, and 8 of copper."[419] What is interesting is that this was the identical formula the West Africans used. Is this a coincidence, or does it show a metallurgical connection between West Africans and the people of the Western Hemisphere? That is indeed interesting, and it does seem to tie both groups together.

There is a mathematical formula that will be used to clarify this point. It is called the "Transitive Property of Equality:" If A=B and B=C, then A=C. If the Egyptians and the Manding are related, and the Manding and the

416 Winters, Clyde. *Atlantis in Mexico*, p. 10.

417 Winters, Clyde. *African Empires in Ancient America*, p. 27.

418 Van Sertima, Ivan. *Early America Revisited*, p. 199.

419 Ibid.

Olmecs are related, then the Egyptians and the Olmecs are related. They are all the same people from the same area. Hereafter, when one of these groups is mentioned, the reference includes all three. Further evidence will show a Manding,/Olmec/Egyptian bond. While the complete list is far too comprehensive to include in this volume, a selection will illustrate the logic. "Nicholas Leon, an eminent Mexican authority, reports on the oral traditions of his people according to some of whom that say, 'the oldest inhabitants in Mexico were Blacks."[420] That gives us more evidence that the Olmecs predated the Asians' arrival into the Americas. There is still a pre-Columbian African presence in Mexico today. There is an ancient people, called the Huicholes, still living in the Mexican Sierra Madre Mountains. While most are of medium height with varied skin shades, some have retained their darker skin tone and are diminutive in stature. The Huicholes people are said to have migrated from the eastern part of Mexico, near the ocean, before the Aztec's reign.

The Huichol are a small tribe of approximately 35,000 living in central western Mexico, near Ixtlan in the Sierra Madre Mountains. They are said to be the last tribe in North America to have maintained their pre-Columbian traditions.[421] It was also the Huicholes who first made the "Tepari," a stone disk constructed to conceal an offering chamber of the underworld:

The Tepari was engraved with the image of an eagle eating a serpent. The entourage of divine ancestors took it to Mexico City, where they gave it to the Aztecs. Antonio related that the Aztecs (not the Spaniards or the Mestizos, as one might think) then placed the image of the eagle and serpent into the currency of Mexico as the ubiquitous national seal.[422]

420 Van Sertima, Ivan. (1976). *African Presence in Early America*, p. 79.

421 "The Huichol Indians of the Sierra Madre" (2014) Accessed September 4, 2014. http://www.shamanism.com/huichol-indians/.

422 Sleeper-Smith, Susan. *Contesting Knowledge* (Nebraska: University of Nebraska Press, 2009), p. 197.

Yes, it was the Huicholes who were the first to make the famous Mexican seal. They were short and dark complected. The Huicholes are found to have African Haplotype L1 and L2 chromosomes.[423]

A review of the literature shows more African chromosomes found than European. Lisker et al., noted:

The variation of Indian ancestry among the studied Indians shows in general a higher proportion in the more isolated groups, except for the Cora, who are as isolated as the Huichol and have not only a lower frequency but also a certain degree of black admixture. The black admixture is difficult to explain because the Cora resides in a mountainous region away from the west coast. (1) Green, et al. also found Indians with African genes in North Central Mexico, including the L1 and L2 clusters. (2) Green et al. observed that the discovery of a proportion of African haplotypes roughly equivalent to the proportion of European haplotypes among North Central Mexican Indians cannot be explained by recent admixture of African Americans from the United States. This is especially the case for the Ojinaga area, which presently is, and historically has been, largely isolated from U.S. African Americans. In the Ojinaga sample set, the frequency of African haplotypes was higher than that of European haplotypes (3).[424]

See Fig. 19: Dr. Imhotep with a short Mexican nurse who was from a group called the Chichimecas, who "The Huicholes say was another group of people who predated them and were even darker and shorter than they were; the little people,"[425] who were spread out over 1000 miles across the Sierra Madre Mountains north of the Huicholes. We are told, however, that the Spanish enslaved them, and they did not survive in their homeland.

---

423 Winters, Clyde. "Dr. Clyde Winters says Mexicans are Black!" February 6, 2015. Accessed January 25, 2017. htpps://plus.google.com/117489061122831424612/posts.

424 Winters, C. A. (n,d.). "Race and Identity: Ancient relations between Africans and Mexicans." Accessed October 18, 2010. http://olmec98.net/RacePaper.pdf.

425 Conversations with Patricia Gonzalez, Historian at the Four Seasons Resort's Cultural Center, Punta Mita, Mexico in August 2009.

Another Mexican population, comprising 70,000 people with obvious African roots today, is concentrated on Mexico's Pacific coast. It is one of two areas in Mexico with a significant Black population today.

Fig. 19: Dr. Imhotep and a short Costa Chican Mexican nurse. *Photography by Teresa Gray-Jones.*

One of the reasons we took these two photos (Fig. 19 & 20) was to show the height of many Mexicans. I am 5'9" tall. The guide is in the 4' range. They obviously received their short stature from the "Grandmother civilization" of the Americas, the Southern African: ancient Anu, Twa, San, Khoisan, Koi Koi—all very diminutive peoples.

Please notice that these two people are not children but full-grownMexican ladies. They are the same size as their ancient African ancestors, the short Twa/Anu. Their short relatives can be still found all across the planet in South America, Hawaii, the Pacific Islands (excluding Australia where they were all massacred by the slowly encroaching Europeans).

You shall find them in India, China and of course Africa, where their ancestors began and are also there today.

The Negro-Costachicanos claim that they have never been slaves. Could it be that the Costachicanos are related to the North American
138

Chahta Indians? This comment had to be made, for neither tribe has ever tasted defeat in battle by their enemies! The traditions of Mexican Indians make it clear that the founders of civilization in Mexico came from the East and arrived in Mexico as a result of a shipwreck[426] rather than beginning the descendants of slaves.

Fig. 20: Dr. & Mrs. Imhotep with another short Costachican guide.

The largest rock-carving connection in Mexico would be the famous Olmec heads. In La Venta, Mexico, there were four giant heads. They were carved out of a single block of basalt each weighing approximately forty tons. They were six-to-nine feet in height. The sculptures are obviously Negroid heads with wide noses, very thick lips, typical prognathic jaws (jutting out).[427] One of the heads at Tres Zapotes has seven African-type braids on the back of his head.[428] The side view of the statue in Mexico has a clear example of African earlobe stretching. There are seventeen Olmec heads in Mexico[429] that have been found so far.

426 Ibid.

427 Winters, Clyde. *Atlantis in Mexico*, p. 10.

428 Van Sertima, Ivan. *Early America Revisited*, p. 74.

429 Winters, Clyde. (2017). "Olmec Heads. Slide 4. Slide show" presented by Dr. Winters at Governors State University. http://www.academia.edu/8457889/Names_of_Olmec_Heads_deciphered.

Here again, are phenomenal, large stone heads that exist in America and Africa, but not in Asia. Yes, the Proto-Manding also made many giant stone heads in Africa.

Those stone heads are over 2000 years old and predate the Olmec Stone Heads that have been found in the Ivory Coast and in Senegal. These giant stone heads were made of granite and laterite hard stone. The heads in Africa are three feet high and may have been the prototype for the Olmec heads made by the Olmec people in Mexico.[430]

Viewing the Olmec Stone Heads is like magically looking back in time and being able to see just what the Olmec people looked like before they mixed with the natives. Besides seeing the Olmec people through the stone heads, they may also be seen through their clay sculptures of themselves:

...an examination of them reveals the unmistakable combination of kinky hair, broad nose, generous lips, frequency of prognathous (abnormally projecting jaws), occasional goatee beard, and sometimes distinctively African ear pendants, hairstyles, tattoo markings and coloration.[431]

Professor Harun Kofi Wangara, formerly known as Harold Glyn Lawrence (1928–1989), was born in Detroit, Michigan. After making many research trips to Africa, he wrote *African Explorers of the New World*. In that book he noted: "We can now positively state that the Mandingoes of the Mali and Songhay Empires, and possibly other Africans, crossed the Atlantic to carry on trade with the Western Hemisphere Indians and further succeeded in establishing colonies throughout the Americas."[432]

We Find the Africans in the Americas Trading as Well

From Mexico came the ability to farm beans and corn. From the southeast came conch shells, from the northeast came obsidian,

---

430 Winters, Clyde. *Atlantis in Mexico*, p. 85.

431 Van Sertima, Ivan. *African Presence in Early America*, p. 63.

432 Lawrence, Harold. "African Explorers of the New World." *Crisis Magazine*, June-July 1962, p. 2.; Rodgers, J. A. (2010). World's Great Men of Color - Volume 2 (New York, Collier Books), p. xiii.

from the Great Lakes came copper. Much of the trade was done by water routes. The ability to travel great distances was made known to Columbus as well. We know that the Carob people, whom Columbus had encountered, had canoes, complete with masts, that held twenty-five to seventy people just like the Nigerian Dufuna canoe. Columbus seized a ship from the Putun Mayans larger than his own.... On the other side of the continent, the Kwakiutl in the northwest would have the oceangoing "canoes" that held 70–100 individuals. Clearly trade was established in America before Columbus arrived.[433]

These attributes and more can be seen in Alexander von Wuthenau's book, *Unexpected Faces in Ancient America.* For thirty years he served as the Chair of Pre-Columbian Art History at the University of the Americas, and he founded the Humanitas Americanas collection in his studio at San Angel. Here is some background data on the Manding:

Manding—a major ethnic group in the Nile Valley that migrated early to West Africa.

Manding—built mounds along the Niger River and in Mauritania.

Manding—used the same gold spear formula in Africa as the Africans Columbus found across the Atlantic using in Haiti.

Manding—and Olmecs used identical-sounding words, for example: guanin/ghanin and ghana/goanna.

Manding—formed the base of the Olmec people.

Manding—most likely taught the Micmac how to write using Egyptian hieroglyphics.

Manding—in 1311 A.D., thousands of years after the Olmec arrival, the Mandinkan Muslim, Abubakari II sailed a fleet ships from Mali, Africa, in the Atlantic headed west.[434] When they reached South America, they left signs on the rocks at the mouths of rivers warning followers of dangerous or friendly natives.

433 "Discovery of the old world by native Americans," *Atlantis Rising* #80, (March/April 2010). Accessed October 14, 2016. http://atlantis risingmagazine.com/article/the-discovery-of-the-old-world-by-native-americans/.

434 Van Sertima, Ivan. (1976). *They Came Before Columbus: The African Presence in Ancient America* (NY, Random House), p. 47.

Algonquin Connection to the Egyptians

The next example brings us full circle with the Algonquin. It identifies an Egyptian-Algonquin relationship. "As was now quite obvious, the Micmac writing system (and also part of their language) is derived from the ancient Egyptian."[435] Another item the early Algonquin had in common with the Egyptians and the early peoples of the Nile Valley, as well as the Picts of Britain, is that they were all short and dark complexioned, as the Mexican people we just left in the previous chapter. Further, the Micmac were found to be even "shorter than their neighbors, and both had dark complexions."[436] One of the native tribes the French navigator, Jacques Cartier, met is described as the Micmac...a shorter, darker people. Do you feel a hint of a possibility that these short people are related?

Over in Europe. when they landed in Scotland, the taller Celtic peoples called them "pixies," a name that still exists in the folklore of the British Isles. The Romans in the British Isles called them Picts. Roman historian Gildas said they came from across the sea.[437] The Mediterranean Sea? Further descriptions of what the Picks and Micmacs looked like were recorded by explorers of the New World:

Racial characteristics are also shared among the Picts and Micmacs. They were both shorter than their neighbors, and both had darker complexions. The Celts in comparison were more likely to be taller, red or blond haired, blue-eyed inhabitants of the later British Isles. The expression "dark Irish" or "Black Irish" survived today to distinguish them from the Celtic cousins...On both sides of the Atlantic, there were places where it appears the inhabitants were very small people.[438]

Next, we were always taught that the Native Americans were great hunters but they did not farm,[R] nor could they read or write. None of this was true. French Catholic priest, Pierre Maillard, wrote a 450-page book

435 Fell, Barry. *America B.C.: Ancient Settlers in the New World.*

436 Sora, Steven. (2010). "The Discovery of the Old World by Native Americans," *Atlantis Rising*, # 80, March/April. p. 315.

437 Kenyon, J. Douglas. *Missing Connections*, p. 224.

438 Ibid., p. 67.

in Micmac hieroglyphics in 1767 A.D. The Spanish said he was one of the priests Richelieu sent to civilize the Indians.

Sixty-one years after Maillard published his book, the French historian, Champollion-Figeac (also the very first French Egyptologist, in 1839 A.D.) published his first book on the decipherment of Egyptian hieroglyphics. What this means is Maillard wrote his book sixty-one years before Champollion-Figeac's book was published. Consequently, Maillard could not have copied the Egyptian script. His book, therefore, had to be an original.

Let's open the Micmac book. In the Micmac script there were:

Hundreds of different hieroglyphic signs, a considerable portion of which are clearly derived from, or even identical with, ancient Egyptian or their hieratic equivalents.... He also says he has met older people among the Indians at Old Town, Maine, who remember a time when writing was inscribed vertically, and also horizontally.[439]

The vertical or horizontal form of writing is identical to the way the ancient Egyptians wrote. The Micmac-Algonquian speakers most likely had much contact with the Egyptian, Olmec, Manding people, due to the amount of knowledge about Egyptian writing and Egyptian words incorporated into their language.

In the American Midwest, the Amerinds in Oklahoma are part of the Great Plains Tribes. According to Levi-Strauss (1978), the Algonquin tribes of the Great Plains share similar mythologies with the Shoshone, which means there is some sort of relation.[440] The Utes are part of the Shoshone language family, but complexion-wise, they also had something else in common with the early Algonquins. Tradition says the Utes were so dark-complexioned that the neighboring Amerinds created a special name for them:

They were so dark-skinned that other tribes referred to them as the "black Indians."...One has only to compare the mythologies of the Plains Indians with that of the Shoshone to be convinced that they both derive from some ancient syncretism" (syncretism means

439 Fell, Barry. *America B.C.: Ancient Settlers in the New World*, pp. 253-27. Quoted in http://www. flavinscorner.com/abctext.htm. Accessed January 12, 2017.

440 Levi-Strauss, Claude. (1978). *The Origin of Table Manners: Mythologiques Volume Three* (Illinois, University of Chicago Press), p. 204.

combining different religions, cultures, or languages). The actual name of the state of Utah is derived from the Utes.[441]

The Algonquin and Shoshone language-speaking peoples of North America are most likely related because of similar mythologies. Native American spirituality and mythologies are very important to them. This makes a lot of sense for the tradition of the Algonquin, which says their ancestors crossed the sea to come to the Americas. This probably makes them older than any of the Amerinds in the Americas. Their contact with the Mande and the Egyptians in North America (along with their similarities in their mythologies or religious practices) is further evidence that shall be covered later in this work.

They were connected genetically. In closing this section, the Transitive Property of Equilibrium equation shall be applied here for clarity: If A=B and B=C then A=C. The Manding, Egyptian, Olmec, and Algonquin peoples are all most probably related. Just as in a family there are parents, sisters and brothers, but they are still in the same family.

A summary of evidence displaying an Algonquin link with Africa and the Manding/Egyptians: They came from across the sea and some kept yearly sacrifices for their safe arrival on the East Coast of North America. They were the most heavily populated and wide-spread of all Amerinds, suggesting they were in the Americas before all other tribes. Some of the Micmac-Algonquin's written language was identical to ancient Egyptian hieroglyphics. Early on, the Micmac-Algonquin were short in stature and dark complexioned as the Proto-Manding and the Anu/Twa. Some of their oral languages were Manding/ Egyptian. Eastern Algonquin skulls were of the elongated, dolichocephalic African shape. Some of their descendants, as late as the early 1900s, still resembled Africans. They were here before the first Asians entered the Americas in 2600 B.C., settling in New England at least 10,000 years ago. Leo Wiener wrote about the connections between the Algonquin and the Manding.[442]

441 McPherson, R. S. (1988). "Ute Indians-Southern." Accessed August 24, 2009. http://www.media.utah.edu/UHE/u/UTES, SOUTHERN.html.

442 Mroueh, Y. (n.d.). "Precolumbian Muslims in the Americas." Accessed May 29, 2010. http://www.themodernreligion.com/ht/precolumbus.html.

Could the Algonquin Be Related to the Skraelings?

Hodge's quote below seems to be surprisingly accurate:

The type of the Atlantic coast Algonquians can hardly be determined from living individuals, as no full-bloods survive, but skulls found in old burial grounds show that they were tall, the skulls, their faces not quite so broad, their heads much more elongated and remarkably high resembling in this respect the Eskimo and suggesting the possibility that on the New England coast there may have been some mixture with that type.[443]

The Atlantic coast's Algonquin skulls were tall [but their stature was short], the faces narrow, rather than the wide-flat faces of the Mongolian, and their "heads much more elongate."[444] Hodge is describing a dolichocephalic skull rather than a brachycephalic round skull in that example. Then, he brings in a comparison to the Eskimo long skull type. The original Algonquin's similarities are with the Skraeling/Anu. The first Algonquin did not have a Mongolian skull type.

The early Algonquin lived in the New England and eastern Canadian areas of North America. These were the same regional areas as the Skraeling were reported to have been. They both were in North America during the same time period.

Before they began mixing with Mongolians, both groups began with an African heritage. The Algonquin resembles the Eskimo who resembled and was also related to the Skraelings. The evidence showed the first Skraelings entering from the east. The Algonquin held festivals and made sacrifices for their safe trip from their eastern origin across the sea.

It seems that the Skraelings could also have been the first Algonquin, just as the Skraelings were the first Eskimos. In Chapter 1, Oleson wrote that the Eskimo was a mixture of the Tunnit (Caucasian), Icelander, and the Dorset/Skraelings. The evidence shows that there is a very good possibility the Algonquin were related to the Skraelings.

---

443 Hodge, F. W. "Handbook of American Indians North of Mexico." (1906). Accessed February 17, 2010. http://www.access- genealogy.com/native/ tribes/algonquian/algonhist1.htm.

444 Ibid.

The Hopi/Pueblo(Anaszi)/Dogon/ Navajo/Apache Relationship

Contrary to popular belief, the Dogon are not just a small tribe that lives in Mali; the Dogon are composed of many different bloodlines that represent the elite of the Egyptian Pharaonic Society. The Dogons once lived in the Nile Valley, but they migrated to Mali just before the invasion around 400 BC.[445]

According to the oral tradition, the Dogon are originally members of the Keta, a Mande speaking group from the headwaters of the Niger River.[446] **The Dogon migration myth claims that they are of Manding [Mande, Mandingo] origin and that they settled in the Seno Plains after their separation from the Dyon and Arou tribes.**[447] Eventually, parts of both the Dogon and Manding migrated to the Americas. On a similar note, the groups of Dogon from Mali have another connection in America. It seems that the Hopi (one of the Pueblo tribes) and the Dogon have similar clothing, ornaments, ceremonial masks, and a three-prong headdress that is shaped like the letter "W." The Hopi also paint their faces, not just in a similar way to the Dogon, but identical to them.[448] Very interesting. Even today, they both "separately" participate in a ceremonial Bado dance. In part of their individual costumes, they wear a colorful skirt. As a matter of fact, the "The ceremonial dance of the Hopi Indians is identical to the Dogon's Bado dance of Africa, using the same symbols and spirit names."[449]

This dance may goes back before the Proto-Hopi left Africa. The only Africans who used to wear skirts were the Egyptians! This ritual and

---

445 Morodenibig, Naba. *Philosophy Podium*. (Illinois, Firefly Productions, 2008). Back Cover.; Appiah, A., and Henry Louis Gates. (1999). *Africana: The Encyclopedia of the African and African American Experience* (West Sussex, John Wiley and Son Inc.), p. 415.

446 Blom, Huib. (2011). *Dogon Images and Traditions* (Brussels, Momentum Publication), p. 64.

447 Ibid., p. 164.

448 Nu, Ra. (8/3/13). African origins of America. Accessed on May, 1, 2016 from https://blacktoday.wordpress.com/2013/08/03/african-origins-of-america/.

449 Ibid.

ceremonial costume could very well date to the Nile Valley before both groups separated.

Let us revisit the relations in the Americas. Given that the Hopi and Pueblo must be related, they also have other striking identical similarities with the Dogon. They have identical cliff dwellings to those in Mali that can be found in Canyon de Chelly National Monument in Arizona (see Fig. 39). Additionally, the findings of a hereditary study of the Hopi and Navajo "confirms the genetic similarity of the two populations."[450]

These are not one or two, but several undeniable similarities. Interestingly, the Navajo and Apache have related linguistic and ethnic similarities. Just as the Hopi and Navajo are genetically related. "Genetically, Navajos are more closely related to the Apache."[451]

Using the Transitive Property of Equality, the large family of Hopi-Pueblo-Dogon-Navajo and Apache are all related. Coincidently, the Hopi (one of the Pueblo tribes), the Apache and Navajo all live in the same region in eastern Arizona. The coincidence of the entire ceremony, the skirt, and especially the Apache wearing a headdress that is identical to the Dogon headdresses is very interesting. The part that is over the top is that the Apache ceremonial dance is amazingly like the Dogon's Bado Dance. The Apache's descendants still perform the Dogon Bado Dance in Arizona.[452]

Around fifty miles northwest of the Canyon de Chelly Monument, more Pueblo cliff dwellings can be found in Colorado in Mesa Verde National Park, also built by descendants of the Telem/Dogon. Do you see a connection here? The Hopi are another fly-in-the-ointment to the theory that the first Americans came from Asia through the Bering Strait. "According to their legends, the Hopi or their Proto-American ancestors

450 Williams, R. C. et al. (27 Apr 2005). "The HLA loci of the Hopi and Navajo." *American Journal of Physical Anthropology*, Volume 56 Issue 3, pp. 291-296.

451 Lapahie, H. (1999). "Navajo Nation." Accessed February 19, 2010. http://www.lapahie.com/Dine_Photos.cfm.

452 Nu, R. (8/3/13). African origins of America. Accessed on May, 1, 2016 from https://blacktoday.wordpress.com/2013/08/03/african-origins-of-america/.

migrated north to Arizona from...South America, Central America and Mexico."[453]

The Hopi are related to the Pueblo-Dogon-Navajo and Apache. If their ancestors are related, then their southern origins are related. Following the evidence, this again suggests the first Americans did not come through the Bering Strait. Other overwhelming evidence shows only the eastern part of North, Central and South America have the majority of the oldest archaeological sites as seen on the Fig. 5 map. This data further sinks the Bering Strait-first entry theory. Here is another piece of the south-to-north migration puzzle. Remember, the Dogon (from Mali or Burkina Faso) trace their descendants to the Manding.[454]

The Manding formed the base of the Olmecs as they entered Central and South America. This line of reasoning points to the probability that some of the Olmec/Manding, migrated north from Central America to the American Southwest exactly as the Hopi. The Manding (who were related to the Dogon in Africa) became the Olmec in the Americas when they landed and mixed with the natives. So again, the Dogon have direct similarities to their Hopi/Pueblo and Apache brothers and sisters, who in turn are related to the Navaho. This evidence demonstrates the relationship between the large family of Hopi-Pueblo-Apache-Navajo-Dogon-Manding-Olmec.

At the end of Chapter 2, there is a nine-point summary that shows the Algonquin connection with Africans, i.e. Egyptian/Manding. We also covered the Algonquin connection to the Skraelings, and the Skraeling connection to the Eskimos. We therefore have a relationship connection among Manding-Egyptian-Algonquin-Skraeling-Eskimo. The Manding are the common thread tying both large families together. So now that we know the two large families are related, they now form the super family of Eskimo/Skraeling/Algonquin/Egyptian/Manding/Olmec/Dogon/Pueblo/Hopi/Navaho/Apache. Even with all these super relationships, we are still leaving out two other groups from the extreme east and west.

Do not forget that after 2600 B.C.—when the Asians crossed the Bering Strait for the first time—the Hopi-Pueblo-Apache-Navajo family became

453 Inter-Tribal Council. (n.d.). "Hopi Tribe." Accessed June 5, 2015. http://itcaonline.com/?page_id=1162.

454 Winters, Clyde. (2015). "Malians in Ancient America." Accessed January 5, 2014. https://ww w.academia.edu/8505600/Malians_ in_ Ancient_ America

a part of the Mongolian/Asian group. Then after the Proto-Americans mixed with the Mongolians, that created the Hopi-Pueblo-Apache-Navajo Amerinds. They are on the extreme western side of the human family from Asia.

Then there are the Eskimo who were the offspring of the Skraeling and Tunnit-Icelander-Caucasians from the extreme eastern side of the family in Scandinavia. The Caucasians were the offspring of the Khoisan from Africa—who traveled to Europe and lost their dark skin color during the long Ice Age from 115,000 until circa 8000 B.C.—and the DNA from the South American Fuegians matched that of the Khoisan people from South.

Section Notes

N. Mounds

At least 10,000 years ago during the African Aqualithic period, the Mound Builders of Africa, the Proto-Manding, were building habitation mounds to live upon even before the Manding built their mounds along the Niger River. These Proto-Saharan people also built dams, boats and mounds to escape the waters in case of flooding. There are also large erections formerly called "Native American mounds" (now known to be—African mounds), that are shaped like pyramids that are found across North America. The largest ones surviving today are in the Mississippi Valley area. The largest of all was the Cahokia mound near the area where the Mississippi and Missouri rivers converge.[455]

One of the great cities of the world, Cahokia, was actually larger than London in 1250 A.D.! **More than 10,000 people—estimates are as high as 20,000 people**—are thought to have lived in that settlement between 1050 and 1200 A.D.[456]

Author and editor of *Ancient American* magazine, Frank Joseph, believes Cahokia's population was far greater than previous estimates. He indicates the count was closer to 200,000 people. Joseph came to this conclusion

---

455 Winters, Clyde. *Atlantis in Mexico*, pp. 71, 85.

456 Mulvihill, Keith. (2008). "Ancient Midwest." *The New York Times*. Accessed February 2, 2010 from http://travel.nytimes. com/2008/08/15/travel/escapes/15mile.html.

"after factoring in Mound City and its affiliated, outlying areas.[457] Mound City stood near where the modern city of St. Louis now stands. Cahokia is thought to have been the largest ancient North American city built before Columbus arrived. Cahokia had 120 earthen mounds.[458] Several of the mounds were massive, with square bottoms:

> *This is the largest prehistoric earthwork in all the Americas, covering more than 14 acres at its base. It stands 100 feet high and was built in a series of stages over a period close to 200 years. That's probably more than 15 million basket loads of soil—dug out with clamshells.... Nearby, an ancient sun calendar has been reconstructed on the site where its remnants were found: an enormous ring of tall tree trunks stuck in the ground, called Woodhenge.[459]*

Around the city of Cahokia, crops were grown to feed the city's residents, who included: government officials and religious leaders, as well as skilled trades workers, astronomers and artisans. Cahokia, center of a large trading network, was linked with other societies covering a great part of North America.[460] Childress supports Joseph writing, "Originally there were over 120 pyramids and mounds at the Cahokia site."[461] "Its largest mound's base is larger than the Great Pyramid at Giza. It is as tall as a 10-story building."[462]

North of Cahokia's southwestern Illinois location was the city of Aztalan in southern Wisconsin: "Aztalan was the home of an aristocratic population of priests, architects, astronomers and engineers."[463] They built

457 Joseph, Frank. *Advanced Civilizations of Prehistoric America*, p. 138.

458 Carlton, J. "Explaining the Phenomenon of Cahokia" *American Archaeology*, Spring 2007, Vol. 11, No. 1., p. 13.

459 Little, Gregory. *The Illustrated Encyclopedia of Native American Mounds & Earthworks* (Tennessee, Eagle Wing Books, 2009, p. 62.

460 Seppa, Nathan. (Wednesday, 3/12/97). "Metropolitan Life on the Mississippi" March 12, 1997, p.101. Special to *The Washington Post*.

461 Childress, David. H. *Lost Cities of North & Central America*, p. 350.

462 Little, Gregory. *The Illustrated Encyclopedia*, p. 62.

463 Joseph, F. *Advanced Civilizations of Prehistoric America*, p.155.

walls and rectangular towers for protection. Their enormous walls were completely plastered with a mixture of shell-clay as in Cahokia:

> *The people who settled Aztalan built large, flat-topped pyramidal mounds and a stockade around their village. Mentioned earlier is that Cahokia was famous for their flat-topped pyramid mounds. It is believed that the Aztalan Indians moved north to Wisconsin from the large mound settlement at Cahokia near St. Louis, Illinois.*[464]

These people built something for their city that was a one-of-a-kind in America. It was similar to what the Carthaginians built in Africa before they were built in Rome: "The city itself was connected at its north end to nearby Rock Lake via a stone aqueduct three miles long."[465] For three miles, the level of the aqueduct had to continually decrease so the water would continue to flow through a gravitational pull the entire distance from Rock Lake to Aztalan. That was quite an engineering feat for people who were described by insurgent Europeans as "savages." Yes, aqueduct technology was also a part of ancient America too. The probability of these people in the Americas building a one-of-its-kind aqueduct, halfway around the world from the aqueduct in Carthage, Africa—before those in Rome—is astronomical.

Towards the west is another complex of ancient pyramids, canals, and artificial lakes with paved bottoms just across the Mississippi River from Memphis, Tennessee, in Francis County, Arkansas. It is believed that an ancient Egyptian city once existed there, and apparently it is the reason the modern city of "Memphis" was given the name of the ancient Egyptian city of the same name by Anglo-Americans. On the banks of the Arkansas River near the present-day town of Spiro, Oklahoma, lies another huge pyramid-mound complex known today as the Spiro Mounds Site. In southern Wisconsin (near the Illinois border, between Milwaukee and Madison) is the Aztalan pyramid site. The two main pyramids face each other across a broad plaza much like a miniature version of Teotihuacan near Mexico City.[466] This would be an Olmec/Manding/Egyptian influence.

---

464 "Ancient Aztalan Village" (No. 408)" (n.d.) Accessed on September 10, 2010. http://dnr.wi.gov/org/land/er/sna/index.asp?SNA=408.

465 Joseph, Frank. *Advanced Civilizations of Prehistoric America*, p. 35.

466 Childress, D. H. (1992). *Lost Cities of North & Central America*, pp. 336-7.

O. Credible Sources of Ancient Copper Mining

Archaeometric Study of Native Copper in Prehistoric North America, Ph.D. Dissertation (Anthropology), State University of New York at Stony Brook, 1979 (University Microfilms: Ann Arbor, MI 1981), 145 pages, text with footnoted sources, 16-page bibliography E99. A6 V39. Bastian, by Tyler Johnson.

Copper mining in Isle Royale National Park, Michigan, from a thesis in Anthropology, University of Utah, 1963 (Photocopy available at Michigan Tech Archives), 77 pages, text with footnoted sources, 11-page bibliography F572. I8 B3. Aboriginal Research Club (various authors).

The Ancient Copper Mines of Northern Michigan Aboriginal Research Club: Detroit, MI 1940. Collection of 21 papers, mostly reprints of earlier publications, 112 pages, few footnoted sources, 2-page Bibliography (Photocopy available at Michigan Tech Archives) E98. I5 A23. Drier, Roy W., and Octave J. Du Temple.

Prehistoric Copper Mining in the Lake Superior Region. Published privately by the Authors: Calumet, MI 1961. Collection of 25 papers, mostly reprints of earlier publications 213 pages, few footnoted sources, 5-page Bibliography E98 I5 D7.

For more on this subject, 57 more articles can be found online about raw material and mining.

P. Egypt in the Grand Canyon

Author David H. Childress tells a story that dates back to April 5, 1909. An article appeared in the *Phoenix Gazette* stating that an Egyptian rock-cut cave had been found in the Grand Canyon. It goes on to say that G. E. Kinkaid claims to have found a cave cut out of solid rock as the ancient Egyptians used to make in the Valley of the Kings. The story claims that archaeologists from the Smithsonian Institute agreed to finance the exploration of the cave. Professor S. A. Jordan is said to have pursued the explorations for the Institute. The cave was found to extend a mile down into the bowels of the earth and contain hundreds of rooms in a series of catacombs. Some of the objects found were "War weapons, copper instruments, sharp-edged and hard as steel indicate the high state of civilization reached by these strange people."[467]

---

467 Ibid.

This Egyptian cave was not an anomaly. There are several other places in the Americas where caves are cut from solid rock and mummies are kept in a crypt or catacombs underground. In Springerville, Arizona, catacombs were found underground, two to three acres in size. One room was thirty feet long and thirty feet high. Archaeologist John Hohmann said the catacomb contained hundreds of skeletons. Another place where mummies were found was in tunnels beneath the modern city of Lexington, Kentucky:

In a chamber 300 feet long, 100 feet wide, and 18 feet high lay idols, altars.... The oldest mummies found so far in the Americas are the... sophisticated mummies found in the desert of northern Chile that are dated at 11,000 years old.[468]

Q. The Manding

Mandingo, by the way, is the name currently given to a very important division of Black peoples in West Africa. It is seemingly a corruption of a term applied to an important section of this group, the Mande-nka or Mande-nga (Mandinka, Mandinga, Mandingo). Dr. Imhotep has heard this word pronounced by the Mandingo as "Mandina," or even "Madina." It seems to be derived from the racial name Mande, coupled with the suffix -nka or -nke, meaning "people," the people of Mande.[469]

The Mande are an adventurous people. They sailed to the Americas dozens of millennia before Columbus, leaving many artifacts for us to examine. Al-Umari documents two more recent trips made by Muslim sailors from Mali. These voyages, "would have taken place in either 1307 or 1312 [A.D.]"[470] It seems hard to believe that the Muslim Emperor of Mali, Abubakari II, arose one morning, and out of nowhere sent 400 ships without knowing where he was going or why.

Mansa Abubakari II, also known as Mansa Qi, was the ninth mansa of the Malia Empire. He probably found out about the Americas from

468 Ibid.

469 "Mandingo" (n.d). Accessed from on-line Encyclopedia Britannica. Accessed January 5, 2011 https://en.wikisource.org/wiki/1911_ Encyclop%C3%A6dia_Britannica/Mandingo.

470 Ortiz de Montellano, Bernard., G. Haslip-Viera, and W. Barbour. (1997). They were NOT here before Columbus. Ethnohistory. Accessed August 10, 2009 from http://www.jstor.org/pss/483368.

other Africans who had actually traveled there, or who had heard of the Americas and wanted to investigate.

Mansa Abubakari II had a brother by the name of Mansa (Gonga) Musa who was the second most famous of the Mandinga explorers of Mali. When he stopped in Cairo on his way to Mecca in 1324, he reported that his predecessors had launched two expeditions to discover the limits of the Atlantic. A few decades after Musa's Cairo visit, Al-'umari was writing about Musa's ventures. He left the following notice of these voyages:

> *Sultan Musa said he wanted to discover the limits of the neighboring sea the Atlantic. He had two hundred ships equipped and filled them with men and others with the same number, 200 more ships filled with gold, water and supplies in enough quantity to last for years. He told those who commanded them: "return only when you have reached the extremity of the ocean, or when you have exhausted your food and water." They went away; their absence was long before any of them returned. Finally, a sole ship reappeared. We asked the captain about their adventures. "Prince," he replied, "we sailed for a long time, up to the moment when we encountered in mid-ocean something like a river with a violent current. My ship was the last. The others sailed on, and gradually as each one entered this place, they disappeared and did not come back. We did not know what had happened to them. As for me, I returned to where I was and did not enter that current." But the emperor did not want to believe him. He equipped **two thousand vessels**, a thousand for himself and the men who accompanied him, and a thousand for water and supplies. He confirmed power on me, Mansa Musa, and left with his companions on the ocean. This is the last time that I saw him and the others... somewhere between 1307 and 1312.*[471]

Obviously, this captain had heard the well-known rumors about how the world was flat, and if one sailed too far to the end, his ship would fall off the edge and all would be lost. The emperor was upset, but probably said nothing to this captain.

Those two accounts of African maritime expeditions were well documented—but not alone. Another well-known expedition to the Americas appeared in the journals of Christopher Columbus. On Columbus' third trip to the Americas he specifically mentions that Africans had a habit of leaving the Guinea Coast and sailing to the West

471 Van Sertima, Ivan. *African Presence in Early America*, p. 170.

conducting trading expeditions. Obviously, this practice had gone on for many thousands of years before Mansa Abubakari II, the Vikings, Amerigo Vespucci and Christopher Columbus.

The history of Eastern Hemisphere contacts with the Western Hemisphere must be made known and revisited. To repeat, "In 1311, Abubakari II appointed his brother Kankan Musa (i.e., Mansa Musa) as regent and then departed. "He was never seen again."[472] But there is evidence to show that may not be true. The author of that quote seems to have been quite agitated by the title he gives his book: FYI, there are one thousand Eurocentric views of this story, however, you may read the title of his book for yourself: *Invented Knowledge: False History, Fake Science and Pseudo-religious,* by Ronald H. Fritze.

There is evidence, however, that **does** actually show that we **do know exactly** what happened to Mansa Abubakari II. They say his fleet most probably sailed to South America. In the Foreword of this book, Dr. Clyde Winters wrote that after these Africans from Abubakari II's expedition landed in the Americas, they left their Mande inscriptions. However, they not only made inscriptions, but left them in several different places they traveled in the Americas.

There is quite another group of ancient Americans who also had a great maritime presence, and they were "the Carrib people, whom Columbus encountered, had large canoes, complete with masts, that held twenty-five to seventy people."[473] So we now see that evidence has reversed the Eurocentrists' unsubstantiated claim that, "**it is not known what happened to Abubakari II's fleet, nor were they ever seen or heard from again!**" The first Abubakari II expedition of Manding sailed from Mali, Africa, and reached South America. Here is the evidence:

Upon arrival in America the Manding sailed along the coast until they found rivers like the Orinoco in Venezuela, and Amazon in Brazil, which they used to move into the inland parts of South America. Along these rivers the Manding have left many inscriptions to point the way to good campsites for Abubakari and the main expeditionary

---

472 Fritze, R. H. (2009). *Invented Knowledge: False History, Fake Science and Pseudo-religious*, footnote #51 (the book has no page numbers). Reaktion Books: London, UK.

473 Sora, S. (2010). "The Discovery of the Old World by Native Americans." *Atlantis Rising*, # 80, March/April, p. 41.

force. Many of these inscriptions have been found along the Rio Chao River in the State of Alagos in Brazil. These inscriptions are of two kinds. One group of inscriptions was meant to warn the Manding expeditionary force not to camp in certain areas. Inscriptions in this category are found at Piraicaba, Brazil. Another group of inscriptions was left in areas suitable for settlement.[474]

One of the safe settlements developed into a stone city. This lost city was rediscovered in 1753 A.D. Similar inscriptions were found by Padre Tellesde Menezes in Marajo, which is near the Une and Paraoaca Rivers in the territory of Bahia, Brazil. A royal tomb of "Pe" was found there.

Col. P. H. Fawcett found an ancient tablet close to the Culuene River in Brazil. The tablet had an actual carving of an aristocrat with dark skin and African features who belonged to a colony of people from Mali, Africa, in Brazil! The evidence proving that this artifact was from the Malalian (Mali) culture was the crown that the man on the tablet was wearing, the inscriptions on his chest and feet, as well as his Manding styled pants. When living near rivers these Malians built mounds to live upon just as they had done in Africa on the Niger River. To see more mounds in Africa, look just to the south of Africa's Lake Chad. Actually, these are only part of a group of 822 known mounds that also extend across Cameroon and into southwestern Chad. (Hollmann, 1966: 581)[475]

Permit us to enter a sidebar here. As wonderful as this discovery of the 1307 B.C. trip of the Mansa Abubakari II to South America is, we must also remember they were definitely not the first Africans to reach the Americas. Evidence of Africans was found in South Carolina by Dr. Goodyear dating back to 51,700 years ago; Nadine Guidon's date for Africans in South America is 100,000 years ago, and Micah Hanks' Hueyatlaco site near Pubela, Mexico is "peer-reviewed evidence of 250,000 YBP!" **It is therefore, in this vein, that we must insist that Africans were the first Americans.**

Moving forward, in the last three chapters the reader shall find a well-documented account of an artificial harbor found one mile off the west coast of the island of Bimini, Bahamas: A 600-yard-long pier and

474 Winters, Clyde. (2015). "Malians in Ancient America."

475 Connah, Graham. (1987). *African Civilizations: An Archaeological Perspective* (Cambridge University Press), p.124.

breakwater that can be seen in 25–30 feet of water. But this is not the only evidence of artificial harbors built in the Western Hemisphere. There have been several ancient piers found underwater off the coast of South America. Not to mention an actual city found in deep water three and one-half miles off the western coast of Cuba.

The accounts of Abubakari II, the Vikings, Amerigo Vespucci and Christopher Columbus are late news to the academics who have actually studied the historic evidence of maritime travel. Christopher Columbus was a definite late comer to the Americas, as well as being the last to discover it for Europe. Other evidence of Africans in early America can be found in the mounds that we have continually presented in this book. But we must always give the mounds found in Africa the prize for preceding all others.

Both in Scotland and Morocco, we meet with artificial mounds in which there are chambers. In Southern Morocco they are inhabited by dwarfs. The name "Pecht," which is used in Scotland for dwarf and is more familiar to us as "Pict," is to be found south of the Atlas Mountains in Algeria as well as Morocco. My informant there said dwarf click sound made the name sound like Psecht. She gave me an account of the dwelling places of the Nanos of Aledo, which she said were built of large stones covered with earth, which were evidently similar to those of the "Adwarfi" and to the Pict houses of Scotland.[476]

To follow the progression of mound building, first look in Africa along the Niger River; then look in Portugal, the British Isles, Denmark, Eastern Canada, New England and all over the rest of North America. Columbus was most likely unaware of mounds but was familiar with Africans in the New World:

A renowned American historian and linguist, Leo Wiener of Harvard University, in his book, Africa and the Discovery of America *(1920) wrote that Columbus was well aware of the Mandinka presence in the New World and that the West African Muslims had spread throughout the Caribbean, Central, South and North American*

---

476 Haliburton, R. G. *The Dwarfs of Mount Atlas* (Ohio, Coachwhip Publications, 2009), p. 190.

territories, including Canada, where they were trading and intermarrying with the Iroquois and Algonquin Indians.[477]

R. Indians Farming

Something that has never been taught nor publicized is that some of the peoples in the ancient Americas were great farmers. The following evidence of farming is an account witnessed by an American general in the 18th century. General George John Sullivan (and his troops in Wyoming) witnessed the following gigantic Indian farm just before they **destroyed it** on May 1, 1779 A.D.; unfortunately, its destruction was what made it memorable.

As the weary columns of soldiers slowly emerged from a dark forest and filed into this open space, they were startled to see what seemed to be an area transformed into an Eden! The tall, ripe grass bent before the wind—cornfield after cornfield waved in the sun—orchards that had been growing for *generations*, were weighed down under a profusion of fruit— cattle grazed on the banks of a river, and all was luxuriant and beautiful. All about were scattered a hundred and twenty-eight houses—not miserable huts huddled together, but large airy buildings, situated in the most pleasant spots, surrounded by fruit trees and exhibiting a civilization level on the part of the Indians never witnessed before.[478]

This account is not the only instance of ancient civilization in pre-Columbian North America:

The first Europeans to visit the Northern Mississippi Valley reported groves of nut and fruit trees being managed as orchards, in addition to gardens and more expansive agricultural fields. Further away, prescribed burning (sometimes known as slash-and-burn agriculture) was used for the prairie areas, which helped the growth of herbs and berry-producing plants, which were important to food and medicine.[479]

477 Mroueh, Y. (n.d.). "Precolumbian Muslims in the Americas." Accessed May 29, 2010 http://www.themodernreligion.com/ht/precolumbus.html.

478 Sora, S. (2010). "The Discovery of the Old World by Native Americans." *Atlantis Rising*, # 80, March/April, p. 41.

479 Mayfield, Marlys. *Thinking for Yourself*, (Boston: Thomson-Wadsworth, 2007)), p. 319.

Speaking of medicine, in 1534 Europeans were camped along the St. Lawrence River. Scurvy broke out amongst them. The Algonquins helped them:

> *The medicine man boiled the bark of a certain tree...and the men drank it. To a man, all were saved, their scurvy cured by the concoction. The British would not "discover" the cure for scurvy until 1795.*[480]

Here in another region of ancient North America, this time in Arizona, we see more evidence of pre-Columbian farming:

> *In the desert area of Arizona, an area now occupied by the greater Phoenix metro area, Indian people were farming corn, beans, squash, and cotton more than 2,500 years ago. Called Hohokam by archaeologists, these people developed a system of irrigation that carried water for many miles to their productive fields, which yielded two harvests per year. In the Phoenix Basin, the Hohokam brought some 70,000 acres under cultivation with their elaborate networks of irrigation canals. Along the canals were interdependent villages whose residents shared the work of constructing, maintaining, and managing the canals.*[481]

These examples of farming in ancient America are not anomalies. Between Phoenix and Tucson lies the remains of another large ancient city. The people there grew beans, squash, corn and cotton.[482] Not all occupants of ancient America were just hunter-gatherers or nomads as Hollywood has led us to believe. Furthermore, they were not just farming for foodstuffs, they were also farming cotton for clothing. And no, all ancient Americans did not wear only buckskin:

> *The Indians made simple clothing from animal skins and plant fibers. Villagers wore breechcloths and aprons. In winter, they wore buckskin shirts, cloth ponchos, and blankets. For foot protection,*

480 Lentz, D.L. (2000). *Imperfect Balance Landscape transformations in the pre-Columbian Americas* (Columbia University Press).

481 Ojibwa Indians. "Ancient-America-Hohokam - Ball-Courts." Feb 16, 2014. *Daily Kos*. Accessed August 28 from http://www.dailykos.com/story/2014/02/16/1278031/Ancient-America-Hohokam-Ball-Courts.

482 Gregonis, L. M., and K. J. Reinhard. (1979). "Hohokam Indians of the Tucson Basin." Accessed on August 29, 2009. From http://www. uapress. arizona. edu/onlinebks/HOHOKAM/CHAP1.HTM.

sandals were worn. On festive occasions they donned headdresses, turbans, headbands, belts and kilts.[483]

One interesting note is that cotton, Gossypium herbaceum, *is indigenous to Africa, and the ancestor of America's cotton varieties. It is a New World cotton, G. hirsutum var. punctatum. It is clear that if the feral cottons today are the descendants of the cottons introduced from Guinea between 1462 and 1466, then a New World cotton must have been established in Africa approximately thirty years before Columbus' first voyage.*[484]

These Amerinds must have either been in contact with indigenous Africans or it was passed down from their African ancestors to them. Here is yet another example of how these first Americans were living and farming:

The first encounters between Europeans and Indians living in what is now Arkansas took place in 1541, when Hernando de Soto's army camped on the eastern side of the Mississippi River. The Spaniards were visited on or about May 22 (on the Julian calendar) by Aquixo, the leader of a large community on the other side of the river. Aquixo arrived with a fleet of 200 canoes outfitted with banners and shields and filled with powerful teams of paddlers and painted warriors wearing colorful feathered regalia. The warriors were organized in ranks, and Aquixo was seated beneath a canopy erected over the stern of a very large canoe. He presented a gift of fish and plum loaves, but the Spaniards, alarmed at the size of Aquixo's force, fired their crossbows and killed five or six Indians. So begins the history of relations between Europeans and Arkansas Indians:

When they crossed over to the western bank of the Mississippi, the Spaniards described the lands they observed as among the most agriculturally productive of any they had seen. Groves of nut and fruit trees and extensive fields of corn separated compact, fortified towns with populations numbering in the thousands. A system of roads and trails connected one town to the next. Many towns contained hundreds of square, thatch-covered houses. Open plazas provided space for public ceremonies. Flat-topped earthen mounds supported

---

483 Riley C. L. et. al (1971). *Man across the Sea: Problems of Pre-Columbian Contact.* Riley Kelley Pennington, Pennington & Rands All rights reserved.

484 Sabo III. (2017). "Native Americans." From *The Encyclopedia of Arkansas History & Culture.*

leaders' residences and temples containing the remains of revered ancestors and finely crafted artifacts used in sacred ceremonies.[485]

Another explorer has written about his experience witnessing ancient American civilizations. When DeSoto made his 1540s A.D. excursion into the American southeast he found that:

Towns in Mississippian culture serving as boundaries to the chiefdom were often fortified with palisade walls, defensive towers, and defensive ditches. The capital town contained the cacique's house, a temple or temples, and other important public buildings. Natives built most of these public buildings atop pyramid shaped, flat-topped, earthen mounds that took several years to construct.[486]

Yet another advanced civilization in ancient Americas was that of the Hohokam. *Hohokam* is a Pima Indian name referring to them as the "Ancient Ones."[487]

Like their Hopi neighbors, rather than entering North America from the northwest:

The Hohokam people occupied the valley and much of southern Arizona from A.D. 1 to 1450....The Hohokam migrated north from what is now Mexico and settled in southern Arizona. There is strong evidence that they maintained ties with communities in Mexico.

485 "Coosa" (2011). National Park Service, U.S. Department of the Interior. Accessed on July 6, 2011 from http://www.nps.gov/chch/historyculture/coosa.htm.

486 Joseph, Frank. (2010). Water Wizards of Ancient Arizona. Atlantis, No. 83, September/October, p. 45.

487 "The Hohokam" (1994-2011) Who were the Hohokam? Accessed on August 9, 2011 from http://www.tempe.gov/museum/Tempe_ history/basics/hohokam.htm.

Trade items such as parrots and copper bells have been traced to their origins in Mexico[488] from in 300 B.C.[489]

This date, however, is suspected to be much too late for the Ancient Ones. This most likely meant the Hohokam were ancestors of the most ancient civilization in Central America, the Olmec. But…why Olmec? A little further down here will be an Olmec connection.

We have some interesting data about these people. They are said to have brought:

Some aspects of the higher civilization of Mesoamerica.... The Hohokam arrived in Arizona with the knowledge of pottery manufacturing and canal irrigation...for a peak population of 50,000 inhabitants who were directly supplied with fresh water...needed for their crops of cotton and corn, as well as several types of beans and squash."[490]

Irrigation was paramount for their crops for this was a desert region, which would otherwise be uninhabited. The most elaborate structure the Hohokam built was "more than a thousand miles of canals...for irrigating their crops. The canals were made of cement-like clay. The bottom of much of the canals were covered with a thick calcareous coat of caliche... which would render it practically watertight."[491] This canal was a ready-made watercraft highway through one thousand miles of territory that was heavily used. It seems that Proto-Americans and Amerinds were farming in different areas all over America.

---

488 Vision Internet. (2018). The Hohokam From: http://www.tempe. gov/ city-hall/community-services/tempe-history-museum/tempe-history/the-hohokam.

489 Royo, A. R. (n.d.) Prehistoric Desert Peoples: The Hohokam. Accessed on August 9, 2011 from http://www.desertusa.com/ind1/du_peo_ hoh. html; Grogginess, L .M., and K. J. Reinland. (1979). "Hohokam Indians of the Tucson Basin." Accessed August 4, 2010 from http://www. uapress.arizona. eduonlinebks/hohokam/chap2htm#agri culture7.

490 Arizona Museum of Natural History. (n.d). Hohokam Canals: Prehistoric Engineering http://arizonaexperience.org/remember/hohokam-canals-prehistoric-engineering.

491 Childress, D. H. (1992). *Lost Cities of North & Central America*, p.297.

These Hohokam people did not wear buckskin outfits. Instead, they wore clothes they made from cotton and lived in long Pueblo-type buildings instead of teepees.

They did play sports back then! They played a ball game called Pokta Pok with a rubber ball, which can be seen today at the "Arizona State Museum in Phoenix. More than 100 Hohokam ball courts have been identified."[492]

"A ball field was also found in the Cahokia complex in Illinois. The rubber ball is evidence of contact and a relationship with the rubber-producing Olmecs in Mexico, just on the other side of the Arizona border."[493] Here we find another Olmec contact with Proto-Americans and Amerinds. Most researchers believed it was a game the Olmecs played, followed by others.

It was complicated. To score a goal, a player could not throw, shoot or kick the ball through a horizontal hoop like in modern basketball. He would have to hit the ball through a vertical hoop with a stick. To make it even harder, the ball player could also strike the ball with his hips. In some other versions, they were allowed to use their forearms. In even other versions they used bats, rackets or even hand-stones.

"Ball courts and the Olmec-Mayan ball game: they were popular even as far north as Arizona and Utah and as far south as Costa Rica and Panama."[494] As you can see the hoops are turned vertically rather than the horizontally the way basketball hoops are. Also notice that the hoops are not at the ends of the court but to the left and right sides of the court.

We have even found a picture of one of the ancient ball courts they used to play the game.

These Hohokam people seemed to be a different culture than the typical Amerinds. There is another game that was played, also invented by the first Americans. This was the game of lacrosse. Originally, the game was a little different, however. They did play with a netted stick, but the ball was made of deerskin stuffed with hair, and the field was a few miles

492 Ibid.

493 Childress, D. H. (2007). *The Mystery of the Olmecs.* (Stelle, IL: Adventures Unlimited), p. 15.

494 Cartwright, M. (9/16/18) The Ball Game of Mesoamerica. https://www. ancient.eu/article/604/the-ball-game-of-mesoamerica/.

long. Many times, it was played to resolve conflicts and prevent outright war.[495] Was that not something to admire? Therefore, lacrosse was also appropriately named, "The Little Brother of War." They also played quite another game that is the origin of lacrosse. It was played with a stick at night, so the ball and the goals were the only source of light on the field. It was called "Pelota Phurepecha," now called "Fire Hockey." The goal was at the end of either side of the field. It was shaped like a soup dish about 5'x 5' wide and it was also on fire.

In one or both games, one of three things happened:

- The losers were sacrificed.
- The winners were sacrificed.
- Both teams were sacrificed.

It is said that was an honor for them to be sacrificed as a result of playing this game.[496]

Were these people more civilized than our so-called "modern" civilizations? More evidence of trade with the people from whom they originated is seen here: "They were connected to an expanding commercial web actively trading with contemporary Mound Builders of the Mississippi Valley, most notably in the form of ceramic containers, and as far south as the Valley of Mexico."[497]

495 Collage Sports Scholarships. "How Lacrosse Began." (2001-2018). The Origins and Roots of Lacrosse. Accessed on September 1, 2009 from http://www.collegesportsscholarships.com/history-lacrosse-rules.htm.

496 DeMain, P. (2011). Lacrosse: Little Brother of War. Accessed on January 5, 2011.http://www.indiancountrynews.com/index. php/tv/Indian-country-tv-com/4411-lacrosse-little-brother-of-war-interview-with-tom-vennum.

497 Joseph, F. (2010). *Advanced Civilizations of Prehistoric America*, p.201.

Fig. 21: Ancient ball court in the Yucatan Peninsula. Accessed August 4, 2016, from http://scoreboredsports.com/tag/chichen-itza/.

Chapter 4

African Structures Left in North American Mounds

Evidence shows dwarfs (short Africans) entered Britain at least by 14,000 years ago.[498] Their ancestors left something for us to see, but there are not many left. In the Americas, strange structures erected in ancient times can be found in 41 states in North America today. They are the "Native American mounds," which have been incorrectly labeled.

By the time the European Pilgrims pushed west into North America, the mounds were covered with dense growth and the Mound Building culture was soon forgotten. When they were asked, "Who built the mounds?" many tribes related they did not know. And a great myth was soon concocted about the builders of these amazing structures.[499]

Diminutive Africans were the primary builders of the mounds in the Americas. They eventually sailed directly from the Old World or pushed North into Scandinavia and went island hopping as the Vikings would later do on their way to the Americas. If they island hopped from Scandinavia, they would have landed in modern day Canada. Once in the Americas, the Africans were reported to have built and lived in subterranean mound chambers as they did in Britain to avoid the cold weather of Canada.

The interior was a megalithic stone slab skeleton frame and roof made with either large stone slabs laid horizontally, or a corbeled-vaulted roof— meaning the slabs were laid progressively overlapping each other toward the center. In the Great Pyramid of Giza, the Grand Gallery hallway is supported by the identical architectural technique. Today, this technique is called a masonry arch (or Pelasgic Arch) and is used over large doors or hallway entrances. Most of the interior, stone and structures inside the mounds was covered by tremendous amounts of earth. There were some areas not covered with earth such as those at the American Stonehenge in New Hampshire (see Fig. 35 in Chapter 5).

---

498 Hayworth, J. Scotland's most ancient home found - at 14,000 years old, *The Scotsman*, Apr. 10, 2009.

499 Little, Gregory. *The Illustrated Encyclopedia*, p. 2.

As mentioned several times in this work, writers have been quoted using the names of the Skraelings and Eskimos interchangeably. The next quote surprisingly speaks of "a race of human beings not unlike the Eskimos" in Iowa.[500] The state of Iowa is just about on the same latitude as Pennsylvania, which is far below Canada and the Arctic:

> *Ages ago, when Iowa was much different in aspect from that which it bore when the whites first saw the country, a race of human beings not unlike the Eskimos inhabited this territory.... On its edge lived a race of short, stout, flat-featured men and women. Of them we know little. We know more of the Mound Builders, who succeeded this short people.... In Iowa, groups of mounds are found. The Mound Builders evidently preferred the banks of the rivers for their works.*[501]

Rivers were used for transportation. The *Illustrated Encyclopedia of Native American Mounds & Earthworks* (2009) map illustrates the mounds in eastern North America. It is immediately noticeable that the majority of mound communities were found along the rivers of eastern America. Here again hinting that the Americas were peopled from the east.

The probability of any tall people arriving in the Americas before the diminutive Africans is miniscule. We see that the small African Skraelings were the first people (the Vikings say they saw) in the extreme Northern part of the Americas, the Arctic and Canada, according to Oleson's (1962) 17-volume set.

Then we see the diminutive African people of Tierra del Fuego—the last remnants of the first Americans—seen at the extreme southern part of the Americas by the British in H.M.S. *Challenger*. (That trip took place during the British voyage there in the 19th century. If one wishes to see exactly how they looked, just find a copy of the first edition of my 2011 book, *The First Americans Were Africans*, and on the cover you shall see a realistic photo of the last generation of the first Americans.) The evidence seems to present a picture of the first Americans populating the Western Hemisphere from the Arctic regions down to Tierra del Fuego.

---

500 Sabin, Edwin L. (1900). *The Making of Iowa: Iowa's Indians.* From the Iowa History Project, Chapter 4.

501 Ibid.

Earlier we saw Cyrus Thomas' statement that Native Americans could not have been Mound Builders.[502] Consequently, the mounds must have been built by some other peoples.

Revisiting the Red Record's statement of the Mongolians' journey into North America, "from Asia into the New World," we see the encounters of the people who were already living there.[503] Speaking of the Mongolians, Childress writes, "they were Mound Builder attackers, and mound destroyers, not mound builders."[504] This data makes it plain that the Mongolians were not the Mound Builders.

Could the Vikings have been the Mound Builders? The Vikings or other Scandinavians are the least of all the groups mentioned to have been the Mound Builders because they arrived far after them all.

"The short people...the race of short, stout, flat-featured men and women" to whom the quote above refers, were in the Americas 100,000 years ago, tens of millennia before their later diminutive ancestors began to build mounds in the Americas. Based on this evidence, it is probable that these "short people" did not predate the "Mound Builders" but were one and the same people.

There are thousands of mound dwellings in the British Isles alone.[505] It seems that these mounds in ancient Britain were built by diminutive Africans as well. These small-statured Africans were renowned for their architectural skills. For example, in the British Isles they built:

Megalithic mound dwellings with, "dry-stone walls and Pelasgic arch" stone ceilings (p. 155); towers (p. 66); cathedrals (p. 72); and forts (p. 73); to their castles (pp. 67, 145) which they would later build. When describing the "Round Tower of Ardmore"...the Rev. J. Ferench...tells us...these "Hottentots" brought stones from the Mountain of Slieve-Grain, some four or five miles distant...without "horse or wheel."[506]

502 Childress, David. H. "Archaeological Coverups." *Nexus New Times Magazine*, Vol 2, No 13, 1992.

503 McCutchen, David. The Red Record.

504 Childress, David. H. *Lost Cities of North & Central America*, p. 376.

505 MacRitchie, David. *The Testimony of Tradition*, p. 114.

506 Ibid., p.71.

The "Hottentots" statement directly refers to diminutive African stonemasons. Their megalithic mound chambers in New England and Canada can still be seen today. There are over forty chambers in Vermont alone.[507] A mound seen in the film version of Tolkien's book trilogy, *The Lord of the Rings*, is very similar to the mound sketch in Fig. 36 (Chapter 5). This authentic mound chamber can still be seen today in Vermont, but a significantly larger number of them exist in New England and Canada. For example, one typical structure is:

> Located on the Nashoba Brook Conservation area.... The chamber, 11' x 6' x 6' (at its highest point), is built into the bottom of a small hillside, mounded over with earth and entered via a 17' tunnel. A stone pillar supports the roof of the L-shaped room. Five 1-ton (or greater) stone slabs averaging 3" thick overlap to comprise the roof... This chamber, the only such in Acton, is one of 350 to 400 similar structures scattered throughout New England, Putnam County, New York, and eastern Canada that still stand. Many more have been destroyed for their stones and to make way for development.[508]

Additionally, some of these stones were carried long distances from quarries as far as four of five miles away. There are stones found in the structures in Canada and New England as large as those in the Forfarshire Fortress in Scotland, which the small-statured Pechts built. There are also similar megalithic structures in Africa, especially in the Nile Valley. There is very little or no evidence that the White Celts built with megalithic stone in the Americas.

As mentioned earlier, in Fell's *Bronze Age America*, African or Eskimo mound chambers were not confined to New England but have been found in Canada as well. There were small underground chambers like the one Fell mentioned in Markand, Canada. Where was Markland?

According to J. L. Burpee's *Atlas* of 1927, Markland was in "New-found-land and Vinland was in Nova Scotia.[509] But Alastair Sweeny, Vice President of Development at Northern Blue Publishing, says, "because of

507 Mid-Atlantic Geomancy, (n.d.). Accessed on November 22, 2009.

508 McElroy, L. "Action [Acton] Historical Stone Chamber" March 27, 2006. Accessed May, 2, 2014.

509 Burpee, J. L. (1927). "A Historical Atlas of Canada." Montreal: Thomas Nelson and Sons Limited.

recent archaeological discoveries" his map puts Markland in Nova Scotia and Vinland in the Cape Cod area.[510]

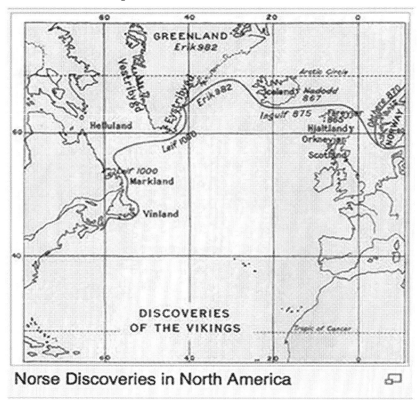

Norse Discoveries in North America

Fig. 22: Norse map to America. *Courtesy of Alastair Sweeny Northern Blue Publishing*

Another small structure was found in North Salem, New Hampshire, at America's Stonehenge complex. Dated to 4000 years ago, it is a beehive-shaped structure built out of stone without mortar. As in most of these structures, it has a large stone lintel above the entrance that leads down a cramped corridor to the main room. One of these beehive structures had a "75-ton anchor stone"[511] supporting it. Who was building in North America with stones weighing 75 tons back then? There is no record of Amerinds building on such a colossal scale in North America.

Though many if not most of the chambers date back to that pre-Columbian period, others do not fit the colonial mold. The Pearson

510 Burpee, J. L. 2010. Email.

511 Gage, M. E., and J. E. Gage. (2006). "America's Stonehenge." Accessed December 21, 2009. http://www.stonestructures.org/html/solar_align.

Chamber at Upton, Massachusetts, for example is a 4-foot, 6-inch tall, the height of most dwarfs...3-foot wide stone corridor that runs for 20 feet into the side of a sloping hill. According to researchers J. W. Mavor Jr. and B. E. Dix, five large adjacent boulders, each weighing 30 to 40 tons, form a portion of one of the walls. The chamber itself is a large stone "beehive," architecturally like some in Ireland and Scotland. Capped with a flat lentil, this beehive chamber itself rises 10 feet in nearly a corbelled vaulted form.[512]

Some mound structures have only one room with the whole structure shaped like a large Eskimo Igloo. Others have one main room with a few antechambers off the centered larger room. The corridors leading to the rooms are usually very small and difficult to enter. "Others point out that the structures are best suited for a race of people not more than three feet tall,"[513] especially the doorways. Enter the diminutive Africans, the Skraelings. This American Stonehenge complex, with its conservative "4000" year date, is still 300 years older than Fell's mysterious Celtic King who supposedly visited America in 1700 B.C.

The Mound Builders did not just build small structures. There are also large structures like the one in Hopedale, Labrador (southeastern Canada), which "more than one hundred persons...inhabited."[514] There is a sketch of a subterranean chamber mound in Upton Massachusetts, in Childress' (1992) book. From the top and side view it was shaped exactly like an Eskimo igloo, but it was built with stone instead of ice. The chamber is crowned with another corbel-vaulted ceiling built with overlapping stones.

The entrance tunnel is 14 feet long, three feet wide and four feet six inches high, exactly like an igloo entrance. The diameter of the chamber is eleven feet around and the highest point of the vaulted ceiling seems to be about ten feet high.[515]

Tolkien based his hobbit people on real-life diminutive Africans, who lived in mound-homes. These small Africans built homes like the half-underground homes of the hobbits in the book. "The beginning of the book explains that the hobbit lived in 'a hole in the ground...in the

512 Joseph, Frank. *Advanced Civilizations of Prehistoric America.*

513 Childress, David H. *Lost Cities of North & Central America*, p. 442.

514 MacRitchie, David. *The Testimony of Tradition*, p. 155.

515 Childress, David H. *Lost Cities of North & Central America*, p. 462.

Shire.'"[516] The real mound dwellings are found in chronological succession, in Africa, Europe, Greenland, Canada, Northeastern America, Virginia, West Virginia and Ohio.

The major difference between these two types of mound homes is that the entrance was very small. Sometimes, the entrance was two feet by two feet, which is too small and inconvenient for a normal-sized man to use as the only entrance. A diminutive person, however, could enter very easily. As stated earlier, the center chambers of some of the structures had corbeled-vaulted ceilings identical—on a smaller scale—to the one at the Great Pyramid of Giza in Egypt. As in the Great Pyramid, this type of engineered architecture was designed to support a tremendous amount of weight. These American mound structures in the northeast were covered with a large amount of earth in most cases.

The British chambers were not the only mounds with arched ceilings, "In one of the mounds opened in the Ohio Valley, two chambers were found...with arched ceilings precisely like those in Central America, even to the overlapping stones."[517] This unusual architectural style links the structures in America to those from the British Isles down to the Nile Valley.

Why would people build mound homes to begin with? The answer is purely speculative, but sound. When Blacks left Africa for Europe and Asia, the weather was far cooler than they were used to. Building an earthen structure provided effective and efficient insulation. The long entrance tunnel kept the cold from entering the dwelling. The opposite is true for the interior's heat loss in the winter. Then, in the summer, the cool of the night air remains throughout the heat of the day.

The aerodynamic dome shape would easily withstand the high winds of a tornado or hurricane. The harder the wind blows, the more the shape of the dome holds it down. The tiny tunnel entrance was also a safety factor, providing protection from large wild beasts, as well as human predators. Enemies could not file in side by side en masse; they would have to crawl in one by one allowing their progression to be stopped much easier.

---

516 Tolkien, J. R. R. (1937). *The Hobbit.*

517 Baldwin, J. D. (1871). *Ancient America and the Mound Builders* (Pennsylavania, Kissinger Publishing, republished 2009), pp. 70-71; Baldwin, John D. (1871). *ANCIENT AMERICA in Notes on American Archaeology* (Harper & Brothers Publishers).

There are more mound sites along the Mississippi and Ohio Rivers than anywhere else in North America.[518] This is because they used the rivers as their expressways...especially the Ohio and Mississippi Rivers. Baldwin (1871) stated that there were 500 mounds in Rose County, Ohio, alone at the time he wrote his book.[519]

Cyrus Thomas reported that they had "found 100,000 mound sites, many with complexes containing 2 to 10 mounds"[520] each, in North America. Dr. Gregory Little, the author of *The Illustrated Encyclopedia of Native American Mounds & Earthworks* (2009), wrote that "After visiting several thousand mounds and reviewing the literature, I am fairly certain over 1,000,000 mounds once existed, and perhaps over 100,000 still exist."[521]

There are several types of pre-Columbus mounds built in North America: burial mounds; subterranean mound dwellings; mega mounds; and animal-shaped mounds. "Most are heaped burial mounds or 'effigy' mounds built in the shape of animals."[522] As mentioned above, however, there are subterranean mound chambers still in existence. They are mostly found in Europe and the northeastern areas of North America.

Looking toward the South, to a town called Epps in West Carroll Parish, Louisiana, there is a massive mound site called Poverty Point that contains several mounds. One huge mound there, that Little found, is dated "as early as 3800 B.C."[523] 800 years before the Mongolian Asian invasion of North America. At the southern end of the continent, Louisiana borders the Gulf of Mexico.

However, the oldest mounds found in North America are not found at Poverty Point, Louisiana. There may be even older mounds off the southeastern Florida coast, under water. They appear at Horrs

---

518 Little, Gregory, (2009). *The Illustrated Encyclopedia*, p. 3.

519 Baldwin, J. D. *Ancient America and the Mound Builders*, pp. 24.

520 Little, Gregory, (2009). *The Illustrated Encyclopedia*, p. 2.

521 Ibid.

522 Bear, David. Ohio earthen embankments show evidence of sophisticated ancient culture. *Pittsburgh Post-Gazette*, May 2006.

523 Little, Gregory, *The Illustrated Encyclopedia*, p.107.

Island—now Marco Island—in Southwestern Florida, off the Gulf Coast. These mounds have been carbon dated and "could be as old as 4380 B.C." That 4380 B.C. date is 1780 years before the Mongolians entered the Americas, so they could not have built the first mounds in the Americans nor possibly any others. They were Mound Builder attackers, and mound destroyers, not mound builders.[524]

Additionally, it seems that in this case, that the oldest mounds are on the southeastern side of North America. Archaeologists suspect an Olmec influence at Poverty Point. It is just across the Gulf of Mexico from the Olmec capital. Some of the unique artifacts found at Poverty Point are like the artifacts found farther south at Olmec sites along the Gulf in Mexico. The people at Poverty Point engaged in extensive trading. Materials from Lake Michigan, Lake Superior, Ohio and North Carolina have been excavated from the site.[525] Some mound sites were laid out scientifically, displaying the presence of a sophisticated culture.

A reproduction of the Marco Island mounds just off the southwestern Florida coast makes it apparent they were purposely laid out mathematically in "geometric embankments deliberately shaped."[526] Similarly, in Central Florida near Lake Okeechobee the "Ortona Indian Mounds located north of La Belle, Florida...are 17 mounds and distinctive, geometric earthworks."[527] Most of the mounds in Ohio have not been measured, except for the earthworks at the Hopewell site. The mounds at Marco Island, Central Florida and Ohio were laid out mathematically in geometric forms. "The Hopewell site was utilized in the period between 500 B.C. to A.D. 500."[528]

Clearly, North America's so-called Indian Mounds were not crude poles of dirt heaped up by primitive savages. They were instead examples of applied geometry, materials handling, advance planning, design, an organized workforce and construction skills...public works engineers, astronomers and metal-smiths, the land's first farmers and potters. Note workforce and construction skills...public works

---

524 Childress, David H. *Lost Cities of North & Central America*, p. 366.

525 Little, Gregory, *The Illustrated Encyclopedia*, p.108.

526 Ibid., p.32.

527 Ibid., p.33.

528 Ibid., p.182.

engineers, astronomers and metal-smiths, the land's first farmers and potters.[529]

There are no known Amerind structures that are laid out using geometry or astronomy. Africans, on the other hand, are on record building mounds in ancient times found from along the Niger River to mounds south of Lake Chad: "The builders of the mounds in the United States were people from West Africa,[530] across the Straits of Gibraltar to Portugal, to Northern Europe, and to the Americas. North American mounds are linked to Africa in several ways. The first link is that "…the builders of the mounds in the United States were people from West Africa."[531] The second is that author Leo Wiener says that, "Similar mounds were used for the protection of Mandingo trading posts."[532] Tracing the mounds and Mound Builders is evidenced based.

Fig. 23: Portuguese Mound and Dolmen. *Courtesy of Alex Whitaker; Ancient-wisdom.co.uk.*

529 Joseph, Frank. *Advanced Civilizations of Prehistoric America.*

530 Connah, Graham. (1987). African Civilizations: *An Archaeological Perspective* (Cambridge University Press).

531 Gronerborn, Dettlef. (1998). Archaeological and Ethnohistorical Investigation Along the Southern Fringes of Lake Chad 1993-1996. *African Archaeological Review* Vol 15, No 4.

532 Winters, Clyde, *Atlantis in Mexico.*

The Celts

Let us next confirm the African connection to Canada through the architecture. There are small mound chambers all over eastern Canada and New England—as seen above—that were built with megalithic stone before Columbus or the Vikings visited America.

In his first book, *America B.C.* (1976), Dr. Barry Fell opens his book to Chapter One, claiming that Celtic mariners left Spain and Portugal and passed through the Canary Islands in 1000 B.C. These Celts left Europe "to discover, and then to colonize, North America. They built villages and temples and raised Druids' circles"[533] in New Hampshire and Vermont. Then in his second book, *Bronze Age America* (1982), Fell claims that 700 years earlier than the Celts:

> *A Royal Visitor in 1700 B.C....a Nordic king named Woden-lithi, sailed across the Atlantic and entered the St. Lawrence River. He reached the neighborhood of where Toronto now stands and remained in Canada for five months. He left colonists with essentials, then he sailed back to Scandinavia and disappears.*[534]

Disappears? Other than the claims of inscriptions on rocks that someone made, the king, his Norse colonists, the Celts (and any solid evidence of their presence in the Americas) have mysteriously all "disappeared" as the Nordic King "disappeared...no evidence, no argument!"[535] Speaking of Norse colonists, "the only scientifically authenticated remains ever found in America of the Vikings were on the northern tip of Newfoundland Island. around 1000 A.D."[536] Not in 1000 B.C.

Frank Joseph says, "The early Adena stone mounds do not show themselves in the Keltic sphere of influence."[537] In plain words, the mounds were not under the Nordic king's control for he was not responsible for building them. Additionally, "Not one example of the Celts' most

---

533 Van Sertima, Ivan. "They Came Before Columbus."

534 Fell, Barry. *America B.C.: Ancient Settlers in the New World*, pp. 5-7.

535 Ibid., pp. 5-7.

536 Fell, Barry. *Bronze Age America* (Massachusetts, Little Brown & Company, 1982), p. 36.

537 Conner, William D. *Iron Age America Before Columbus*, pp. 33-34.

iconographic artifact—the torque—had been found in prehistoric America. The torque was a ornament of twisted precious or semiprecious metal worn around the wrist or neck."[538]

Where is Fell's evidence of Europeans building anything in the Americas in 1700 or 1000 B.C.? A French eyewitness, Jacques Cartier, wrote that when he "explored the St. Lawrence River region in the middle of the sixteenth century, he met no Vikings or Celts, and he also saw no traces of their culture."[539] On the other hand, there is a significant trail of evidence that the first Americans left behind, namely: epigraphy (writing on rocks), rock sculptures, artifacts, megalithic mound chambers, dolmen, stone circles, and phallic monoliths in New England and Canada. Winters wrote in the foreword of this book:

Evidence shows that the followers of the Mali expedition wrote in the Manding writing system to read—which is understood by using the Vai script—the Mande inscriptions, the Malians left in the Americas.[540]

In other words:

These were Mande inscriptions left by the Mande of Africa that appear from Northern America to Mexico. Luke [as seen in Van Sertima, 1985] appropriately wrote that Fell (1982) deals with a whole complex of cultural artifacts, which bear an unmistakable African imprint, yet he tries desperately to assign the entire assemblage, lock-stock-and-barrel, to mythological Scandinavians or "Celt-Iberians."[541]

Europeans have built the giant technological world we live in today. However, some people try to attribute all great works and thoughts exclusively to Europeans. The Asian Chinese had a time of greatness as the Caucasians have today. There was, however, also a time when Africans had their period of brilliance as well. All past great civilizations have made some positive contributions to the world. But to try to exclusively attribute all greatness to one group is not logical.

---

538 Joseph, Frank. *Advanced Civilizations of Prehistoric America*, p. 81.

539 Ibid.

540 Mallery, Arlington H., *Lost America*.

541 Haynes, Jr. C. V. "Geofacts and Fancy." Natural History Magazine, (February 1988) pp.4-12. http://hdl.handle.net/2246/6494.

The Celts were originally Black people. Ephorus (c. 405 B.C.) claimed that the Celts were Blacks or Ethiopians.[542] The Celts continued to be recognized as Blacks by Tacitus, who wrote about the Black Celts and Picts in 80 A.D. The Celts on the mainland of Europe were called Iberians from Spain or Silures.[543]

> Though the original Celts were Black, overtime their name was **stolen by Europeans**. Father O'Growney has discussed the history of the Celts. He makes it clear that the original Celts were the Iberians. The Iberians were probably conquered by the Ligurians. It is suggested that the Ligurians may be represented by the modern Basque of Spain. The Ligurians took the name Celt. Then, the Ligurians/Celts were conquered by the Gaulish speaking people.[544]

Dr. Clyde Winters arranged the previous paragraph, and is a brilliant teacher, writer and historian. He has shown that there is genetic and linguistic evidence that proves that the Celts were Black or African people. An examination of the language spoken by the Basque has a Niger-Congo substratum. C. J. K. Cambell-Dunn has found a Niger-Congo substratum in Basque.[545]

> Dr. Cambell-Dunn found that the Niger-Congo and Basque languages share personal pronouns, numerals and vocabulary items. There is also genetic evidence linking the Basque and Niger-Congo speakers. Both groups share the genetic evidence of: SRY10831.1, YAP, M2, M173(xR1a, R1b3), E3*-P2, E3b2-M81. This linguistic and genetic evidence supports the African origin of the Celts. This is made clear by the Oseberg 8th-century Vikings, on the Norway Sledge Carving of the Black seafarers that populated the region at this time. It is clear from this carving that the 8th-century Vikings were different from the Blond, big bodied folk of Viking legends.[546]

---

542 Van Sertima, Ivan. *African Presence in Early Europe*, p. 232.

543 Haynes, Cyrus V., *Geofacts and Fancy*.

544 Ibid., pp. 4-12.

545 Ibid., pp. 4-12.

546 Ibid., pp. 4-12.

So, we now have genetic and linguistic evidence that the Celts or Kelts were a Black African people. Now that the sensationalism of the Celts is out of the way let us take a closer look as to where they began.

"Celts" appears to be a local name for Phoenician settlers of Western Europe who by nature of heritage were Canaanites and therefore sons of Ham, Semetic and Hebrew, all minorities; and centuries later were called Moors. They are locally known as Celts of Gaul, Celts of ancient Briton, Romantic Celts, Celts of Germany, France, the Netherlands and so on.[547]

---

547 Ibid., pp. 4-12.

Chapter 5

African Structures in Central and South America

Before beginning this chapter on specific structures in Central America, let us look at some non-specific structures. It is well-known that Brazil has the largest population of Black people outside Africa and India. It is a myth and a mathematical impossibility that all, or even most Brazilian Africans came over on slave ships, during the Transatlantic Slave Trade.

"Slavery in the North America lasted from 1619 to 1865. An estimate of the amount of Africans brought to the American colonies is 597,000"[548] However, "according to conservative estimates by archaeologists, Folsom & Folsom, there were **over 57 million people already living in the Americas when Columbus arrived**" in **1492**.[549] If that is true, how did all the Africans (already in the Americas in 1492) arrive there before Columbus? Secondly, since there are three Americas—North, Central, and South—one-third of 57 million is 19 million. With all things being equal, how could 19 million Africans be in North America when Columbus and later the Dutch slavers arrived?

The "Why" they wish for us to believe, is that Africans were all brought over on slave ships. This is a question that inevitably leads to politics and religion, which are two subjects that this author does not discuss. As mentioned earlier, Africans have been coming to the Americas for at least 250,000 years, and we are talking millions of them. Some of the same structures they built in North America were first built in South America. Why? Because the first Americans landed in South America, long before entering North America.

One series of books that is highly recommended by this author is *When The World Was Black*, by Dr. Sujan Dass. In it, the author says Francisco de Orellano was one of the Spanish explorers, who in 1542 explored the Amazon Basin and the Rio Negro. He found a complex of cities, villages

---

548 Miller, Randall, and John Smith. (eds). *Dictionary of Afro-American Slavery* (Praeger, 1988), p. 678.

549 Little, Greg. (2009). *The Illustrated Encyclopedia*, p. 2.

and farms. The villages were described to be just as large, which involved a long-range trade with other networks of villages.

The Amazon was highly populated then. What Orellano found was nothing compared to the more than 100 different sites across the Amazon. Evidence that was uncovered and studied by scientists, shows that earlier civilizations were much further advanced, more broadly connected, and much more densely populated than the Spanish thought they would be. They were very surprised.

Also, in Brazil, in the Xingu Basin, was one village with a very large plaza, canals, roads, and causeways. They had bridges that joined two large prehistoric collections of villages. Each cluster of villages had many large towns surrounded by walls. Each cluster seemed to be able to house approximately 50,000 people. Roads were jutting out in four of the cardinal directions. These roads connected to smaller satellite villages, of which many had built agricultural sites and fish ponds.

Believe it or not, these ancient localities were close to ten times the size that local villages in that area are today! Anthropologist Michael Heckenburger and a team of archeologists unearthed 28 villages, towns and hamlets that covered 7700 square miles of land that is now covered by forests. That is a larger area than the state of Connecticut today! Heckenburger even expresses, in his writings, that these cities' fractal organization contained planning that was superior to that of medieval Europe!

These people were also mound builders, who not surprisingly, built earthen mounds along their miles of canals constructed for "travel and fish farming." It comes as no surprise that all of these mounds were built for the same reason: to avoid floods, which were a problem along the Niger River for their African ancestors. Further, it was early in the 1900s that Thomas Griffith Taylor, a British anthropologist, and Joseph Deniker, a French anthropologist studied the frizzy or wavy hair of the indigenous people of the Xingu River, and their Arawak neighbors. They could be related to our first Americans from Africa. These two anthropologists were not alone. Several other first explorers commented on seeing so-called "Negroes" near the Central and South American coasts: Enter—the Olmecs.

Soon after their arrival in the 12th century A.D., the Olmecs began to infiltrate the valley of Mexico.

ORIGINAL: OLMECS-MAYANS-AZTECS

"The Olmecs"

<Any Doubts?
He's African?

Dred Locks
Behind Head>

Are they different, similar, or just the same folks at different periods?

Fig. 24: Olmecs-Mayans-Toltec-Aztecs Constructed. "A picture is worth 1000 words."

1. Top Left Photo: Stone Face. www.grahamhancock.com; filename: p1-sml.jpg
2. Top Right Photo: Stone Head Locks. www.crystalinks.com; filename: olmecbraids.jpg
3. Middle Left Photo: Renovated Olmec Art. 2012.caliwali.com/map/htm#2
4. Middle Right Photo: Black Mayans; painted by Tod B. Williams.
5. Bottom Photo: Last Full-Blooded Mayans. https://www.tineye.com/

The Olmecs were the Mother Culture of Central America and predated the Mayans and Aztecs. The Olmecs were a conglomeration of three different peoples, when they stumbled upon Teotihuacan. Michael D. Coe is an American archaeologist, anthropologist, epigrapher and author.

Coe says that today it is generally accepted that all later civilizations in Mesoamerica ultimately rest on an Olmec base:

> Coe further stated **the Olmecs not only influenced the Mayans, but they actually <u>were</u> the early Mayans!** *Some even see Olmec influence in the art of Peru's Chavin civilization, which developed later – 1000 (meaning 1000 B.C.).*[550]

To put it bluntly, most of the arts that are attributed to the Mayans have come from the loins of the Olmecs: spiritual concepts, calendars, architecture, art forms, and even their language. The first of the three groups in Central America were the Paleoamericans—originally Africans described by Dr. Imhotep as the "Grandmother Culture"—the short people—whose descendants were still in Central America when the Mande, the second group arrived. The Mande brought different skills and religious beliefs and practices from Africa. The third group to arrive was the Amerinds, who were a blend of Africans and Asians. They were the ones given the name "Red-Skins" as seen on cowboy shows.

The ancient African geometrical city, Teotihuacan, in Central America had fallen into ruins by the time the Aztecs arrived. Nevertheless, the Aztecs had preserved distinct traditions concerning it.[551]

Back to the pyramids at Teotihuaco, Mexico. The Pyramid of the Sun, which is dated at 200 A.D.[552] This date is very, very controversial. It could possibly be too late for the construction of this and other large step pyramids in the Americas. The Great Giza Pyramid of Egypt and Teotihuacan's Pyramid of the Sun's base perimeter measurements are almost the same, but the Giza pyramid is much taller.

> *Professor Michael D. Coe of Yale University has pointed out that the Pyramid of the Moon and the Pyramid of the Sun are both "explicitly named in old legends" and concludes: "there was no reason to doubt that they were dedicated to those divinities." The same names were <u>adopted by the Aztecs</u> when they stumbled upon Teotihuacan soon after they had begun to infiltrate the Valley of Mexico in the twelfth*

---

550 Hancock, Graham, and Santha Faiia. *Heaven's Mirror*, p. 14.

551 Ibid.

552 Department of the Arts of Africa, Oceania, and the Americas. "Teotihuacan: Pyramids of the Sun and the Moon." In Heilbrunn Timeline of Art History. New York: The Metropolitan Museum of Art, 2000.

century A.D. The giant geometrical city, already very ancient, had by then fallen into ruins.[553]

1. This Teotihuacan complex contains a carving that represents the dwarf Egyptian god Bes, with his tongue sticking out of his mouth. This site is found 224 miles southeast of Mexico in Palenque (then Olmec territory), where there is the Temple of the Sun. Inside this temple is a dwarf—the god Bes. So it was Bes, and Nubians/or Egyptians who actually built this temple. There is a *relief depicting Chan Balum and his father, the famous Pacal* at those pyramids.[554]

2. *Votan, showing two crossed arrows and a symbolic shield hovering between them. There is a face on the shield with his tongue out in Bes/Kali fashion.*[555]

There are four more images of "the tongue out of the mouth."

3. Face of the Nubian god Bes with his tongue out is carved into an ivory headrest (an Egyptian pillow) which is in the Egyptian Museum Cairo today (see Fig. 25). It was made to protect the head of a deceased person in the afterlife. In ancient Egypt small headrests could also protect the person's head while sleeping. They are still used in some parts of Africa to enable circulation of air around the person's head on a hot summer night. A soft cushion or pillow would make it more comfortable for the ancient sleepers.[556]

4. Another illustration is found 224 miles southeast of Mexico City in Palenque, where there is the Temple of the Sun. Inside this temple is a relief depicting Chan Balum and his father, the famous Pacal Votan. There is a face on the shield with his tongue out in Bes/Kali fashion.[557]

---

553 Hancock, Graham, and Faiia, Santha. *Heaven's Mirror.*

554 "Welcome to Palenque Park, Tours, Lodging and Transportation." Welcome to Palenque. ecotourism-adventure. Accessed April 27, 2020. http://palenquepark.com/#!/walkpalenque.

555 Defenestrate, Orryelle. "Magic Mushrooms and Mayan Temples in Mexico." (2000). Accessed February 15, 2010.

556 Carr, Karen. (2015). Who was the Egyptian god Bes? Accessed: May 22, 2015.

557 Defenestrate, Orryelle. "Magic Mushrooms & Mayan Temples in Mexico."

Notice the detailed woodwork: the hair design on the back of his head; see how the first string of the neck support is just a bit lower than the others to adjust for the shape and slant of the neck to comfort; see the finely designed duck heads; notice the detail of the Black Gods' people of New Zealand.[558] New Zealand, Samoa and Hawaii, all sticking out their tongues.[559]

5. On any so-called "Mayan" calendar, there is a picture of a deity with his tongue out. However, it was the Olmecs who first brought this calendar to Central America.[560] The Mayans later adopted it.

6. This is an authentic "*Australian War Dance with Tongue stuck out by the Mâori!*" It smacks of Egyptian/African roots.

Just see what the god Bes is doing below:

Fig. 25: Egyptian God Bes' Headrest. © *Sandro Vannini/Corbis*.

558 Phillips, Charles. (2002). *The Complete Illustrated History: Aztec and Maya* (New York, Annes Pub. Ltd.), p. 74.

559 Krokk. "Haka Maori Australian War Dance" (2007), New Zealand.

560 "The Psychology of Satan and the Unfathomable Mind of God." (n.d.). Explaining the Meaning of Sticking Out the Tongue https:// theunfathomablemindofgod.wordpress. com/2014/05/31/explaining-the-meaning-of-sticking-out-the-tongue/

Then see how this tradition has carried on from its Egyptian/African roots:

Fig. 26: New Zealand's Maori in the "Haka Championships." *Source: Smale, A. & Pietrasik 2/9/04 aka championships in New Zealand. The Guardian. https://www.theguardian.com/travel/gallery/2009/feb/18/haka-championships-new-zealand-travel.*

This custom is also known in Egypt, Mexico two times (numbers 1 and 2 above), then in Australia, New Zealand, Samoa and Hawaii. This "facial expression" seems to express some type of aggression.

Is this a different meaning than is seen by the god Bes? As stated just above, is this fellow's face that is shown with the tongue out really a sign of aggression? No, it is not. In this case, it is not a war dance, it is being done just before a sport is being played that is used to intimidate their opponents. It is a "ceremonial challenge dance" done just in front of the opposing team as they begin their "pre-game warm-up" exercises. But unlike the pre-game warm-up exercises done in the USA to prepare for a sport. This very interesting ancient dance they are duplicating was done just before battle!

But luckily, during this very emotional physical dance, no one is killed (smile). What they are doing is psychologically challenging the other team with loud yells, stomping their feet vigorously on the ground while making very loud rhythmical grunts and yells at their opponents. This, my friends, is called the "Haka Dance," obviously done to intimidate anyone who is around!

186

New Zealand teams perform this dance before international matches around the world, and it has made the Haka dance more popular all around the world. This tradition started in the 1888–1889 New Zealand football team and has been continued by the New Zealand rugby team today [and I quote] of "all Blacks" since 1905.[561] What a sight to see!

Central America's Huge Pyramids and Temples

The Maya, during their Pre-Classic period, built pyramids over the top covering of the older Olmec pyramids to **disguise the Olmec origin of the pyramids**.[562]

It was the (Manding) Olmecs who brought the pyramid building, religious technology and writing to the Mayans[563] from Africa in the beginning. The evidence shows that **it did not originate** from the Mayans.

The largest pyramid at Teotihuacao is 31 miles northeast of Mexico City. It is the step pyramid complex at Teotihuacan, Mexico, containing the Pyramids of the Sun and the Moon. It stands 65.5 meters high; its base is 220x230 meters, and its total volume is 41, 841, 817 cubic meters. It is located about 30 miles northeast of Mexico City.

However, the largest pyramid in the Americas is the Great Pyramid of Cholula, located in southeast Mexico in the state of Puebla, adjacent to the Olmec heartland of Veracruz and Tabasco. The Cholula Pyramid stands 55 meters high, but its base is 450x450 meters, and its volume is 88, 121, 125 cubic meters—more than twice that of the pyramid at Teotihuacao.

Black Gods of Ancient Central America

The major Black god was Quetzalcoatl. The Mayan gods Xaman and Ekchuah are depicted in the Codex Troano.[564] Sahagun tells us that

561 Aualiitia, Tahlea. "Rugby World Cup: They're Not All Called 'Haka' — the Differences between Pacific War Dances." *ABC News.* September 1, 2019. https://www.abc.net.au/news/2019-09-01/rugby-world-cup-haka-pacific-war-dances-dwayne-the-rock-johnson/11456828.

562 Winters, Clyde. *African Empires in Ancient America*, p.27.

563 Winters, Clyde. *Atlantis in Mexico.*

564 Wiener, Leo. (1921). *Africa and the Discovery of America* Vol.3. (U.K., A Traffic Output Publication), p. 258.

Ekchuah was also the god of the Amanteca. The Nahuatl term Amanteca, was probably the name of the Mandinka or Mandinga people who were the foundation of the Olmec people.[565] "The gods in the Maya and Aztec manuscript illustrated as blacks, include Kulkulkan, Ek Chuan,"[566] Chuai, Zac Cimi and nine other dark deities lived.[567]

From: Wikipedia--https://en.wikipedia.org/wiki/Homo,

Fig. 27: Aztec God Ixlilton, "The Little Black One."

Here is another example of Ancient Mexico's Black gods, this time, Ixlilton. He was the god of medicine and healing. You can see his little bag of medicinal herbs and instruments in a case with wheels just in front of him. Of course, that means he was a pretty important and intelligent god if he was a medicine man. The evidence that he was of African heritage can be seen in his wide, fleshy nose, and his lips are also large and fleshy. His entire nose, lips and jaw protrude out in front of his forehead, which is seen in African physiognomy.

Similarities across early American and African religions also indicate significant cross-cultural contact. Again, the Mayans, Aztecs and Incas all were worshipping black gods and the surviving portraits of the black deities are revealing. For instance, ancient portraits of the Quetzalcoatl, a messiah serpent god, and Ek-ahua, the god of war, are unquestionably Negro, with very dark skin and wooly hair. Why would Native Americans

565 Winters, Clyde. *Atlantis in Mexico*, p. 5.

566 Wiener, Leo. *Africa and the Discovery of America*, pp. 269-271.

567 "Mayan Foundation Laakee." yucatanadventure. Accessed February 16, 2016. http://www.yucatanadventure.com.mxmaya-gods.htm.

venerate images so unmistakably African if they had never seen them before? Numerous wall paintings in caves in Juxtlahuaca depict the famous ancient Egyptian "opening of the mouth" and cross libation rituals. All these religious similarities are too large and occur far too often to be mere coincidences.

But over time, racists have erased the Aztec god Quetzalcoatl's original dark skin color and have now painted his skin color to appear as a White man. This is nothing new as someone has also begun to portray the Ancient Egyptians and Hannibal as White too. If we don't watch out, before you know it, the history books could start portraying the boxer Jack Johnson, the Harlem Globe Trotters and Martin Luther King as White fellas.

Yes, before the Aztecs, the Maya also had Black gods. Due to contributions of Africans to Mesoamerican civilization, many of the Mayan gods and several kings were depicted as Black Africans: Fish Fin, Itzamnnj B'alam II, Quirigua Izabel, K'inich Ahkal Mo'Naab III, K'inich Tatb'u Slull III, K'inich Janaab 'Pakal II, Yaxuun B'alam IV, Chaan Muan.[568] There are also several vases in existence that have pictures of blue-black Mayan rulers or gods. The list of the Negroid Mayan gods and Kings fall in line with what this book is all about.

Were the First Mayans, Olmecs?

Far beyond pictures of Black Mayans on vases, there are the tremendous Bonampak murals, which can be found in The Temple of the Murals in the Mexican state of Chiapas. They are seen in a small, three-room temple on the step pyramid. These marvelously colored pictures are displayed about two-thirds of actual life size of an average man. Most of the Mayans portrayed in "Room 1" were painted with a chocolate-to-black skin color by the first Mayans.

The ancient Mayan site of Bonampak, located within the deep tropical rainforest of Chiapas, Mexico, is home to the most complete and important mural program of the ancient Americas. These three murals first came to modern attention in 1946, when Lacandon Maya, who lived in the region, showed photographer Giles Healey what they had not previously shown to any outsider, a small temple with murals creating a gallery of art.[569]

568 Winters, Clyde. *Ancient African Writing Systems and Knowledge.*

569 The Maya Murals of Bonampak: Windows on an Ancient Culture (n.d.) Accessed: January 13, 2017.

Jim Budd is a Caucasian writer for *The Herald Mexico*, a daily newspaper published in Mexico City, who does not see color. Mr. Budd calls the Bonampak Mural Pyramid a well-deserved "Sistine Chapel of the Americas." On the cover of this book, see for yourself what the first Mayans were telling the world inside the painting. In "First Civilization," another Caucasian, Michael D. Coe, from Yale University, makes this case even clearer in his *America's First Civilization: Discovering the Olmec*. The Olmec influence is the "key" to a study of the pyramids in Mesoamerica.

Fig. 28: Bonampak Mural Pyramid containing the Mural. *Public Domain at Wikipedia*

It is generally accepted that all later civilizations in Mesoamerica ultimately rest on an Olmec base. However, "**Coe goes further and says that the Olmecs not only influenced the Mayans, but they actually <u>were</u> the early Mayans.**"[570] Coe was stating in words, what Fig. 24 shows pictorially. It should now be very clear to the reader that:

There was a connection between the Maya and the Olmecs. This is supported by the evidence from the Pre-classic Maya sites of Olmec Jaguar pyramids and inscriptions. The Olmec taught the Maya architecture and all the related sciences. Moreover, throughout Mayan history, depicted in its monuments and art, we see the presence of Africans. ***The figurines found at the sight of the Ocos illustrate***

---

570 Coe, Michael. (1968). *America's First Civilization. Discovering the Olmec*. American Heritage Association/Smithsonian.

quite clearly, and in color that the earliest Mayans were Africans.
They used a ceramic type at Ocos that was used by other African
communities in Mexico between 850 and 155 B.C. The presence of
Africans at early Mayan sites may explain the presence of African
words (e.g., Manding) appearing in the Mayan languages.[571]

Fig. 29: Bonampak Mural: The Musicians. *Public Domain, Wikipedia.*

Adding to that statement, the dark-skinned people wearing long African locks pictured inside the Bonampak Pyramid, featured on the back cover of this book, depict the very first Mayans, as Michael Coe suspected.

But this is not all, Coe goes on to explain that in Mexico:

During the Pre-classic period, the Maya, with assistance from African Mexicans, developed mathematics, non-telescopic astronomy and calendrical calculations more advanced than any other Mesoamerican civilization <u>except</u> for the Olmec. The Mayan cities, Copan, Tikal, and Peten, had thousands of inhabitants and were built on the foundations first constructed by the Olmec and other African groups settled in Mexico when the Maya arrived on the scene.[572] *The Lacandon people are descendants of the Yucatan Maya, who fled from the Spanish. They are shorter and of a darker complexion than other native people in the area, revealing their Anu/ Twa heritage.*

571 Winters, Clyde. *African Empires in Ancient America*, p. 14.

572 Van Sertima, Ivan. *African Presence in Early America*, p. 148.

In 1975, geneticist Alfonzo Garay identified the gene for malaria resistance (which also produces sickle cells, an African trait) among the Lacandon; a 10,000-year old gene "usually found only in the blood of Black people."[573] Furthermore, Chapas Mexico is adjacent to Veracruz and Tabasco, Mexico, where many Olmec heads were found. So, Mexico's "Sistine Chapel" temple was found in the heart of ancient Olmec territory. Does this fact give us a hint as to who may have built it?

Fig. 30: Bonampak Mural: Diplomats. *Public Domain.*

It can now be seen that the Mayans inherited their short height and darker complexions from the Olmecs, and/or African dwarfs, and passed it down to their Lacandon relatives. A very deliberate question must be asked at this point. How does one account for the Pyramid of the Sun—

573 Winters, Clyde. *African Empires in Ancient America*, p. 14.

and the other step pyramids in that complex in Teotihuaco—only being dated to 200 A.D.?[574]

Also, how does one then account for the late dates of the step pyramids today under the waters—just 3.5 miles off the southwestern coast of Cuba? Since they are far beneath the water level, they had to be built before the Ice Age flood, at least 10,000 years ago. Are they also to be dated at 200 A.D. as well?

For these step pyramids off Cuba—and an entire city surrounding them also containing roads, bridges and temples—to be underwater now, would they not have had to have been erected before the last Ice Age melt, that flooded them 11,000 years ago?

Furthermore, how does one account for the Pyramid of the Sun—and the other step pyramids in that complex in Teotihuaco—only being dated to 200 A.D.?[575] Are they not all "step pyramids, which predated the smooth-sided pyramids in that complex? Is that not true for the Giza pyramids, which were built long after the step pyramid in Sakkara, Egypt—designed by Imhotep, the multi-genius? Does this fact not push the dates of the step pyramids much further back in history?

The existence of pyramidal structures deep beneath Cuban waters is verified. We only needed to gather the details."[576] The last Ice Age melt of 11,000 years ago is a date that has already been validated by Professor Lemke's dissertation. So, with that in mind, how do we justify such a late date of 200 A.D. for the Pyramid of the Sun complex that has an identical architectural design as those found underwater off Cuba?

"What we have here is another failure to communicate." For these step-pyramids off Cuba—and an entire city surrounding them also containing roads, bridges and temples—to be underwater now, would they not had to have been erected before the last Ice Age melt that flooded them 11,000 years ago? Makes sense, right?

---

574 Department of the Arts of Africa, Oceania, and the Americas. (October 2001). "Teotihuacan: Pyramids of the Sun and the Moon." quoted in Heilbrunn, *Timeline of Art History*. New York: The Metropolitan Museum of Art, p. 2000.

575 Ibid.

576 Camera, Herman. (2005). "New National Geographic/Zelitsky Expedition to Cuba "Underwater City."

Central America's 40+ Temples and Pyramids

The following is a list of the pyramids or ceremonial structures in Central and South America—that we know of currently. Why is the statement, "that we know of" used? These are newly discovered sites in the lush, dense jungles of Central America, where such discoveries are being made all the time. On August 22, 2014, *The World Post* released a story in partnership with the Huffington Post and Berggruen Institute on Governance entitled, "Ancient Mayan Cities Found in Mexican Jungle."

How is this new discovery immediately stamped with the idea that it is so old that the whole city—not just one structure—was enveloped like a mummy with centuries of plant overgrowth? In this case, the foliage was so dense, it swallowed the entire ancient city, not just a couple of pyramids "hidden in the jungle in southeastern Mexico"[577] for millennia. So, one now sees how a new pyramid or temple turns up from, "out of nowhere," from time to time.

In several cases, these structures are not true pyramids, but pyramids nonetheless. Also, some of these sites are not just one structure, but a group of structures. Again, here is a list of cites "that we know of" at this moment:

1. Altun Ha in Belize.
2. Caracol in Belize, also called the Temple of the Wooden Lintel Maya.
3. Lamanai in Belize: the Mask Temple, High Temple, Temple of the Jaguar. (The Mask Temple has a very large carving at the bottom of the temple that looks suspiciously like a few of the Olmec heads.)
4. Lubaantun in Belize is a structure that is built of mostly stone blocks without any mortar; it is accompanied by one larger pyramid and several step pyramids.
5. Nim Li Punit in Belize is accompanied by several step pyramids.
6. Xunantunich is in Belize.
7. San Andrés in El Salvador, is accompanied by several other structures similar to pyramids.
8. Tazumal is in El Salvador.
9. Aguateca is in Guatemala. This temple/pyramid was abandoned and left unfinished.

---

577 Burnstein, Joanna. "Ancient Mayan Cities Found In Mexican Jungle." *The World Post*, August 22, 2014.

10. Dos Pilas is in Guatemala. This temple/pyramid looks like one massive structure, but was built by expanding a natural hill. Its principal stairway has at least 18 hieroglyphic steps.
11. Kaminaljuyu in Guatemala is accompanied by 200 pyramidal mounds and platforms.
12. El Mirador La Danta is in Guatemala and is also a huge pyramid temple.
13. El Mirador El Tigre is in Guatemala.
14. Mixco Viejo is in Guatemala.
15. Tikal is in Guatemala.
16. Copán in Honduras is accompanied by several overlapping step pyramids.
17. Bonampak is in Mexico.
18. Calakmul is in Mexico.
19. Chichen Itza pyramid temple complex is in Mexico.
20. Cholula has the Great Pyramid of Mexico.
21. Coba Nohoch Mul pyramid is in Mexico.
22. Coba La Iglesia is in Mexico.
23. Coba Crossroads Temple is in Mexico.
24. La Venta Great Pyramid in Mexico is one of the first pyramids in Central America.
25. Palenque Temple of the Cross is in Mexico.
26. Palenque Temple of the Inscriptions is in Mexico.
27. Santa Cecilia Acatitlan is in Mexico.
28. Tenayuca is in Mexico.
29. Tenochtitlan is in Mexico. This site contains at least a dozen pyramids.
30. Teotihuacan Pyramid of the Sun is in Mexico.
31. Teotihuacan Pyramid of the Moon is in Mexico.
32. El Tepozteco is in Mexico.
33. Tula in Hidalgo is in Mexico.
34. Uxmal Pyramid of the Magician is in Mexico.
35. Uxmal La Gran Pyramid is in Mexico.
36. Xochicalco Temple of the Feather Serpent is in Mexico.
37. Xochitecatl Pyramid of Flowers is in Mexico.
38. Xochitecatl Spiral Stepped Pyramid building is in Mexico.
39. Yaxchilan is in Mexico.
40. Calixtlahuaca, Mexico has a Pyramid and Ankh Temple.

This list contains 40+ pyramids. Some of these structures do not exist alone but belong to an entire pyramid complex containing several other pyramids. A good example is Kaminaljuyu, which alone contains 200 platforms, as well as pyramidal mounds. But it is counted as one single complex. There are even more in the jungle waiting to be uncovered as we speak. By sheer volume, Central America has the largest group of pyramid temples in the world.

The Lamanai Mask Temple in Belize is, "UnBelizeable"

At Mexico's Laventa site, the 40-ton Olmec heads are phenomenal, but they are eclipsed by a larger Olmec face just across the Yucatan Peninsula. It is an Olmec face carved on the Lamanai Mask Temple in Belize, which is definitely "unbelizeable"! TripAdvisor says, "the Mask Temple's gigantic face is an Olmec head."[578] The head is modeled after an Olmec God— some think it is Kinich Ahau. The Jaguar is also an Olmec symbol:

There are traces of jaguar carvings dating as far back as the Olmecs, the earliest organized society of Central America, and continuing all the way through to the Aztecs. For the Mesoamerican cultures, the jaguar symbolized power, ferociousness and association with the gods. The Olmecs support the idea that if a person is dressed in a jaguar-like costume, he acquired special powers that were usually associated with the jaguar. For the Olmecs, the jaguar was the most ferocious animal that would overpower any living creature.[579]

Like the Olmec, the Egyptians also had a high regard for cats and represented them anthropomorphically, i.e. half god-half animal. Bastet was an Egyptian lioness goddess and later a cat goddess in ancient Lower Egypt. In Upper Egypt, Sekhmet was the warrior lioness deity. There was no higher respect for an animal than to represent them anthropomorphically.

The Mande carried this idea to their Olmec culture in the Western Hemisphere. The colossal Olmec heads of San Lorenzo sometimes displayed jaguar paws on their headgear. Later, the pre-Inca Peruvians, in their Mochica civilization, actually worshipped Ai-Apaec, their ancient

578 Trip Advisor New River Tour. (2014) Accessed August 292016. http://www.tripadvisor.com/LocationPhotoDirectLink-g291967-d2160015-i94042982.

579 University of Florida. (n.d.). The Jaguar Is Symbolic. Accessed August 26, 2015. plaza.ufl.edu/akathy/personal/Papers/Jaguar%20 symbolism.doc.

cat god. The pre-Columbian Maya had various jaguar gods.[580] We found this temple deep in the Belize jungle. Let us take a closer look at the Mask Temple at Lamanai and what some of the features on the gigantic temple carving represent.

Fig. 31: Mask Temple in Belize at Lamanai. *Photo taken by the author.*

Archaeology of Lamanai, by The Institute of Archaeology:

The exposed mask and its concealed counterpart at the left side of the stair, is unique in the Maya area because they are cut from blocks of limestone rather than sculpted from plaster over a stone core. The facial features of the masks are clearly related to characteristics of Olmec iconography as seen in the Gulf Coast of Mexico, particularly in the upturned lip and broad nose. The masks are each adorned with a headdress representing a crocodile. This symbol validated the ancient site name recorded by the Spaniards as Lamanay ("place of the crocodile").[581]

A closer look at the Mask Temple at Lamanai reveals:

580 Trip Advisor New River Tour. (2014) Accessed August 292016. http://www.tripadvisor.com/LocationPhotoDirectLink-g291967-d2160015-i94042982-Lamanai_Mayan_Site_and_New_River_ Tour-Belize_District.html.

581 "Institute of Archaeology" (n.d.). Archaeology of Lamanai.

Some of Lamanai's ruins are some of the oldest in Belize. Archaeologists believe this site was of moderate size as early as 1500 B.C. With a population exceeding 35,000 at the height of the city's power, Lamanai's trading influence extended over the borders of present-day Guatemala, Honduras, Mexico and Belize. Still, of the around 800 buildings within the complex, less than five percent have been excavated and explored. Aside from the central pyramid, thick forest has consumed many of the limestone mounds. Unlike other ancient ruins, much of the Lamanai Belize archaeological site was built in layers. Successive populations built upon the temples of their ancestors, instead of destroying them.[582]

Continuing with the quote above, we see that the Olmecs at Lamanai brought with them a ball game and built game courts that would later spread to the North American Midwest at Hohokam. In Central America:

Ballplayers wore protective equipment during the game to prevent bodily damage by the hard rubber ball. The balls were made of solid rubber and weighed up to 4 kg (9 lbs) or more, and sizes differed greatly over time or according to the version played. Players would attempt to bounce the ball without using their hands and only touch the ball with their elbows, knees or hips through stone hoops attached to the sides of the ball court.[583]

In the ancient North American Hohokam ball courts—as seen in Fig. 21 in Chapter 3—they played with rubber balls showing a possible connection to the Olmecs, who brought rubber to the Western Hemisphere. These balls traveled, following the ballgames from Mesoamerica to the North American Southwest:

In the larger communities there were basin-like structures which archaeologists have identified as ball courts. Balls courts were an important part of the ancient civilizations of Mesoamerica (Mexico, Guatemala, Honduras), such as the Maya. In Mesoamerica, the ball game which was played on these courts was often a ceremonial event, which tied different communities together.[584] *Archaeologists have*

---

582 "Guide to Belize - Lamanai." (2015). Accessed on August 25 from http://www.guidetobelize.info/en/maya/belize-mayan-lamanai- guide.shml.

583 Ibid.

584 "OjibwaIndians" Ancient-America-Hohokam-Ball-Courts (2014).

uncovered rubber balls similar to those used in Mesoamerica at sites in the Southwest. The Hohokam (in the North American Southwest) managed to create large public works, such as their canal systems and ball courts, but there is no evidence of any ruling elites. The ball game may have integrated the communities, brought together for feasting, dancing, trade and sport and in so doing reduced the need for social coercion and a ruling class. In 1100, however, they stopped building the ball courts and began building mounds, suggesting a change in their social and religious organization.[585]

The Ankh Temple

The last in the list of cities above, of a pyramid and temple complex, warrants a separate notation. In Calixtlahuaca, 35 miles southwest of Mexico City today, you can see the shape of an Egyptian Ankh. This is yet another similarity between the ancient Egyptians and the ancient peoples of Central America:

The Ankh Temple is perfectly aligned with an Egyptian-like stone pyramid at the same archaeological site.... Both cultures built pyramids, both used solar symbolism, and both believed in life after death, preparing their dead for a journey to the afterlife via an elaborate and highly ritualistic ceremony.... The meaning of this ankh seems suspiciously parallel to the meaning behind Egypt's ankh cross.... Both cultures also used a very similar "tau" cross symbol—for the very same purpose: To signify the forces and interplay between physical life (which they saw as temporary, material) and spiritual life (which they saw as eternal, spiritual). In Egypt, this cross was called "ankh," which was formed by a "tau" cross (looks like the letter "T") with a loop on top of it.[586]

Instead of building a rectangular shaped doorway, several pre-Columbian American cultures in Central America, as well as in North America used the following:

A T-shaped doorway or window appears as a common architectural motif in stone masonry across Mesoamerica. It is found, for instance,

---

585 "Hohokam Ball Courts." Native American Netroots (2014).

586 Donnelly, Ignatius. (2012). *Atlantis: The Antediluvian World: Atlantean Megalithic Civilization* (CreateSpace Independent Publishing Platform), p. 176.

at *Chaco Canyon* in northern New Mexico and *Mesa Verde* in southwestern Colorado.[587]

Another author has also written of a worldwide, super-civilization that is extremely congruent with Cassaro's work. In his classic book, *Atlantis: The Antediluvian World*, Ignatius Donnelly says the tau was an important icon signifying "hidden wisdom for Mexicans, as well as for Peruvians, Egyptians, Phoenicians and Chaldeans."[588] Donnelly says it was "emblematic of rejuvenation, freedom from physical suffering, hope, immortality and divine unity."[589] Cassaro does an exceptional job of explaining the current attitude of anthropologists when judging ancient people:

> *Today, the prevailing anthropological view of antiquity among scholars is that ancient and indigenous peoples worldwide developed their own complex cultures independent of outside influence or inspiration. Any suggestions to the contrary have been generally dismissed as either fanciful, racist or demeaning. Ancient peoples worldwide, and scholars have argued, they were fully capable of developing their own civilizations. But, nagging evidence still remains; evidence like the ankh cross and tau cross symbols being found worldwide, and particularly among the Egyptians and pre-Columbian American cultures.*[590]

It is well known and it has been documented more than once. This is yet another visible piece of evidence of the ancient worldwide "super-civilization," as it has been labeled. It has been left for our modern society to see and not forget about "a lost Wisdom Tradition that was practiced globally in antiquity, found memorialized in pyramids, triptychs, and identical images worldwide."[591]

---

587 Cassaro, R. Unexplained Mystical Structure: Egyptian "Ankh Cross" Temple. November 13, 2012.

588 Donnelly, Ignatius. *Atlantis: The Antediluvian World*, p. 176.

589 Cassaro, R. Unexplained Mystical Structure: Egyptian "Ankh Cross" Temple. November 13, 2012.

590 Ibid.

591 Cassaro, Richard. (2011). *Written in Stone* (Deeper Truth Books. LLC.).

Gulf of Mexico Structures

The Olmec civilization has been labeled as the first in America. A theoretical date for its origin is 1500 B.C., "the glottochronological time depth of 3,500 years (around 1500 B.C.) correlates with the first glimmerings of Olmec civilization."[592] This date is far too late and is now being challenged by new evidence at the bottom of the Gulf of Mexico that appears to possibly be Olmec in origin—based on pyramidal architectural similarities.

One of the many challengers to the current status quo is Boston University Professor Robert Schoch, who wrote:

Another underwater suggested Atlantis location possibility has been suggested by scientists exploring the sea off the west coast of Cuba. Researchers using sonar equipment have found a large submarine plateau and have produced images that look much like pyramids, roads and buildings viewed from above.[593]

These submerged pyramids that Schoch writes about are **almost identical** to the pyramids of the nearby Yucatan Peninsula. One of the people in charge of the exploratory expedition is Paulina Zelitsky:

Russian-Canadian oceanographer Paulina Zelitsky, who reported that according to the investigators, these structures seem to be remains of streets, pyramids and buildings. Most of these blocks have **gigantic dimensions,** *reaching to five meters of height and several tons of weight... The scientists managed to film a pyramid of almost 35 meters height (approximately 115 feet)... "We think that this is no longer a hypothesis; it is a fact, supported by scientists who specialize in geology and archaeology," says the investigator. "The existence of pyramidal structures deep underneath Cuban waters is verified. We only needed to gather the details."*[594]

Believe it or not, cities have sunk in relatively modern times too. The sinking of Port Royal, Jamaica, is real and sets the precedent in the

592 Schoch, Robert. (2003). *Voyages of the Pyramid Builders* (New York: Tarcher/Putnam), pp. 52-53.

593 Schoch, Robert M. (2004). *Voyages of the Pyramid Builders* (New York: Penguin).

594 Camera, Herman. C. (2005). "New National Geographic/Zelitsky Expedition to Cuba "Underwater City."

same hemisphere as Cuba just a few centuries ago. This city's catastrophe occurred not far from Cuba in 1692 A.D. "Shortly before noon on 7 June, 33 acres (66 percent) of the 'storehouse and treasury of the West Indies' sank into Kingston's harbor in a disastrous earthquake."[595] That was a terrible catastrophe. However, that was just a drop in the ocean compared to the flooding at the end of the last Ice Age:

> *The end of the last Ice Age, terrible things happened to the world our ancestors lived in. Great ice caps over northern Europe and North America melted down, huge floods, about 25 million square kilometers of formerly habitable lands were swallowed up by the waves...unfortunately vast areas of the Earth's surface—the Sahara Desert, for example (which was green for 4000 years at the end of the Ice Age)—have hardly benefited from the attentions of archaeologists at all.*[596]

Therefore, the pyramids just off Cuba would probably have flooded around the same 11,000 years before present time frame, unless they just sank without the help of a catastrophic flood. Cuba is only 120 miles from the Yucatan Peninsula. Again, these pyramids (seen underwater near Cuba) are almost identical to the pyramids still above ground at nearby Yucatan Peninsula and others in Central America. Therefore, it seems logical that these structures were probably built by some group from the Nile Valley because they were the only people to build pyramids in such an early period. If the pyramids just off Cuba are at least 11,000 years old, then logic would require the Yucatan Peninsula step pyramids to be near 11,000 years old as well.

1. The Yucatan Peninsula and Cuban underwater pyramids are identical in that they are both step pyramids.
2. Both locations are not that far apart.
3. Only people from the Nile Valley were building pyramids at such an early date.
4. They were possibly built by the same people.

Therefore, the theoretical date of 1500 B.C. given the Olmec civilization is either tremendously wrong, or another people from the Nile Valley with

595 Hamilton, Donny L. (2001). The Port Royal Project. Accessed on September 12, 2010 from http://nautarch.tamu.edu/portroyal/ PRhist.htm

596 Hancock, Graham. "Graham Hancock Website." (2015). Accessed on March 10, 2015 from http://www.grahamhancock.com/archive/ underworld/

architectural knowledge traveled there and built these ancient structures much earlier.

Fig. 32: Temple & Pyramid, Calixtlahuaca, Mexico. *Courtesy Richard Cassaro.*

On an investigative trip in December 2014, Dr. Imhotep traveled to Central Mexico, specifically the Yucatan Peninsula (Y.P.), to gather new data. Dr. Imhotep found the modern Mayan survivors to be a kind, proud, caring people who are serious about their history. Unfortunately, when taking several bus tours to three of the ruins visited on the Y.P., the official tour guides completely ignored and made no mention of the "Olmecs," the "Mother Civilization" of Central America. The only mention of the Olmecs was in passing, as one of the 300-some different peoples they say make up the peoples of Central America.

203

Fig. 33: Dr. & Mrs. Imhotep standing in front of a large step-pyramid park in the Yucatan Peninsula.

Unbelievably, the tour guides continuously repeated that there were no Olmecs in the Yucatan Peninsula. We were also told that all the temples and pyramids were built by the Mayans. This statement is partially true, in that the Mayans repaired and heightened the original pyramids that the Olmecs had built; those pyramids had suffered from many years of neglect by the time the Mayans arrived. The tour guides do, however, fail to tell the public about the Olmec origins of the pyramid base. It was the Olmecs who originally built the ancient structure.

Here we have several interesting scientific studies covering the historic truth about Mayan history:

For many hundreds of years, the Maya, Zapotecs and Toltecs were considered by many to be the first Indians of Mexico. However, within the last 100 years a newly discovered culture has come to the forefront of scientific and historical inquiry. Evidence shows that the Mother Culture of Mexico is the ancient Olmec civilization.... Researchers prior to this time attributed many of the discoveries now associated with the Olmecs to Mayan, Toltec, or even Chichimecan cultures. However, due to advances in scientific dating, scientists were able to determine that the art, artifacts and miscellaneous objects found at La Venta, Tres Zapotes, and San Lorenzo were from a period earlier than the Maya.[597]

So, now we see that the Olmecs *were* the Mother Culture of Mexico.

The Olmec Heads: You can see one today at the De Young Museum in San Francisco. We know they (not the Mayans or Aztecs) were the builders of ancient American pyramids. Dozens of their enormous Olmec heads have been found throughout Central and South America. Why don't they look like modern Native Americans?... There is now undisputed scientific proof that the first Americans were descended from Africans or Australian aborigines, according to evidence in a new BBC documentary. Dozens of their skulls and cave writings have been found dating back 50,000 years.[598]

The Olmecs were the "Mother Culture." But again, we ask a question: What African group was the "*Grand*mother Culture" who entered South America at least 250,000 years ago or more, and afterword entered Central America before the Olmecs? Even though the major Afrocoid group in Mexico pre-Columbus were the Olmecs, there were other Blacks who lived in the Chiapas highlands as well as Talapacoya. There were ceramic heads in Central Mexico found at Chalcatzingo, which prove that there was a large community of Blacks living in that area before the Olmecs arrived.

Remember, we traced the Anu/Twa DNA coming to North America from two directions: earlier from Africa by way of South America, or later from Scandinavia by way of Canada. Their mode of transportation—when traveling over water—came from papyrus reed boats. This is the Grandmother Culture that reached the Americas.

Stone tools and charcoal from one site in Brazil show evidence of human habitation as long ago as 50,000 years, and artifacts previously called Mayan or Aztec. The Aztecs and Mayans used the pyramids for blood- letting and human sacrifice, but archeologists agree that the Mayan and Aztec civilizations—which began thousands of years after the Olmec

597 Villescas, Daniel. (2005). "Mother Culture Mexico: The Olmecs."

598 The Olmecs. Accessed November 16, 2015. (2012). http://2012.caliwali. com/theolmecs.htm.

civilization ended, definitely inherited the bulk of ancient pyramids and advanced pre-Columbian art and artifacts.[599]

While the Olmec were never involved in blood-letting, there is one item the Mayans did inherit from their Olmec ancestors:

Some Mayan skeletal remains indicate that they suffered anemia, an illness associated with Sub-Saharan Africans (Moore, 1929; Whittington, 1977; Wailoo, 2002). Antigens of the Rhesus system, HLA alleles and haplotypes in the immune system in humans are different among various ethnic groups. "The HLA in indigenous American populations, found among Indians in Belize and Mexico at centers associated with the Mayan Civilization (Allsopp, et al., 1992)."...and six Mayan groups show the B Allele of the Otomi people, that is of African origin" (Gather, 2006; Winters 2011a, 2015b). This means that these Mayan groups' immune systems originate from African peoples. Underhill, et al. noted that: "One Mayan male, previously has been shown to have an African Y chromosome" (7). This is very interesting because the Mayan language illustrates a Mande substratum, in addition to African genetic markers.[600]

An additional fact that links the Olmec with the Mayans is the jaguar symbol:

In many of the Mexican pyramids found in Guatamala and Belize we find Stockomala Jaguar Pyramids. These pyramids with Jaguar masks and large earrings predate all the Mayan pyramids. And these pyramids suggest they were built by Africans who worshiped the Jaguar Cult.[601]

Yes, Africans have been known to wear large earrings. Again, which gods did these ancient Central Mexican people worship? The major Black gods of the Mexicans were Quetzalcoatl, and the Mayan gods L and M, Xaman

599 Winters, Clyde. "The Africans Who Discovered America Thousands Of Years Before Columbus." (2014). Accessed May 2, 2015 from http://howafrica.com.

600 Winters, Clyde. (2015). "HLA-B*35 In Mexican Amerindians and African Populations."

601 Winters, Clyde. "Harappan Fish Signs" (2012). Accessed on January 13, 2017 from https://africancivilizations.wordpress.com.

and Ekchuah. These gods are depicted in the Codex Troano.[602] Sahagun tells us that Ekchuah was also the god of the Amanteca. The Nahuatl term *Amanteca* was probably the name of the Mandinka or Mandinga people who were the foundation of the Olmec people.[603] Ekchuah is depicted with a long nose. Researchers have found that some Mayan people have genetic markers that point to African ancestors. For example: Underhill, et al. noted that: "One Mayan male, previously has been shown to have an African Y chromosome."[604]

This genetic report is proof positive, highlighting direct genetic evidence of Mayans containing African DNA from their direct ancestors. From the linguistic branch of scientific evidence, we have new information that strengthens Dr. Imhotep's hypothesis:

There is linguistic evidence for pre-Columbian contact between African and Amerind languages, which is considered an indication of African ancestry. There is "evidence from the Otomi and Mayan languages which indicate the borrowing/copying of Manding/Mande lexical items by speakers of these languages in pre-Columbian times." The Olmec were the first Americans to develop a number and math system, influenced their Mayan neighbors. The Olmec are recognized as the "madre cultura" Mother Culture of Mexican civilizations. The Mayans borrowed much of their art and architecture from the Olmecs, including the calendar and pyramid structures that the Mayans are so famous for. The first of these great Mayan structures appeared between 400 B.C. and 150 A.D. The Manding origin for the Mayan term for writing leads to a corollary hypothesis. This hypothesis stated simply is that an examination of the Mayan language will probably indicate a number of Olmec-Manding loans in Mayan. Many of the Mayan sites were first settled by the Olmec. This is supported by the fact that the Mayan inscriptions from Palenque claim that the first ruler of this city was the Olmec leader U-Kix-chan. There are "seventy plus loans in the Mayan languages from the Olmec Mande language."

602 Wiener, Leo. (1921). *Africa and the Discovery of America*, p. 258.

603 Winters, Clyde. *Atlantis in Mexico*.

604 Winters, Clyde. "Inference of Ancient Black Mexican Tribes and DNA" (2015). Accessed on January 13, 2017 from https://www.webmed- central. com/article_view/4856.; Winters, Clyde. (2015). "HLA-B*35 In Mexican Amerindians And African Populations."

Many of these loan words...support the view that in ancient times Mayan speakers lived in intimate contact with the Mande speaking Olmec people. Moreover, this is further confirmation of Leo Wiener's theory in Africa and the Discovery of America *that the religion and culture of the Mesoamericans was influenced by Mande speaking people from West Africa. These Mande speaking people were the Olmec.*[605]

"Most experts believe that the Mayan writing systems came from the Olmecs."[606] Another author wrote:

Tozzer (1941) claimed that the Yucatec Maya said that the Tutul Xia, a group of foreigners from Zuiva, in Nonoualoco territory taught the Maya how to read and write. This term Xui agrees with the name Si, for the Manding people.[607]

In summary, we see ten items between the Mayans and the Olmec:

1. Olmecs predated the Mayans.
2. Mayans made blood sacrifices but the Olmec did not.
3. Mayans skeletal remains showed evidence of sickle cell anemia, a sub-African illness the Olmecs inherited.
4. Mayan groups' immune systems originate from Africa.
5. Mayans built on top of older Olmec pyramids.
6. Mayans had Black gods.
7. Mayans were shown to have an African Y chromosome.
8. Linguistic evidence shows pre-Columbian contact between African and Amerind languages, which is considered an indication of African ancestry.

605 Winters, Clyde. "Olmec (Mande) Loan Words in the Mayan, Mixe-Zoque and Taino Languages." Accessed May 2, 2015. http://maxwellsci.com/print/crjss/v3-152-179.pdf (Cache), (2011). Current Research Journal of Social Sciences 3(3): 152-179, 2011 ISSN: 2014-3-246 Maxwell Scientific Organization, 2011.

606 Underhill, et al. (1996). A pre-Columbian Y chromosome-specific transition with its implications for human evolutionary history. *Proceedings of the National Academy of Sciences USA*, Vol.93, pp. 196-200.

607 Tozzer, A. M. (1941). "Relacion de las Casa de Yucatan." Peabody Museum of American Archaeology and Ethnology; Winters, Clyde. (2005). "Race and Identity: Ancient relations between Africans and Mexicans." Accessed May 2, 2015. http://olmec98.net/RacePaper.pdf.

9. Mayans borrowed much of their art and architecture from the Olmecs.
10. Seventy-plus loans in the Mayan languages originate from the Olmec Mande language.
11. Mayan writing systems came from the Olmecs.

50 Underwater Structures near Bimini

While we are studying the Caribbean—just outside and adjacent to the Gulf of Mexico heading northeast and turning the corner around the Florida Keys, we head in a northern direction towards the Bahamas. Our conversation now points to a different location, and we shall sneak to Bimini for a moment. The outcome of the cataclysm that covered this site was the rise of a phenomenal amount of melted ice water. The civilization that existed on the large Bahamian island was wiped out leaving only the mountain tops, which is all we see today. That island—some call it Atlantis— did not sink in an earthquake as many writers have told us since Plato wrote about it in his Timaeus around 355 B.C.:

"It requires no great stretch of the imagination to believe that this manuscript reached the hands of Solon's successor and descendant, Plato."[608] Solon, who brought the story to Greece from Egypt, learned of it from an Egyptian priest named Senchis. So, it was Plato who finally told the world about Atlantis' so-called "sinking." However, what the evidence actually shows us now is that Atlantis did not sink! It was flooded by the melting of the last Ice Age. This was also the event that ended the age of Zep Tepi.

Atlantis was not the only site that was covered by the flood. More underwater structures have also been found two miles west of Bimini;[609] this time in 100 feet of water. Dr. Little tells us what he saw:

Our one dive at the stone-block rectangles, conducted with the History Channel...pointed to these odd stone piles as probably man-made. These formations, generally 10 by 45 feet...numbered about

---

608 Donnelly, Ignatius. (1882). "PLATO'S HISTORY OF ATLANTIS."

609 Little, Gregory. "Underwater Stone Formation at Bimini: Ancient Harbor Evidence." *Alternate Perceptions Magazine* online.

50, are laid out in straight, parallel lines, and are located at the edge of the 10,000 B.C. shoreline.[610]

If South America was the first area in the Western Hemisphere where people landed 100,000 years ago, then logic demands it must be where the first structures were built. The first country on the northwest side of South America, which is connected to Central America, is Colombia. Just below the western side of Colombia is the small coastal country of Ecuador. Then, south is the coastal country of Peru.

The continental mountain range of the Andes is the longest in the world. It extends 4,300 miles down the western coast of South America. The Andes begin in Venezuela and run all the way down to Chile.

The Six-Step-Pyramid City of Caral

This 5,000-year-old city sits approximately 20 miles from the Pacific coast in Peru. The first modern-day discovery of this pyramid city was made in 1905. In 2001 researchers and archaeologists working on-site dated the city at 2627 B.C. The plaza is larger than a football field and surrounded by:

A complex of mostly flat-top pyramids, circular plazas and staircases that demonstrate the knowledge and might of this important ancient culture. It covers a mighty 165 acres and it is one of the largest in Peru... The main pyramid found at Caral covers a staggering area nearly the size of four football fields, and it is 18 meters(almost 20 yards high).[611]

The city also has a gigantic circular amphitheater large enough to fit one of the smaller step pyramids inside. "Musicians played flutes crafted from pelican and condor skeletons and horns made from llama or alpaca bones in the city's amphitheater."[612]

---

610 Soustelle, Jacques. (1984). *The Olmecs: The Oldest Civilization in Mexico* (Doubleday), p. 191.

611 Petricevic, Ivan. "The Ancient City of Caral." (2002). Accessed May 28, 2014.

612 Josephs, Leslie. "Explore Peru's 5,000 year old city, Caral." Associated Press. October 16, 2016. NY. http://agutie.homestead.com/files/incas/caral_ruins_pre_inca_1.html

Since these people put so much time and effort into creating such a stupendous amphitheater, they probably had other entertainment besides music. The Mesoamerican Aztecs and Olmecs had at least one kind of sport covered earlier. "The sport known simply as the Ball Game was popular across Mesoamerica and was played by all the major civilizations from the Olmecs to the Aztecs."[613] It was played from South America through Central America to North America. There are the Egyptians who had theatrical performances, so, why not the people of Caral?

The Greeks may have believed that they were the inventors of theatre, but that depends on how one defines "theatre" and interprets ancient records. It can be claimed that the Egyptians—while it is not known if they had special venues for their plays—preceded Greece in the public performance of shows, which were mostly pageant-like, religious in character, ritualistic, and to a large extent, devoid of dramatic narrative.[614]

It seems that these were a fun-loving, peaceful people. As hard as excavators worked, they could find:

No weapons and no evidence of violence or warfare (p. 174). We don't see evidence of bloodshed or human sacrifice, yet the rulers were able to motivate large numbers of their citizens to come together in massive construction projects.[615]

In Peru, there are many examples of Egyptian architecture. **The largest group of ancient buildings that have ever been found in the Americas is now claimed to be in northern Peru**. A well-known explorer, Gene Savoy, discovered a "lost city" in 1985, deep in northern Peru's jungle-covered mountains. Savoy named this citadel of stone buildings "Gran Vilaya." It is located close to 400 miles northeast of Lima. Gran Vilaya is not found in the lowlands but on top of a mountain range extending 9000 feet high. When interviewed, Savoy said:

The city's buildings ran along the ridge for at least 25 miles. He said the expedition calculated that there were 10,350 stone structures in the

613 Cartwright, Mark. "The Ball Game of Mesoamerica." (9/16/13). Accessed on May 28, 2014.

614 Dollinger, Andre. (2009). "The ancient Egyptian theatre." Accessed May 28, 2014.

615 Understanding, Supreme. *When the World was Black* (Georgia, Proven Publishing, 2013), p. 176.

defensive network along the ridge and 13,000 other stone buildings in three major city layouts. The stone structures, some measuring 140 feet in length, were built atop terraces that go up the mountain doorways, windows, and niched walls. "The walls," he said, "soar up as high as a 15-story building."[616]

South American Nazca's Enormous Geoglyphs

South America and Egypt have so many similarities. These major parallels are pyramids, megaliths, mummies and the belief in reincarnation.[617] The most well-known ancient artifacts in Peru are unique to Nazca, near the southern coast. They come in the form of geometrical patterns and abstract lines. The ancient Nazca Lines are the oldest and largest geoglyphs in the world. There are hundreds of geometrically shaped lines. At least seventy of them are bird, fish, other animal or human figures. These large geoglyphs are amazingly proportionate and well drawn.

Criss-crossed all over the 37-mile-long plain at Nazca are an assortment of geometrically straight lines, some running parallel, others crossing over and intersecting other lines. These large drawings on the surface of the earth are known as geoglyphs, but they make no sense at all to those who view them from the ground. Aerial archaeology, involving aerial photography and mapping, has brought the recognition of several kinds of animal figures—monkeys, birds, fish—even a whale, as well as insect forms, such as spiders and a variety of plants.

Aerial observation has shown that the lines continue along the ground for more than 800 miles.[618] Dr. Phyllis Pitluga has written a paper about the lines: the gist of which appears to be that a wide-ranging plan of celestial imitation lies at the heart of the Nazca enigma, which may be carried down from remote antiquity, and follows a distinct doctrine of sky-ground dualism ("as above so below").[619]

---

616 Fawcett, Percy. Gran Vilaya. (1999). Accessed on July 29, 2011 from http://www.phfawcettsweb.org/vilaya.htm.

617 Ibid.

618 Johnston, Grahame. (2014). "Nazca Lines and the Nazca Culture."

619 Fawcett, Percy. Gran Vilaya.

This is yet another example of dualism we can see in the first representation of the "as we" in Egypt's Giza Pyramid complex, which is also written about in Bauval's *The Orion Mystery* (1994). Another example of dualism in Latin America is found in Dr. Imhotep's dissertation.[620] It is the Mexican flag. It has a picture of a feathered serpent. The dualism here is between a bird and a snake. If we go to Egypt, we find a connection in the symbolism of the Feathered Serpent there. He was Wadjet, the winged serpent of Egypt. He protected the Pharaohs and controlled the waters of the Nile. The ancient Mesoamericans and Egyptians who had never met and lived centuries and thousands of miles apart both worshiped feathered-serpent deities.[621]

A dualism inside a dualism is the Mexican god, Quetzalcoatl. Was he depicted as a Black or White god?

In the book, *Fair Gods and Stone Faces*, author Constance Irwin says it is a "flat contradiction"[622] to other descriptions of Quetzalcoatl that refer specifically to his black hair or black beard. Several scholars have inferred that some nameless Aztec poet (who may have never existed) employed poetic license (he stretched the truth) and bleached the black beard of Quetzalcoatl to present him as a sun symbol. In his book, Basil Hedrick says, "The Quetzalcoatl of the Mexican Valley documents was never blond or fair, as stated by the (Catholic) friars, but virtually always pictured as black-bearded, and in illustrations (paintings) had his face painted black."[623]

Back then represented as Ehecatl the wind god, Quetzalcoatl was painted black with prominently bulging nose and heavy, protruding lips.[624] A black-haired, black-bearded figure in white robes, one of the representations of Quetzalcoatl modeled after a dark-skinned outsider

620 Imhotep, (Jones) D. The Origin of Civilization.

621 Leonard, R. C. (2010). "THE FEATHERED SERPENT." Accessed September 20, 2015.

622 Irwin, Constance. (1963). *Fair Gods and Stone Faces* (New York: St. Martin's Press), p. 38.

623 Hedrick, Basil.(1971). "Quetzalcoatl: European or Indigene?" Man across the Sea. (Riley Kelley Pennington, Pennington & Rands All rights reserved), p. 66.

624 Ibid.

can be seen in paintings in Mexico. The Aztecs worshiped a Negroid figure mistaken for their god Tezcatlipoca because he had the right (black) ceremonial color too.[625]

By the way, an ancient feathered serpent can also be seen today in North America, at Alabama's Moundville, in Hale County, near the city of Tuscaloosa. Also, did you know that Alabama's city of Tuscaloosa is named after the Black Chatah Chief Tuscaloosa? His name in western Muskogean vocabulary "Tusca" means "Black" and "loosa" means "warrior."

Advanced Black civilizations etched hundreds of complex geoglyphs into the Earth about 150 miles inland of South Africa, near the west of the port of Maputo. These geoglyphs were located using satellite imagery and mapping software.[626] As we have witnessed from the scientific community—humanity began in Africa. We have also seen that the first civilizations began there. So, it should be no surprise that the first giant glyphs have been found there as well. Also, in our own North American back yard, there are ancient geoglyphs to see:

Throughout the American Southwest, glyphs and pictographs sites (a petroglyph is an engraving made on rock by pecking at or grinding the surface, while a pictograph is a painting on a rock) are referred to as rock art. The most famous examples of rock art are Painted Rocks in Petroglyph State Park near Gila Bend, Arizona, and the Petroglyph National Monument near Albuquerque, New Mexico. Far rarer are geoglyphs or intaglios (in-tal-yos), which are large figures found on the Colorado desert floor.[627]

Continuing on with Colorado, we see:

Along the Colorado River, a number of geoglyphs are carved out of the desert floor that are on par with the mysterious markings in the Peruvian desert near Nazca. However, the American "intaglios" are far less famous... Near two of the human shapes are figures of

625 Irwin, Constance. *Fair Gods and Stone Faces*, p. 38.

626 "Lost Advanced Civilizations Inhabited Earth Over 100,000 Years Ago" http://www.rvwest.com/article/united_states/the_fascinating_mojave_ desert_rock_pictures.

627 Coppens, Phillip. (n.d.). America's Nazca Lines. Accessed June 7, 2015.

serpents and four-legged animals with long tails. One giant, or god, appears to have just stepped out of a large dance ring.[628]

Could the same people who began drawing petroglyphs in Africa have also drawn them in South America and then North America? The modern city of Trujillo is also in northern Peru. There are two large pyramids a short drive east of Trujillo. As in Mexico, these step pyramids made of adobe bricks are also called the Pyramids of the Sun and Moon. This Pyramid of the Moon is close to the Pyramid of the Sun. From the top of the Pyramid of the Sun, a vast, empty desert can be seen. The exterior of these once great monuments has now turned to dust.

Nazca not only has geoglyphs, but also pyramids (plural) that are related to the lines:

> *The Nazca lines are in connection with the pyramids because some lines are pointing directly to the pyramids. It is perfectly possible that the lines were a calendar, or when there were 30 pyramids...and there were detected remnants of the so called "Man of Pyramid 2" from pre-ceramic times (from the year 4282 B.C.).[629]*

This date is another one that precedes the Mongolians in the Americas, this time by 1682 years. Are there still ruins of other Nazca pyramids? Yes, but only a few of the **30 pyramids** just mentioned are accounted for. Some researchers have entered "Peru's Cahuachi desert to reveal an ancient adobe pyramid."[630] This is one pyramid that you do not have "to look hard to find because just behind this pyramid are a significant number of lines as well as figural drawings."[631] This data comes from a booklet attained from the Antonini Pyramid Museum, Nazca.

The excavations under the leadership of Dr. Orefici show that there were many columns on the stairs-like platforms with roofs. Under the protection of the roofs, the priests performed their ritual acts. The walls were made of conical or bread-formed mud bricks and painted indifferent

628 Ibid.

629 "Nazca: History of the pyramids of Cahuachi." Accessed on August 17, 2010.

630 Lorenzi, R. Ancient Peru Pyramid Spotted by Satellite. (October 6, 2008)

631 Aveni, Anthony, and Helainie Silverman. (2000). Between the Lines. *The Sciences*, 31: 36-42. doi:10.1002/j.2326-1951.1991.tb02320.x.

colors of clay. Striking were above all the rose color, or dark red, or glaring red.[632]

Tiahuanaco's Age
and Many Egyptian Similarities

Moving on from lines in Peru to structures in Bolivia, right next door, we see that Tiahuanaco has some very ancient structures. "What is distinctly odd is the fact that both the Giza Plateau in Egypt and Tiahuanaco have been suggested, on reasonable geological and astronomical grounds, to be more than 12,000 years old."[633] At that date, some say that Tiahuanaco has one of the oldest megalithic structures in South America:

The geology of the site at Tiahuanaco is showing a relationship to Lake Titicaca that last prevailed more than 10,000 years ago...geologically, zoologically and astronomically speaking, at Tiahuanaco's Semi-Subterranean Temple there is a representation of...a large hippo-like animal that became extinct in the Tiahuanaco area more than 12,000 years ago. And on the eastern side of the Gateway to the Sun there is a representation of an elephant-like creature...that became extinct 12,000 years ago.... There are also astrological alignments which speak of an extremely ancient date for Tiahuanaco.[634]

In an interview in January 1997, a scholar who is known to be a mainstream figure was interviewed. During the interview:

Dr. Oswaldo Rivera, Director of the Bolivian National Institute of Archaeology...confirmed what he told Daichi—that the date of 12,000 years ago, suggested for the Kalasasaya temple in Tiahuanaco by astronomical calculations was beginning to look as though it might be correct.[635]

---

632 Palomino, M. (2009). "Nazca: History of the Pyramids of Cahuachi." Accessed June 8, 2015. http://www.am-sur.com/am-sur/peru/Nasca/Rojas_piramides-Cahuachi-02-great-pyramid-ENGL.html.

633 Aveni, Anthony, and Helainie Silverman. Between the Lines. pp. 36-42.

634 Hancock and Faiia. *Heaven's Mirror*, pp. 305, 306.

635 Ibid.

Does Egypt's Civilization Predate South America's?

According to Louis Leakey and other paleoanthropologists, the first people came out of Africa. Did pyramid and temple building first begin in Africa as well? It is also logical that evidence of the antiquity of the Nile Valley civilization, predates the Mesopotamian civilization. It also goes back long before South America's date of 10,000 B.C.[636]

We have established that Africans have been traveling to South America for 250,000 years. After Africans, the next closest group were the Caucasians in 3000 B.C, then there were the Mongolians in 2600 B.C. The question is: "Can the ancient Egyptian builders be trusted for their accuracy?" To answer this question there is a piece from project engineer and machinist Christopher Dunn's book, *Lost Technologies of Ancient Egypt*:

> *In these pages, Chris Dunn demonstrates an underlying system of incredible features, ranging from the tool mark details in the "Rose Red Rosetta Stone of Abu Roash" to the symmetries of the giant heads of Ramses at the temples in Luxor, to the layout of the column capitals at the great Hypostyle Hall at Denderah and the base of the Great Pyramid itself. Thanks to this work, the modern reader sits back in the awe and admiration of the Egyptian geniuses of five thousand years ago.[637]*

The next question that inevitably arises is, "How long did their civilization—that included such precision—last?" This cycle of civilization, the longest in history, presumably lasted 10,000 years. This is a reasonable compromise between the long chronology [based on data provided by Egyptian priests, given to Herodotus and Manetho that places the beginning at 17,000 B.C.] and the short chronology of the moderns—for the latter are obliged to admit that by 4245 B.C., the Egyptians had already

---

636 Ibid.

637 Dunn, Christopher. (2010). *Lost Technologies of Ancient Egypt* (Vermont, Bear & Company).

invented the calendar [which necessarily requires the passage of thousands of years].[638]

Professional astronomers have dated the Temple of Karnak, which still stands in modern Luxor, Egypt. As Norman Lockyer observed, the axis of Karnak is best understood as an immense "instrument"—in some ways like a telescope—designed to focus light and "to carry it to the...extremity of the temple, into the sanctuary, so that once a year...at the absolute moment of sunrise...a 'flash'...would have remained visible for perhaps as long as a 'couple of moments'.... Understand that the summer solstice is not fixed and immutable but rather modeled mathematically, so it is theoretically possible, if you trust the accuracy of the ancient builders, to work out...the date at which it must originally have been surveyed."[639]

As Chris Dunn explained earlier, it is logical to trust the builders of ancient Egypt. We shall now progress to the very latest date Karnak could have been in existence to have an astronomical event, such as the "flash" to occur:

> It was the opinion of nineteenth century British astronomer Sir J. Norman Lockyer...that in the case of Karnak this date has been variously calculated at 11,700 B.C., 3700 B.C., and anywhere between 2000 and 1000 B.C.... Thirty years later, in 1921, the astronomer F. S. Richards—using more refined observations and formulae —came up with the earlier date of 11,700 B.C. [agreeing with Lockyer] as well.... Yet if Lockyer is correct...about 11,700 B.C., as F.S. Richards [also] calculated in 1921...the earlier date of 11,700 B.C., 13,700 years ago predates Tiahuanaco by 1700 years.[640]

Notice that Lockyer and Richards have given the Temple of Karnak a similar date of existence to at least 11,700 B.C., which is just 300 years shy of 12,000 years ago. Understand that Karnack is older than the 11,700 date because that was not its date of original construction. It was just a date in which the flash in the sanctuary of the temple was recorded. This date has

---

638 Jones, D. C., (2007). *The Origin of Civilization.*(Self-Published: Roanoke, VA) p. 186; Brophy, Thomas G. (2002) *The Origin Map: Discovery of a Prehistoric, Megalithic, Astrophysical Map and Sculpture of the Universe* (New England: Writers Club Press), back cover, p. 109.

639 Hancock and Faiia. *Heaven's Mirror*, pp. 305, 306.

640 Ibid., p. 58.

startled modern Egyptologists, but we cannot stop there, for there is far more for them to see.

Ta-Seti was a city in ancient Nubia, part of the Great Kushite Empire, which predated Egypt and is credited with moving north from Nubia into Egypt creating the Egyptian civilization. Then again, at the very end of Egyptian civilization, the Nubians saved an aging Egyptian nation postponing its doom for almost 100 more years. But that certainly was not the beginning of this civilization. Many of the pieces of Ta-Seti's and Egypt's civilization are seen in Nabta Playa, which is given a starting date of between 17,700 and 43,000 years ago.[641]

This 43,000-year date does not seem too unreasonable when you look to the Africans in the Americas 250,000 years ago. Hunter-gatherers do not sail repeatedly across the ocean and build civilizations...and even if they did, they had hundreds of thousands of years to do so.

We shall yield to the 17,700-year date, the most conservative of the two given by the astrophysicist Dr. Thomas Brophy. This date is practically congruent with the date the Egyptian priests gave Herodotus and Manetho. The historical deception about who the first Americans were is similar to the inaccurate start date of 3100 B.C. given to Egypt by Egyptologists. The type of engineering seen in the construction of the Temple of Karnak has been shown to exist in at least one North American mound.

A flash of sunlight enters and ends at the other end of the structure once a year, identical to the Karnak flash. The New England forests in general, and Windham, Vermont specifically, are packed with stone chambers. Most of the time they are dismissed as root cellars or pig pens made by colonial farmers. There was one chamber, however, that was different than the rest. All the chambers checked in this article were made of stone, not wood. Some of the stones were huge:

Why would settlers have invested such enormous effort and moved such massive stones (some of which must have weighed over a ton) to put a roof over swine? Why did they gouge a groove over an inch deep into the bedrock that comprised the door sill? Was it a coincidence that the Pig Pen is positioned to capture the sun as it rises over Mount Monadnock on the morning of the winter solstice?[642]

---

641 Ibid., p. 58.

642 Lord, Benjamin. (2013). "Lost Histories: The Story of New England's Stone Chambers."

No, moving massive stones weighing tons just to keep pigs warm seems kind of ridiculous. This chamber had a hole in the front and a flat wall in the rear of the room, directly across from the hole. During Winter Solstice:

A beam of light shot through the entrance to illuminate an unusual stone in the back of the chamber and the cramped space filled with a fiery glow.[643]

That is exactly what occurred in Egypt at the Temple of Karnak, on a much smaller scale, of course. Why would people build such a structure with stone that weighed more than a ton...and build it in the wilderness? Also, why is it "The ceiling was no more than three feet high?" (Could it have been constructed by the same short "Mound Builders" covered in this book?)

To find out, Muller enlisted the help of Tom Wessels, author of Reading the Forested Landscape, *and they visited Glastonbury during the summer of 2007. They mapped and measured the mounds and observed the surrounding forests. They measured the depth to which forest debris and soil had accumulated. They noted the thick layer of moss covering the rocks, suggesting that the stone structures might be far older than the mountain's trails.*[644]

Unfortunately for academia, they must have thought incorrectly just like Barry Fell:

Ancient European mariners were the ones who built these hard-to-explain stone structures. As we walked through the woods behind his home, he pointed out impressive dry-masonry structures with unusual features. The stones were enormous. The largest ones must have weighed several tons each. And they were all meticulously oriented 22° north of east. When we came upon a particularly massive and beautifully crafted stack of stones, he stated passionately, "' bunch of hardscrabble, backwoods farmers did not build this. Nor did Native American builders," Johnston believes. "I think they're Celts."[645]

---

643 Hancock and Faiia. *Heaven's Mirror*, p. 58.

644 Brophy, Thomas G. (2002). *The Origin Map: Discovery of a Prehistoric, Megalithic, Astrophysical Map and Sculpture of the Universe.* (New England: Writers Club Press).

645 Lord, Benjamin. "Lost Histories: The Story of New England's Stone Chambers."

Tiahuanaco's Blocks and Megalithic Walls of Sacsayhuaman

Back to South America—as in Egypt—at Tiahuanaco, we shall find:

Massive blocks of stone, many weighing 100 tons, carved with such exactitude that a knife could not be inserted between the blocks. Where the blocks had been separated, as in Puma Punku, it could be seen that they were often joined by metal clamps, obviously to prevent them from coming apart in an earthquake.[646]

The Spanish came showing their superiority in concrete technology. A similar scenario is beginning to appear. In each case listed, similar clamps are being found in Egypt or the Nile Valley first rather than in the Americas. This example is no different than the rest. Yes, metal clamps were found in Egypt, and not in just one location. Clamps were found "on ruins on Elephantine Island in Aswan, and in Dendera, Egypt."[647]

Just outside of Cuzco, at Sacsayhuaman, there are three tiers of zigzagging rows of megalithic stones, "many in the range of 200 tonnes [sic]. Here again, they are so well-fitted together that you could not slip the point of a knife between two of them."[648] This is the second reference to the proximity of one megalithic stone to the next stone joining it exemplifying the exact craftsmanship of these ancient South American builders. It sounds exactly like the space between the mega-blocks some of the Egyptian pyramids were built with. Another amazing feat is that many of these huge stone blocks came from over sixty miles away, like in Egypt. However, these stones are not the largest dressed stones in South America. In Tiahuanaco at "...Puma Punku,...there is a block that weighs 447 tonnes [sic]."[649]

In contrast to the large Puma Punku block, in Egypt next to the Sphinx and Valley Temple at Giza, there are no stones weighing less than 50 tons, and some weigh as much as 200 tons. The Temple's granite facing stones (called ashlars) were brought all the way from southern Egypt in Aswan.

646 Ibid.

647 Hancock and Faiia. *Heaven's Mirror*, pp. 305, 306.

648 Lord, Benjamin. "Lost Histories: The Story of New England's Stone Chambers."

649 Hancock and Faiia. *Heaven's Mirror*, pp. 305, 306.

All the stones covered so far in this work are dwarfed by the unfinished obelisk of Aswan, Egypt, which measures 120 feet (42m) and would have weighed over 1,168 tons when complete. That megalith, however, was never completed or moved. The next largest megalith from ancient Egypt is the statue of Ramses at the Ramesseum:

> *Only fragments of the base and torso remain of the colossal statue of the enthroned Ramesses (19 m high and weighing around 1000 tons). The stone for the statue was moved this time and transported 170 miles over land from Aswan to Thebes.*[650]

South American and Egyptian Religious and Writing Similarities

Before leaving Tiahuanaco, it must be mentioned that many of the religious practices the Inca had are identical with the Egyptians:

> *The Incas mummified the remains of their deceased god-kings (p. 280); they possessed similar creation stories; their primary gods emerged from bodies of water (p. 276); Incas had a meteorite clan, and symbols of fertility and rebirth (p. 279); God-Kings (p. 280); Astronomer-Priests who had direct communication with celestial powers and quest for the immortality of the soul (p. 281); and Priests wearing Leopard skins/or spotted animal skins (p. 310).*[651]

On Bolivia's eastern border is the country of Paraguay:

> *On one mound structure in Yariguaa Paraguay, stones were discovered with inscriptions resembling the old Egyptian hieroglyphics. The well-known South American ethnologist, Dr. Mbertoni, affirms that at least one-half of the Yariguaa hieroglyphics are identical with the old Egyptian hieroglyphics.*[652]

Just over the northern border of Peru is Ecuador. Although there is a lack of large structures there, small items, like artifacts from ancient Egypt have been found:

---

650 Whitaker, Alex. The top 50 megaliths. Scott and Elaine Jones, n.d. http://www.ancient-wisdom.com/top50stones.htm.

651 Hancock and Faiia. *Heaven's Mirror*, pp. 305, 306.

652 Ibid.

Certain excavations in Ecuador have sometimes yielded a highly developed prehistoric culture... Excavators have found many ancient statuettes that resemble the ancient Egyptian by their headdress, clothes, and the breast-adornments on the statues of the priest.[653]

Tying in the connection between Central and South America:

The kinship of prehistoric American and ancient Egyptian cultures is demonstrated very eloquently in the ruins of Palenque, Ocochingo, the Mitla palaces, the Xochicalco, Teotihuacan, and Sihuatan pyramids, by the decorations of the Sun Temple of Cuzco, by the monolithic portal of the cyclopean temple-observatory of Tiahuanaco, and by many other monuments throughout Central and Southern America.[654]

Astronomically Aligned Structures

One of the attributes that tie these lines to our story, besides the South American location, are the astronomical implications:

Like the Native Americans, the Egyptians placed great importance on the sun.... The orientation of Egyptian pyramids suggests that their knowledge of geography and astronomy was impressive. The four corners of most pyramids line up almost exactly with the four cardinal directions, only deviating by about six hundredths of a percent.[655]

The Bimini Breakwater—covered in Chapters 6 to 8—and some of the mounds in North America have astronomical ties as well. As in ancient Egypt, these orientations were of great importance in Nazca:

In 1941, history professor Paul Kosok traveled to Nazca to see the famous geoglyphs and happened to observe the sun setting directly over one of the long pampa lines. He was struck by the idea that the lines could be linked to the positions of the sun and other stars at different times of the year—an immense astronomical calendar

653 Whitaker, Alex. *The top 50 megaliths.*

654 Braghine, Alexander. *The Shadow of Atlantis*, p. 181.

655 Belmonte, Izpisúa, "The Origin of the Universe" (answer key, Science for the Contemporary World, Institute for the International Education of Students, Hellín, Spain, May 6, 2015).

written on the ground, or as Kosok put it, "the largest astronomy book in the world."[656]

Yet again, we see that the pre-Columbian and pre-Mongolian connection between South America and Egypt is evident and indisputable. In the end, however, South America's civilizations must all bow to their mother civilization somewhere in the Nile Valley. The idea that the Incas built all the magnificent structures in South America shall now be silenced here, once and for all:

Fig. 34: Caracol at Chichen Itza, an ancient domed astronomical observatory, Yucatan Peninsula. *A Public Domain photo.*

> *In the sixteenth century the Spanish chronicler Cieza de Lion asked the Aymara...Indians, who have lived in the vicinity of Tiahuanaco since the times immemorial...whether the city's many megalithic structures were the work of the Incas: They laughed at the question, affirming that they were made long before the Inca reign.*[657]

> *The layout suggests a temple or an observatory. Well preserved and each weighing several tons, the stones were arranged upright and evenly spaced...What impressed researchers was the sophistication*

656 Braghine, Alexander. *The Shadow of Atlantis*, p. 260.

657 Ibid., p. 220.

of the construction. The stones appear to have been laid out to help pinpoint the winter solstice, when the sun is at its lowest in the sky. The site, thought to be an observatory or place of worship, predates European colonization and is said to suggest a sophisticated knowledge of astronomy. Its appearance is being compared to the English site of Stonehenge. It was traditionally thought that before European colonization, the Amazon had no advanced societies.[658]

We know differently now because of the existence of this and many other ancient structures in South America. We know it was built before European colonization. The pre-Columbian Brazilian Amazon has been stereotyped as a jungle filled with big snakes, large cats and hunter-gathering nomads with bones in their noses. The combination of satellite imaging surveys and corporations destroying the Amazon rainforest can now be seen:

This has revealed a sophisticated pre-Columbian monument-building society with sophisticated landscape management techniques, such as elevated terraces for agriculture and living, as well as dams and fishponds to manage aquatic fauna in order to guarantee the necessary protein intake. This is in the upper Amazon Basin on the east side of the Andes. An unknown people constructed earthworks of a precise geometric plan connected by straight orthogonal right angles roads that stretch over a region more than 250 km across.[659]

Brazilian Stonehenge: Dams, Roads and Earthworks

Archaeologists have found ruins of the Brazilian Stonehenge in the most northeastern corner of Brazil, in a remote section in the state of Ampia. In the first decade of the 21st century, archaeologists working on a hillside north of Lima, Peru, announced the discovery of the oldest astronomical

---

658 Kingstone, Steve. (Saturday, May 2006). "'Brazilian Stonehenge' discovered."

659 Parssinen, M., D. Schaan, and A. Ranzi (2009). "Pre-Columbian geometric earthworks in the upper Purus: a complex society in western Amazonia." *Antiquity*, Vol. 83, No. 322, p. 1084.

observatory in the Western Hemisphere—giant stone carvings, apparently 4,200 years old, that align with sunrise and sunset on Dec. 21.[660]

Archaeologists have also found evidence of several complex pre-Columbian societies that built other earthworks, such as sunken plazas and mounds. Bridges, roads and moats were found connected to some earthworks. Anthropogenic earthworks, geometrically patterned, have caused debates and arguments. As of today, 200 such sites have been discovered over an expansive area, extending from northern Bolivia down to the southern state of the Amazon. The earthworks have been shaped into perfect rectangles, circles and composite figures that have been sculpted, appearing to be used for protection and/or ceremonial enclosures.

A site named Fazenda Colorado has three structures. There is an opening in the southwestern corner that connects to a 180-foot broad avenue. On each side of the entrance, one may notice two high mounds reminding one of towers. The road extends for about 160 yards, until it is no longer visible.

Since most of the areas have been discovered because of deforestation, there is a possibility that many more sites may still be found inside the existing forests. Because of the advantages of river travel, geometric earthworks that were linked by roads were found near the junction of the Purus and Acre Rivers. This enlarged the development of the glyph-type sites by more than 124 miles. Whether these sites were mostly defensive or ceremonial, it is clear that the area was highly populated by a sedentary population by the time of European contact.

It is possible that the Proto-Manding or the Manding, who were responsible for the technology they brought to Central America, built a civilization there at the time when Bimini was part of the larger island. It is most likely that it was the Proto-Manding who built Schoch's underwater city just off southwestern Cuba, and the structures around the corner in the Bahamas. Further discussion for a more accurate, earlier, realistic date for the "first glimmerings of Olmec civilization," is unfortunately beyond the scope of this book.

The structures in Central and South America were not built just before Columbus arrived, nor were the Bimini Breakwater and pier. The Olmecs have been designated the "Mother Culture" and first civilization

660 Lehman, Stan. (2006). "Another 'Stonehenge' discovered in Amazon: Centuries-old granite may have served as observatory."

of the Americas.[661] Remember, in the Americas, they constructed the first pyramids, temples, "grand ceremonial centers to sculpt bas reliefs, to carve hard stone and to invent writing."[662] Maya rest upon an Olmec base."[663] As stated by historian Michael Coe, "There is not the slightest doubt that all later civilizations in Mesoamerica, whether Mexican or the presence of the ancient Egyptians in the Americas and the age of the oldest structures in the Americas, predate the Asians in the Americas by many thousands of years. As the title of this book designates, neither the Vikings nor the Mongolians can claim primacy, "the first Americans were Africans."

Migration of Structures, Artifacts, and Dolmen

A dolmen is a very large stone (usually flat) forming a sort of table or stage that is laid on top of smaller, vertical support stones. Let us follow the path of dolmen from the Nile Valley to New England, as we followed the mounds to the Americas. Dolmens are very ancient and widespread: "A Dolmen surrounded by a circle was found by... de Morgan in the desert near Edfu in Southern Egypt, then... Wilson and Felkin describe a number of simple dolmens which exist near Lado in the Southern Sudan."[664] They are also found at several sites all over North Africa, namely in Morocco, Tunis and Algeria.[665]

There are also dolmens in Spain, France and Ireland. The oldest European examples are found in Brittany in northern France, and date to the 5th millennium B.C. Dolmens are also present in the Middle East, North Africa, and Asia, and especially large numbers exist in Korea.[666]

661 Flannery, K.V., and J. Marcus. "Formative Mexican Chiefdoms and the Myth of the "Mother Culture." *Journal of Anthropological Archaeology*, Vol. 19. Issue 1, March 2000, Pages 1-37.

662 Winters, Clyde. "Malinke-Bambara Loan Words in the Mayan Languages."

663 Cartwright, Mark. "Olmec Civilization." *Ancient History Encyclopedia*. August 30, 2013. https://www.ancient.eu/Olmec_Civilization.

664 Peet, T. Eric. (2006). *Rough Stone Monuments and Their Builders* (England, The Echo Library), p.62.

665 Susani, Crowley, & Parker. (2016). Boulder Center for Master Builders. https://bouldermasterbuilders.com/resources/definitions/.

666 Whitaker, A. (April 2012). Exploring the Frontiers of Pre-History. http://www.ancient-wisdom.com/dolmen.htm.

Below we have more evidence. This time, instead of ancient people migrating, we have stone circles that follow the same familiar design as the dolmen, from the southern to northern Nile Valley and North Africa, as well as from southern to northwestern Europe into the Americas.

Stonehenges and Stone Circles

The African Stonehenge, at Nabta Playa in Southern Egypt, predates the 14,000-year-old British Stonehenge by thousands of years.[T] Stonehenge is Britain's most famous prehistoric icon. It is a megalithic circle of stones. "These blocks weigh up to fifty or sixty tons, and the tallest stands 23 feet (7 m) above ground."[667] "D. Q. Bowen, Professor of Earth Sciences at Cardiff University, has applied Chlorine-36 dating on a sample of igneous rock, or bluestone from Stonehenge...and found the rock was cut and used 14,000 years ago."[668] In there was mention of the American Stonehenge in New England labeled "Mystery Hill" near Salem, New Hampshire.

David Brody, a local lawyer and mystery novelist, explains that "a complex of cairns, walls, chambers and huts was encircled, at a distance of approximately 100 yards, by notched 'sighting stones' that lined up with the sunrise and sunset on important dates like the summer and winter solstices. You'll find the same type of construction in Scotland, Ireland and England, as well as other North American sites stretching from eastern Canada down to the Hudson River Valley," he said as we walked along.[669]

The trail of Africans moving into Europe, penetrating the Arctic, and then the Americas, is very transparent. With the entrance of the American Stonehenge dwellings being so very small, it leaves little doubt that the people who built those structures were very short as well. This is another "smoking gun" that leads us back to the short Anu/Twa from Africa.

The approximate 4000-year old date given the American Stonehenge puts it at the beginning of the Bronze Age—beginning in the Near East

667 "Primitive Stone Monuments" (n.d). Accessed on January 12, 2010 from http://1911encyclopedia.orgPrimitive_Stone_Monuments.

668 Talboys, Dean. "Stonehenge: Geological feature indicates the site was constructed at the end of the last Ice Age, 14,000 Years Ago." (2008). Accessed November 21, 2009. https://www.pr.com/press-release/107717.

669 Atkinson, J. "America's Stonehenge: A Classic Whodunit and Whydunit." NYTimes.com (2009).

and Southeastern Europe in the late 4th and early 3rd millennium B.C. After making a complete study of the American Stonehenge in Salem New Hampshire, CAS Archaeology Professor Curtis Runnels at Boston University said:

> *The theory that America's Stonehenge was built by Celts in ancient times has absolutely no credibility. No Bronze Age artifacts have been found there.... In fact, no one has found a single artifact of European origin from that period anywhere in the New World.*[670]

(See Fig. 35. Dr. Imhotep, stands 5 feet, 9 inches. But even at that height he must actually bend down and kneel at the entrance of one of the dwellings at the "Mystery Hill" site.)

Fig. 35: Dr. Imhotep at American Stonehenge, Salem, New Hampshire. *Photography by Teresa Gray-Jones.*

In the same vein, Fell acknowledges that this assessment has been made about his work: "My book *America B.C.* was dismissed by most

---

670 Fitzgerald, C. (2002). Stonehenge in America? Archaeology professor debunks claims for ancient rock structures a pseudo-science fallacy. B.U. Bridge, February, 1, 2002, Vil. V, No.21 http://www.bu.edu/bridge/archive/2002/02-01/archaeology.htm.

archaeologists as ignorant rubbish."[671] There are also stonehenges in areas northwest of Mystery Hill: "The circles of standing stone that occur in large numbers in Europe also span the entire continent of North America from New England to California."[672]

These circles begin in the Nile Valley, up to England, over to Canada, New England, and are found as far away as California. Brophy believes the oldest are in Nabta Playa, Egypt; dated to "17,700 B.C."[673]

In the middle of North America is an ancient 180-foot rock circle in Arizona, northwest of Tucson that is found in the Tortolita Mountains. The site is called Zodiac ridge. The circle contains more than 180 stones. "It contains alignments to the 18.61-year lunar cycle, the solstices, equinox and several stars including the constellation of Orion. Petroglyphs that have Egyptian-like hieroglyphs have been found nearby."[674]

Phallic Symbols

The phallus was a symbol of fertility and regeneration. Phallic symbols of worship are more glaring pieces of evidence that have been traced back to the Nile Valley. The obelisk, or teckenu, is a monolith representing a phallus, which represents fertility, rebirth and regeneration. Its origins lie in ancient Egypt.[675] Phallic symbols can also be found in Nigeria,[676] Spain, and France in the Eastern Hemisphere as well.

Also in the Western Hemisphere, such as in Vermont in New England,[677] as are mounds and dolmen. The largest representation of this

671 U.C.R. Faculty (n.a.). A View from the Bronze Age. www.faculty. edu/~legneref/bronze/bronze4.htm.

672 Fell, Barry. *America B.C.: Ancient Settlers in the New World*, p. 130.

673 Brophy, Thomas G. *The Origin Map*. pp. 109, back cover.

674 Little, Gregory. (2001). *Mound Builders*. (Tennessee, Eagle Wing Books), p. 203.

675 Fell, Barry. *America B.C.: Ancient Settlers in the New World*, p. 130.

676 Brophy, Thomas G. *The Origin Map*, p. 109.

677 Diop, Cheikh A. (1974). *The African Origin of Civilization*, p. 89.

ancient structure in the United States can be seen in Washington D.C. This ancient phallic symbol is "hiding" next to the Smithsonian Institution. It has been given a disguised name. It is not called a giant phallic symbol, representing the regeneration of a human being. It is called the "Washington Monument," secretly representing the rebirth of the English way of life on a different continent, beginning with the 13 colonies and ending with 50 states.

Metallurgy and Ancient Missouri Iron Mine

Was there metallurgy in Ohio before Columbus? Metallurgy was not invented in Ohio, Europe or Asia. Who brought metallurgy to Ohio and where did they first go to practice it? Tracing the history of metallurgy begins in Swaziland, South Africa, with the men of the Upper Paleolithic Age who mined iron *30,000 years ago*. That mine is the most ancient mine in the world.[678] A block of hematite (ore) extracted from this mine, which was found on top of a coal seam, was dated by Yale University. Yes, documentation shows Africans mining iron in 30,000 B.C. and smelting iron at least by 8,000 B.C. Iron was being used by the people in Ta-Seti Nubia, as cited in The Egyptian Book of the Dead.[679]

Much later, "Iron was known to the ancient Egyptians by 3000 B.C. On the monuments of the Temple of Karnak in Egypt are pictures of ancient methods of iron reduction."[680] This 3000-year date is most likely inaccurate because "Author Graham Hancock claims Egypt must be at least 11,700 years old. Be mindful of the fact that Egypt's greatest temple, the Temple of Karnak, is at least that old based on sound astronomy."[681] Iron was used in the Nile Valley at least 10,000 years ago, and very probably even earlier. Diop wrote: "An iron plate was found in the inner joints of the masonry on the south face near the mouth of the air channel of the Great Pyramid (p. 64), and the type of iron found was non-meteoric" (p. 65).[682]

---

678 Diop, Cheikh A. *Civilization or Barbarism*, p. 12.

679 Mallery, Arlington H. *Lost America*, p. 198.

680 Hancock and Faiia. *Heaven's Mirror*, pp. 305, 306.

681 Ibid.

682 Diop, Cheikh A. (1986b). Iron in the Ancient Egyptian Empire, quoted in Van Sertima, Ivan. and L. Williams (Eds.), *Great African Thinkers* (pp. 64-73). (New Jersey, Journal of African Civilizations Ltd., Inc.)

Non-meteoric means it was mined by humans and did not just fall from the sky. That author was not alone in his claims. Two other authors joined Diop:[683]

The iron plate was originally observed in 1837 by J. R. Hill, a British engineer. It was embedded within a joint inside the southern shaft of the King's Chamber of Cheops, the two outer tiers of the stones of the resent surface of the pyramid. Mr. Hill and others with him then presented certificates stating that the iron plate was contemporaneous with the pyramid, and then deposited the ancient relic at the British Museum.[684]

Is it possible that someone could have planted this piece of metal on the surface of the pyramid shaft long after the construction of the pyramid? Ogden wrote:

The most celebrated instance of iron in the Old Kingdom is the supposed iron sheet found in 1837 near an air passage in the Fourth-Dynasty Great Pyramid at Giza, deep within the masonry and revealed after blasting.[685]

Ogden then explains that the iron sheet was very unlikely to have been planted after the construction of this pyramid because it was not found on a surface wall but deep within the structure.

As stated in Chapter 1, only the African part of the human family existed 250,000 years ago in the Americas. They probably were not smelting iron or writing in Egyptian hieroglyphics yet, but they were surely doing both before the Vikings or Columbus visited the Americas, as illustrated below. These short-statured Africans in America were known for their metallurgical skills, just as their ancestors were:

In southwestern Pickaway County, Ohio...these Ohio furnaces are both prehistoric and pre-Columbus.... Artifacts recovered from the Lynn site, along with photos, were examined by Carroll Mobley, a Professor of Metallurgical Engineering of The Ohio State University,

---

683 Bauval, Robert, and A. Gibert. *The Orion Mystery* (New York, Three Rivers Press, 1994), p. 236.

684 Ibid.

685 Nicholson, Paul, and Ian Shaw (Eds.). *Ancient Egyptian Materials and Technology* (Massachusetts, Cambridge University Press, 2000), p. 167.

Columbus, Ohio. The professor told us we had indeed found an iron furnace, based on evidence he was shown.[686]

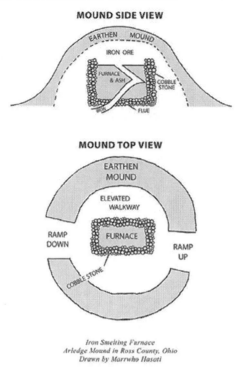

Fig. 36: Arledge Iron Smelting Mound Sketch. *Drawn by Marrwho Hasati.*

As mentioned earlier, these short-statured Africans in America were known for their metallurgical skills, just as their ancestors in the Nile Valley and British Isles. Data has now surfaced that says people were also smelting iron in ancient North America. According to Howe and Mallery, the Mound Builders may have been smelting iron 11,000 to 8,000 B.C.

Iron furnace and Iron artifacts were found by J. V. Howe in Virginia in 1946 in the Roanoke River Valley near Clarksville. In their interpretation of evidence found at the Howe sites, both Howe and Mallery made the suggestion that the iron smelters and associated artifacts might be 10,000 to 13,000 years old because of their close association with Fulsom's spear points on all sites of discovery.[687]

To keep one iron furnace burning takes a tremendous amount of wood, coal or some other type of fuel. The APG Society alone found, "30

686 Conner, William D. *Iron Age America Before Columbus*, pp. 65, 67.

687 Ibid.

plus pit iron furnaces in southern Ohio,"[688] and that is only one group that found iron furnaces.

In Mallery's *Lost America*, he mentions that one iron-smelting furnace was found in Allyn Mound: "near Frankfort, Ohio, was a beehive type mound with charcoal and iron ore found inside."[689] These are essential items to producing iron (see Fig. 36). In "Spruce Hill Ohio, the relics of an ancient Iron Age civilization left hundreds of tons of a particular iron slag."[690] This was no small operation, but evidence of a large, sustained industry.

These ancient ironworkers must have used some other type of fuel in addition to/or instead of just burning wood. If they only used trees for fuel, the number of trees needed to supply the needs of these prehistoric iron furnaces would have been tremendous. There should have been huge areas of open spaces caused by the deforestation the prehistoric iron makers made to feed their hungry furnaces. Yet, when the first White pioneers arrived in North America:

> *It was said that a squirrel could travel tree to tree from the Atlantic Coast to the prairie grasslands of the Great Plains in Midwest America without touching the ground.*[691]

> *It is known from the historic record that huge trees still covered the Arledge and Haskins furnace mounds in the early 1800s.*[692] *The forests returned long after the Mound Builders built their iron smelting mounds. This could also mean that quite an amount of years passed between the time these people were smelting iron and the time the Europeans entered the Americas. Ancient sites containing iron ore "can even be found on many hilltops in Virginia and the Ohio Valley... and deposits of slag (slag is stony waste matter separated from metals during the smelting) found in a similar mound at...Sweden.*[693]

---

688 Mallery, Arlington. H. *Lost America*, p. 192.

689 Ibid.

690 Ibid., p. 193.

691 Ibid., p. 20.

692 Ibid., p. 214.

693 Ibid., p. 184.

Are they authentic? There are other artifacts, such as carbonized axe blades, found in mounds in Virginia and Newfoundland.[694] A real treat was the "iron shovel" which Dr. Imhotep actually found down in the ash of a prehistoric furnace in one of the ancient Ohio mounds. This heavy metal shovel was later tested by Dr. A. M. Hall, a metallurgist of the Battelle Memorial Institute of Columbus Ohio.[695]

Later an iron chisel or celt was found under similar conditions in a mound in a North Carolina burial pit.[696]

"The first artifact uncovered at the Arledge Mound was a shovel.... At first Mallery thought the shovel looked exactly like any modern shovel because of its regular shape."[697] Three more iron shovels were found at Lynn Acres in the south-central part of Ohio. The shovel blades were ten inches wide and 16 inches long. Their thickness could not be determined because of the rust factor.

In the prehistoric Arledge Furnace Mound, two iron shovels and an iron axe were found:

Commenting on a 62-pound cast iron bar he found in the Arledge Mound, Mallery said it was found "lying under the hard unbroken furnace floor" which proves the bar was not formed by intrusion or intruders (p.48). Some readers may be thinking that Mallery found something he thought was shaped something like a shovel.[698]

From a mound furnace in Oak Hill, Virginia, "part of the iron and slag from there, have also been accepted as authentic by the Smithsonian Institute where they are at present stored."[699] The carbon-14 method of dating applied in these detailed studies should put aside all doubts of the pre-Columbus age of these mound-furnace sites. Here again, the trail leading to the truth grows for iron-smelting in mounds. Validation can be found, however, because all these authenticated iron artifacts can be traced

---

694 Conner, William D. *Iron Age America Before Columbus*, pp. 134, 204.

695 Ibid., p. 134.

696 Ibid., p. 184.

697 Mallery, Arlington. H. *Lost America*, p. 193.

698 Joseph, Frank. *Advanced Civilizations of Prehistoric America*, p. 60.

699 Conner, William D. *Iron Age America Before Columbus*, pp. 134, 204.

back to the ancient Nile Valley in Egypt, Sudan, Liberia, India, England, Germany, Belgium, Scandinavia, Sweden, Greenland, North America, Virginia and Ohio.[700]

The Book of the Dead, whose doctrine is earlier than any in the history of Egypt, teaches us that Isis was a Negro woman, and Osiris was a Negro man, who was an Anu. Thus, in the oldest Egyptian texts, his name is accompanied by an ethnic designation to indicate his Nubian origin.[701]

In Diop's (1974) book, Budge is quoted as having said that the ancient Anu were metal producers from Nubia. Osiris and Isis' son Horus was Anu.[702] Their son Horus and his followers were metal workers. Bauval (2007) agrees with Diop in that "a small metal cutting tool, a sort of carpenter's adze, was used on the mummy in a ceremony known as 'the opening of the mouth ceremony.'"[703] This adze was made of iron. The Egyptian Book of the Dead reveals that the god Horus used this instrument in the ceremony.[704]

The reader should be told that the most sacred and ancient book of the Egyptians was their Book of the Dead. That ancient book actually predates Dynastic Egypt; it is older than any other written history of Egypt.[705]

The book originated in Nubia, which is the home of Isis, Osiris and Horus. This takes iron forging back to the beginning of history, and it occurs in Africa. These short African people were making metal before Egypt existed.

---

700 Diop, Cheikh A. *The African Origin of Civilization*, pp. 197-209.

701 Ibid., p. 89.

702 Budge, E. A. (1902). *A History of Egypt*, Vol. I (London: Kegan, PAUL, Trench, Trubner & Co. LTD), quoted in Finch, Charles. S. (1998). *The Star of Deep Beginnings* (Georgia, Khenti Press), p. 25.

703 Bauval, Robert. *The Egypt Code*, p. 11.

704 Ibid., p. 11.

705 Wainwright, G. A. Letopolis. (1932). *The Journal of Egyptian Archaeology*, Vol. 18, pp. 159-172.

In 1839 A.D., Champollion-Figeac, a French Egyptologist, was the first person to decipher ancient hieroglyphics. His work put the beginning date for Egypt at 5867 B.C.[706] Macleod, a *Time Magazine* writer says that Kendall has found that "Nubia, not Egypt, may have been the first true African civilization in 8000 B.C."[707] So, iron was being made by the Anu in the Nile Valley before Dynastic Egypt even existed. We therefore see that the Anu have a tradition of metalsmithing that their descendants continued. "These little people made bronze[708]...and 'metal swords of magic temper' including body armor."[709]

There is a compelling structural, as well as cultural trail that links these small Africans in the Americas to their ancestors in Africa. After a deep study of ancient iron-smelting furnaces in North America, Africa, Europe and Asia, Mallery[710] came "to the conclusion that the iron industry developed from a common origin."[711]

The oldest iron mines dating back to "30,000 B.C. furnaces,"[712] "on the monuments on the Temple of Karnak in Egypt...can be seen in pictures of the ancient methods of iron reduction,[713] and writings about iron implements[714] appear in the Nile Valley. It seems that Mallery's "common origin" for metal making may have been found. This trail leads us to the Nile Valley in Africa.

---

706 Jackson, John G. (1972). *Man, God, and Civilization* (New York, Carol Publishing Group), p. 219.

707 Macleod, Scott. (1997). "The Nile's other Kingdom." Time, Vol. 150, No. 11, p. 102. http://content.time.com/time/magazine/article/0,9171,138301.00.html.

708 Ibid., p. 102.

709 Budge, E. A. *A History of Egypt*.

710 Ibid., p. 44.

711 Mallery, Arlington. H. *Lost America*, p. 197.

712 Ibid., pp. 156, 197.

713 Diop, Cheikh A. *Civilization or Barbarism*, p. 12.

714 Del Grande, Nino. "Prehistoric Iron Smelting in Africa." *Natural History Magazine*, Vol. 32,. No 1. Sept/Oct. (1932). pp. 531-539.

While we are dealing with iron, there is one more ancient iron mine worth mentioning in pre-Columbus North America, even though it was on the other side of the Mississippi River from Ohio's Adena iron smelters. Where there is one there are likely to be others that have not yet been discovered. The ancient iron smelters of Missouri probably used this iron mine.

> *A Smithsonian Institute archaeologist, W. H. Holmes, and the city archaeologist for St. Louis, D. L. Bushnell, confirmed the pre-Columbus operation of an iron mine in Franklin County, near Leslie, Missouri.... They found the prehistoric mine was about 100 feet wide, running about 150 feet long to a depth of 20 feet..."the passageways extended even below the present floor of the mine." The scientists recovered some one thousand stone mining tools— sleighs, hammerheads, and weights—that had been piled near the entrance.*[715]

According to the Medieval Technology department of the American History of the Center for Medieval Studies at the Pennsylvania State University, the "Native Americans or Amerinds had some experience with extracting precious metals but had not mastered the art of iron extraction; that knowledge was to arrive with the Europeans."[716]

Black dwarfs in Europe were well known for their iron smelting abilities. Amerinds were not. Also, if the reader remembers, Cyrus Thomas from the Smithsonian Institute commented on "Indian Mounds" in America: "There was a race of mound builders in America distinct from the American Indians."[717] "Distinct from" means the Amerinds did not build mounds. A dwarf skeleton was found in "another mound in Waverly, Ohio which did contain the presence of a dwarf."[718]

> *The artifacts excavated in the ancient mounds of the New World indicate that Africans built many of these mounds. The fact that many art styles and artifacts recovered from these mounds illustrate*

715 Joseph, Frank. *Advanced Civilizations of Prehistoric America*, p. 62.

716 Wainwright, G. A. Letopolis. The *Journal of Egyptian Archaeology*, pp. 159-172.

717 Joseph, Frank. *Advanced Civilizations of Prehistoric America*, p. 62.

718 Walton, Steven. (n.d.). "Iron Beginnings in America." Accessed on May 9, 2015. http://www.engr.psu.edu/mtah/articles/iron_ beginnings.htm.

similar themes, suggest an origin for the mound builders from a common ideological system.[719]

Lastly, we have the pipe in question. During the 1901, Ohio Historical Society archaeologists were excavating Chillico, and in Burial Mound #12, they found an extraordinary effigy pipe of a man dressed in Adena attire exhibiting dwarfism.[720] We, therefore have four pieces of evidence that suggest that the people responsible for smelting iron in ancient Illinois were dwarfs:

1. Amerinds did not smelt iron in pre-Columbian times.
2. Amerinds did not build mounds.
3. The presence of dwarfs was found in two separate mounds, in ancient Illinois a dwarf skeleton.
4. An effigy pipe of a dwarf dressed in Adena attire.

Over and over in his book, Mallery insists that the Viking Norsemen built all the mounds and iron-smelting furnaces, but just as with Fell, where is the evidence to prove his case? To Mallery's credit, he admits that, "no genuine artifacts...used by the Norse have ever been found in America."[721] Unfortunately for Mr. Mallery, no evidence, no argument. Just as in Fell's (1982) case, neither his Celts, the mythical King, nor the Viking Norsemen could have built megalithic mounds with or without the iron-smelting furnaces in ancient America.

There is, however, a story that the Vikings have admitted to. When they needed iron, they had no problem going to the Black dwarfs, just as the Viking god of thunder, Thor went to the mythical dwarves for their iron:

In Viking mythology even the god Thor went to the Black Dwarf blacksmith masters to have his hammer made. Thor's hammer...in the Eddaic (i.e. Scandinavian people before their Christianization) tradition it is an iron weapon forged by Svartálfar (black elves, correlated with the dvergar dwarves) named Sindri and Brokkr.[722]

---

719 Childress, David H. (1992). "Archaeological Coverups." *Nexus Magazine*, Volume 2, #13. Mapelton Qld: Australia: Nexus.

720 Joseph, Frank. *Advanced Civilizations of Prehistoric America*, p. 62.

721 Mallery, Arlington. *H. Lost America*, p. 136.

722 "Thor's Hammer: A Norse Viking Symbol." (2009).

Thor was Viking mythology, but the Viking's message to us is obvious. They either did not make iron in those early times during the formation of Viking mythological tales, or the dwarves' iron was so well made, that they found it best for the dwarves to make it for them. The fact that they were so specific that they even named the dwarves blacksmiths shows how they relied on these experts. In reality, these were probably short-statured men who actually made metal for the Vikings.

There is, however, actual physical evidence of these dwarfs making iron in Scandinavia. The Oseberg Sleigh can be seen today at the Viking Ship Museum in Oslo, Norway. This sleigh's runners were made of iron (see Fig. 37).

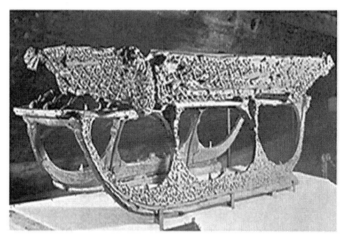

Fig. 37: Entire Oseberg Viking Sleigh: *Courtesy of Tre Tryckare. ©2015 Kulturhistorisk Museum, Oslo, Norway.*

When you observe the carvings on the sleigh (see Fig. 38), you will see the dwarfs themselves depicted. These dwarfs' ancestors, the Khoisan, are a testament to diminutive Africans entering Europe 40,000–45,000 years ago, bringing their metalsmithing skills with them from Africa. Some of their descendants were most likely the mound builders who built the iron smelting furnaces along the Ohio River.

Notice the short height of these people with an African corn-rolled hair style. Also see the female's projecting-prognathic jaw structure and protruding fleshy lips. On their sleighs these first Europeans had wooden runners. Years later the "blacksmiths" forged and began to make metal runners which were smoother, creating less resistance, producing a faster sleigh and a longer lasting runner.

Fig. 38: Enlarged Photo of Oseberg Viking Sleigh. *Courtesy of Tre Tryckare.*

Flint Arrowheads

Flint arrowheads were being made at a site in ancient Britain. Dr. Saville and his colleagues officially identified this site. What Saville found was that in Scotland 14,000 years ago, tools and flint arrowheads[723] were being used by the "dwarf races" in the British Isles.[724] These flint arrowheads are what the pre-dynastic Anu/Twa had used in Egypt, and the Sudan[725] tens of thousands of years earlier. They found stone and flint axes and arrowheads,[726] just like the pre-dynastic people in the Sudan, south of Egypt[727] used. The fact that short Blacks were the first to use flint arrowheads in Britain was so well known years ago, that when someone was found shot with a flint arrowhead, they were said to have been "elf-

723 Haworth, J. (2009). "Scotland's most ancient home found—at 14,000 years old." Accessed December 15, 2009.

724 MacRitchie, David. *The Testimony of Tradition*, p. 156.

725 Brunson, James E. (1991). *Predynastic Egypt: An African Centric View* (Illinois, Brunson), p. 36.

726 Haworth, J. "Scotland's most ancient home found—at 14,000 years old."

727 Brunson, James E. *Predynastic Egypt: An African Centric View*, p. 36.

shot."[728] The reason for this difference is the arrowheads the Europeans were using were always made of denser stone. Flint, however, is lighter and slices through the air faster than heavier arrowheads. They are also much sharper. The flint arrowheads connect the small Africans in the British Isles with their ancestors in the Nile Valley.

Boomerangs

We have all heard of Australian boomerangs, but African boomerangs? Yes, yet another artifact that gives us evidence of the Anu in America are boomerangs. Amerinds were never known to make use of a boomerang. In Egypt's Cairo museum on the second floor is the King Tut exhibit, and there are two boomerangs from King Tut's Tomb in a glass case on the wall:

> The second volume of Gaston Maspero's History of Egypt clearly showed as early as 1906 an illustration of an Egyptian with a boomerang, accompanied by the specific caption, "Hunting with a boomerang...." Dr. Carl Clausen...found boomerangs in Denmark as well...then Clausen's discovery both in western Texas and Little Salt Springs, Florida...boomerangs...carbon-dated between 9,080 and 9,572 years old.[729]

These North American boomerangs are further evidence of the Anu leaving the Nile Valley and venturing into northwestern Europe—Denmark in this case—and then on to North America.

Adobe Cliff Dwellings

Many Manding lived in ancient Egypt. Years later, when they migrated and reached western Africa, instead of building stone pyramids, they built dirt pyramids, called mounds. The proto-Manding lived on mounds along the Niger River to escape flooding. They also built dams and boats. It was most likely the Africans who built the mound cultures of ancient America

---

728 MacRitchie, David. *The Testimony of Tradition*, p. 156.

729 Rux, Bruce. (1996). *Architects of the Underworld: Unriddling Atlantis, Anomalies of Mars, and the Mystery of the Sphinx* (California, Frog, Ltd.), p. 389-90.

(primarily the Manding).[730] Although the Manding built some of the mounds in Africa, they were not the first. The Dogon were not the first to build cliff dwellings in Mali either. It was the shorter Tellem Africans who predate taller Africans who built the first cliff dwellings.

• Pueblo
(Ruins in
Southern
Colorado)

Both peoples
were short

• Dogon
(Tellum Ruins
in Mali, Africa)

Fig. 39: Upper image: Tellem Cliff Dwellings in Mali, Africa. *Courtesy of Peter Adams and Laini Torgerson.* Lower image: Pueblo Cliff Dwellings in SW Colorado, U.S.A. *Courtesy of Ron Reznick, Digital Images.*

Who were these Tellem people and from where did they originate? One of the regions to which the short-statured Anu or Twa migrated after leaving the Nile Valley was West Africa. It was they who were called the Tellem people and were "short statured."[731] Later, when the Dogon moved into that area, they coexisted for a few centuries and then the Tellem migrated to Burkina Faso. The tiny cliff dwellings of the short Tellem

---

730 Winters, Clyde. *Atlantis in Mexico*, p. 85.

731 Ibid.

people can be seen now just as in ancient times.[732] The Tellem people have a connection with America. The connection is that the so-called "Pueblo Indian" adobe cliff dwellings in the Four Corners area of the U.S. Southwest are amazingly like the Tellem's dwellings—almost identical! (see Fig. 39) How is that? There are no adobe cliff dwellings in all of Asia, so it seems there is no Asian connection or intrusion. So, the only cliff-house duplications are in the Four Corners area of the American Southwest. The builders must have come from the east.

The Dogon, descendants of the Proto-Manding people, have the obvious link of identical architecture with the Pueblo people. The Pueblo dwellings are just about identical to the adobe houses with wood roof supports that can be seen today in Mali on cliffs and in the flatlands. Since there is no identical cliff-dwelling architecture in all of Europe, these architects must have come from Africa (Alkebulan).

The cliff dwellings may not be the only feature the Pueblo have in common with the short Tellem. Eyewitnesses have described them as, "stocky Pueblos...squat, and robust Pueblo."[733] (*Squat* used as an adjective, is defined as "short and thickset.")

This is the same way the dwarf-looking Skraelings have been described. The reader must also realize that "The name "Anasazi" is used interchangeably with Pueblo."[734] Therefore, by deduction, the Anasazi must have at least begun as dwarfs, if not also remaining short statured.

Back to the architecture. To be fair, the Pueblos could have been mixed with one or several Amerind groups. But the evidence illustrates that the people who first built the cliff dwellings in the Four Corners area were probably the migrating Proto-Manding (the Tellem). So, who does the evidence show most that probably built these adobe cliff dwellings in Colorado, Mongolians or Africans?

---

732 "Mali" (2009-2015) Accessed December 17, 2009. http://us-africa. tripod.com/mali.html; Enderle, Melissa. The Dogon of Mali. (2005). Accessed on February 2, 2010. http://www.melissaenderle.com/ dogon.html.

733 Joseph, Frank. *Advanced Civilizations of Prehistoric America*, p. 138.

734 "What does Anasazi Mean?" Northern Arizona University. Accessed May, 2, 2015. http://www2.nau.edu/~sw-ptry/anasazi.htm.

Section Notes

S. Watercraft and the Popol Vuh

Just what kind of watercraft did these Africans use to sail to the Americas? In the far north they probably used seal-skinned boats and kayaks. In the other areas, they probably used a different craft. Thousands of years later the Popol Vuh was written, which was the sacred book of the ancient Quiché Mayan Indians.[735] This book "claims that the Olmec came to Mexico in "ships of bark."[736] This refers to ships made of wood, but as opposed to what? Why was it necessary to make that distinction of ships of bark? Could it be because Africans first probably came to the Americas in ships made of papyrus reeds from the shores of the Nile or Niger Rivers?

The African voyagers to the New World came here in papyrus boats. A stone stela from Izapas in southern Mexico shows the boats these Africans came in when they sailed to the Americas. These boats were carried across the Atlantic Ocean to Mexico and Brazil by the North Equatorial Current, which meets the Canaries Current off the Senegambian coast. It is interesting to note that papyrus boats are still being built in West Africa today.[737]

Papyrus boats predated those made of wood. To still be around since time immemorial, this type of watercraft must have been constructed efficiently enough to last since the time Africans used to make dugout canoes. The small Africans probably first arrived in the Americas many millennia ago in papyrus reed sail boats. You may wish to ask if there is any evidence of reed boats in the ancient Americas. Reed boats have indeed been found in the Western Hemisphere. They have been found by Lake Titicaca in South America but are known to have originated on the Nile River. Could reed boats venture out into the wide, turbulent, open ocean? Yes, Thor Heyerdahl proved it several times by crossing first from Australia to South America, and then from Africa to the Americas in reed vessels!

---

735 Goetz, Delia., and Sylvanus G. Morley. (1950). *Popol Vuh: The Sacred Book of The Ancient Quiche Maya*. (Oklahoma, University of Oklahoma Press). Accessed August 12, 2009. http://www. oocities.org/athens/academy/3088/ popol.html.

736 Winters, Clyde. "African Empires of Ancient America."

737 Ibid., p. 44.

Is this going too far? Is there really a connection of Central and South America to Ancient Egypt?

The kinship of prehistoric American and ancient Egyptian cultures is demonstrated very eloquently in the ruins of Palenque, Ocochingo, the Mitla palaces, the Xochicalco, Teotihuacan, and Sihuatan pyramids, by the decorations of the Sun Temple of Cuzco, by the monolithic portal of the cyclopean temple-observatory of Tiahuanaco, and by many other monuments throughout Central and Southern America.[738]

T. Nabta Playa Stonehenge

To go into depth on this subject is beyond the scope of this book. An in-depth analysis can be found in Thomas G. Brophy's book, *The Origin Map*. A brief explanation is appropriate here, however. Brophy is a physicist with impeccable credentials. His book supplies evidence that this ancient circle of stones, some weighing ten tons:

*is a unified and detailed astrophysical map of truly astonishing accuracy, with no less than staggering implications...**these bedrock sculptures date from much earlier than Briton's Stonehenge, from 17,700 BC to 43,000 BC.**[739]*

On a desolate plain in the Egyptian Saharan desert, west of Aswan, there is a very remote prehistoric site called Nabta Playa. There, a recently discovered complex of extremely ancient man-made megalithic structures have baffled the archaeologists who excavated them. An insight into the meaning and use of these megaliths led to a step-by-step sequence of discoveries, verified by measure and calculation, revealing that the megalithic architecture at Nabta Playa is a unified and detailed astrophysical map of truly astonishing accuracy, with staggering implications. Nabta Playa appears to be an accurate depiction of the Milky Way Galaxy, as it was oriented astronomically at a specific time: vernal equinox heliacal rising of the galactic center of the Milky Way galaxy in 17,700 B.C. The designers of the megaliths had a basic understanding of physics and knowledge of astronomy that rivaled or surpassed ours today.[740]

---

738 Braghine, Alexander. *The Shadow of Atlantis*, p. 181.

739 Brophy, Thomas G. *The Origin Map*, p. 109.

740 Ibid.

U. Reed Boats

Some of the earliest rock drawings in the Nile Valley are of boats made from papyrus reeds that grew wild and in abundance beside African rivers and lakes in ancient times. As they were in ancient times, papyrus boats are still made and used by the Buduma boat builders, who built Thor Heyerdahl's Ra I and II and still live in Africa's Lake Chad area today.[741]

According to Ballard (2004), reed boats are still being made using freshly cut green papyrus reeds just as in ancient Egypt. They use "green" papyrus reeds because they do not absorb water, for they are filled with thick resin. The older brown reeds are dry and thirsty for moisture. When introduced to water, they would swell, adding weight to the craft which would weigh it down or even eventually sink it. In Lake Chad, and "Lake Tana in Ethiopia the indigenous people still make reed boats there today."[742] The papyrus boats in South America of the Suriqui people used on Lake Titicaca were:

1. Almost identical both in the method of construction and in finished appearance, to the beautifully crafted papyrus reed boats.
2. The pharaohs had sailed using reed boats on the Nile thousands of years previously.[743]
3. Remarkably, reed boats can still be seen today in Lake Chad, which lies in Niger, Nigeria, Cameroon, and Chad.

In Peru, Heyerdahl had become acquainted with the use of small reed boats on Lake Titicaca. Then, while making excavations there, Rapa Nui believed he had uncovered images of three-masted reed boats. This led Heyerdahl to speculate whether such vessels were known in ancient Egypt, were constructed by the Buduma people from Lake Chad back then, and could they have crossed the Atlantic?[744] In Africa, the more common papyrus boats were built for the Nile River and for open ocean voyages as well.

---

741 Van Sertima, Ivan. *Early America Revisited*, p. 14.

742 Dejen Dresilign, Eshete. "ECOLOGY AND POTENTIAL FOR FISHERY OF THE SMALL BARBS (CYPRINIDAE, TELEOSTEI) OF LAKE TANA, ETHIOPIA." September 2, 2003. Wageningen University; Accessed July 29, 2011. http://edepot.wur.nl/121430.

743 Hancock, Graham. Fingerprints of the Gods, p 70.

744 Van Tilburg, JoAnne. "Thor Heyerdahl" The Guardian April 19, 2002.

One papyrus boat from the Old Kingdom's 6th dynasty had 32 oars, illustrating that some of the papyrus boats were large crafts.[745] So, large or small, Papyrus reed boats were used by Africans during Zep Tepe to cross the world's oceans, creating new civilizations on every continent in the world. What about Antarctica, you ask? Did they reach Antarctica in those reed boats as well? Someone may have.

Pyramids and Sunken Cities

Google Earth images have shown photos of three pyramids in Antarctica, of all places: two of them are approximately 10 miles inland and the other is near the coastline where part of Antarctica juts out like a slightly curved finger. When they were covered with snow and ice people thought they were just mountains. However, on all of the photos the snow has melted halfway down to the base of these pyramids and the top halves· are now visible.

Fig. 40: Photo of a pyramid in Antarctica, by Ruth Doherty. https://www. msn.com/en-ca/news/world/mysterious-pyramids-found-in-antarctica/ar-AAkIAvE. *All 3 pyramid images from: ©2019 DigitalGlobe U.S. Geological Survey. Map data United Kingdom and Image credits from Richard Hoagland and NASA/JPL.*

---

745 Van Sertima, Ivan. Early America Revisited, p. 14.

Of course, there are some critics who have come out with "alternative facts" about this story. But, "time tells all tales." Some of the pyramids in the beginning were taken down off the Internet, but new pyramid finds are still popping up in Antarctica, so they evidently have left them alone. Suspiciously, they still have not announced them, or let the world know about these incredible finds for some reason.

Some people do not believe there are pyramids in Antarctica, so we use these documented pyramids as evidence. Of the three pyramids, one has been chosen to show three different photos of it. You can actually check to see this pyramid is not a Photoshop prank photo for yourself, by going to the Google Earth's site: 79 58 39.2S 81 57 32.2W shown in the next three photos.

In Figs. 40 & 41 ground-level photos showing the exact same Antarctic pyramid's location at different angles. Again, notice Fig. 41 just where the mountain range is creeping into the photo on the bottom left side.

Fig. 41: Another photo of a pyramid in Antarctica, from a satellite.

The Fig. 41 photo is just above the pyramids in question: it shows this particular photo was taken from a satellite. Whereas, the photos in figures 40 and 42 were taken from the ground level. From the bottom-left side of this photo the viewers can see a tiny rock structure first. Then look at the first pyramid where the snow drifts can be seen to have been blowing snow from the south-west corner, towards the northeast corner.

The wind blows the snow towards the side of the pyramid. Combined with the steep slope down the side of this pyramid, the snow at the top blows in a downward motion. When the wind reaches the bottom, it blows snow away from the pyramid like a slide. This lateral blowing motion away from the bottom eventually reveals a deeper amount of snow has been blown. It continues to blow away from the pyramid. See the forming snow trench on the bottom that is blowing the snow away from the side and bottom of the structure. As it blows, the sides of the trench begin to accumulate snow from the pyramid in a straight northeast direction, blowing and forming a trench. The snow from the trench then blows next to the right side of the growing snow mound at the side of the structure.

Now notice the arc-shaped, wind-blown dark line on the bottom right side, beginning to grow darker because it is forming a snowless trench at the windward side of the trench. All the snow, however, is not blown out of the trench but some accumulates on the top of the windward side of the trench. Notice the growing elevation of snow beginning on the upper lip of the trench.

If you look at the twin sister pyramid to the immediate right, it is sitting directly in the direction of the wind path. The snow surrounding it, has accumulated during the hours before, is still sitting in situ. The first pyramid is blocking most of the wind current's blasts, thus, much less snow is lost around the base of that second pyramid. That accumulation of snow causes this second pyramid to look like it is sinking into the snow; when it has not lost the amount of snow that the first pyramid has. Thus, making it look taller.

Again, what this shows is that more snow has blown off the first pyramid than the one to the right piling up around it, thus making the illusion of the second pyramid looking smaller than the first. However, one can plainly see from the next photo (in Fig. 42), taken from ground-level, that the pyramid on the right is a large pyramid as well.

Then on the side of the first pyramid on the bottom left, the snow drift has been blown away from the south side of the structure. So, now we see that more snow has blown off and around the second pyramid, making the illusion that the first pyramid is larger.

Enter the pyramid climbers (see Fig. 42). Below, on the side of the twin pyramid mountains is a hiking team passing by. On the right side of the photo, closest to the camera there is a hiker. He seems to be walking down a slope out the mountains towards the pyramid. Then, looking in front of him, other hikers are seen walking down the slope towards the pyramid.

Fig. 42: Hikers walking down around a large out-cropping part of the mountain at the side of the pyramid.

These "snow pyramids," as they have been dubbed, have been a definite surprise to everyone who sees them. They are just a part of that extremely old civilization that existed on Earth before Noah's flood, called "Zep Tepi." We mustn't forget the surprise we all had when they began finding pyramids and entire cities under the waters of the ocean, all around the world.

For confirmation, just go to "Google Earth" to check these directional numerals yourself at: World's Treasures, pub. 3/31/2018/. https://www.youtube.com/watch?v=cJJZULxr33a

Scientists discovered on the territory of the Antarctic shelf three pyramidal objects. According to a preliminary version of geologists, the pyramids are of unnatural origin. They could not have formed by nature. They were built by man, scientists concluded.

Moving right along, to the biggest and most phenomenal surprise: the face and **pyramids on Mars**! In the next frame, you shall see the human face near a pyramid. This gigantic stone-mountain-top carving is an obvious message to those who view it. This face is obviously human and built by humans, as these pyramids were!

Given…humans do not carve giant faces of Martians on Earth. Conversely, and obviously, Martians do not carve human faces on Mars! This carved face was an obvious message. Do these photos not visually declare that humans were here? It was we who built those pyramids and signed the proof by carving a gigantic human face on the top of a near-by mountain![746]

About the Face & Pyramid Found on Mars

Published July 26, 2017 by Arjun Walia in *Alternative News*

In 1976, the United States sent a pair of space probes, known as Viking 1 and Viking 2, to Mars (https:www.youtube.com/watch?v=cJJZULxr33a). Viking 1 was launched on August 20th, 1975, and Viking 2 was launched in September of the same year. Both probes photographed the surface of Mars from orbit, and one studied the planet from the surface.

As Viking 1 spacecraft was circling the planet, it spotted the shadowy likeness of a human face. An enormous head nearly two miles from end to end seemed to be staring back at the cameras from a region of the Red Planet called Cydonia. A pyramid structure was also seen.

Bob Dean, a retired United States Army Command Sergeant Major who also served at the Supreme Headquarters Allied Powers Europe (SHAPE) of NATO as an intelligence analyst, gave a lecture on footage and photos that had been erased and kept hidden for decades.

Dr. John Brandenburg worked for the government with top-secret security clearances on various projects. Brandenburg was also the Deputy Manager of the Clementine Mission to the Moon.

"Someone complained to me, John, why do you have to bring Cydonia into this? And I said, because I can read a map. Here's what's at Cydonia Mensa. There's the face on Mars, there's the D & M pyramid… Here it is in a second shot, this was taken July 25th, this was taken 30 days later, the government was apparently doing a follow-up investigation. These two pictures...tell you everything you need to know about what's at Cydonia Mensa (region of Mars). If you see on a planet that used to be Earth-like, a

---

746 Wilcock, David. https://www.youtube.com/watch?v=S-nHYzK-Bvg.22"08. From RICHARD HOAGLAND and the MESSAGE of CYDONIA": https://divinecosmos.com/books-free-online/the-shift-of-the-ages/64-the-shift-of-the-ages-chapter-08-richard-hoagland-and-the-message-of-cydonia/.

carved human face and a pyramid within 5 km of each other, it doesn't take a rocket scientist to figure out what this all means."[747]

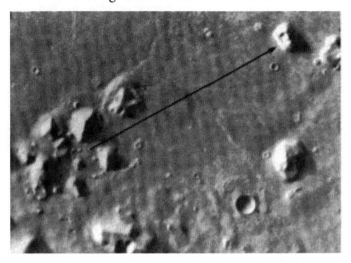

Fig. 43: Pyramids and human face on Mars.

747 Friedman, Janice. "Cydonia, the Face & Pyramid on Mars Are Real, Claim Former NASA Scientists." *Ancient Code*, June 16, 2018. https://www. ancient-code.com/cydonia-the-face-pyramid-on-mars-are-real-claim-former-nasa-scientists/.

Chapter 6

The Largest African Underwater Site, 55 Miles East of Miami

Moving right along, several pyramids have also been found under water on Earth. There is an entire city under water 3.5 miles southwest of Cuba. There sunken city is complete with pyramidal structures, buildings, and bridges still intact! There are two pyramids underwater just off New Providence Island in the Bahamas as well. Their exact location is 21° 56'26.50"N 77º19'39.35"W. A military presence is always near and will let no one near above or below the waves. But it can be seen from far above the Earth.

Underwater cities have been well known for years. The last Ice Age flood raised our oceans 200–300 feet. There is another underwater city just off the southwestern coast of India; another sunken pyramid and entire city off the coast of Japan's Yonaguni Jima that was sunk by an earthquake 2000 years ago. In the end, there are ancient pyramids all over the Earth, above and below the waves, and now, no longer unknown.

The movement of Africans to the Americas did not happen overnight, of course. The evidence of this movement traced in this book shows the earliest known contact began 100,000 years ago, attested to by the discovery made by Nadine Guido. Ever since then, people have been sailing to the Americas. Countless millennia later the Egyptian/Manding could most likely be credited with building a relationship between Africa, the Bahamas and the Americas. The link to this relationship is an extremely large, ancient, underwater structure.

This one structure has more pieces connecting it to ancient Egypt and is larger than any other artifact in North America. This relic is larger than life—it is as large as six football fields. Specific equipment is not needed for you to view. It can be easily seen with the naked eye. This structure is a relic from the "Pyramid Age," when some of mankind's greatest accomplishments were being built. That is not an idle statement. The evidence for that statement will be given in the pages that follow.

This structure was constructed with massive blocks, like those used to construct the Great Pyramid. The Bimini Road blocks are held together without cement just as in the Great Pyramid. To hold some of the blocks in place, the connectors used are obviously waterproof: dovetails, talons, keystones, tongue and groove joints, or they used blocks so large and precisely cut, that their sheer volume of weight holds them in place, similar to the pyramids. Many of the connectors were made of metal.

The Bimini Road (hereafter known as the B.R.) is complete with science evidence and pictures to back Dr. Gregory Little's thesis: that the B.R. is not a natural formation, but a man-made, megalithic site. There are professionals who believe the B.R. is a man-made structure. They have studied it and back its provenance, just as the cosmic event that caused the Ice Age to end has its backers. Many of the sources used came from respected institutions and professionals.

If you study the footnotes in this book, you will see the painstaking list used includes organizations such as *The National Institute of Science, indirectly from the Royal Observatory in Edinburgh, the University of Oxford, and the Armagh Observatory*. Along with the professionals already mentioned, there are three scientists who wrote one of the main resources used by Dr. Imhotep: *The Cycle of Cosmic Catastrophes*, which was written by Dr. Firestone, a nuclear physicist, Dr. West, a scientific consultant, and Warwick-Smith, a field exploration geologist. We also have another eminent scientist on board:

> *Dr. W. M. Napier, a professional astronomer currently an Honorary Professor of Astrobiology at Cardiff University. He has also worked at the Royal Observatory in Edinburgh, the University of Oxford, and Armagh Observatory. His collaboration with fellow astronomer Victor Clube and others on the role of comets in Earth history, is known as "coherent catastrophism."*[748] *The three authors mentioned on page one are trained researchers who have worked as government researchers, are joined in our quest for the truth by a wide variety of other experts, including a retired NASA section chief and others who are researchers at well-known universities.*[749]

So, what happened to cause this calamity—this cataclysm? Out of the heavens came a gigantic fiery ball leading to a disaster that would cause

---

748 Napier, William. "The Velikovsky Encyclopedia-William Napier." October 4, 2009. Accessed September 27, 2015 http://www.velikovsky.info/Bill Napier.

749 Napier, W. M. "Paleolithic extinctions and the Taurid Complex." Accessed March 10, 2010 http://arxiv.org/pdf/1003.07.

the world to pause and observe the change that occurred. Here is how it began. A large comet entered the Earth's atmosphere and splintered in many pieces. The pieces that caused the destruction of the "Great Bahama Bank" where:

"two deep wounds inflicted on the Earth's crust by the impact of a celestial body of considerable size...It must have been an indescribably powerful force that drove these deep holes in the sema of the Atlantic basin... In the age of the atom bomb, one is tempted to think of it in terms of a colossal submarine nuclear explosion...headed on their northwest to southeast orientation..." [750]

When they hit the ocean, they caused a tidal wave that pushed out in many directions. One headed for and hit the Bahamas with devastating power:

"The cataclysms recounted so vividly by the indigenous people and Afro-Caribbean communities of the Antilles speak of a breakup of a former land mass through disaster and flood, followed by the sudden emergence of individual islands that were all that was left of the "former land mass." The Chilam Balam of Chumayel's reference to "sea waves" covering the "sandy shores," in "one watery blow" seems remarkably like a description of super-tsunamis that unquestionably have accompanied such a catastrophic event." [751]

Let us turn and now examine the evidence to see which Old World civilization most likely could have built the B.R.:

Rome began in 753 B.C.[752]
Greece began in 1500 B.C.[753]

---

750 Collins, Andrew. *ATLANTIS in the Caribbean: and the Comet that Changed the World* (Vermont, Bear & Company, 2016), pp. 326-338.

751 Ibid., p. 341.

752 "Roman Civilization: Timeline, Facts & Contributions" Accessed September 24, 2015. http://study.com/academy/lesson/roman-civilization-timeline-facts-contributions.html.

753 "History of Greece" (n.d.). Accessed September 10, 2015. http://www.cs.mcgill.ca/~rwest/wikispeedia/wpcd/wp/h/History_of_ Greece.htm.

China began in 2100 B.C.[754]
Mesopotamia in 3000 B.C.[755]
Phoenicia in 3200 B.C.[756]

They all arrive on the scene too late to have built the B.R. Let us look at the evidence that will clearly name the only civilization that could have built the B.R. at its early date of construction. Later in this book, we shall discuss in detail the fact that the B.R. is not now found on land but under 25–30 feet of ocean water just off the western coast of Bimini in the Bahamas. The very fact that it now lies under water clearly indicates it had to have been constructed before the last Ice Age melted and flooded it. That should be as plain as if I asked you where the Brooklyn Bridge is located and what is under it. The question at hand now would invariably be, why is it now under water and how did this happen?

Gigantic glaciers formed in the Arctic and Antarctica in the last Ice Age. How did they form?

Zillions of gallons of water were sucked up and frozen into icebergs and glaciers. This caused the water levels of the Earth's oceans not to just drop in the Atlantic Ocean, but in all oceans around the world; this included the water around the Bahamian Islands. The shallow water separating the many islands naturally ran off as the ocean levels lowered. The smaller islands merged, and a larger island was formed.

This new land probably looked as if it were being raised out of the primal muck from the bowels of the Earth. This ancient, large island probably stretched from 70 miles north of Freeport south to Ragged Island. It also stretched from Bimini in the west, to Eleuthera Island in the east. Today, the large island is under water and surrounded by the current Bahamian Islands. It did not sink like Atlantis was said to sink. It was covered by the melting of the Ice Age glaciers and the flood that resulted. The current Bahamian Islands were probably large hills or small mountains when the water levels were higher.

754 "Timeline of Chinese History and Dynasties." Accessed September 24, 2016 http://afe.easia.columbia.edu/timelines/china_timeline. htm.

755 Mesopotamia. Accessed September 24, 2016. http://ftp.collin.edu/andrade/WorldLitI2332/SlidesofMesopotamia.html.

756 "PHOENICIAN." Accessed September 24, 2016. http://www.aut.edu/phoenician.html.

The "large island" would have extended to and connected with the pier before the Ice Age melt occurred, flooding the oceans and raising water levels worldwide. The problem that any researchers may have with the ideas presented here, are that there is insufficient evidence to formulate a history of the Bahamas before 11,000 B.C. This is the case because the event that caused the last Ice Age glaciers to melt was cataclysmic. Nevertheless, this event did not go unnoticed, and the evidence can now be provided.

The climate around the world was changed by that cataclysmic cosmic event that caused the Ice Age to end. Part of it was a comet that "was ten to twenty miles across, and left the LARGEST CRATER ON THE PLANET... It left a depression 300 miles in diameter in Canada's Hudson Bay, leaving... multiple impacts of comet like objects hit the northern Hemisphere,"[757] meaning Canada, the northern half of North America, Europe and the northwestern part of Asia.

> *This climate change is actually described in the ancient Egyptian Ipuwer Papyrus, secular proof that the Ice Age was ending at that time of the Exodus of the Jews, the climate change, plagues, and anarchy corroborating the report in the Bible, with the submerged ruins of Menouthis and Heraklion at the mouth of the extinct Canopic branch of the Nile bearing testament to that great loss to the sea and all over the world for the Ice Age flood affected all oceans and seas when it ended.[758]*

This was an extremely turbulent time on planet Earth for all those souls who did survive. The quote below is another of the many testaments to the major effects of the Ice Age ending:

> *The end of the Ice Age; (13,000 BC) Slowly the great ice sheets melt away, from Chicago and Boston and Seattle and London, under the influence of an 'altithermal' climate several degrees warmer than today. The sea level, which has remained some 350 feet below its*

---

757 Firestone, Richard et al. *The Cycle of Cosmic Catastrophes*, pp. 147, 288-289.

758 Genesis Veracity Foundation" (n.d.). Post Ice Age Migration. Accessed July 10, 2014. http://www.genesisveracityfoundation. com/posticeage.html

present level for 100,000 years, begins to rise at a rate of ten feet a century.[759]

We do not recognize day-to-day sea level rises. But there was a time when it rose tremendously:

There was once, "a great world catastrophe during the infancy of mankind." Most writers refer to it as "Noah's Flood." The melting the ice glaciers where different authorities give different dates for the same event... Authorities of the caliber of Runcorn and Mulholland have admitted that axial shifts could be expected to occur on such occasions.[760]

So, did Noah's flood cause an "Axial Shift" that caused the last Ice Age to end?

*While there is still a lot of debate on **what causes Ice Ages to end suddenly, the most excepted explanation for the glacial retreat 13,000 years ago** concerns long-term cyclical changes of the Earth's rotation and its orbit around the sun. These are called Milankovitch cycles, after the scientist who named them, but there is a growing debate about the effect on Earth's climate caused by these cycles. Some scientists believe the effect is too small to cause the event of the Ice Age. Whatever the cause, we think that was another contributing factor this last time: the sudden occurrence of the event.*[761]

However, overwhelming evidence on what caused the last Ice Age:

A carbon-rich black layer, dating around 12,900 years ago, has been previously identified at around 50 Clovis-age sites across North America and appears contemporaneous with the abrupt onset of Younger Dryas cooling. The in-situ bones of extinct Pleistocene large mammals along with Clovis tool assemblages, occur below this black layer but not within or above it. Causes for the extinctions, Younger Dryas cooling, and termination of Clovis culture have long been

---

759 Meehan/Donnell. (1999). "Climate, Culture, and Catastrophe in the Ancient World." Accessed September 10, 2015. http://web. stanford. edu/~meehan/donnellyr/summary.html.

760 Allan, D. S., and J. B. Delair. *Cataclysm!: Compelling Evidence of a Cosmic Catastrophe in 9500 B.C* (Vermont, Bear & Company, 1997), pp. 186, 191.

761 Firestone, Richard et al. *The Cycle of Cosmic Catastrophes*, pp. 24-25.

controversial. In this paper, we provide evidence for an extraterrestrial impact event at 12,900 years ago, which we hypothesize caused abrupt environmental changes that contributed to Younger Dryas cooling, major ecological reorganization, broad-scale extinctions, and rapid human behavioral shifts at the end of the Clovis Period. Clovis-age sites in North American are overlain by a thin, discrete layer with varying peak abundances of (i) magnetic grains with iridium, (ii) magnetic microspherules, (iii) charcoal, (iv) soot, (v) carbon spherules, (vi) glass-like carbon containing nanodiamonds, and (vii) fullerenes with extraterrestrial helium, all of which are evidence for an extraterrestrial impact and associated biomass burning at 12,900 years ago. This layer also extends throughout at least 15 Carolina Bays, are unique, elliptical depressions, oriented to the northwest across the Atlantic Coastal Plain. We propose that one or more large, low-density extraterrestrial objects exploded over northern North America, partially destabilizing the Laurentide Ice Sheet and triggering Younger Dryas cooling. The shock wave, thermal pulse, and event-related environmental effects (e.g., extensive biomass burning and food limitations) contributed to end-Pleistocene large mammals' extinctions and adaptive shifts among Paleoamericans in North America.[762]

This was a very disastrous time to be alive. But some made it and actually recorded the events we read about today.

The Bible vividly describes torrential rains and an immense flood in which most of humanity perished. Plato wrote about the catastrophic destruction of Atlantis, which occurred in a day and night about 11,600 years ago. Native Americans have many stories about an enormous cataclysm involving worldwide fires and flooding. Altogether, the myth and folklore of as many as fifty different cultures around the planet tell of similar global devastations, during which humanity went through a trial by fire and flood.[763]

Yes, the Greek Philosopher/author Plato wrote about Atlantis in 330 B.C.:

---

762 Ibid., pp. 1, 8.

763 Collins, M. (Jan.-Feb. 2017). "Clues to the Great Catastrophe." *Atlantis Rising Magazine*, pp. 13, 50, 60.

The mechanism for the destruction of Plato's fabled island empire was the Younger Dryas comet...which I refer to as the Carolina Bays impact...they were created as a direct result of the catastrophic events of 12,800 years ago...Firestone provides brand new evidence to suggest that the Carolina Bays are, as I propose in Atlantis in the Caribbean, *the result of massive air blasts caused by disintegrating comet fragments impacting the Earth...Did Plato go on to use these stories, which came originally from indigenous people from the opposite side of the Atlantic ocean, to construct his detailed account of Atlantis?*[764]

Firestone calls this particular global devastation the "event." The event had a lethal effect on people and animals 13,000 years ago; far more species of North American land mammals died out in the last part of the Ice Age than had gone extinct in the previous 3.5 million years.[765] This is quite an extraordinary statement that needs to be backed up by evidence. What it implies is that "something extraordinary must have happened at the end of the last Ice Age—something that had not occurred for millions of years."[766] The evidence available is not in just one, but three ancient Papyri recording the event.

The ancient Egyptian Ipuwer Papyrus, for example, describes terrible devastation created by an early cataclysm that "turned the Earth upside down." The Ermitage Papyrus, now preserved in St. Petersburg, refers to a similar ancient world convulsion; a third Egyptian papyrus tells how the Earth was nearly destroyed by fire and water from a tremendous celestial upheaval long ago when south became north and the world turned over.[767]

In other words, if the Egyptians were writing and recording events at the time of this cosmic event 13,000 years ago, Egypt is far older than that. There is one historian who wrote about Egypt being much older:

764 Firestone, Richard et al. *The Cycle of Cosmic Catastrophes*, p. 8.

765 Ibid., pp. 8, 113.

766 Collins, M. "Clues to the Great Catastrophe." pp. 13, 50, 60.

767 Allan, D. S. et al. *Cataclysm!: Compelling Evidence of a Cosmic Catastrophe in 9500 B.C.*, p. 191; Carson-Priede, E. "Atlantis- Shift of Axis" (2014). Accessed June 5, 2007. http://www.blavatsky.net/index. php/37topics/atlantis/50-atlantis-shift-of-axis.

The Chronicler of Manetho who served as a priest in the temples at Sebennytos and Heliopolis lived 300 years before Christ, has also been the foundation of claims of ante-Mosaic antiquity predating Moses for the Egyptian nation. These chronicles are records of Egyptian dynasties running back 30,000 years.[768]

On what grounds does Evans, the modern-day author of the quote above, have to support the claim that this priest is lying? Would an Egyptian priest, whose life was sworn to the spiritual world, lie or "pretend" to make claims about Egypt's history going back 30,000 years? The real age of Egypt is now being recorded as far more ancient because of the B.R.

New scientific evidence has shown that the Ice Age was over and melting between 13,000 and 11,500 years ago. Egypt was not affected by the Ice Age's frigid temperatures and snow. Three different scribes, at three different locations recorded the event on papyrus paper—the world's first paper. These scribes were not sub-humans, but advanced humans, who had received special training to write and to make paper out of papyrus reeds. The Egyptian civilization was obviously a logical and civilized people.

The Ice Age areas were under ice, suffering subzero temperatures and frigid winds from the Arctic. The European Ice Age environment did not permit civilization—people striving after the finer things in life. They were in survival mode and experienced differentiation. The people in Egypt and Nubia did not go through the Ice Age hardships and continued with their advanced society. The evidence shows that the Egyptians most probably built the B.R. This is the key element that the last few pages have been leading up to.

It is now clear that Egypt was in existence at least by the time of the event 13,000 years ago. There is no evidence of an older civilization, outside of Africa, with that much antiquity, who could have built all the Egyptian artifacts, statues and structures found in the water around the Bahamas. Therefore, it is not Rome, Greece, China, Phoenicia, but Egypt, who must logically be the civilization that built the B.R.

We believe that the data given here suggests that Africans—specifically the ancient Egyptians, considering the evidence presented here—are the most logical candidates to engineer and construct the B.R.

---

768 Evans, David M. (1873). *Landmarks of Truth, Or Harmony of the Holy Scriptures* (Pennsylvania, Quaker City Publishing Company), p. 24.

When was the B.R. rediscovered and by whom? On the second of September in 1968, two pilots flying over Bimini in the Bahamas, rediscovered what has been incorrectly labeled the "Bimini Road." It was, "about one mile off the west coast of north Bimini, Bahamas...under 15-20 feet of water."[769] It does look like a short, wide, ancient road from the surface. The "B.R.," also referred to as "the structure," is not a road. (see Fig. 43) It is an ancient breakwater protecting a pier from the force of the ocean waves, which created an artificial harbor. Much of this pier is brilliantly split in half so that large cargo ships can be unloaded. simultaneously making it possible to finish twice as fast!

The question now is, why is this structure now underwater? During the last Ice Age, the water levels of the Earth's oceans dropped. This included the water around the Bahamian Islands. The shallow water separating the many islands naturally ran off as the ocean levels lowered. Because of the lower water level, some of the islands merged, and a larger island was formed.

On most world maps the ocean depths are a deep blue color. When looking at a map of the Bahamas, the light blue area represents the shallow waters. The light blue areas on maps were not covered by water before the Ice Age ended, close to 10,000 years ago.

If observed closely, the light blue area (around the Bahamian Islands), is shaped something like a wreath. The Lucayan people were the Amerinds who inhabited the Bahamian Islands when the Spanish arrived. "The Lucayans knew Bimini as "the Place of the Wreath or Crown," which may refer to the ancient, large island's original circular configuration."[770] This evidence supports the theory that before the Ice Age ended, Bimini was one large island shaped like the letter "U," sitting on its side.

In one area, the blue color on the map of the Bahamas is dark blue, for it represents a deep-water area located between Nassau and Andros islands. It is referred to as the "Tongue of the Ocean."[771] The ancient large

---

769 Little, Gregory. "Underwater Stone Formation at Bimini."

770 Joseph, Frank. "The 'Bimini' of Japan." *Atlantis Rising*, No. 28, July/August (2001), p. 61.

771 Little, Gregory and Lori Little. *The A.R.E.'s Search for Atlantis: The Ongoing Search for Edgar Cayce's Atlantis in the Bahamas* (Tennessee, Eagle Wing Books, 2003), p. 106.

breakwater that is currently just off Bimini's western shore is 600 yards long and 30 yards wide, built with huge megaton stones.

Exactly what purpose did this breakwater serve? In 2003, the husband and wife team, Drs. Greg and Lori Little, dove into the water next to the structure and took hundreds of photos. After many dives they found that it was certainly not a road. Looking towards the east from the breakwater, 50 yards from the island of Bimini, they found another long stone structure, not quite as large as the first, running parallel to both the breakwater and the shore. After much research, they decided the larger formation was indeed a breakwater that protected the pier from the mountainous waves.

After taking hundreds of pictures, as well as measuring and studying, the Littles were sure of what it was. The smaller structure was a pier built with large blocks as the breakwater. These two structures together created an artificial harbor. Its function was to enable ships to dock at the pier and unload their cargo. It turns out there are several sites around the world like this breakwater, and a few that are identical to it.

Fig. 44: Bimini Breakwater & Pier Reconstruction, Dee Thurman. *Courtesy of Dr. Greg Little.*

The breakwater broke up the ocean waves instead of allowing them to break on the smaller pier. Since the waves broke on the larger structure, the water was calm by the pier that was connected to the shore. The ships were then able to load and unload without the ebb and flow of the waves raising and lowering the ship every few seconds. This allowed ships to remain in calm water just as a naturally formed harbor creates.

The reason for the split-pier architecture in both the breakwater and pier was to allow ships to pull in and be unloaded or loaded on both sides at once, to hurry the docking procedures of large ships.

What caused Bimini Road
to become covered by water?

The "large island" would have extended to and connected with the pier before the Ice Age melt occurred. The problem that any researchers may have with the ideas presented here is that there is insufficient evidence to formulate a history of the Bahamas before 11,000 B.C. This is the case because the event that caused the last Ice Age glaciers to melt was a cataclysmic, earth-changing event that caused a depopulation of North America. Dr. Bill Topping believes the event was so catastrophic, that it caused a mass extinction of the larger animals in ancient North America. He also believes that this event was the cause of, "the sudden disappearance 11,000 to 13,000 years ago of the Paleoamericans."[772]

This event did not go unnoticed. The Egyptian civilization was old enough and civilized enough to record this cosmic event in the Ipuwer Papyrus. "In the early 19th century a papyrus, dating from the end of the Middle Kingdom, was found in Egypt."[773]

For the Egyptians to be around recording this event that occurred 13,000 years ago, is as surprising as hearing about this cataclysm itself. It alters the age we are now given for Egypt's beginning at 3100 B.C. However, a debate on Egypt's age is beyond the scope of this book.

Again, this cataclysm took portions of the Earth and turned it into a raging hell for those affected. Egypt's Ipuwer Papyri said it seemed like it was "the world appearing to turn upside down in a cosmic cataclysm" from the sky.[774]

---

772 Firestone, Richard et al. *The Cycle of Cosmic Catastrophes*, p. 8.

773 Becher, Rabbi M. (1995-2015). The Ten Plagues-Live From Egypt. Accessed May, 2, 2015. http://ohr.edu/838.

774 Joseph, Frank. (2002). *The Destruction of Atlantis* (New York, Bear & Company), p. 152.

The dating of ancient spear points shows us that at Blackwater Draw, a well-known Paleo-Indian site near Clovis, New Mexico, where the first Clovis points were found...it was quiet and empty for 1,000 years before any other people showed up.[775]

There must have been survivors in another parts of North America. How do we know this? The Algonquin survivors and others passed down the story of the cataclysm that has survived[V] to this day. If it were not for the cataclysmic event that occurred in North America and killed so many of its ancient Paleoamerican inhabitants, the look of the modern Amerinds would have been different. They would probably have looked more African.

The depopulation of the Black Protoamericans killed by the cataclysm 13,000 years ago did not last. Despite the devastating loss of life, 11,508 years later, there were millions of people living in the Americas. If you remember, "according to conservative estimates by archaeologists (Fulsom and Fulsom, 1983) there were over 57 million people already living in the Americas when Columbus arrived."[776]

Yes, after the Mongolians from Asia began arriving between 3000 and 2600 B.C., they repopulated North America along with the remnants of the Protoamericans already in North America. To be thorough, one must mention that after the heat dissipated, the Ice Age temporarily returned for another 1300 years as mentioned in Napier's (2010) study.[777] The cause of this temporary drop in temperature is not exactly known. One theory is based on the fact that all the dust, smoke, gasses, etc., were caused by the cataclysm, and rose into the atmosphere blocking the sun's rays—it was similar to a nuclear winter. This was possibly the cause of the temperature dropping, and the Ice Age returning until the atmosphere cleared.

---

775 Firestone, Richard et al. *The Cycle of Cosmic Catastrophes*, pp. 6, 144.

776 Little, Gregory L. (2009). *The Illustrated Encyclopedia of Native American Mounds & Earthworks*. (Tennessee, Eagle Wing Books Inc.), p. 2.

777 Powell, Joseph F., and Walter A. Neves. "Craniofacial Morphology of the First Americans," pp. 153-88.

The Wisconsin Ice Age—the last one before our time—began around 115,000 years ago and ended 10,000 years ago.[778] Another source says the Ice Age ended between 11,000 and 8,000 B.C.[779] (That is equal to 10,000 to 13,000 years ago and still in the same range); the melting ice began to raise the levels of all the oceans. Yet a third source, Firestone et al., wrote that the Ice Age melt began 11,000 B.C. (13,000 years ago) when the comets struck Earth initiating the great catastrophic Ice Age ending melt.[780]

New discoveries now show that **people erected buildings back then that were two miles west of Bimini's breakwater. After the Ice Age's tremendous glacial melt, today those structures are now flooded in 90 feet of water.**

There is no doubt that this intriguing set of formations sits just above the shoreline that was present off Bimini in 10,000 B.C.[781] The people who erected the buildings in 10,000 B.C. had to be Africans as well, for they preceded the 1200 B.C. Greek civilization by 8800 years; and they preceded the Mongolian entry date of 2600 B.C. into the Americans, by approximately 7400 years. Also, Chapter 1 says that the Native Americans did not build using large stone blocks, "The Algonquins did not use stone in their constructions."[782]

What exactly was found two miles west of Bimini that dated back to 10,000 B.C.?

Thirty-five man-made underwater constructions have been found four miles west of Bimini's eastern coast, facing Florida. This also

778 Lemke, K .A. (2009). Ice Age Chronology. Accessed on June 10, 2009 from http://www.uwsp.edu/geo/faculty/lemke/geol370/lecture_ note15_ice_age_chronology.html.

779 Lioubimtseva, E. U., S. P. Gorshkov, and J. M. Adams. (1998). "A Giant Siberian Lake during the Last Glacial: Evidence and Implications." Accessed June 10, 2009. https://www.esd.ornl.gov/projects/gen/ lake.html.

780 Firestone, Richard et al. *The Cycle of Cosmic Catastrophes*, p. 136.

781 Little, Gregory. "Has Atlantis Finally Been Found at Bimini?" Atlantis Rising, No. 77, (2009). September/October. Accessed June 10, 2009. http://atlantisrisingmagazine.com/article/ has-atlantis-finally-been-found-at-bimini/.

782 Fell, Barry. Bronze Age America, p. 51.

means it is two miles west of the B.R. The farther west one travels away from Bimini's coast, the deeper the water becomes, and the older any other erections become.

It took four years for the data about this discovery to be circulated to the general public—the original find was in 2006. Anthropologist Bill Donato was the person who found the 35 structures in 90 feet of water. A year later (in 2007) the Littles were working with a History Channel television crew preparing for a future television show and would film the 35 stone buildings again. What the Littles found was that:

All but one or two of these are square or rectangular...the largest are about 25 by 15 feet with many being about 12 by 20 feet. Almost all the formations have distinctive outer walls...there is no doubt that this intriguing set of formations that sit just above the shoreline was present off Bimini 10,000 B.C.[783]

After further investigation, Dr. Gregory Little wrote in a later article:

The deep area called the "Rectangles," which is a widespread area of uniformly arranged square and rectangular formations... The coral encrusted stone formations are found on a mile-long swath, a strip about 200 feet wide. These formations, generally 10 by 45 feet or so in size, appear to number about 50, are laid out in straight parallel lines; and are located at the edge of the 10,000 BC shoreline.[784]

These 50 buildings were obviously part of a small city! This work and study have been investigated, and then reports have been based on scientific evidence. However, the next short statement should not be overlooked. The well-respected psychic, Edgar Cayce, lived well after these structures/buildings/civilization existed back before the 10,000 B.C. shoreline flooded it. However, **before they were recently discovered**, somehow he knew they were there because he made the following revealing statement: "**a highly developed pre-Ice Age culture once lived off the coast of the Bahamas** and operated throughout the region."[785]

This is right in line with the account that appeared in the Introduction of this work, mentioning that there were not only people living off the

---

783 Ibid.

784 Little, Gregory. "Has Atlantis Finally Been Found at Bimini?"

785 Little, Gregory. (2011). "Man-Made Bahamas Structure Dated to Before the Ice Age."

coast of Bimini, but it was a highly developed culture. Cayce then went on even further to say that it existed before the Ice Age melted, which takes us back to where? Zep Tepi. This is very uncanny, but it is absolutely right on the money. Some could call it coincidence, and then there are others who believe that some people have the gift that Mr. Cayce showcased in this example. In ancient times, people with this gift were revered and respected. Today many just look the other way because they only depend on scientific reasoning. The author included Cayce's quote above in this work to be thorough, because sometimes these folks quite right. A new man-made structure has also been found in the Bahamas just a few miles southwest of Bimini. This area was investigated by Drs. Greg and Lori Little. They made the first carbon-14 dating on this structure that they found near "Pino Turolla's Columns" in 20 feet of water:

> *A complex, man-made, underwater...**multi-room structure in the Bahamas has been carbon to over 20,000 years B.C.**....a sample of beach rock from a long, straight foundation.... Clearly man-made, the building's foundation has mitered limestone corners and other debris inside the outer walls. In the new dating report, according to an A.R.E. press release, a sample of beach rock from a long, straight foundation wall was carbon dated to between 21,520 B.C. and 20,610 B.C. Conventional archaeological wisdom holds that the oldest dates for humans in the area go back to only about 1,000 B.C. The conclusion is that the structure was built on high ground sometime between 21,000 B.C. and well before 4,000 B.C. This is the first site to be carbon dated, and to a time long before the last Ice Age ended, strongly indicating that, contrary to standard academic theory, a highly developed pre-Ice Age culture once lived off the coast of the Bahamas and operated throughout the region.[786]*

According to Little, the building and wall were constructed **more than 20,000 years ago**. For your information:

> *Pino Turolla's Columns is an unnamed area 10 miles south of Bimini that contains granite slabs, stone steps and cut rooms. Each is uniquely interesting and together they seem to provide the "smoking*

---

786 Little, Gregory. (2011). "Man-Made Bahamas Structure Dated To Before Ice Age."

gun" that proves the existence of an ancient maritime culture which flourished in the area more than 10,000 years ago.[787]

Sometime afterwards, Dr. Little made another dive at this site and further added that his friend, Elsie, and his wife, had noticed something very unusual off South Bimini that had previously been discovered. Back in the 1970s a report had been made by Pino Turolla detailing the following:

[The] discovery of about 30 long stone columns off South Bimini. Some of these were described as rectangular beams over 30 feet in length. It is now clear that this underwater area contains the ruins of a stone building or buildings. The outside "edges" (the outer walls of the ends) of the structure are formed by well-defined rectangular foundations still in place...in 20 feet of water.[788]

This was most likely part of the civilization of Zep Tepi that is translated as the "First Time or The Golden Era..."[789] We covered the fact that people have been traveling to the Americas for more than 250,000 years. The Bimini Breakwater and Pier—made from stone—were most likely connected to the very last "transfer port" or "way station" in the ancient Bahamas before the cataclysm.

In ancient times, the first peoples traveling west must have been caught in the natural east-west ocean current, sailing west across the middle Atlantic ending in the Bahamas. Eventually, they learned how to navigate back-and-forth trading with each other. They probably began building small transfer ports made of wood and ended building with large stone structures. The large wood structures were replaced with stone in ancient times. A logical example would be that the first Stonehenge in ancient England was made from wood and was called "Woodhenge."[790]

787 Archer, R. J. "Ancient Underwater Structures in the Bahamas." November 12, 2010. Accessed November 5, 2015 https://www. goodreads. com/author_blog_posts/3024676-ancient-Sunderwa-ter-structures-in-the-bahamas.

788 Little, Gregory. "Man-Made Bahamas Structure Dated to Before the Ice Age", p. 23.

789 Bauval, Robert, and Thomas Brophy. *Black Genesis*, p. 299.

790 Owen, James. "Stonehenge Had Neighboring Wooden Twin—More to Come?" *National Geographic News*, July 24, 2010. Accessed October 14, 2011. http://news.nationalgeographic.com/news/2010/07/100723-stonehenge-woodhenge-twin-timber-circle-gaffney-science/.

Some of the structures, if not most, that are covered above are most likely the remnants of the: Peaceful/Ancient/African/Antediluvian/ Worldwide/Maritime/Megalithic/Mercantile/Super-Civilization™ of Zep Tepi, which was known to Egyptians as "The First Time." Yes, it is true that this:

Pre-catastrophic Golden Age traditionally existed during the childhood of humanity in northern latitudes, where life existed in serenity. The traditional end of this paradisiacal world is consistently described as a sudden and violent.[791] This was the "abrupt destruction of a primeval earthly paradise widely known as the Golden Age." Yes, it was "reminiscence of a sinless Golden Age."[792]

British Egyptologist Rundle T. Clark concluded this about Zep Tepi:

All that is good or efficacious was established on the principals laid down in the First Time—which was, therefore, a golden age of absolute perfection. If the Vedic cycle is properly calibrated to the procession cycle in the same way, then we can conclude that Zep Tepi was coincident with the center of the Satya Yuga, which the Vedas identified as the perfect time or Golden Age of humanity. Here we trace the physical archaeological and astro-ceremonial evidence to identify that the ancients themselves placed that golden age in the epoch around 12,000 B.C.[793]

It is so interesting that Dr. Little, after his thorough investigation with the History Channel, would agree with Edgar Cayce and write:

*Before the last Ice Age ended, the evidence has strongly indicated that, contrary to standard academic theory, a **highly developed pre-Ice Age culture once lived off the coast of the Bahamas and operated throughout the region**.[794]*

After the age of Zep Tepi it seems that most of those advanced civilizations were severely crippled by the cataclysm that wiped out a good deal of their "worldwide super-civilization" from the face of this Earth.

---

791 Allan, D. S., and J. B. Delair. *Cataclysm!*, p. 191.

792 Ibid.

793 Bauval, Robert, and Thomas Brophy. *Black Genesis*, pp. 298, 299.

794 Little, Gregory. "Man-Made Bahamas Structure Dated to Before the Ice Age," p. 10.

Not only Christian and Jewish savants, but others of the pagan pre-classical and oriental worlds agree that the Deluge had terminated the earlier Golden Age.... The numerous traditions descriptive of a vast genial friendly prehistoric world...terminated abruptly by world-embracing disturbances.[795]

We are told that these worldwide events were not just happening in one small area of this planet; but "several widely-scattered traditions described the catastrophic termination of this wonderful primeval age" that affected the entire world.[796] Those ancient statements make perfect logical sense. For example, during any period on Earth, most cities are found at riverside or consisting of ports on the oceanfront. Logically, the ancient times were no different. It seems that most of them in the North American continent were destroyed by the floodwaters. "From every existing river and stream, frigid freshwater flowed into the Atlantic, Pacific and Arctic Oceans."[797]

All together the world's oceans rose an incredible 200 feet during the event from 17,000 to 13,000 years ago, inundating millions of square miles of the world's most fertile land area mostly along the shelf shore of each continent.[798]

The Mercyhurst Institute corroborates Firestone's ocean rise data, which actually was found to be quite conservative. Mercyhurst calculated their data:

By analyzing ancient DNA found at an archaeological dig in Vero Beach Florida..."humans were on this continent much longer than originally thought," said Greg O'Corry-Crowe, an FAU associate research professor. It was about 13,000 to 14,000 years ago, as the Pleistocene Epoch and the last Ice Age were drawing to an end. At the time, **Florida was almost double its current size,** *extending out into the Gulf of Mexico and the Atlantic, and much of the state*

---

795 Allan, D. S., and J. B. Delair. *Cataclysm!*, pp. 3, 14.

796 Ibid., pp. 174-175.

797 Firestone, Richard et al. *The Cycle of Cosmic Catastrophes*, p. 144.

798 Ibid., p. 324.

was more than 300 feet above sea level, said Andy Hemmings, lead archaeologist for the Mercyhurst Institute.[799]

They were all destroyed by the flood that followed the cataclysm. Their inhabitants would have been mostly destroyed for there was no warning. The cataclysm began and the meteors hit traveling from 25,000 to 160,000 mph,[800] creating tremendous heat and fires.

This ancient worldwide civilization was ended by the cataclysm and flood—covered in the book, *The Cycle of Cosmic Catastrophes* by Firestone et al. (2006)—that brought Zep Tepi to a screeching halt.

The theory that the cataclysm ended the civilization of Zep Tepi is backed by trusted evidence, "physical evidence." The evidence for this ancient civilization of Zep Tepi can also be found in Graham Hancock's book, *Underworld* (2002), which has many actual pictures covering man-made, underwater structures all over the world that can actually be seen today. That book is well written and researched, containing 740 pages and filled with many pictures in color of ancient underwater remains.

The Holy Bible actually covers this flood

Genesis 6:17 "For behold, I will bring a flood of waters upon the earth to destroy all flesh in which is the breath of life under heaven."

Genesis 6:5 "And God saw that the wickedness of man was great in the earth, and that every imagination of the thoughts of his heart was only evil continually."

Genesis 6:11-13 "The earth also was corrupt before God, and the earth was filled with violence. And God looked upon the earth, and, behold, it was corrupt; for all flesh had corrupted his way upon the earth. And God said unto Noah, the end of all flesh is come before me; for the earth is filled with violence through them; and, behold, I will destroy them with the earth."

But wait a minute—we have two opposing sides here. At the beginning, both sides do agree that the flood was caused by a cataclysmic

799 Kaye, Ken. "Ancient DNA could unlock South Florida secrets." *Sun Sentinel*. September 9, 2014. Accessed November 12, 2015. http://www.sun-sentinel.com/local/palm-beach/fl-fau-ice-age-20140919-story.html.

800 "How fast are meteorites traveling when they reach the ground?" American Meteor Society (2013-2016). Accessed September 9, 2016. https://www.amsmeteors.org/fireballs/faqf/#12.

event. Where the difference begins is where the biblical verses (above) say that God destroyed because, "The Earth also was corrupt before God" due to man's wickedness, violence and corruption. On the other hand, a completely different position must again be stated:

Pre-Catastrophic Golden Age traditionally existed during the childhood of humanity in northern latitudes, where life existed in serenity. The traditional end of this paradisiacal world is consistently described as sudden and violent.[801]

*All that is good or efficacious was established on the principals laid down in the First Time—which was, therefore, a golden age of absolute perfection.[802]

*The numerous traditions descriptive of a vast genial friendly prehistoric world.[803]

*Before the flood it was "reminiscence of a sinless Golden Age center of the Satya Yuga, which the Vedas identified as the perfect time or Golden Age of humanity.[804]

*Not only Christian and Jewish savants, but also others of the pagan pre-classical and oriental worlds agree that the Deluge had terminated the earlier Golden Age.[805]

If the Vedic Yoga cycle is properly calibrated to the procession cycle in the same way, then we can conclude that Zep Tepi was coincident with the catastrophe:

*The numerous traditions descriptive of a vast genial friendly prehistoric world...terminated abruptly by world-embracing disturbances.[806]

The reader may make up their own mind as to what they choose to believe. Let us now completely switch gears and fly way back to the Bahamas.

---

801 Allan, D. S., and J. B. Delair. *Cataclysm!*, p. 191.

802 Bauval, Robert, and Thomas Brophy. *Black Genesis*, p. 298.

803 Allan, D. S., and J. B. Delair. *Cataclysm!*, p. 174.

804 Ibid., pp. 3, 174-175.

805 Ibid., p. 3.

806 Ibid., pp. 174-175.

Evidence of a Very Large
Ancient Bahamian Island

While diving near Andros (a Bahamian Island just southeast of Bimini), Jacques Cousteau made a significant discovery. He found a cave that contained stalactites and stalagmites 160 feet below the ocean surface (see Note W in chapter 8). **With this discovery in mind, this evidence shows that the cave had to have been on dry land for thousands of years**[807] **for the stalactites and stalagmites to develop!** It is *scientifically impossible* that they could have developed underwater. **The cave's mineralized deposits <u>provide confirmation</u> that this very large Bahamian Island was once above water for thousands of years.** This very large island was one of the several Atlantises that are being found now all over the world at the time of Zep Tepi.

Since the pier that accompanied the breakwater was connected to dry land at least 6,700 years ago, one wonders why is there only one layer of blocks existing there now? Further, why are they no longer tightly fitted together?

In 1926, a hurricane blasted Miami. Much beachfront and some of the harbor was lost due to erosion and was reclaimed by the ocean. To prevent this erosion from happening again, Miami engineers decided to build a sea barrier to block the waves and prevent them from robbing such real estate again. **They sailed to Bimini and floated a large barge over it and looted the B.R. of hundreds of large blocks down to the last layer.**[808] Unfortunately, they thought this looting was a lot more cost effective than quarrying the blocks themselves. That is why today some the blocks do not fit tightly together.

Dr. Zink was a member of the U.S. Air Force Academy. Zinc reported that his guide told him, when he was young (back in the 1920s) the breakwater was built with blocks that were ten or so stories high. The blocks were huge limestone slabs. Zink confirmed the fact that nine or ten of the medium-sized blocks would be approximately thirty feet high.[809] This

---

807 Joseph, Frank. "The 'Bimini' of Japan," p. 62.

808 Little, Gregory and Lora Little. *The A.R.E.'s Search for Atlantis*, p. 174.

809 Zink, David. (1978). *Stones of Atlantis* (New Jersey, Prentice Hall), p.174.

means that before the B.R. was looted of its stones, it was approximately 30 feet high from the seabed to the top level.

Underwater Structures and Objects

The B.R. is not the only anomaly in the Bahamas. There is not just one long underwater formation there, but three. The one we are covering here is the best-known large formation, which is just off Paradise Point in Bimini.

About one mile north of the B.R., a second site was discovered in 1979 and named after Steven Proctor. He was co-founder of the Scientific Exploration and Archaeological Society. Proctor's Road is as large a formation as the Bimini and Andros structures. It is also "called the Paradise Point Pier, which is clearly a previously unknown man-made pier or breakwater extending from the shoreline."[810] At Proctor's Road there are also several piles of stones on the ocean floor. They form a line so perfect that the stones just could not be a natural formation. This evidence suggests it must be man-made.[811]

There is a third formation in the water just east of Andros Island about one quarter of a mile[812] that is 900 feet long. Since it was not disturbed, the surface is flat and in its original state. Dr. Imhotep measured one of the blocks and agreed with Dr. Greg Little's measurements—many of the stones are 25 feet by 30 feet by 2 feet long. This platform did not require a breakwater to protect it from the waves for it is situated inside the area called, "The Tongue of the Ocean." The northern part of the The Tongue rests between the land areas called Nicholas Town and New Providence. The Andros Platform is not pounded directly by oceanic wave action, as is the breakwater in Bimini.

Was the modern discovery of the B.R. a natural formation or man-made? In 2005, Dr. Greg Little wrote two definitive articles in *Atlantis Rising Magazine* that settled the argument conclusively. The first article in issue 51 was entitled "Astonishing Discoveries of Ancient Port Facilities Challenge the Conventional Wisdom and Raise Important New Questions."

---

810 Little, Gregory L. *The Illustrated Encyclopedia*, p. 174.

811 Ibid., p. 56.

812 Little, Gregory and Lora Little. *The A.R.E.'s Search for Atlantis*, p. 208.

The second article was "Exposing a 'Skeptical Hoax,'" in issue 57. Here, **Little explained how some skeptics actually perpetrated a hoax and tried to convince the public that the B.R. was just a natural formation and not man-made.** The probable reason for the hoax is that if these dates are even slightly off, then it is likely that the history of the entire Western Hemisphere will have to be rewritten.

Little's prima facie evidence included hundreds of photographs of undeniably-man-made objects that were part of the structure and culture of the builders. A few of the items beg to be noted here. **One is a wedge-shaped prop stone found by archaeologist Bill Donato.** It was probably used to level out a large block on top of it that was crooked.[813] **There are a number of tool marks on the Andros platform blocks. Identical tongue-and-groove cuts were found on stones at Bimini.**[814] These tongue-and-groove cuts reveal a very sophisticated pattern that was part of the formation.[815] One B.R. stone has an obvious "U" shape cut while others were part of a triple tier of stones.[816] In addition, "an Egyptian-style anchor was found at Proctor's Road."[817]

One of the most convincing arguments against the B.R. being a natural structure is that one end of the structure has a "J" shape. Natural formations do not end in such a distinctive shape. Many such harbor breakwaters were shaped in that fashion in the Mediterranean Sea. There are two reports that suggest another possible Egyptian presence off the Bimini coast in ancient times. An obelisk is a symbol of resurrection and can be observed at most any graveyard. The first report of such an **arrangement of stones is at Bimini at the Paradise Point site. Zink reports seeing two cylinders cut from stone that "looked very much like obelisks."**[818] The second report made in 1973 contained photographs taken of one column

813 Little, Gregory. "Exposing a 'Skeptical Hoax.'" *Atlantis Rising*, March 2006, p. 42.

814 Ibid., p. 69.

815 Zink, David. *Stones of Atlantis*, p. 174.

816 Donato, W. M. "Proof: The Bimini Road is an Ancient Ruin." *Ancient American* Vol. 10, Issue #66, (2006), p. 34.

817 Zink, David. *Stones of Atlantis*, p. 37.

818 Ibid., pp. 156-161.

standing vertically in the mud just off South Bimini in water forty feet deep. There's no telling how tall this object is because it is embedded into the mud. It is suspected to be extremely tall, however.[819]

The next find is second only to the Bimini and Andros formations. **In 1968, the two pilots also reported spotting a temple site in shallow water just north of Andros Island."**[820] The pilots reported their find to Dimitri Rebikoff, and an archaeologist, Dr. Valentine, who then visited the site off Andros. They both described the walls of the temple as three feet thick and made of limestone that was skillfully worked. Dr. Valentine could not help recognizing the temple's proportions and size, which invariably mirrored a Mayan Temple's floor plan.

The temple's foundation was one hundred by sixty feet and was in water six feet deep. **Rebikoff and Valentine found twelve other underwater structures in the area around Andros no more than a mile away.**[821] There was also another strange find regarding foreign stone at the Bimini breakwater. In 1995, divers at this formation found granite stones. Granite, like marble, is also not a stone native to the Bahamas."[822]

How did it come to rest in the Bahamas?

Twelve years later (in June of 2007), a discovery was made about seven miles north of Bimini, in water 28-feet deep. **It was an elaborate well-polished triangular building apex.** It looked as if it were part of the roof of the temple whose walls were three feet thick. The divers removed a small piece of the slab, and it turned out to be white marble of such a high quality that when the sun struck the slab it shined like quartz.[823]

Pillars have been found at several other underwater locations. When Valentine and Rebikoff joined the "MARS (Marine Archaeological Research

819 Ibid.

820 Ibid., p.9.

821 Zink, David. *Stones of Atlantis*, p.10.

822 Joseph, Frank. "The 'Bimini' of Japan," p. 61.

823 Little, Gregory, and Lora Little. "Lost Civilization & the Bermuda Triangle." *Atlantis Rising* #66 (2007), p. 71.

Society)," expedition[824] between July and November of 1969, they made a great find. They **discovered 44, 3-to-5-foot pillars, with diameters of three feet just west of the B.R., this time in 15 feet of water**. An article in Argosy magazine described the very same pillars, but they had entirely different measurements. The Argosy article said the largest pillars were up to 6 feet in diameter, and the longest pillars measured 14 feet. The exciting thing about it is that some of the pillars were still standing upright forming a circle.[825]

The destructive tidal waves, icebergs and tremendous hurricane-force winds obviously were powerful enough to tear down these temples, leaving scattered pillars that supported the temples; a triangular building apex of a roof, and actual remains of structures and foundations of buildings three feet thick. For pillars to have been found at several other underwater locations means that these buildings were not in just one location but spread around the large island, which means there were several communities or cities. That story is to be found under the waves now.

These wonderful pieces of evidence of these advanced Nile Valley people's presence in the Bahamas are truly wonderful. Yet, there are people saying that the Romans, English kings, or the Vikings could have built these ancient underwater structures. Then they ask, "Who knows who built the breakwater and pier?" As always, if one is patient, and waits long enough, good things happen—and this is the case. **Early in 2014 an Egyptian Sphinx, as large as a small automobile van was found.** In a third article, the author reports of the B.R.'s columns (also called pillars) found under water as being, "Short stone columns still bear traces of fluted grooves, although eroded and encrusted."[826]

The oldest fluted pillars known in the world today can still be seen today in the Egyptian Temple of Sakkara next to—arguably—the first pyramid in the world. The Step Pyramid built by Pharaoh Zoser of the Third Egyptian Dynasty. The underwater temple pillars were built before the end of the Ice Age in 8,000 B.C. and are probably copied from the

824 Zink, David. *Stones of Atlantis*, p.10.

825 Donato, W. M. "Proof: The Bimini Road is an Ancient Ruin," p. 34.

826 Archeology, Archeology, Science, (2014), "Mysterious Antique Sphinx Discovered in the Bahamas." Accessed January 15, 2017. http:// worldnewsdailyreport.com/mysterious-antique- sphinx-discovered-in-the-bahamas/.

Sakkara Temple's pillars. This means the Sakkara Temple and Sakkara Step Pyramid must be older than 10,000 years old—from what we have been told—but that subject is beyond the scope of this book.

Just imagine, this large island had many buildings made out of limestone blocks and temples, at least partly built with marble, shinning in the sun like quartz. The temple also had fluted marble columns as tall as trees. These ancient builders must have had very large ships as well to carry these heavy blocks, and large harbors with enormous breakwaters and piers. Can you imagine how large the ship had to be to carry a temple roof and gigantic pillars? These were anything but primitive peoples.

The destructive tidal waves, icebergs and tremendous hurricane force winds obviously were off the eastern coast of the Bahamas. The chemical analysis of the stone demonstrated that it was almost certainly extracted from a quarry near Wadi Rahanu, an Egyptian region known for its quarrying industry since 3500 B.C. The erosion caused by the natural elements and the various corals and other life-forms that settled on it, has been disturbing our scientific dating attempts, but the nature of the mineral used in its construction confirms beyond the shadow of a doubt that the statue is of Middle Eastern origin.[827]

Unfortunately, Egypt is still considered as being in the Middle East although it has always been in Africa. On the other hand, this is what we have been waiting for. Neither the Assyrians, Persians, Greeks, Romans, nor the later Hebrews were ever in the business of building a Sphinx of their own. Their religious beliefs did not include "Hor-em-Akhet," the Egyptian name for the Sphinx; which translated means, "Horus in the horizon." In the Egyptian religion, Heru—or who the Greeks call Horus— was the son of Wsr (Osiris) and Isis. The Egyptians did not make idols of other people's gods, so why would others make idols of Egyptian gods?

Given the fact that the stone was quarried in the so-called "Middle East," should settle all debate on who this artifact belonged to. It also settles who most probably built the breakwater and pier. That argument should be closed.

---

827 Little, Gregory and Lora Little. *The A.R.E.'s Search for Atlantis*, p. 219.

Bahamian Similarities with Egypt

Science requires eight similarities to prove contact. Here are a dozen:

1. Obelisks
2. The name "Bimini"
3. Egyptian anchors
4. Egyptian keystones
5. Tongue and groove technology
6. Sacred geometry/Golden ratio—which was found and used by the Egyptians
7. The use of megalithic blocks before 7000 B.C.
8. The use of fluted marble columns
9. Identical stone mooring circles to those in the Mediterranean
10. The J-shaped breakwater identical to the pre-Greek, Nile Delta breakwater
11. Metallurgy
12. The Bahamian Sphinx

From the evidence above, we see that the Bimini Pier and Breakwater were most likely built by Egyptians. The B.R. construction is the largest underwater evidence, illustrating the African presence near the Americas before the end of the last Ice Age. The first Bahamians were African.

Section Notes

V. Algonquin Survivors of the Cataclysm

Scientists differ on what caused the cataclysm, but the one point where they all agree is that it did, indeed, occur and was an Earth-changing, Ice Age-ending catastrophe. Firestone, et. al. (2006), in a total of 368 pages, goes to considerable lengths to cover all the angles with undeniable scientific and eyewitness accounts of what caused the cataclysm and what it created. Briefly, Firestone says, **the cause of the catastrophe was a series of blistering, red-hot meteorites and small iron pellets that rained down on many parts of North America from Canada to Mexico, including a small portion of Northwestern Europe, and Siberia. Every northern continent took direct hits. The National Institute of Science (NIS) dates this catastrophe to approximately 10,400 B.C.**[828]

---

828 Firestone, Richard et al. *The Cycle of Cosmic Catastrophes.*

This horrible event probably destroyed most of the ancient civilization that built the breakwater and pier in the Bahamas and only remnants have remained. Since the Americas are so much larger not all of them were in "harm's way," as the Bahamas were during the Cataclysm. So the Americas shall be used as a reference.

To learn more about this catastrophic event, there is a masterful book written by three scientists entitled *The Cycle of Cosmic Catastrophes* by Dr. Firestone, a nuclear physicist, Dr. West, a scientific consultant, and Warwick-Smith, a field exploration geologist.[829] This is the most comprehensive book with much scientific evidence to back their story. Similar to NIS, this group dates the Earth-changing catastrophic event just 600 years earlier than 11,000 B.C. A corroborating report written by Dr. Robert M. Schoch says:

> *Circa 9700 BC our sun "woke up" and erupted with a mighty outburst—probably followed by a series of closely spaced outbursts... therefore in my assessment the isotope and geochemical data, sediment data, and archaeological evidence (such as ancient petroglyphs; see A. Peratt 2003 IEE Trans. Plasma Science) all converge to corroborate that a major solar outburst ended the last Ice Age.*[830]

In other words, our sun erupted and ejected several pieces of itself out towards and eventually hitting the Earth. When the scientists studied the ground where they landed on the Earth, they found atomic elements in the chemical composition of the Earth, matter deposited on the Earth's surface or the bottom of bodies of water; which all support the theory that it was a major solar explosion that ended the last Ice Age.

In 2010 another study was conducted. Dr. W. M. Napier, who then wrote a journal article that corroborates the Firestone, et al. story. Napier is a professional astronomer who has worked at the Royal Observatory in Edinburgh, the University of Oxford, and the Ramah Observatory.[831] Many of the first Algonquin, or Protoamericans, survived the cataclysm of 11,000 B.C. that ended the Ice Age. Because they survived, they were able

829 Ibid., p. 8.

830 Schoch, Robert M. (n.d.). "Plasma, Solar Outbursts, and the End of the Last Ice Age." Accessed January 16, 2017. http://www.robert-schoch.com/youngerdryas.html.

831 Napier, W. M. Paleolithic extinctions and the Taurid Complex, pp. 1901-1906.

to pass down stories about it. These Algonquin speakers, back in 11,000 B.C., were the Mattamuskeets, who had migrated down to North Carolina. They witnessed a horrifying meteor shower that was so large that it rained down on select areas as far north as Hudson Bay in Northern Canada. These meteors hit the ground with such an impact that they made elliptical craters that resembled teardrops.

When the meteors hit the ground, they made terrifying loud noises and shook the ground like an earthquake. This event caused very large fires all over the northern Western Hemisphere, and death was all around. As the night wore on, it began to rain. If it rained every day for thirteen days, that would seem like it would never stop. But worse, **this storm continued raining every day for thirteen months, which equals ninety-one days in a row!** *The rains filled the craters creating the Carolina Bays. One crater was so large it created an inland lake that was fifteen miles long, and the ocean levels began to slowly rise. One group named it "Mattamuskeets, 'the lake on the hill,' and named their tribe after it."*[832]

832 Firestone, Richard. et al. *The Cycle of Cosmic Catastrophes,* pp. 193, 194.

Chapter 7

Who Built Bimini's Ancient Underwater Structures?

The answer to this question is problematic. Therefore, to obtain the answer, critical thinking and deductive reasoning will be employed, which will help solve the question of who built the ancient structures. In deductive reasoning, the evidence is followed from the general to the specific. One by one, each piece of evidence is eliminated until the field of possibilities is reduced to the only remaining answer. For clarity, we shall begin with the most recent and proceed to the most ancient civilization to determine who built the structure.

First, the Ice Age began to flood the oceans and the Bimini Road (B.R.) thousands of years before Columbus. Secondly, who built the other structures two miles west of Bimini in 10,000 B.C., at least 11,492 years earlier? No, Columbus could not have built either structure for these structures were under water many thousands of years before his journeys.

The Vikings as B.R. Builders?

The Scandinavian Vikings were the first documented group of Europeans to enter the Americas. If it were not for one group of Paleoamericans, "the Skraelings," Scandinavian Vikings would have been the first people to expand and try their hand at colonizing the Americas. The flag we fly today would probably look a little different.

No one knows why, but after the Holy Roman Empire peacefully assimilated the German barbarians, between 500 and 600 A.D., there was a bloody invasion of Italy. Into what remained of the classical culture of the emerging Christian society "came a violent eruption from the north."[833] From Norway, Denmark and possibly Sweden, came the "last and the fiercest of the Germanic Barbarians,"[834] the Vikings.

---

833 Oleson, Tryggvi J. (1963). *Early Voyages and Northern Approaches 1000-1632* (Toronto, McClelland, and Stewart Limited), p. 1.

834 Ibid.

No one knows if overcrowding or something else caused the Viking raids to come, but come they did to Northern and then Southern Europe and eventually into the Mediterranean. These are the areas where most history books discuss how the Vikings raided, raped and pillaged. After invading western Russia in the East, the Vikings began looking to the West. Most history books do not cover the area we are about to investigate.

The first recorded Caucasian Europeans to venture west towards the Americas were Scandinavian Vikings in 1000 A.D.[835] who reached Iceland 590 miles[836] west of Scandinavia. Then they colonized Greenland, which is 190 miles west [of Iceland]. Erik "The Red" Thorvaldsson, is remembered today as a trailblazing Viking explorer and the founder of Greenland. Erik's second son was Leif Erikson; "Leif the Fortunate" is best known as the first European ever to set foot on the North American continent. [Leif] Erikson explored lands he called "Helluland, Markland, and Vinland." Historians believe that these may be the Canadian maritime areas now known as Baffin Island, Labrador, and Newfoundland.[837]

So that you will have a frame of reference for how far they travelled and how long it took the Vikings to get from Norway to Canada: Erik the Red began in Norway and made his way to Greenland. From there, his son made it the rest of the way to Canada. The "distance from Canada to Norway...is 5,871 kilometers. That is, the air travel distance is equal to 3,648 miles."[838]

"No matter which version is accepted, there can be no question that Leif Erikson was the first European to set foot on American soil"[839] on his first voyage to the Americas in 1000 A.D.[840] Some others report the Vikings came in 850 A.D. Eventually, Leif Erikson supposedly landed in Vinland. "Vinland is the entire island of Newfoundland, as shown herein

835 Ibid.

836 "Geography Of Iceland" (n.d.). Accessed May 21, 2009. http://www.travelnet.is/geographyoficeland.html.

837 Oleson, Tryggvi J. *Early Voyages and Northern Approaches*, p. 17.

838 Ibid., p. 13.

839 Ibid., p. 18.

840 Guest Contributor. 5/21/2017. From https://www.zegrahm.com/blog/viking-history-how-erik-red-settled-greenland.

by evidence from three separate disciplines: navigation, geography and history"[841] says author Paul H. Chapman, who was a former navigator with the Army Air Corps Ferry Command. He believes Newfoundland is Erikson's "Vinland." Therefore, Erikson was the first documented European to enter the Americas. Vinland got its name because when the Vikings first landed there, they found grapes growing.[842] Vinland had to be in Southeastern Canada or New England, for Northern Canada was too cold to accommodate grape growing.

Leif's brother **Thorfinn** made a third voyage, but no date is mentioned. The writings did not specify how far the Vikings might have sailed south. All the writings about Thorfinn say he and his crew sailed south for quite a while until they reached a place they called "Hop," which might have been somewhere between Baffin Island and Vinland. This is where they saw the **diminutive Skraelings** for the first time, paddling towards them in skin' boats and kayaks. The Vikings described these Skraelings as being **swarthy or dark-skinned men with coarse hair, broad cheeks, large eyes, and large nostrils**; they had high cheekbones with pointed chins. They were also described as being a **Black, dwarf people who lived in subterranean dwellings accessed by holes in the ground.**[843]

The Vikings identify these people as "Pygmies," meaning none of them were taller than four feet.[844] In fact, the Vikings met so many of these "Black Dwarves" (also referred to as Skraelings or Protoamericans) in one geographical treatise we see this quote appear: "Vinland the good, which some men think is a projection of Africa...because all over Vinland.... Both east and west in the country they found human habitations of people whom the Greenlanders called Skraelings.[845] These Skraelings were also known as the "Dorset people." **They predate the Eskimos of the Arctic regions and were still in eastern Canada when the Vikings arrived.**[W]

841 "Distance from and to." (2009-18). Distance from Canada to Norway. From: https://www.distancefromto.net/distance-from-canada-to-norway.

842 Oleson, Tryggvi J. *Early Voyages and Northern Approaches*, p. 19.

843 Chapman, Paul. H. "Where in North America did the Vikings Settle?" *The Official Journal of the Ensign Trust*. Accessed December 12, 2009. http://www.ensignmessage.com/archives/vikings.html.

844 Oleson, Tryggvi J. *Early Voyages and Northern Approaches*, p. 6.

845 Chapman, Paul. H. "Where in North America did the Vikings Settle?"

On that Viking's third voyage, they recorded that this was the first time they came into contact with the Skraelings. Out of the nine Skraelings they saw, eight were killed and the ninth escaped in his boat. There are several other reports of the Vikings killing Skraelings. In one battle, large numbers of Skraelings were killed. The Skraelings did eventually, and fearlessly fight back. They used war slings, that rained down large amounts of marine animals. The projectiles were probably the teeth of marine animals. They also made a device that launched a catapulted ball, which terrified the Vikings. There was no mention of the bow and arrow in Oleson's book (1963), however, the Skraelings must have had the bow because Leif Erikson's brother Thorvald was killed with an arrow in a battle with the Skraelings.[846] *The Skraelings did eventually, and fearlessly fight back, however. They used war slings that rained down large amounts of sharp objects.*[847]

There is much mentioned in Mallery's book (1951) of the Skraelings using arrows and defeating the Vikings:

By keeping up constant and vigorous volleys of arrows and darts, the Eskimo Skraelings forced the Norse Vikings to hide behind their shields.... Then came the surprise.... The Skraelings raised up several poles on each of which was a very large shaped body balista...This they hurled from the pole...when a balista hit a shield the shield broke into pieces.... The only way the Norse could save themselves was by running away.[848]

Oleson wrote, "The Vikings were cruel and fierce barbarians."[849] They were known across Europe for their fighting nature, so there is no surprise they did not get along with the Skraelings either.

The place the Vikings called "Vinland the Good" had ample game; "there was scarcely any frost in the winter and cattle could forage year-round. Grapes were found in abundance and self-sown wheat...salmon were very plentiful.[850] A settlement was built which lasted three years. At

---

846 Ibid., pp. 23, 47-50.

847 Oleson, Tryggvi J. *Early Voyages and Northern Approaches*, p. 45.

848 Ibid., p. 48.

849 Ibid., p. 46.

850 Mallery, Arlington. H. *Lost America*, p. 92.

the end of the fifth voyage to Vinland, the Viking expedition returned home to Greenland with a rich cargo of grapes, vines and furs. During the sixth voyage to Vinland "talk continued about huge profits to be made in Vinland."[851]

After the sixth voyage was over, however, the Vikings finally left Vinland for good. Why was that, when they wrote about the huge profits to be made in Vinland? Further, why is it that, "After returning to Europe, no more Europeans tried to colonize it or even travel there until Columbus' time. Although there have been claims to the contrary, the longest documented period an Icelander settlement stayed in Vinland was three years.[852] There is no date given as to why or when the Vikings left Vinland for good" says Oleson, who wrote *Early Voyages and Northern Approaches*. Oleson did say that the Vikings were in Vinland for three years. Could it have been because of the Skraelings that they gave up?

Since Leif Erikson, supposedly landed in Vinland in 1000 A.D., a calculated guess would be that they left Vinland in the Western Hemisphere in 1003 A.D. The Skraelings did not want to be colonized and fought for their freedom. It seems that there is no other plausible explanation, other than these short people, called the Skraelings, halted the spread of Europeans to the Western Hemisphere, and they did not return until 1492, 489 years later!

The prevailing question here is: "From whence did the Skraelings come?" A full explanation is beyond the scope of this book, but a short answer may be read in the Section Notes at the end of this chapter.

It is often asked why the Scandinavian Vikings failed to stay in "Vinland the Good," having found such a paradise there. Oleson gave the most probable reason the Vikings left the Western Hemisphere. The Vikings reported that the native population Skraelings were even more hostile in Vinland than in Greenland![853]

After the Vikings tried out Vinland in the Western Hemisphere they seem to have abandoned it. They then set their sights back to northwestern Europe (south of Scandinavia), and began to rape and pillage in a southerly direction. Their raids were successful in most places on their venture south

---

851 Ibid., p. 4.

852 Ibid, pp. 19, 29.

853 Ibid., p. 25.

until they approached Spain. They did not end up fighting the Spanish in Spain. They found a very different, far more formidable opponent. This time they were not fighting tiny Black men. They were fighting tall muscular Africans. They had to fight the Moors of North Africa who had been there in Spain since 711 A.D. Just as the tiny Skralings did, **the Moors also defeated the Vikings**. Some Vikings escaped and sailed into the Mediterranean Sea to plaque communities there, but never returned to Spain.

It therefore seems that the Vikings could not have built the B.R. either. Firstly, for the Vikings to have built the B.R., they would have had to have arrived before the flood. Secondly, after arriving in Canada, they were not there long enough to expand almost a continent away, down to the Bahamas. It is perfectly clear that the answer to the question at hand, is that the Vikings did not build the B.R. structure.

The Romans as B.R. Builders?

Rome is believed to have been established in 753 B.C. The first Europeans confirmed to have sailed out of the Mediterranean Sea were the Romans. The Republic of Rome was later founded in 509 B.C., but the Romans were not the first civilization in Italy. The African-Etruscans predated the European Romans by thousands of years. The Etruscans drained the valleys and swamps around Palatine Hill and built the first city of Rome,[854] the first Caucasian civilization in Italy.

The Romans did sail out of the Mediterranean to England, however. In England, one of the last remaining structures the Romans built is a wall that stretches across the breadth of England for 70 miles. It is called Hadrian's Wall, and it was built in approximately 120 A.D. It stretches east to west from England's eastern shore at Tyne West to Solway Firth at the Irish Sea. It was built with regular-sized stones rather than megalithic stones weighing several tons.[855] It was built to keep out the same type of people, indigenous to the British Isles, that the Vikings fought and lost to in Canada. Even at Rome's earlier rise of 753 B.C., the Romans were 3247 years too late to have built anything in the Bahamas, even using the latest date of the B.R.'s construction. Therefore, the Romans did not build Bimini's breakwater and pier.

854 Ibid., pp. 19, 34.

855 Oleson, Tryggvi J. *Early Voyages and Northern Approaches*, p. 35.

The Greeks as B.R. Builders?

It has been hard to get the scientific community to establish a start-date for the origin of the Grecian civilization, but it seems to have begun sometime between the Trojan war in 1200 B.C.[856] and 776 B.C., when the first Olympic games began.[857] However, most people do not know that Caucasians were not the first civilization in Greece.

The "Pelasgians were Africans from Crete,"[858] and built the first civilization in Greece. "The Greek historical works make it clear that many ancient settlers of the Aegean came from Africa, especially the Garamantes and Pelasgians."[859] Then in the end of the Pelasgian saga we see that, "It was the Pelasgians who first founded Athens and Thebes."[860]

From the evidence above we see that post-Pelasgian Greece was the first European civilization. There are no records, however, of the Caucasian Greeks sailing out of the Mediterranean Sea during either period (1200 B.C. or 776 B.C.). The Greeks could not have sailed out of the Mediterranean before Indo-European Greece was born. Her earliest possible start date is 1200 B.C.[861]

Therefore, Greece, the first European civilization, could not have built the ancient harbor because Greece's start date was over 2800 years after the date of 4000 B.C. for the B.R.'s construction.[x]

---

856 "Rome," (n.d.). Accessed on July 2, 2009 at Wikipedia.

857 Mallory, J. P.(1989). *In Search of the Indo-Europeans* (New York, Thames & Hudson), p. 93.

858 Zweifel, C. (2002). Hadrian's Wall. From http://www.american.edu/ted/ice/hadrian.htm.

859 Martin, T.R. (1999). Introduction to the Historical Overview in Perseus. Accessed on July 2, 2009 from http://www.perseus.tufts. edu/hopper/text. jsp?doc=Perseus:text:1999.04.0009.

860 Rice, R.S. (2008). Ancient History 26. Accessed July 2, 2009 from http:// ccat.sas.upenn.edu/ rrice/026913.htm.

861 "Pelasgians." (1963). *Encyclopedia Britannica*, pp. 448-9.

The Phoenicians as B.R. Builders?

Most people do not know that the first Phoenicians were Africans from the Nile Valley, who much later integrated and became multicultural, as well as multinational. Farther east and long before Greece, we see that the first anatomically modern humans to leave Africa for the Levant/ Cannon/ Palestine, were the Qafzeh peoples. Skhul has dates that are barely within the Late Pleistocene. Thermo luminescence dates for Skhul level B are 119 plus/minus 18,000 years and for Qafzeh they range between 102,000 and 85,000 years ago (Valladas et. al., 1998).[862]

Then, during the Qafzeh occupation of the Levant 40,000 years ago, the Aurignacian people moved in through the Levant on their way to Europe from Africa followed by the Gravettians 25,000 years ago. The last two groups mentioned left their African "genetic template for European men" labeled Y marker M173 and M170 that living Europeans carry in their blood today.[863]

Natufians followed for thousands of years before they were labeled Phoenician. The Natufian/Phoenicians were the first permanent culture to settle in the Levant, or in Mesopotamia for that matter. A "new life style" in the Levant, arguably had a slow start, but really took off during the Epipaleolithic period (EP): from c. 23,000–11,500 years ago. Recently, archaeologists have considered the early parts of the EP to be more culturally dynamic and similar to the later phase (Natufian) than was previously thought.[864]

The Phoenicians did not leave the Nile Valley and enter their homeland of modern-day Israel until circa 1450 B.C.[865] The Cretan (Minoan) and Phoenician people were both under the political domination of Egypt.

---

862 Winters, Clyde. (n.d.) "The Black Greeks." Accessed May 3, 2015. http://clyde.winters.tripod.com/chapter6.html.

863 Ibid.

864 Martin, T. R. (1999). Introduction to the Historical Overview in Perseus. Accessed on July 2, 2009 from http://www.perseus.tufts. edu/hopper/text. jsp?doc=Perseus:text:1999.04.0009.

865 Kramer, Andrew, Tracey L. Crummett, and Milford H. Wolpoff. "Out of Africa and into the Levant: replacement or admixture in Western Asia?" (2001). p. 52. *Quaternary International* 75 (2001) 51-63. Accessed May 5, 2014. http://www.personal.umich.edu/~wolpoff/Papers/levant.pdf.

Neither of these peoples were inventors because both were doing nothing but transmitting Egyptian cultural values including the domain of navigation and writing,[866] not to mention their first civilization there.

The next reference attributes the name "Canaan" to all lands between Asia Minor and Egypt prior to 1200 B.C. and states, "Phoenicia now generally refers to this region in the Iron Age (c. 1200–332 B.C.), even though the culture had earlier antecedents."[867] Maher confirmed his hypothesis that the replacements for the Neanderthal people were Sub-Saharan Africans. We clearly see the continuity between African culture from Nubia to the Levant. The Natufians used the Ibero-Maurusian tool industry. They took the Ibero-Maurusian tools from Nubia into Europe, North Africa and the Middle East.[868] Artifacts found in that region, which was called, "The Capsian tool industry...[were] of Negroid origin."[869] Again, this time in the Middle East. these Natufians—according to Christopher Ehret—were small-statured folk who spread agriculture throughout Nubia into the Red Sea,[870] and then into North Africa and Europe.

Later ancient western Eurasians, especially the Natufian populations when plotted, fall within the range of Sub-Saharan populations like the

866 Gibbons, Ann. "Europeans Trace Ancestry to Paleolithic People." *Science*, 10 Nov 2000: Vol. 290, Issue 5494, pp. 1080-1081. Accessed August 3, 2016. DOI: 10.1126/science.290.5494.1080.

867 Maher, Lisa A., T. Richter, and J. Stock. (2012). "The Pre-Natufian Epipaleolithic: Long-Term Behavioral Trends in the Levant." *Evolutionary Anthropology* 21:69-81. doi:10.1002/evan.21307.

868 Diop, Cheikh A. *Civilization or barbarism*, pp. 95, 109.

869 Holst, Sanford. (2004). "Origin of the Phoenician Empire— Accurately Dating Phoenician History." A paper presented to the Annual Conference of World History Association at Fairfax, Va. Accessed June 9, 2015. http://phoenicia.org/datingchronology. html.

870 Wendorf, Fred. (1968). Prehistory of Nubia (Dallas, Southern Methodist University Press), pp. 941-46.

Niger-Congo speakers.[871] The modern civilizations of the Middle East were created by the Africans, from the Aurignacians to the Natufians. Also, "Since the Natufians came from Nubia, they cannot be classified as Europeans."[872]

In review, Phoenicia and Canaan were the same place. The ancient city of Ugarit (which lies on the Syrian coast), will place the original habitat of the Phoenicians to the south, which is in Egypt's frontier. This comes from the Ras Shamra text—which are Akkadian.[873] Akkadia is the second African civilization in Mesopotamia. Sumer was the first.

Phoenician history is, therefore, incomprehensible only if we ignore the biblical information, according to which the Phoenicians, in other words, the Canaanites, were originally Negroes already civilized, with whom nomadic, uncultured white tribes later mixed.[874]

The Phoenicians did not enter their homeland of modern-day Israel until circa 1450 B.C. It therefore makes sense to say that—even though the first Phoenician ships were probably made by Africans—the Phoenicians in 1450 B.C., were too late to have built the B.R.

The Amerinds as B.R. Builders?

Most sources agree that the first Amerinds who entered the Bahamas from South America sometime before 5000 B.C. were called the "Ciboney"[875] or "Siboney." Archeologists have discovered that an extinct

871 "The origins of domestication in Ethiopia." Pan-African Congress on Prehistory and Quaternary Studies (8th:1977:Nairobi:, Kenya); Ogot, Bethwell A & Leakey, Richard E (1980). Proceedings of the 8th Panafrican Congress of Prehistory and Quaternary Studies, Nairobi, 5 to 10 September 1977; Holliday, Trenton W. (2014) Evolution at the Crossroads: Modern Human Emergence in Western Asia, American Anthropologist, Vol. 102, No. 1 (2000); The Natufians. http://www.exposingblacktruth.org/the-natufians/.

872 Diop, Cheikh A. The African Origin of Civilization, p. 107.

873 Ehret, Christopher. "On the Antiquity of Agriculture in Ethiopia." The Journal of African History Vol. 20, No. 2 (1979), p p.161 -177.

874 Winters, Clyde. "Origin and Spread of Haplogroup N." 2010. Accessed May 22, 2015. https://www.academia.edu/1898557/Origin_and_ Spread_of_Haplogroup_N.

875 Holliday, T. W. (2000). Evolution at the Crossroads: Modern Human Emergence in Western Asia. American Anthropologist, 102(1)).

group of Paleoamericans called the "Guanajatabeys" once populated the entire West Indies and Cuba. They became extinct before anyone could study them, but sources also referred to them as the Ciboney.[876]

The Lucayans entered the West Indies from South America in 5000[877] after the Ciboney. The Lucayans "are best known as Taínos, which is the term chosen by scholars to refer to their language and their culture."[878] "The term Arawak, which is also substituted for Taíno in the British West Indies, is a misnomer and should be abandoned."[879] To simplify matters, the Lucayan, Taíno and Arawak are the same people who were recognized by different names, just as the Ciboney were also called the Guanajatabey. Furthermore, "Tahino and Manding/Olmec languages share many points of phonology and morphology sounds and arrangements of words."[880]

Some of you may ask, "What about the Carib Indians, after whom the Caribbean Sea was named?" We are told that they probably first lived inside the Amazon River Valley in South America. After migrating to the northern coast, the Caribs expanded north into the Caribbean around 1000 CE. In the process, they drove out the resident Indians.[881] There is a definite Egyptian/Carib Indian connection…but did they speak Manding?[Y] Before ending this section on the Amerinds's potential for building the Bimini Breakwater, the Algonquin must be considered. Mentioned earlier, "The people of this nation have a tradition that their ancestors crossed the sea"

---

876 "Ras Shamra Texts Volume II." (1981). Edited by Rummel, S. Published by IURA EDITIONIS ET VERSIONIS RESERVANTUR: Italy.

877 Diop, Cheikh A. *The African Origin of Civilization*, p. 108.

878 Aarons, George A. "The Lucayans: The People Whom Columbus Discovered in the Bahamas." (1990). Accessed August 3, 2016. http://libertyparkusafd.org/Columbus/papers/The%20Lucayans%20-%20%20The%20People%20Whom%20Columbus%20Discovered%20in%20the%20Bahamas.htm.

879 Rouse, Irving. "Origin and Development of the Indians Discovered by Columbus." Accessed August 3, 2016. 1987. http://www.gerace-researchcentre.com/pdfs/1stColumbus/.

880 Aarons, George A. "The Lucayans."

881 Ibid.

to reach the Americas.[882] This is similar to the Mayan legend from their sacred book "Popol Vuh, the ancient religious and historical text compiled by the Quiche Mayan Indians...claims that the Olmec came to Mexico in 'ships of bark.'"[883]

The Yucatan was part of the Olmec Nation. "Friar Diego de Landa said that: 'Some old men of the Yucatan say that they heard from their ancestors that this country was peopled by a certain race from the East, whom God delivered by opening for them twelve roads through the sea.'"[884] There is no evidence of Amerinds building with stone blocks, even though they may have been of African descent when they first entered the Americas, before mixing their blood with the Mongolians. Realistically, Amerinds building with megalithic blocks weighing several tons is even more improbable. Amerinds are ruled out as the builders of the B.R.

It is now evident that the natives in the Bahamas did not build the structures. As a side note, it seems that the first documented Paleoamericans in the Bahamas were Guanajatabey or Ciboney. They were most likely Africans, because they were in the Americas in 5000 B.C.,[885] two thousand years before the Mongolians entered the Americas in 3000 B.C.[886] The Lucayans probably looked like the Carib Indians, a dark brown-skinned people.

In summary, the groups that have been ruled out for building the Bahamian structures are the Spanish (Columbus), Vikings, Romans, Greeks, Phoenicians and Amerinds. It seems that the Egyptian/Proto-Manding people, who originated in the Nile Valley, had several characteristics that make them the best candidates for having built these sites in the Bahamas. However, this does not mean they did or did not partner with other peoples from the Nile Valley.

---

882 Fell, Barry. *America B.C.: Ancient Settlers in the New World*, p. 279.

883 Winters, Clyde. "Race and Identity."

884 Winters, Clyde. *Atlantis in Mexico*, p. 6.

885 Aarons, George A. "The Lucayans."

886 Powell, Joseph F., and Walter A. Neves. "Craniofacial Morphology of the First Americans," pp. 153-88.

10 Characteristics of the Manding

1. They had a civilization old enough and sophisticated enough to build "The Bimini Road."
2. They had ships and the knowledge of the Americas to take them there.
3. They had the ability to build with megalithic blocks.
4. They had built temples and used fluted columns exactly like those in Egypt.
5. They built mounds along the Niger River in Africa similar to the mounds along the Mississippi and Ohio Rivers.
6. They used the same gold spear formula as the Africans Columbus found in Haiti.
7. They had words matching pre-Columbus–Paleoamerican and West African words for gold, such as guanin/ghanin.
8. They formed the base of the Olmec people.
9. They understood and used metallurgy.
10. The Egyptian Sphinx was present.

Science only requires eight coincidences to establish contact between two cultures.[887] It therefore seems that the people who built the ancient sites in the Americas were most likely Egyptian/Manding people. The ten characteristics above make a logical argument for the first Bahamians to have been related to Egyptians, Mande and Olmecs.

The Manding either partnered with Egyptians, or they built the structures without other Egyptian ethnic groups' help. In review, the Manding were the base of the Olmec, and the Manding originally began in the Southern Nile Valley. With so much contact between all three groups, they probably became the same people after a while, or at the least, they were related.

In conclusion, it is accurate to say that Africans built the megalithic structures in the Bahamas.[888]

---

887 Van Sertima, Ivan. *Early America Revisited*, p. 157.

888 Little, Gregory. "Proof: The Bimini Road is an Ancient Ruin," p. 34.

Section Notes

W. Where did Eskimos come from and when did they arrive in the Arctic?

The renowned scholar Franz Boas, writing in 1910 stated that "the much discussed theory of the Asiatic origin of the Eskimo must be entirely abandoned"...investigators seem to show that the Eskimo must be considered as, comparatively speaking, new arrivals in Alaska, which they reached coming from the east.[889]

Anthropologist H. P. Steenby agrees with McGhee's data on the Eastern origin of the Eskimo.

In the conclusion of his book (the first of 17 volumes), Oleson (1963) wrote that everything indicates that the Eskimos did not migrate from Alaska in the west, to eastern Canada, bringing with them new iron-age developments, like whaling (sleighs) and sleigh dogs to pull loads. After reading this new information, think about it logically. Eskimos did not migrate from anywhere. Eskimos are the offspring of two separate groups,[890] the Skraelings and the Caucasian Scandinavians, who originated from the East in different time periods. They predate the Vikings by at least 10,000 or more years. The Scandinavian Vikings met a completely different Skraeling people in Greenland. Physically they were the same, but obviously they got along with the Scandinavian Viking people. Both groups mixed their blood and it was their offspring that became the Eskimo.

We have been taught that Eskimos from Asia crossed the Bering Strait, across the glaciers of Alaska, and entered Canada:

From Alaska is one of the most astounding myths in the whole of history. One is asked to believe that the centuries preceding 1000 CE before the Vikings, the bearers of a new culture different from the Skraelings migrated from Alaska, gradually moved across the Canadian Arctic and coincidentally reached Greenland at the same time as the Icelanders. One is asked to believe this, although the

---

889 McGhee, Robert. (1941). *Ancient People of the Arctic* (British Columbia, UBC Press), p. 20.

890 Oleson, Tryggvi J. *Early Voyages and Northern Approaches*, p. 175.

oldest Thule Eskimo sites are to be found in Greenland as opposed to Alaska or Asia.[891]

X. Were the Greeks native to Greece?

Oxford graduate, Sir Arthur Evans (one of the fathers of Mediterranean archaeology), made a world-shaking statement:

Whether they like it or not, classical students must consider [origins]. The Grecians whom we discern in the new dawn were not the pale-skinned Northerners...but essentially a dark haired, brown-complexioned race.[892]

That would also make sense to J. P. Mallory, who agrees with that statement:

J. P. Mallory says the Greeks were not native to Greece but were Indo-European invaders from the North. He adds that they gradually absorbed an earlier culture, the Pelasgians. This invasion is confirmed by the Greek's own traditions. It, therefore, makes sense that a good deal of the Greek language itself, is not Indo-European.[893]

The people who lived in Greece before the Indo-Europeans built the huge Egyptian-style granaries, a massive Bronze Age dam, dikes and channels controlled by hydraulic engineering of a very high level. A style of engineering, found in Egypt, was a sophisticated and complicated network of channels and dikes used in draining Lake Kopis. They built the step pyramid—says archaeologist Theodore Spyropoulos who excavated the site in 1971—and below the pyramid, the Tomb of Amphon and Zethos at Thebes before the arrival of the Indo-Europeans. "There was a substantial Egyptian influence on the construction of the pyramid of the twins Amphon and Zethos at Thebes early in the Helladic II period...from 3000–2400 B.C.," which predates the arrival of the Indo-Europeans.[894] The pyramid of Amphon and Zethos—a step pyramid dated during the reign of Mentuhotep's Pharaonic Dynasty XI—was uncovered in recent

---

891 Ibid., pp. 60, 174-175.

892 Brunson, James E. *Predynastic Egypt: An African Centric View*, p. 36.

893 Mallory, J. P. (1989). *In Search of the Indo-Europeans* (New York, Thames & Hudson), pp. 68-69.

894 Bernal, Martin. (1991). *Black Athena: The Afroasiatic roots of classical civilization* (Texas, Reuters University Press), pp. 124 135, 129, 130, 131.

excavations[895] in Greece. This is yet another connection with the Nile Valley.

Y. The Caribs spoke Manding and Ta-Seti/Qustul.

At different times in history, the same land was given different names. For example, Spain was once known as Iberia. Not only have the names been changed but the borders of the countries have also changed. In Walker's book, *Shades of Memnon* (2001), eminent historian and linguist, Dr. Clyde A. Winters wrote that, "A major ethnic group among the Kushites were the Manding...people."[896] The Kushite people were from Kush, comprising parts of Southern Egypt, Sudan, and Northern Ethiopia that ran along the Nile River.

Ta-Seti was in Northern Sudan bordering Southern Egypt. It was the people of Ta-Seti who built the Egyptian civilization.[897] This proximity makes the Manding an Egyptian people, even though they were just one of several ethnic groups of ancient Egypt. In Chapter 1, we discussed that during the African Aqualithic period, the Proto-Manding migrated west to Mauritania in eastern Africa and lived along the wandering Niger River.[898] Manding is also the language of Mali, which is a major language group in western Africa today. The Manding were later found in the Americas, especially Central and South America.

It is Ta-Seti that is called "Qustul" by historian Bruce Williams of the Oriental Institute, in an attempt to make this wording simpler. Qustul is found on maps today, whereas Ta-Seti is not found on maps today. The country of Ta-Seti/Qustul sat within the boundaries of Kush[899] (and southern Egypt). Some of the people of Ta-Seti left Kush and migrated to

---

895 Brunson, James E. *Predynastic Egypt: An African Centric View*, p. 37.

896 Walker, Gregory. (2001). *Shades of Memnon* (Illinois, Seker Nefer Press), p. 13.

897 Jones, David. *The Origin of Civilization*, p. 146.

898 Winters, Clyde. *Atlantis in Mexico*, p. 102.

899 Williams, Bruce B. Excavations Between Abu Simbel and The Sudan Frontier: The A-Group Royal Cemetery at Qustul: Cemetery L. (1986). Accessed August 3, 2016. http://oi.uchicago.edu/sites/oi.uchicago.edu/files/uploads/shared/docs/oine3.pdf.

western Africa, while some settled in Mali and surrounding areas, before sailing to the Americas.

Z. Were Europe's first farmers short Africans?

Early farmers' remains from the ancient Levant and Europe exhibit Sub-Saharan craniofacial features. Qafzeh-Skhul hominids of 20,000-10,000 B.C., were part of the Sub-Saharan population, along with the Natufian people in early Europe.[900]

Holliday (2000) confirmed his hypothesis that the replacements of the Neanderthal people in the Levant were Sub-Saharan Africans. This finding, similar to Brace et.al.'s (2006) findings for the Levant and Europe.

At this point we are almost finished with Europe. One group that has been only briefly mentioned in this work earlier was the Neanderthal. However, here are a couple of articles we had to bring to the forefront that shall reveal a part of history that "some historians" do not cover for some reason.

Let us look at this a little further. There are five excellent sources that answer the question as to who they were and also where the Homo neanderthalensis first appeared:

Geneticists obtained the oldest DNA ever sequenced from a human species. It confirmed fossils in a cave in Spain belonged to an early Neanderthal.

Aurignacian dates for Europe.[901] The spread of Aurignacian culture from Spain north, to France and then into Central Europe, suggest that there were two exits out of Africa. One from the west, an out-of-Africa event across the Straits of Gibraltar 40,000 years ago. Then 15,000 years later, another migration out of Africa through the Levant were the Gravettians, 25,000 years ago.

In conclusion, the genetic, archaeological and craniometric evidence that the Aurignacians (Boule & Vallois, 1957), Natufians (Brace et al.), suggests the species is **300,000 years older than previously thought.**

---

900 Winters, Clyde. (2015). "HLA-B*35 In Mexican Amerindians and African Populations."

901 Ray, C.C., Neanderthals: The Original Globetrotters. From *Science Magazine* in the *New York Times*, 12/11/17 https://www.nytimes.com/2017/12/11/science/where-did-neanderthals-come-from.html.

AA. National Geographic "admits" that Africans were the Original Europeans.

When people first migrated out of Africa circa 250,000–350,000 years ago they did not leave alone. There were at least two other hominid-related species who migrated throughout Eurasia: Neanmderthal and Denisovans. They ran into Neanderthal and interbred. A small amount of Neanderthal blood was then mixed with the modern gene pool.

Note: But the original population of Africans were in Europe long before the Ice Age began in 115,000 B.C.[902]

Let's take another look at the Neanderthal:

From The Smithsonian Institution, October 17, 2018:

Scientifically speaking, it was once thought that were all one part of a family tree. We are part of a diverse family tree. Since the famed "Lucy" skeleton was discovered back in 1974, our evolutionary tree has nearly doubled.

There was a time when there were three or even four different hominid species. But now we Homo sapiens are the only species to stand the test of time. Who knows, next with us landing on the Moon, and rocketing to Mars, with all that we have learned…we may not be all alone!

These are the sources that give some of the best and most updated story of how and where Neanderthal began:

- National Geographic
- Science Magazine
- Discover Magazine

Neanderthals probably evolved in Europe from African ancestors.

Modern humans and Neanderthals shared a common ancestor in Africa about 700,000 years ago. But the **ancestors of Neanderthals left Africa first, expanding to the Near East and then to Europe and Central Asia.** They were followed by modern humans, who emerged in Africa at least 250,000 years ago and remained there until roughly 70,000 years ago, venturing into other parts of the world.

Recent genetic studies have concluded that modern humans and Neanderthals met up again in Europe and interbred. As a result, the genes

---

902 National Geographic Editors (2018). Why Am I Neanderthal? https://genographic.nationalgeographic.com/neanderthal/

of all living non-Africans are roughly 1% Neanderthal. Our cousins went extinct about 40,000 years ago.

When our ancestors first migrated out of Africa they were not alone. Indigenous sub-Saharan Africans have none, or very little Homo neandethalensis DNA because their ancestors did not migrate through Eurasia.

There were great symbols of settler-colonialism from some of the respondents, but the images make no sense in the context of the question. Here's what we know:

- The first Neanderthals and the modern humans split from a common ancestor in Africa.
- Neanderthals migrated out of Africa.
- Neanderthals and modern humans mated outside of Africa.

The first modern humans **everywhere on Earth were Black Africans**:

- Modern humans
- 51,700 YBP South Carolina, from Dr. Albert Goodyear in 2004
- 100,000 YBP Piedra Fuera, Brazil from from Niede Guidon in 2014
- 130,000 YBP California from Science Magazine in 2017
- 250,00–350,000 YBP Mexico from U.S Geological Survey in 2012[903]

Geneticists have released a new study saying that several fossilized bones were discovered in northern Spain that belonged to an earlier member of the Neanderthal ancestral group. That makes this the oldest partial genome coming from an early human fossil that has been sequenced. This find now precedes the earlier dates for the beginning of the Neanderthal evolutionary tree by nearly 300,000 years earlier.[904]

According to paleogenetic Dr. Matthias Meyer, from Germany's Max Planck Institute for Evolutionary Anthropology, Neanderthals and their close relatives, the Denisovans, may have split from a common ancestor with modern humans about 765,000 years ago.

---

903 Solange, Tony. What Race were Neanderthals? https://www.quora.com/What-race-were-Neanderthals.

904 Gray, Richard. Neanderthals are TWICE as Old as Thought. *Daily Mail.* https://www.dailymail.co.uk/sciencetech/article-3233727/Neanderthals-TWICE-old-thought-DNA-suggests-extinct-human-species-emerged-700-000-yes-ago.html.

Previous morphological analysis agrees that they show Neanderthal/ Denisovan population split predates 430,000 years ago, which is the same geological age of the Sima remains.

These findings came in just days after anthropologists announced the discovery of a new species of early humans called Homo naledi, which was found in a cave in South Africa's Gauteng province.[905]

In summation, these articles say that:

The ancestors of Neanderthals left Africa first, expanding to the Near East and then to Europe and Central Asia. Neanderthals probably evolved in Europe from African ancestors.

When our ancestors first migrated out of Africa they were not alone. It is quite interesting that indigenous Sub-Saharan Africans have none, or very little Homo neanderthalensis DNA because their ancestors did not migrate through Eurasia.

If you're Asian or Caucasian, your ancestors interbred with Neanderthals. Neanderthals are almost *twice* as old as first thought: DNA suggests this now-extinct human species emerged 700,000 years ago.[906]

BB. Oldest DNA from Africa offers clues to mysterious ancient culture.

Around 15,000 years ago, in the oldest cemetery known in the world, folks buried their dead in a sitting position. They were dressed with animal horns, beads, and sophisticated stone arrowheads and points. 20th century archaeologists just assumed they belonged to an advanced European culture that migrated across the Mediterranean Sea to North Africa.

But now, through their ancient DNA—the oldest that has ever been collected from Africans—it became evident they had non-European ancestry. Instead, they were related to both Sub-Saharian Africans and Middle Easterners. Evolutionary geneticist Sarah Tishkoff of the University of Pennsylvania says the DNA shows that North Africa has always been an important crossroads, for a lot longer than people have thought.

---

905 Diop, Cheikh A. *Civilization or Barbarism*, p. 40.

906 Ray, C. Claiborne. (2017). "Neanderthals: The Original Globetrotters." *Science Magazine* in the *New York Times:* Dec. 11, 2017. https://www. nytimes.com/2017/12/11/science/where-did-neanderthals-come-from.html.

This suggested that both groups, Sub-Saharian Africans and Middle Easterners, inherited their shared DNA from a larger population that lived in North Africa or the Middle East more than 15,000 years ago.[907]

CC. The Aurignacians: A Different Origin

Finally, the Aurignacians did not come from the Levant. Haplogroup E1b1b (formerly known as E3b) represents the last major direct migration from Africa into Europe. It is believed to have first appeard in the Horn of Africa approximately 26,000 years ago and dispersed to North Africa to North Africa and the Near East during the late Paleolithic and Mesolithic periods. E1b1b lineages are closely linked to the diffusion of Afroasiatic languages. Allthough present throughout Europe, it peaks in the western Balkan region amongst Albians and their neighbors. It is also common in Italy and the Iberian peninsula. According to Cavalli-Sfortza's work,[908] all non-African populations are more closely related to each other than to Africans; supporting the hypothesis that **all non-Africans descend from a single old-African population**.... Europe is formed by contributions from Asia and Africa.[909]

The archaeological evidence clearly shows that the Aurignacian culture appears fully developed in France and Spain (Caramelli et. al, 2003). The archaeological evidence also makes it clear that the Aurignacian culture moved from west to east (Diop, 1974, 1991; Verneaux, 1926). As a result, the dates for the Near Eastern Aurignacian are later than the 2006; Holliday, 2000) and other groups who inhabited the Levant and Europe belonged to Sub-Saharan populations at this time suggest that these farmers carried haplogroup N into western Eurasia between 40,000–7500 years ago (Winters, 2010) and confirms Quintana-Murci et. al. (1999) hypothesis that haplogroup N originated in Africa.

That is to say, we see these ancient Natufians living in the Levant, sharing DNA with the Aurignacians, who were both former Sub-Saharan residents. Now we show the relationship of the Aurignacians to the Khoisan:

---

907 Winters, Clyde "Ancient African Writing Systems and Knowledge."

908 Cavalli-Sforza, L. L. (1997, 1993). "Drift, admixture, and selection in human evolution: a study with DNA polymorphisms." Proceedings of the National Academy of Sciences of the USA 88 (3): 839-43, pp. 90-93.

909 Winters, Clyde "Ancient African Writing Systems and Knowledge."

Numerous Sub-Saharan skeletons have been found in Europe dating to the Aurignacian and Neolithic periods. Boule and Vallois claim that these European farmers correspond to the Khoisan population. There are also N hgs found in Africa. Haplogroups N, N* and N1 is found in low frequencies within Sub-Saharan groups.

Earlier in this work, we saw that the Khoisan were related to the Anu, Twa, and San. In the end, we see that all of these groups were related from a Sub-Saharan origin.

Chapter 8

The Magic of Bimini in the Bahamas

The Bahamas are a group of islands due east of Florida. One of those islands is called Bimini. The first people known in the Bahamas were called the Lucayans. They were known to have migrated to the Bahamas from Puerto Rico, Haiti, Cuba, Dominican Republic, and Jamaica. All of the inhabitants originated from Alkebulan (Africa). Translated, Alkebulan means, "Garden of Eden," or "Mother of Mankind."

The Island of Bimini gets its name from its circular configuration, which is that of a crown or wreath.

We now move on to the most famous structure, which is located just about half of a mile off of the west coast of the Island of Bimini. It is a "man-made structure" lying in 18 feet of water. It is as long as 6 football fields (600 yards long laid out end-to-end) and 50 yards wide with slits for ships to pull into and dock.

On the shore there is a stone pier. Half of it has a slit that allows people to unload smaller boats on both sides. Just a few yards from the pier is a "J-shaped rock-structure" that also contains a wider slit to accommodate wider-deeper crafts to unload on both sides. The slit in both structures is where the road's "nickname" comes from, for it looks like a country road from the air.

These structures are not original. The first idea, as well as the first build of a similar structure, comes from the ancient Egyptians; it is near the mouth of the Nile River. Its pier had the original "J-shape" at the end that would block any waves that would try to flow laterally across the water break. This would prevent waves from causing the ships that were being loaded or unloaded to rise and fall, thus keeping them stable…brilliant!

Skeptics have tried to deny the fact that the breakwater was man-made and artificial. However, an analysis of pictures from the structure has been made by Dr. Greg Little Ph.D. He proved to our group beyond a shadow of a doubt that this breakwater is not a natural formation caused by wave action over time. It had been entirely built by humans.

Yes, there are several factors that have proven that the structure of the breakwater is a man-made artificial-structure, not part of natural rock formations of any kind. Among other things, there are indentations of tool marks in the blocks made by artisans while making the blocks fit perfectly together. This increases the strength of the blocks to counteract the blows of large waves during a storm.

Do not forget that this peer design is not new, but was first designed and used in Africa's ancient piers along the Nile River Valley's 4132 miles— Bimini's breakwater is just a copy. Lastly, speaking of the name Bimini— it does have another link with Egypt. The very name "Bimini' translates perfectly into Egyptian as the name "Baminini," which means "homage to (ini) the soul of (ba) Min (Min)." This is yet another link with Africa's Egypt!

Dr. Little strikes again. He demonstrates that the piers at Bimini and Andros Island were built long before 8000 B.C. To prove this hypothesis, Dr. Little cut out a small piece of the pier and sent it to a lab to be carbon dated. It was dated to between 4465 and 4585 B.C.

Also, why would hunter-gatherers build a 600 yard pier with 5-ton blocks to dock their canoes, when they could just pull them up to the beach and empty their cargo?

Jacques Cousteau's Evidence of a Large Island

Stalagmites develop in caves that are completely above the water line. Water seeps through the rock ceiling of a cave and drips down to the floor of the cave. As it drips, some of the water and minerals in the dripping water stay on the ceiling. The water evaporates and the minerals dry on the ceiling eventually forming the shape of a muddy icicle called a stalactite. The puddle of water it forms on the cave floor evaporates, leaving the minerals to dry, which form a small hill. As the small hill grows, it becomes much narrower, eventually making the shape of a reverse muddy icicle called a stalagmite.

On the island of Andros next to Bimini, another famous researcher, Jacques Cousteau, found these stalactites and stalagmites while he was diving in an underwater cavern. The only way they could have been formed would have been in dry air conditions when the cavern had been above water. "But the depths at which he found the cavern, in excess of 160 feet, means they were formed thousands of years before the present ..." (p. 62), which had to be before the last Ice Age melted and flooded the cavern in 10,000–12,000 B.C. Because of this early date, also means that the underwater structures had to be built by Africans and not anyone else.

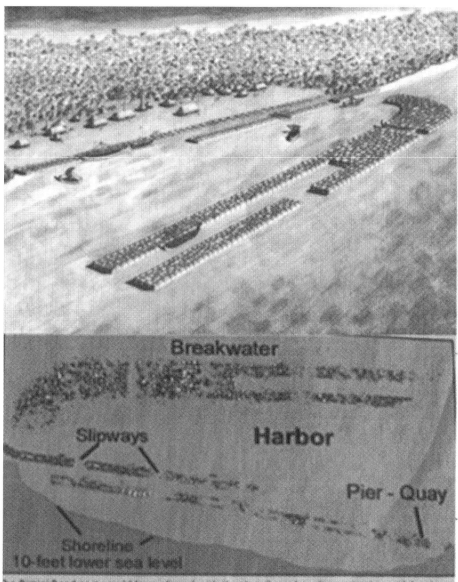

Fig. 45: Breakwater & Harbor. These structures are absolutely man-made, and not by erosion of waves.

Who Discovered the Bahamas and Built the Breakwater/Pier?

Until now we've been studying who the first Bahamians were. We will now find who the first Bahamians were not.

Were they Caucasian-Indo-Europeans? No, because the first Indo-European civilization was not Caucasian nor was it Mesopotamian. That myth was exposed by Dr. David Imhotep's Ph.D. dissertation. Mesopotamia has been falsely labeled the "Cradle of Civilization." So we see that the first Mesopotamian civilization was not Sumer, and furthermore, Sumer's creators were from Africa and not Mesopotamia.

Cretans as B.R. Builders?

No, the first Indo-European civilization was also not from Crete. The first ancestors of the Cretans were also natives of Africa, a branch of the Western Ethiopians who formerly lived in the grasslands of Northern Africa before it dried up, (7,000–10,000 B.C.) and became a great desert—they migrated to Crete.[910]

Additionally, on Crete in 1470 B.C., the non-Indo-European language of Linear A is replaced with the Indo-European Linear B. This is also the same time all the palaces in Crete, except Konossos, are destroyed by fire.

Phoenicians as B.R. Builders?

Was it the Phoenicians? No, the first Phoenicians were not Caucasian-Indo-Europeans.

1. The Bible and other sources say that the Phoenicians were "Hamite," which means Black.
2. The Phoenicians left Africa and migrated to Canaan.
3. The first people found in Canaan in prehistoric times were the African Natufian, who left artifacts found in that region, called the "Caspian tool industry." This was also of African origin.
4. Close to 1450 B.C., the Phoenicians migrated west towards the coast of the Mediterranean Sea where they established their first colony, Boeitia.

---

910 Jackson, John G. (1972). *Man, God and Civilization* (Secaucus, NJ: Carol Publishing Group, 1990), p. 250.

5. The Greeks nickname them "Phoenikes," for the dye they were famous for. Let us not forget, however, that the Phoenicians adopted this purple industry from the Egyptians and ran with it.
6. The most ancient tombs found in Phoenicia were classified by Dr. Valloios to be of Negro persuasion.
7. Great mariners, they establish colonies all over the Mediterranean Sea.
8. They were under the political domain of Egypt.
9. Eventually the Black Canaanites mixed with the Indo-European invaders and became the Jewish people of today.

Even the first Phoenicians, who were Africans in the beginning, did not enter their homeland until circa 1450 B.C. The Phoenicians established their first colony, Boeitia, in 1450 B.C.[911]

Phoenicia was not considered a nation in the modern sense of the word, but rather as a chain of coastal cities. They were a coastal branch of the Canaanites, who according to biblical tradition, were the brothers of Cush (Ethiopia) and Mizraim (Egypt), all members of the Hamite ethnic family.

Therefore, the Bible says they were all Black and are from a Nile Valley origin.

The first people found in Canaan in prehistoric times were the African Natufian. Artifacts found in that region were called the "Capsian tool industry," was also of African origin.[912] The Cretian (Minoan) and Phoenician people were both under the political domination of Egypt: neither one of these people were inventors, they were doing nothing but transmitting Egyptian cultural and economic values, even in the domain of navigation and writing.[913]

Remember, the Phoenicians established their first colony, Boeitia, in 1450 B.C., but the very latest estimates of the age of the Bahamian harbors was 6000 B.C., 4500 years earlier.

So in review, the first civilizations begun in Mesopotamia, Crete or Phoenicia were Africans. However, even they began too late to be the first Bahamians or the people to build the Bimini Breakwater.

911 Diop, Cheikh Anti. *The African Origins of Civilization*, pp. 109-10.

912 Ibid., p. 102.

913 Diop, Cheikh Anta. *Civilization or Barbarism*, p. 95.

Greeks or Romans as B.R. Builders?

Could it have been the Greeks or Romans? No it could not. The first Caucasian Indo-European civilization was the Greek civilization; howevthe Greeks did not build the Bimini Road. Although 1200 B.C. marks the first *Caucasian* Indo-European civilization, it was not Greece's *first* civilization! African Pelasgians were in Greece for thousands of years before the Indo-European hoards invaded and took over the Eastern Mediterranean. The Pelasgians left much megalithic architecture behind—especially in Mycenae—including a couple of small pyramids in Greece.

The Greeks were also said to have never left the Mediterranean. Even if the they had sailed out of the Mediterranean, they could not have done so before Greece 1200 B.C. This first European civilization, which followed Phoenicia, could not have built an ancient harbor whose start date was 4800 years before the current most conservative start date for the harbor's genesis.

The Romans were supposedly the first Indo-Europeans to sail out of the Mediterranean. Rome's start date was 753 B.C. The republic of Rome was founded in 509 B.C.

Here again, the Romans were not the first civilization in Italy. The African-Etruscians predated the Indo-European Romans by many thousands of years. It was the Etruscans who drained the swamps and built the first city of Rome. They also left many structures behind, including three pyramids just discovered in northwestern Italy. Believe it or not, these three pyramids are laid out in the same dimensions as the three Giza pyramids mimicking the three stars in Orion's Belt. The Indo-European Romans could not have built the Bimini Road because the estimate for the Bimini breakwater's construction is 6000 B.C., over 5000 years before Rome existed.

Vikings as B.R. Builders?

It could not have been the Vikings: "Norseman, or North man: member of the Scandinavian seafaring warriors who raided and colonized wide areas of Europe from the 9th to the 11th century."[914]

It is now accepted that Christopher Columbus did not discover America. One popular theory for the discovery of the Americas by Europeans has been the Vikings. A fleet of Danes were actually on their way to colonize

914 "Norseman." *Encyclopedia Britannica* DVD.

Greenland in 986 A.D. They were the first documented Caucasians to see America. One of their ships, captained by merchant Bjarni Herjolfsson, blew far off course to the southwest. The Danes sighted land that they had no idea was there, and sailed back to Greenland without landing in America. It was not until 15 years later that Viking Leif Erikson—Erik the Red's son, Leif the Lucky, outlawed from Iceland—took a ship to the same area Herjolfsson had mistakenly traveled to survey it; he named it Vineland because of its grapes; it is present-day Newfoundland (p. 7). When they landed, they found small Blacks with animal skin canoes living there whom they called Skraelings. Tuck, the author of the book, said the Vikings mercilessly exploited the natives (p. 28) (big surprise) and killed a few of them (p. 60). The Skraelings fought back and finally drove these European settlers out of the Americas, never to return. Dr. Duason and Courtemanche around 1717 CE said the Skraelings "were a black dwarf nation who lived in subterranean dwellings" (p. 49).... They were not Escomes, as we know that people. Indeed the Eskimos themselves have a name for them —Inuarudligkat—which designates a black-complexioned race of dwarfs who lived subterraneously in holes" (Oleson, 1964, p. 50).

So the Caucasians are out of the picture.

Well, if it was not Columbus, Grecians, Romans, Mesopotamians, Cretans or Phoenicians, who discovered the Bahamas and who built the Bahamian breakwaters and piers?

Black Influence on Amerinds

Movies always portray Native Americans with straight hair. People may ask, if the Native Americans have straight hair, how could they be part African? A perfect example is to look at the modern aboriginal Australians, or southern, dark peoples of India. They both have dark skin, yet they have straight hair.

In Africa one finds the straight-haired Negroid type and the kinky haired Negroid type features in the same family. That is so in East Africa and the Sahara. These are Africans who have never mixed with any other race or people. In South India and Australia, Cambodia, Southeast Asia, one finds Australoids with identical facial features but with varying hair textures.[915]

915 Barton, P. A. (2003). The True History of the Black Presence in the Prehistoric and Ancient Americas. Accessed on 8-16-06 from http://community-2.webtv.net/PAULNUBIAEMPIRE/BLACKCIVILIZATIONS.

Were the Native Americans possibly the first people to land in the Bahamas? No. First of all, historians call the first people "Indians." That is incorrect. The so-called "first Indians" in the Americas did not have White skin...but they did not have red skin either! The first Americans were—Africans. The first Africans mixed with the Asians in 2600 B.C. in the Americas.

Pre-Clovis evidence of Africans in Hueyatlaco, which is an archeological site in the Valsequillo Basin near the city of Puebla, Mexico.

Just visit Micah Hanks' work at the **250,000-year-old Hueyatlaco archeological site** . . . where they excavated in the Valsequillo Basin near the city of Puebla, Mexico in 1962. This excavation was carried out be Cynthia Irwin-Williams, who co-discovered the site with Juan Armania Camacho. this excavation was done in association with the U.S. Geological Survey, an *extremely respected organization.*They recovered several ancient stone tools that were found "in situ" next to animal remains.[916]

Interestingly, the biostratigraphic researcher Sam Van Landingham has published **two peer-reviewed analyses that confirm the earlier findings of ca 250,000 years ago** for the tool-bearing strata at Hueyatlaco.

So, the 250,000-year date for the stone tools seems to be a solid find.

By the way, the Clovis culture is a prehistoric Paleoamerican culture, named for distinct stone tools found at their sites. The Clovis sites mostly date between 11,500 and 11,000 radiocarbon years, which means 13,000 years before the present at a minimum. You can find more general information in the Wikipedia article on this subject.

Which so-called "Indians" were in the Bahamas first?

Siboney/Ciboney by 7000 to 5000 B.C.

Lucayan/Arawak by 5000 B.C. their descendants had penetrated into some of the islands of the Caribbean Sea. (Millersville, 1990). The natives of the Bahamas, whom Columbus called Lucayans were Arawak Indians.

---

916 Hanks, Micah. (2017). "Controversial Hueyatlaco Site Suggests Humans Were in the Americas 250,000 Years Ago." Mysterious Universe. 8th Kind Pty Ltd, May 25,2017. Accessed at https://mysteriousuniverse.org/2017/05/controversial-hueyatlaco-site-suggests-humans-were-in-the-americas-250,000-years-ago/.

Carib Indians, whom the Caribbean was named after, entered the Carrabean after 1000 B.C. from Venezuela replacing the the Arawak, Indians.[917]

After reading the several attempts made above to see who was first, there seems to be some lack of clarity among scholars about these natives. Some claim that these Indians were not from the Arawak/Taíno group, but some other tribe. It does seem that an earlier group, the Ciboney/Siboney, did live in this area. But, it's not clear if at the time of Caonabo these were Arawak/ Taino or not.[918]

Why did the Africans visit the Bahamas? Was it for their natural resources? According to Dr. Keith Tinker, their natural resources are salt and argonite, which is a mineral that is added to metals to expand and make a metal alloy harder. Those were the natural resources they were after.

The **Mande people** are otherwise known as the Mandingo, Malinke. Their inscriptions are found in the Sahara, at Tadrart—in the Acacus Mountain Range—between the Fezzan and Libya in North Africa. There are also Berber inscriptions that originated from the ancient Mande people. The Berber inscriptions are written in the Vai script.

They are widespread throughout the whole of West Africa particularly in Gambia, Mali, Senegal and Guinea.

By the way, they are also the people who sailed to the Americas, mixed with the African Anu/Twa—who were the Grandmother Civilization— and much later the Asians. Together, these three groups became the Olmecs, who are called the Mother Civilization of the Americas. See more at: Bimini Road part 2 https://www.youtube.com/watch?v=pmBDXJeeBm4

---

917 Aarons, George A. (1990). "The Lucayans: The People Whom Columbus Discovered in the Bahamas." *Five Hundred Magazine* April 1990, Vol. 2, No. 1), pp. 6-7. Referenced at *Encyclopedia Britannica* DVD. http://muweb. millersville.edu/~columbus/data/ant/AARONS01.ANT.

918 Corbett, Bob. (2005). THE ARAWAK/TAINO NATIVES OF THE ISLAND OF HISPANIOLA (HAITI). http://www.webster.edu/~corbetre/haiti/history/precolumbian/tainover.htm.

Bimini's Sights to See

Bimini Healing Well

An inlet 300 yards wide and 3 feet deep leads to a small swamp. In that Mangrove swamp, there is a fountain of warm fresh water flowing from a source deep below, up into the swamp. Many people with major and minor ailments have soaked in it and have claimed to have been relieved of their ailments: gout (with 3 soakings), small skin cancers, skin inflammations and small growths on their skin disappeared by soaking or using a poultice from water from this fountain. Miami psychologist Aldolpho Villasouso had the water tested by two local laboratories, which found an unusually high amount of the element of lithium.

Fountain of Youth

Explorer Juan Ponce de Leon learned from the Amerinds in the 1500s that Bimini was the site of the Fountain of Youth. According to Native legend, the spring supposedly restored youth to older persons who bathed in or drank its waters. In 1513, Ponce de Leon set sail for Bimini from Puerto Rico with three ships. He found Bimini but failed to find the fabled Fountain of Youth. He then went on to discover the Gulf Stream and Florida instead.

Shark Mound

Indian Mounds are all over the Americas, but there are a couple on the small Island of Bimini in the Bahamas as well. The best recognizable is that of a shark. In 1989, during a flight over East Bimini, a shark-shaped mound was noticed in the dense mangrove swamps. In 1990, some scientists and researchers for the GAEA Project, in cooperation with Atlantic University in Virginia, were in Bimini on an orientation tour of the various archeological sites discovered in past years.

Tongue of the Ocean

One hundred miles north of Bimini in the Berry Islands, the bottom drops to 14,000 feet, and ruins and buildings were found everywhere. Dr. Brown said he found Egyptian-like buildings, some of them having a classic look. Then he saw the tip of a pyramid at bottom 135-feet deep.

Proctors Road

In 2006, just off the north Bimini shoreline, an additional harbor works was found about a mile from the Bimini Road. (It was cleared of sand and exposed by a 2006 hurricane.) Dubbed the "Paradise Point Pier," it appeared to be elevated off the bottom and was constructed from piled stone blocks and also seemed to have numerous "columns" on its surface. This is a mile-long irregular line of stone to the west of the Bimini Road, near the North Bimini shoreline, that has five spaced complete or partial stone circles, circles that look identical to what are called "mooring circles" in the Mediterranean.

Mooring Circles

Mooring circles are a method of ship mooring for boats by chains or anchors, and they are used at several ancient Mediterranean harbors, including the previously mentioned Cosa harbor. Side-scan sonar was used to measure and analyze the circles.

We were able to identify several of these with the side-scan. In addition, the side-scan sonar was used to obtain a complete image of both the Bimini Road and the Paradise Point Pier. When the images were obtained, sand had covered wide portions of the Bimini Road.

White Marble Temple Pediment

In a well-defined area of Bimina Road lies a marble temple pediment (the triangular upper part of the front of a building in classical style, typically surmounting a portico of columns) and also multiple layers of marble beams, slabs, and other marble pieces. This extremely impressive "pile" merits salvage and reconstruction on Bimini as a local attraction.[919]

Marble Ruins

Several years ago the Browns learned of an area about 7 miles north of Bimini, which had some interesting stone blocks on the bottom. Reaching this area, we saw a few dark, coral-encrusted beams of stone and several small piles covered with sand. The side-scan sonar revealed that the area was actually widely littered with apparent stone forms hidden under sand.

Focusing our efforts on one small exposed area, we were astonished to see a triangular, well-polished slab of stone that appeared exactly like

919 The Search for Edgar Cayce's Atlantis (DVD).

the apex at the top tip of a roof on a temple. It was about 7 feet long and its thickness is unknown. The triangular stone was embedded in sand but we were able to confirm that it was at least 3 feet thick. After cleaning this stone of sand and debris, a beautiful, somewhat ornate slab was revealed. Several small pieces off the edge of this apex were removed and brought to the surface. It was white marble, gleaming like quartz in the sun.

Several beams, some as long as 15-feet were found, with one end disappearing into the sand. In addition, columns, polished building slabs, and many smaller blocks were found. Small samples revealed that these were of the same type of white marble. Knowing that the site had been previously known, we then scoured records to see what had been written about it.

We found that in 1970, Richard Wingate and a group of researchers had investigated the marble. Using an underwater sand blower, Wingate found that the marble was widely scattered and had at least three layers of slabs before it reached the bedrock seabed. Under the bottom layer of marble, Wingate found the wooden ribs of an old ship. According to Wingate's group, not far from this site there are massive areas covered with granite slabs, supposedly from two other shipwrecks.

We had previously visited Moselle Shoals, only a few miles away and had found shipwrecks and hundreds of granite blocks. The entire area is literally littered with shipwrecks and such cargo from all sorts of time periods.

In his 1980 book, *Lost Outpost of Atlantis*, Wingate related that at some future date an archaeologist would rediscover the marble and wonder what it was. Indeed.

Donato's Underwater Rectangles

Building foundations? Using GPS location obtained from Donato's side-scan sonar image, we arrived at the area of the underwater rectangles. We then utilized our own side-scan sonar and found them within 5 minutes. We used a setting that yields a bottom image 700-feet wide and could see that there were numerous rectangular formations on the bottom lying in what looked like a nearly straight line.

The rectangular forms sat at the top of a 10-foot dropoff, which led to a narrow flat area. Then it descended quickly toward the deep Gulf Stream.

Intrigued, we dropped a lead weight buoy as we passed over one of the larger rectangular forms. We later found that the weight fell directly into the rectangle and, surprisingly, the boat's anchor fell into another one nearby.

The sizes of the rectangular formations vary somewhat with the largest about 15x30 feet, however, most of them are smaller, 8x10 feet, about the size of small buildings. Their depth (100 feet) is actually just above the sea level estimated in 10,000 B.C. These structures were once elevated just above the ancient shoreline.

Eslie and Krista Brown, both of whom are Master Divers, dived the site and took a series of photographs in the cloudy water near the Gulf Stream. When they reached the surface, they reported that the structures were formed out of coral-encrusted stone.

The photos revealed that the sides of some of the formations seemed to be made from small stone blocks, some of which sat squarely on top of each other. Several square or rectangular stones appeared to be embedded into the bottom, especially at the corners of the rectangular structures.

In addition, several photos show intriguing artifacts, which could be pots or amphorae. However, only a more detailed investigation can prove the actual identity of the artifacts and the structures.

In sum, the preliminary investigation of these rectangular forms shows that they may well be building foundations, perhaps as old as 12,000 years. Plans are now being made for a more thorough investigation of this site.

Stone Anchors near Proctors' Road

In association with the line of stones called Proctor's Road are dozens of stone anchors. These are of several types. Some are simple stones that have bore-holes that were used as throwaway anchors. However, there are also multi-holed, well-carved stone anchors that are identical to Phoenician anchors. The largest we have found was a 600-pound stone in a heart shape. It was carbon dated to 30 B.C. [920]

Marble and Stone Columns near the Bimini Inlet

Nearly 30 columns or cement cylinders were found with two fluted marble columns in shallow water near the inlet between N. and S. Bimini.

---

920 The Ancient Bimini Harbor (DVD).

The marble columns were taken but fully documented by geologists and others. Some of the supposedly lime-kiln cement columns are still there.

Paradise Point Pier

To the East of the Bimini Road, there is clearly a manmade jetty or harbor that is in some ways more interesting than the Road itself. It is a long line of huge stone blocks arranged vertically running for several hundred feet off the coast into deeper water.

Odd Bottom Formations Off North Bimini

In 150–350-foot deep water 6 miles off North Bimini, a large area has been side-scanned and filmed that shows intriguing paths, domes, and unusual shapes. Many of the researchers who have investigated this site believe that it shows man-made features.

Building Ruins Off South Bimini

In 15-feet of water off South Bimini, we reported on this unexpected find in 2010. This is a clearly defined building foundation with the walls extending down into sand at least 4-6 feet. Dating on the site should be available by now.[921]

Basalt Slabs and Carved Enclosures with Steps

In 15 feet of water 8 miles south of Bimini, there were numerous carved slabs of basalt located within what appear to be carved enclosures in this area. There is also what appears to be a long, multilayered wall adjacent to it and carved steps on a wall.[922]

Andros Platform Off North Andros

This is a harbor formation made from 3 separate lines of increasingly high slabs of stone in 10–15 feet of water. It dates to 3000 B.C.[923]

---

921 Search for Edgar Cayce's Atlantis (DVD).

922 Ibid.

923 Ibid.

Wall near Andros Platform

Well-hidden on high land near the Andros Platform is the remains of a stone wall that predates any local knowledge. It may be associated with pirate activity.

Joulter's Wall

North of Andros, a well-defined wall runs in shallow water between two Joulter's islands in this seldom visited, difficult-to-reach location. The wall is made from cut limestone and is clearly man-made, but its function and dating are totally unknown. A large, square platform of stone blocks is attached to the wall. Long-term locals state that it has "always" been there. The water leading to these islands is extremely shallow, essentially several miles long with depths between only 1 and 5 feet.[924]

Temple Remains on Andros at Mangrove Cay

We were led to the remains of a temple that once stood on a high limestone outcrop that runs down Andros. The local owner, Samuel Rolle, who is now deceased, regretted selling most of the blocks from the site to build the local government official's residence. He was credible and related that there was once a stone temple structure there, but all that remained was evidence of a foundation.[925]

Stone Blocks Off the Berry Island Chain

Just above Andros, you can see this anomalous, multi-layered set of huge stone blocks in 30 feet of water. It has not been investigated.

Stone Arrangments at Great Bahama Bank off Andros

We have filmed about four places off western Andros showing odd arrangements of stone blocks. Nothing was definitive on any of these, but they lie in shallow areas where large boats cannot travel. There are another 100 spots we identified in aerial surveys that we have yet to visit.

---

924 Ibid.

925 Ibid.

Anguilla Arc at Cay Sal

Not on Bimini, but a small island in between Bimini and Cuba: On the remote island of Cay Sal is what definitely appears to be a harbor made from cut blocks of beach rock. It is at the same depth as the Andros Platform and the Bimini Road. One stone anchor has been found there. It is the closest island to Cuba at 31 miles away. Cay Sal Bank is the third largest and the westernmost of the Bahama Banks. (Do not forget about the underwater city filled with buildings, roads, bridges, temples, and pyramids 3.5 miles off the southwest corner of the Island of Cuba.)

Was the Bimini Road Built for International Trade Interests?

In the previous chapter, we saw linguistic evidence of Egyptian writing and words that were used by some of the American Algonquin. We also saw that at least 100–500 million tons of ancient copper was mined beyond 3000 B.C.[926]

Also, there were a few other items across the Atlantic that did not come up in the natural flow of the story in the last chapter. The following statements illustrate these other items and the evidence of their origin. Bernal Diaz, who was taken along with Cortez by King Montezuma to see the marketplace at Tlatelulco in the first quarter of the 16th century, listed in his detailed list of merchandise the skins of lions. The bottle gourd that was used to store liquids, was domesticated and then grown by farmers. It was the first canteen in Africa, and it was found that Africans brought it to pre-Columbian, and pre-Mongolian America.[927]

Bouncing over to the Olmecs, we see that they were also called the "rubber people."[928] Among other firsts in Central America, it seems that "The Olmecs were the people who discovered natural rubber."[929] They were

---

926 Childress, David H. *Lost Cities of North & Central America*, p. 376.

927 Van Sertima, Ivan. *They Came Before Columbus*, pp. 77, 197.

928 Memnon, A. R. (n.d.). "The Olmecs", accessed August 17, 2009. https://www.ocf.berkeley.edu/~kennyk/Project/New/Olmecs.html.

929 Lavin, Kimberly. (1999). "The Olmecs: A Mesoamerican Wonder." Accessed July 29, 2013. http://facweb.stvincent.edu/academics/religiousstu/writings/lavin1.htm.

the first to make rubber balls[930] from sap they retrieved from the abundant rubber trees of Central America. They are said to have "supplied the Aztecs with sap from rubber trees."[931] It is therefore logical to believe that since the Olmec/Manding were involved in commerce with the Aztecs, they probably also traded rubber to other countries in the Americas.

The products imported to the Americas from Africa were corn, plantains, sorghum, peanuts, yams, sweet potatoes, Jackbeans, the bottle gourd and lion skins.[932] The other products that were exported in the opposite direction back to Africa, were copper,[933] cotton, tobacco and cocaine.[934] Silver and animal furs were also exported.[935] The land we know of today as the Bahamas was very much involved in international commodity trading.

In 10,000 B.C., Bimini and Andros were part of the same large island. The Tongue of the Ocean was a deep channel running through the middle of this island. Both Bimini and Nicholls Town would have been ideal way stations for ships. We stated the belief that the Bimini Road and the Andros Platform were possibly harbors for small ports.[936]

Even with all this evidence, some people will not believe that people in the Americas before Columbus were involved in international trade. There is one more example that stands far above any others. When examiners were probing the mummy of Ramses II of the 19th Egyptian Dynasty, they found something that threw them for a loop. It was something they just could not accept. Ramses II's mummy had traces of American tobacco

930 Clark, John E., and Mary E. Pye eds. (2009). *Olmec Art and Archaeology in Mesoamerica*. (Washington D.C., National Gallery of Art). Accessed August 12, 2009. http://yalepress.yale.edu/yupbooks/book.asp?isbn9780300085228.

931 Logan, P. (n.d.) "Ancient Olmec and Aztec Civilizations." Accessed August 12, 2009. http://ebsms.wcs.k12.va.us/mexicotrip/patrick. htm.

932 Van Sertima, Ivan. *Early America Revisited*, pp. 106, 167, 187, 188, 240.

933 Childress, David. H. *Lost Cities of North & Central America*, p. 375.

934 Van Sertima, Ivan. *Early America Revisited*, pp. 165, 191.

935 Fell, Barry. *America B.C.: Ancient Settlers in the New World*, p. 279.

936 Little, Gregory. (n.d.). "The A.R.E.'s Search for Atlantis."

and cocaine[937] in his stomach. This was, however, not an anomaly. In 1992, Munich, Germany, acquired 134 mummies from a Sudan cemetery, to be investigated. Each of these 134 mummies tested positive for both cocaine and nicotine as well.

In ancient times, tobacco grew only in the Americas, and cocaine only in Bolivia.[938] This prima facie evidence shows that there is a tradition of Egyptians—and probably people from other parts of the Nile Valley— traveling back and forth to the Americas. This instance is impossible to explain otherwise. Ancient international trade did occur over seas, but also with peoples between the three Americas. Evidence of local trade has also now become available. Historians will just have to get used to the idea that ancient Americans were trading across the Americas using roads, canals, rivers and ocean routes.

The reasoning here is that since thousands of years have passed, it is impossible to know all that was traded between the Americas and Africa. However, as small as it is, the list of items presented here exhibits unmistakable evidence of contact between two peoples and two hemispheres. It also illuminates an even more exciting idea. These African shippers are our earliest example of international trade beyond the Eastern Hemisphere.

It is possible that the 10,000-year-old structures here were the beginning (or even just the continuation) of a trading post between the Americas and Africa and the rest of the Eastern Hemisphere. This ancient trading network is supported by the following facts:

1. People on the island of Crete have been traveling back and forth to Egypt for 130,000 years.
2. The structures found in 90 feet of water, two miles west of present-day Bimini date back at least 10,000 years.
3. Africans have been traveling to the Americas for 100,000 years or more.
4. The current in the Atlantic flows from Africa like a conveyer belt to, and eventually passing, the Bahamas. The reason Africa is

---

937 Van Sertima, Ivan. *Early America Revisited*, pp. 165, 191.

938 Ibid., p. 191.

mentioned first is that it was there that the human race began, and it is there that the first civilizations were founded.[939]

Thousands of years later, as the ocean level continued to rise, we rediscovered the remains of the breakwater and pier, one mile further east of the 10,000-year-old structures towards Bimini. This is evidence of a continuous, or at the least, a semi-continuous, group in the Bahamas between those two points, i.e. the 10,000-year-old structures and the minimum 6000 to 7000-year-old breakwater and pier. It is logical to assume that since the Bahamas was part of a trading network with Africa and the Americas early on, they kept expanding their network as the years passed by. This would provide one of the reasons a large and permanent breakwater and pier would eventually be built on an island, and not on a shore of on of the American continents.

Would it not also be smarter to have a port that is safer on an island, far away from countless other possible raiders on the mainland of the Americas? Another possible reason is that the Bahamas was a hub. Different civilizations in Africa, and later, civilizations from other parts of the Atlantic could make the long trip to the Western Hemisphere, following the ocean current to the Bahamas. Ship's crews could rest for a while there, and then plan which port they would go to trade their goods, and what they would in turn receive to take back home. The Bahamas could have been the hub of trade for both hemispheres. These merchants from the Eastern Hemisphere had their pick of many goods. A few of the places they would visit and the trade goods that we know of include the following:

1. From Canada came furs and hides.
2. From Isle Royal in Lake Superior came copper.
3. From North America came furs, obsidian, quartz, turquoise and iron.
4. From Central America came gold, silver, and turquoise.
5. From South America came tobacco, cocaine, fur and hides.

The list above purposely does not cover the larger list of many foodstuffs available. These are just some of the other goods that are known today to have been available back then. One can only imagine how many more items were traded that we do not know of today.

---

939 Imhotep, David. *The Origin of Civilization*, p. 247.

These people, however, were trading more than goods. They were also trading ideas. The idea of building a breakwater to allow large ships to unload their cargos, rest, and choose their next port of call was brilliant. One specific idea that passed from the Old World to the New World was how to transfer a large ship's cargo to a beach without causing the ship (which was floating low in the water filled with goods) to run aground. **There was a slit in the middle of the breakwater, where a ship needing deeper water could be unloaded.**

A ship requiring less depth would be unloaded at the pier. The breakwater broke up the wave action. Other than international trade, there was also a regional trading network that is not spoken of. From the Mississippi River civilizations to the Ohio River Valley's iron smelting mounds are not the only interesting features making the Ohio Paleoamericans shine. These people were also engaged in a regional American trading network whose range was so large it is staggering.

Obsidian was imported from Wyoming and Montana, Grizzly Bear teeth came from South Dakota, copper and silver came from the Great Lakes, quartz came from Arkansas and Georgia, shells, alligator teeth, shark teeth, fossils came from Florida and Georgia, and mica from the Carolinas.[940]

What this may mean is that people transported their goods on the ancient "I-95" highway—the Mississippi and Ohio Rivers. The Fig. 10 mounds map displays that more mounds were concentrated around the Mississippi and Ohio Rivers than anywhere else.

The dirt road system the people built is likely to be even more amazing. Did these ancient folks exclusively transport their goods by water, or did they use roads as well? The Walam Olum says the Adena/Talegas Mound Builders constructed the following:

Trade networks extended for hundreds of miles, and precious objects might travel for thousands. Shoppers in the ancient markets of the Midwest could choose among items from the East Coast to the Rockies, to Canada to the Gulf of Mexico.[941]

---

940 Little, Gregory. L., John Van Auken, and Lora Little. *Mound Builders: Edgar Cayce's Forgotten Record of Ancient America* (Tenessee, Eagle Wing Books, 2001), p. 117.

941 McCutchen, David. The Red Record, p. 117.

An old Delaware Indian legend says that in ancient times there was a road system of white roads that stretched across America. There was some type of honor system that protected travelers on these roads. As long as travelers stayed on the "White Path" they could not be attacked. Safe conduct was more profitable for everyone and attracted new business as well. These roads were not at all narrow. Some roads were 160–170 feet wide.[942]

Across the continent, in America's southwestern Pueblo country:

The Anasazi Pueblo roads were clearly defined along their edges by earthen beams or rock walls. Anasazi settlements were connected by six road systems accurately surveyed and skillfully engineered over 95,000 square miles.[943]

There must have been a significant number of people utilizing these roads for them to have been built so wide. **These roads were not wide and short, but wide and long running from the Southwest to the Midwest. "Ancient Ohio's Great Hopewell Highway...was 60 miles long, defined by earthen mound walls, replete with ceremonial circles like rest stops existed during prehistoric times in Ohio."**[944]

The Great North Road stretches 60 miles from the San Juan River to Pueblo Alto, the "High Village," so-called because of the 89-room structure's position atop a high mesa. The roads to move turquoise and other trade goods were not crude trails, but a hardened deposit of calcium carbonate that acts like a natural cement and that is still used today in the manufacture of Portland cement.[945]

There was also a road at Millersport that was 30 miles long. Another one of Hopewell's roads ran for 56 miles in a straight line.[946] Looking west, we can see another Pueblo marvel, and this accomplishment was so amazing that it had to be checked three times before publication. **These ancient Americans could send messages faster than the telegraph wires**

942 Ibid.

943 Joseph, Frank. *Advanced Civilizations of Prehistoric America*, p. 182.

944 Hamilton, Ross. (2004). "Ancient Ohio's Great Hopewell Highway." *Ancient American* 4, Issue #29.

945 Ibid.

946 Joseph, Frank. *Advanced Civilizations of Prehistoric America*, p. 183.

the cowboys used centuries later. We think we modern people have a message system via the Internet that has never been rivaled in history. Let's just see...the speed that light travels "approximately 300,000 kilometers per second!"[947] That is equal to 126,411 miles per second. **The Pueblos developed a system of signal posts along their roads that would reflect messages at the speed of light**:

Signaling posts were set up at intervals along the entire network. During daylight hours, data was flashed from one relay station to the next in code by polished obsidian mirrors. From dusk until dawn their places were taken by bonfires able to pass on an equivalent amount of news.[948]

They were sending flashes of light from the sun by day and flashes of bonfires at night at the speed of light reflected by their obsidian mirrors.

All should agree that we know Native Americans also used smoke language to signal each other. This was observed on television every Saturday morning in the 1950s and 1960s. Consequently, they had some sort of code to read the smoke signals. It is as easy as Morse Code. A big puff of smoke could represent a dot and a small puff could be a dash. There are an infinite number of ways to code. Also observed were natives using mirrors to flash each other messages for short distances.

It is, therefore, not too much of a stretch to imagine that they installed poles with reflectors on top and sent each other messages. Again, these were not hunter-gatherers who used this sophisticated system of communication. They had to have a permanent residence to be able to use this communication mode repeatedly.

It is important, when you are trading to know if you will be delivering your goods on time or not. If there has been an attack by some raiders, or if the coast is clear and you can deliver the goods on time, is important to know. Or, maybe the weather caused a delay or the road got washed out causing a long detour. As in modern-day trade, ancient people trading goods wanted to receive their goods in a reasonable time as well. Therefore, communication devices were invaluable.

947 "Measuring the Speed of Light Colorado." (nd,). Accessed May2, 2015. https://www.colorado.edu/physics/phys1230/phys1230_fa01/topic2.html.

948 Bluebell Products. (2018) The Measure of Things. From: http://www.bluebulbprojects.com/MeasureOfThings/results.php?comp=speed&unit=kmsamt=300000&sort=pr&p=1.

Again, these were not hunter-gatherers but sophisticated people who built permanent metropolitan centers. As a matter of fact, they grew, "corn, beans, pumpkins gourds, sunflower and pecans." Before Hopewell or Cahokia, the Adena grew the same crops as their neighbors in Cahokia would later grow. Additionally, Adena grew "raspberries, black walnuts, and hunted catfish, deer, elk, rabbit, turkey grouse and rattle snake, among others."[949] The Adena had a very diversified diet, and eating all that food may have affected their teeth because they also performed dental work.

An ancient skull was recovered from Indiana's C. L. Lewis Stone Mound. Excavators noticed that the skull belonging to one of the interred men featured a metal cap on his tooth; it covered an upper incisor fitted over the bottom to form a sheath-like covering. Subsequent examination revealed that the cap was not ornamental, but more resembled modern bridgework to hold the tooth in place. Archaeologists had discovered the oldest evidence of dentistry in the New World.[950]

Is it not a crime that history sometimes refers to these people as savages? We will now leave the pre-Columbus road systems, and return to the Pueblo, who also built something even more remarkable than their roads. Dams are important for drinking water, farming, as well as watercraft. If there has been a drought, and the water level is too low to send your goods on a larger craft, excess water let lose by a near-by dam may just save the day.

The Pueblo built a spectacular dam in New Mexico's Animas Valley.... Government surveyors measured the dam five and a half miles across.... They estimated that the entire structure, which had "the appearance of great age," was built of 8 million to 10 million cubic yards of material, which made it "almost impossible that it could have been the work of human hands."[951]

These dams did not hold back deep water. The advantage these ancient dams had, was that they did not have to be built as strong as a modern cement dam because the water levels they held were shallow. The disadvantage of a wide dam is that it needed more area to spread out in order to hold an equal volume as a deeper dam.

---

949 Joseph, Frank. *Advanced Civilizations of Prehistoric America*, p. 183.

950 Ibid., p. 3.

951 Ibid., p. 35.

These dams were probably used to irrigate the many crops the people grew. Before Columbus, these ancient people were not static; they traveled extensively:

> With ships as large or larger than that of Columbus, cities certainly greater than many in Europe, and more exacting science of mathematics and timekeeping, the Americas clearly transcended our own previous understanding.[952]

Let us take a look at their city planning. Some of these mound centers were not only astronomically aligned but also mathematically calculated. Take the "Geometry & Alignments of the Octagon Works" at Newark, Ohio.[953] It was probably fed by the 60-mile long road, which was most likely built to make trade more convenient, among other things. At that time and place, a 60-mile, continuous road was a phenomenal feat. For example, many of the Hopewell sites were erected to enable the builders to predict when the equinoxes and solstices would occur. "Newark's Circle and Octagon" were used to chart precisely the moon's 18.61-year cycle.[954]

Other Ancient Harbors

Similar, and in some cases, identical designs for piers were brought from the Nile Valley to the Americas, specifically to the Bahamas.

An Egyptian identity for the Bimini road is strongly seconded by an identically J-shaped wall sea wall or breakwater built by pre-Hellenic—which means before the Greeks—Egyptians at the famous harbor of Alexandria.[955]

Yes, the B.R. Breakwater is shaped like the letter "J," which is the identical shape of the Egyptian breakwater, according to Joseph (2001). What this means is that the Egyptians most likely built the Bimini Road Breakwater, which Joseph said was identical to the breakwater they built much earlier

952 Ibid., pp. 191-192.

953 Sora, Steven. "The Discovery of the Old World by Native Americans." *Atlantis Rising*, # 80, March/April, (2010): p. 41.

954 Hamilton, Ross. (2004). "Ancient Ohio's Great Hopewell Highway." *Ancient American* 4, Issue #29.

955 Little, Gregory L. et al. Mound Builders: Edgar Cayce's Forgotten Record of Ancient America, p. 61.

at the mouth of the Nile River! The famous harbor of Alexandria, should by rights, be known as the harbor of Rhacotis.[956]

Rhacotis is the city Alexander the Great destroyed and rebuilt, then named it Alexandria. Yes, Rhacotis was the pre-Hellenic city that predated Alexandria. In a referenced review, if the J-shaped wall was pre-Hellenic, then the Greek people could not have built it.[957] The J-shaped wall was there before the Greeks first visited Alexandria/Rhacotis.[958] Alexander "arrived in Egypt in 332 BC and was accepted by the native Egyptians as a liberator from Persian occupancy...and founded the city of Alexandria."[959]

There are other ancient harbors in the Americas with breakwaters, possibly built by the same civilization that built the one at Bimini and Andros. The parallels between the Mediterranean and Central American harbors, as well as the Bimini and Andros formations, are striking. In Central America, a recognized ancient harbor site is located off Yucatan at Isla Cerritos, which still has a 1000-foot breakwater.

This breakwater is made the same way as the harbor at Akko, 15-kilometers north of modern-day Haifa, Israel. Akko's breakwater is 1000-feet long by 36-feet wide.[960] This harbor is built in the same design as Bimini's, in that two openings flush silt out of the channel. That way the silt does not build up too much on the ocean floor, prohibiting the passage of ships. This design is another indication of brilliant engineering.

To date, there have been 47 ancient harbors identified in the Mediterranean. [961] The ancient Phoenician Atlit harbor off modern Israel

956 Joseph, Frank. "The 'Bimini' of Japan," p. 61.

957 "History of." History World, accessed March 23, 2015. http://www. historyworld.net/wrldhis/PlainTextHistories. asp?historyid=aa03.

958 Asante, Molefi. K. *The Painful Demise of Eurocentrism* (New Jersey, Africa World Press, 1999), p. 57.

959 King, Richard. *African Origin of Biological Psychiatry* (Virginia, UB & US Comm. Systems, 1994), p. 50.

960 Ferguson, S. "Alexander and Ptolemy" Archaeology of Ancient Egypt. Last modified August 16, 2011. http://anthropology.msu. edu/egyptian-archaeology/category/general/page/2/.

961 Little, Gregory. (2007). "Atlantis in the Bahamas." *Atlantis Rising* #51, p. 69.

has a 400-foot pier, and Cosa, Italy's ancient harbor has another 400-foot long pier. Atlit is 20-kilometers to the south of Haifa. Atlit pier is 100-feet long by 30-feet wide. "The non-astronomical stone circles at Cosa... utilized for mooring tying up ships... are identical in size and shape to those near area of the B.R. known as Proctor's Road."[962]

In the middle of the Mediterranean Sea is Italy's ancient harbor of Claudio. Claudio was also built before there was a Rome. This harbor had a massive breakwater protecting its harbor, which had square indentations, probably the remains of post-holes made for anchoring ships. The architects of this "so-called" Italian structure were probably the African/Etruscans because Roman civilization did not begin until 753 B.C.[963]

The Bimini structure has (what appears to be) slip ways within the break water for ships, like those also seen at Dock in the Mediterranean—27 kilometers from Haifa—near modern day Israel. In addition, the enigmatic, non-astronomical stone circles at Bimini are identical to the size and shape of the mooring stones used to anchor ships at Cosa, Italy.[964] The conclusion seems to be that Bimini is the remains of an ancient harbor that is similar to some of the other harbors discussed above.

Logically, the oldest harbor at the mouth of the oldest navigated river in the world, was built by the oldest navigators, the Nile Valley people. Later, they probably built harbors in the nearby Mediterranean for trading purposes, before they ventured out to the Americas, where they did the same. Evidence confirms that statement, for the Nile Valley civilizations predate all other civilizations that are known of today. They were also the first seamen and ship builders tens of thousands of years or even 100,000 years before Europe, Rome or Greece.

---

962 Little, Gregory. "The Ancient Bimini Harbor: Uncovering the Great Bimini Hoax, Forgotten History Series" (2005: ATA-Memphis Archetypal Productions, Series-#4), DVD.

963 Little, Gregory. "Atlantis in the Bahamas", pp. 70-71.

964 Ibid.

Science agrees that all human life evolved in East, Central Africa, very close to the source of the Nile,[965] "The ancient Egyptians called Africa, South of the Nile Valley Ta-Kenset, literally 'placentaland.'"[966]

Coincidence or Contact?

Great respect should be given to Dr. Greg Little's research on the Bimini Road. Over the years, he published many articles, and has probably made more trips for research—above and under water—as anyone else ever has. However, one author brought up the point that Little has never mentioned who he thinks built the B.R., and here is one author who wonders about that above and under water. In his article, Smith states that, "He [Little] doesn't say who built it," but ever since the pavement-like formation was found in 20 feet of water just off North Bimini in 1968, enthusiasts have tried to link it to the Atlantis myth.[967]

When we look deeper into the avenues that link Bimini with Egypt, we can use the science of etymology to uncover yet another connection. One that may bring all the other evidence together and crown the original builders of this ancient structure with the most obvious evidence. Even linguistically, the very name Bimini has Egyptian roots:

"Bimini" translates into Egyptian as Baminini, which means to the soul (Ba) of Min (Min) we bring Homage (ini). Homage means Tribute or Respect. Min was the Ancient Egyptian god of travelers who appealed to him for guidance and protection whenever they set out on long journeys. Appropriately, Min was also the divine matron of roads in this case, a road in the ocean. After sailing from the continent of Africa, the Bahamas are the closest land in the Western Hemisphere. Could the island of Bimini have been known to the Egyptian seafarers as their first landfall after a long, transatlantic voyage from the Near East?[968]

965 Diop, Cheikh. A. Origin of the Ancient Egyptians, p. 35.

966 Finch, Charles. *The Star of Deep Beginnings*, p. 4.

967 Smith, Larry. "A Rock in the Harbour-Latest Travels on the Bimini Road," Bahama Pundit, April 30, 2005. Accessed December 4, 2005. http://www.bahamapundit.com/2005/12/shes_a_rock_in_.html.

968 Joseph, Frank. "The 'Bimini' of Japan," p. 61.

It is easy to conclude that these travelers were so thankful to see the land (of Bimini) and making the voyage safely, they thanked their god of travel, Min, and named the land appropriately Ba-min-ini or Bimini. This "giving thanks" after a dangerous trip across the ocean is similar to the Algonquin and other Amerinds making sacrifices, thanking their god for their safe trip across the ocean.

Can science be brought to the table to decide who built the structure? Yes, it can. Science only requires eight coincidences to establish contact between two cultures.[969] Although this list is more detailed than the last illustration, below are more than the number required to establish contact:

1. The meaning of the name Bimini
2. Obelisks
3. Egyptian anchors
4. Egyptian keystones
5. The use of fluted marble columns
6. The use of megalithic blocks before 4000 B.C.
7. "Sacred Geometry" evident in the chock stone
8. Moorings to anchor boats are Egyptian in size and shape
9. The J-shaped breakwater identical to pre-Hellenic pre-Greek Nile delta breakwater
10. Similar Giza-pyramid construction using megalithic blocks without the use of cement but using keystones
11. The Egyptian Sphinx found underwater in the Bahamas.

Egypt had at least eleven similarities with the Bahamian structure and artifacts. Therefore, the evidence suggests that the people who built the Bahamian structures were Egyptians.

Why is it so hard for some people to believe the first Americans were Africans? The ancient Greeks, Romans and even Columbus believed it because they witnessed and wrote about it.

As a matter of fact, in chapter two we covered the Atlantic Ocean's other name the Europeans—not Africans—gave it in early times: the Ethiopic Ocean.

The most well known of the ancient Greek and Roman historians who shared the belief that Africans were traveling across the Atlantic Ocean included Homer, Pliny, Virgil, Diodorus Siculus and Scylaxus

---

969 Van Sertima, Ivan. Early America Revisited, p. 1.

of Coriandre,[970] to name a few. They spoke about Ethiopians traveling across the Atlantic in ancient times to some distant civilization. Some of them called it "Western Ethiopia" or "Atlantis." In modern times author/researcher John G. Jackson, wrote that the ancient Greek philosophers spoke of Atlantis:

> *Proclus, who stated in his works that he could present evidence that Atlantis at one time actually existed. He cited as his authority, The Ethiopian History of Marcellus. In referring to: Ethiopian history to prove the existence of Atlantis, Proclus plainly infers that Atlantis was a part of Ethiopia.[971]*

(See Cory's *Ancient Fragments of the Phoenician, Carthaginian, Babylonian, Egyptian and Other Authors*, London, 1876. See also, Maynard Shipley's *New Light on Prehistoric Cultures* and *Bramwell's Lost Atlantis*.)

Lastly, the ancient Egyptians also wrote about this distant land. In the appendix of his remarkable book, *The Chronicle of Akakor*, late German researcher Karl Brugger wrote: "The Egyptian Books of the Dead in the second millennium BC speak about the kingdom of Osiris in a distant country in the west. Rock inscriptions in the region of the Rio Mollar in Argentina are clearly linear in the Egyptian tradition. Symbols and ceramic objects were found in Cuzco that are identified with Egyptian artifacts.[972]

The words from these ancient Greeks, Romans (who represent the two first Caucasian civilizations) and Egyptians, is further evidence illustrating that even ancient peoples were aware of the Africans in the Americas.

Significance of the Bimini Road Pier and Breakwater

Why is this monument important? What is its significance? This site has an item the Pyramids do not. If one stands right in front of any pyramid, just by viewing it, its age cannot be guessed. However, the pier's age can be easily and logically guessed. The reasoning for this is that the Bimini Breakwater and Pier are now under 25–30 feet of water. 600 yards

970 Braghine, Colonel. A. *The Shadow of Atlantis*, p. 214.

971 Jackson, John. 1985). *Ethiopia and the Origin of Civilization* (Black Classic Press), p. 23.

972 Childress, David. (1985). *Lost Cities and Ancient Mysteries of South America* (Adventures Unlimited Press), p. 236.

of dressed blocks could not have been built under water. Therefore, it had to have been built before the last Ice Age melt and flood in 11,000 B.C.[973]

Furthermore, even if they could, why would a hunter-gatherer people build such a megalithic structure, when they could just pull their canoes onto the beach and unload their cargo? What would be the point? Logically, it was built to dock large vessels. A picture of one of ancient Egypt's mega-ships exists as seen on one of the History Channel's episodes. It can also be seen carved into the front of the funerary temple wall of one of ancient Egypt's several female Pharaohs, Queen Pharaoh Hatshepsut. The ship was carrying two obelisks on deck, weighing 750 tons each, which can give you an idea of just how enormous this craft was.

This antediluvian structure was built before the catastrophic Ice Age world flood. Because of this monument's obvious, very ancient age, this discovery also probably pushes back the age of the Great Pyramid's beginning in 3100 B.C. How is that? Why would you come halfway around the planet to the New World and build such a gigantic architecture, but live in primitive huts back home? Does that make any sense? So, this monument logically makes the Great Pyramid even older than the great Bimini structure! When you see the B.R. site you will never forget it.

It's too bad we could not see what this massive structure actually looked like ourselves when it was new—but then again, maybe you can. Dr. Imhotep has done something that has made it possible for people to see this colossal site and witness it for themselves. He has organized a tour called, "Egypt in the Bahamas." It will allow people to ride out a few hundred yards to snorkel or see the site itself through a glass bottom boat. Many other artifacts will also be available to see in this underwater museum. This is a significant and exciting piece of history that has been uncovered and can be enjoyed for the first time in many tens of thousands of years. It was built and used by the people who lived during the "Golden Age of Zep Tepi."

---

973 Little, Gregory. "Man-Made Bahamas Structure Dated to Before the Ice Age," p. 10.

Conclusion

Why is it so important to understand that even the oldest historic stories must be changed and updated when new cutting-edge evidence is presented and verified? Even if the educators are uncomfortable with the new evidence, the old must move out of the way and make way for the new. Politics has no business retarding the process of historical instruction, or any other field in the educational realm for students, or the public at large.

According to an international study, a research team led by Professor Jin Li, of the Fudan University in Shanghai, China, has found modern human remains there from Africa. The Clovis model that has been accepted as a standard since the 1930s is no longer relevant and must be replaced. Our new evidence of the pre-Clovis finds for the first Americans is overwhelming. The evidence presented has unveiled the existence of African people living in the Americas for 100,000 years or more. This demolishes the old 9400-year date for Clovis by a whopping 90,600 years. The evidence for the first Americans being Africans comes from different categories: DNA, anthropology, four different Native American tribes, skulls and skeletons, footprints in lava, ancient campsites, genetic M-174 and D Haploid groups, linguistics, ancient cave paintings, ancient tools, architecture, Egyptian script, artifacts, and ancient structures above and below the oceans.

When the Ice Age ended, there were also structures flooded two miles west of Bimini that were built no later than 10,000 B.C. The Egyptian/Manding left the Nile Valley where the oldest civilizations were built and are documented to have existed. Halfway around the world, in the Bahamas, where "a complex, man-made, now underwater...a multi-room structure in the Bahamas...that was carbon dated to between 21,520 BCE and 20,610 BCE."[974]

These 20,000–21,000-year-old Bahamian structures that were flooded likely belonged to the people who traveled there—either directly, or indirectly, from the Nile Valley, and built the Bimini Breakwater and Pier. It was most likely used to receive and launch international trade expeditions between the Americas and the "Old World," evidenced by a grocery list of items pasted in both directions we covered earlier.

---

974 Little, Gregory. "Man-Made Bahamas Structure Dated To Before The Ice Age," p. 12.

In North America, we saw extremely large pyramid-shaped earthen mounds in Cahokia, the iron smelting mounds in the Ohio Valley, the countless small megalithic stone mound chambers covered by a hill of soil. Then, we discussed who most likely did *not* build the breakwater: Columbus, Vikings, Romans, Greeks, Phoenicians, Algonquins or Amerinds. Lists were produced illustrating that the coincidence of contact were always greater than what science calls for. Who else could have built a breakwater of such antiquity? Were they mysterious people from Atlantis, or aliens from another planet, as the fringe elements propose? Where is the evidence that it was built by aliens from another planet? To date, there is none. Dr. Imhotep challenges anyone to a debate who says they can prove otherwise.

On the other hand, there are many other underwater structures all around the world that were above water before the cosmic cataclysm took place 11,000 B.C. Built by humans. The evidence of ancient structures that exist below the waves today, has been recorded in print as well as photographed. There is evidence of different "Atlantises" all over the world that were flooded by the so-called "Noah's flood."

Could there have been many cities all over the world from the Nubian Techno-Complex during Zep Tepi? See Graham Hancock's book "Underworld" (2002), containing 739 pages of descriptions and phenomenal pictures of evidence of this. There are millions of artifacts, and some entire cities to see underwater, just like the Jamaican earthquake of 1692 and the sunken city off Cuba.

The preponderance of evidence collected, presented, and verified here is overwhelming. It has uncovered the most likely people who could have been the first Americans. Between 250,000 and 350,000 years ago, diminutive Africans entered the Americas, followed much later by the Egyptian/Manding out of the Nile Valley, and those from other parts of Africa. For it was in Africa where the oldest civilizations are documented to have originated.[975] The thesis of this work—backed by seven peer-reviewed articles, 66 pieces of evidence—presented here must, therefore, render any other possible conclusions to the contrary, as unscientific speculation or politically motivated at this point in time.

Built on the foundation laid by Dr. Ivan Van Sertima's groundbreaking book in 1976, this book is likely to inspire more evidence to be found that will further verify that the first Americans were Africans. As more

975 Ibid.

evidence is uncovered in the future, it is my sincere hope that the youth of any color or creed, will pick up the baton of this book and press on. In the words of Marcus Mosiah Garvey, "Up you mighty race, you can accomplish what you will."[976]

In conclusion, we sincerely hope you enjoyed this phenomenal journey into the past; we covered many pieces of history that the public is still woefully unaware of.

---

976 Semaj, Leahcim T. "The African Caribbean Institute of Jamaica/Jamaica Memory Bank." Marcus Garvey Quotes. Accessed March 10, 2016. http://www.ltsemaj.com/specials/marcusgarvey/marcusgarvey-quotes.asp.

Afterword

More than fifty years ago, Cheikh Anta Diop asked a profound question: "When shall we be able to speak of an African Renaissance?" This question laid on the table of human inquiry for a long time. Diop, in his own way, approached an answer to the question that he raised. He would write books, such as *The African Origin of Civilization* as well as *Civilization or Barbarism*, in an effort to suggest a direction. In his well-researched book, *The First Americans Were Africans: Documented Evidence*, Dr. David Imhotep demonstrates that the answer to the question lies in a new orientation to scientific information.

One fact was clear, the renaissance of Africa was not just material. It would have to be something far more powerful than just creating new monuments to the glory of the ancestors. Renaissance could not be brought about by the belief that African people had to master new forms of being Black in the world. It could only be brought about, and Diop suspected this, by a complete re-orientation of the knowledge that the world received about Africa itself.

Who were the first Americans? Here is another question that has begged for an answer, and in this book, as we have seen, David Imhotep brings us the evidence that shows that Africans peopled the American continents before any other people. Furthermore, he establishes that this is not just logical, but it is also demonstrated by the evidence in seventeen different areas. Just as we have seen in the response to Diop's question where there have been numerous respondents in books and articles over the past four decades, there are bound to be many people who will follow the lead of this pioneering scholar.

Africa could not be buried in the past as some museum; it could not be allowed to linger in the disarray of poor scholarship, lack of archaeological resources and researchers, and the inability of African scholars to redirect their thinking away from the common, ordinary Eurocentric manner of viewing reality to a more sustained Afrocentric analysis that sees the profound value of Africa as the core of human civilization. What David Imhotep has given us is a book that speaks to two aspects of Diop's question, the African part and the Renaissance part, together and also separately.

In the first place, Imhotep placed his emphasis on ancient Africa and its influence in America because he believed that was where White scholars first went wrong. They dismissed the possibility that Africans could have come to the Americas. This was an era when Europe thought to change all information into knowledge that elevated others rather than Africans. The Europeans who first met African knowledge started to change the names of towns and cities, scratch as many words off the monuments as they could, and challenge the ancient historical facts staring down at them.

Can you imagine how the first White man who saw the statues of Ramses II at Abu Simbel must have felt? Who are the people who built these great monuments? It is at this moment that Africa suffered its greatest danger; when Whites became conscious of how much Africa had produced and how little Europe understood. It is there in the distant past when humans began to collect data, to discuss it, and to record it that the process of ordering and categorizing Africa met with the chaos of political power and social machinations. Thus, it was essential that Imhotep confound this openly and raise the issues of the distortion of African facts in regard to the peopling of America.

Secondly, he recognized that the way to a Renaissance, that is, a rebirth of thinking, runs through knowing something about naissance, birth. How did Africa get to the place where human beings, especially scholars, would even doubt the sources that were demonstrably African? Who would question the facts about Africans coming to the American continents? What Dr. Imhotep has done is to marshal the sources that show what was under the ground and under the water, the breakwaters, and therefore he has placed us in the best position of any contemporary African scholar to comment on the extent of the robbery of Africa's resources of knowledge.

This book, *The First Americans were Africans: Expanded and Revised*, with its heavy references is an answer that will allow others to read with confidence about the ancient record of African people in the Americas. It puts into context much of the information that has been gathered over the years, organizing it, ordering it in a manner that is accessible to the ordinary reader as well as to the scholarly reader. Imhotep's intent with this book is to burst onto the scene with a follow-up to the best of the works by Diop. Like so many of the books published by scholars who have re-oriented themselves on the Afrocentric road, Imhotep's work must be considered in the forefront of our new awareness of the great depth of African contributions to the world of science and art, and human beginnings on this very continent.

Molefi Kete Asante, Ph.D., Author of *The History of Africa*

Bibliography

Books

African Civilizations: An Archaeological Perspective, by Graham Connah, Cambridge University Press, 1987.

Advanced Civilizations of Prehistoric America: The Lost Kingdoms of the Adena, Hopewell, Mississippians, and Anasazi, by Frank Joseph, Bear and Company, 2010.

African Empires in Ancient America, by Clyde Winters, Uthman dan Fodio Institute, 2013.

African Presence in Early America, by Ivan Van Sertima, Transaction Publishers, 1992.

America B.C.: Ancient Settlers in the New World, by Barry Fell, Pocket Books, 1976.

Atlantis in Mexico: The Mande Discovery of America, by Clyde Winters, 2013.

Civilization or Barbarism: An Authentic Anthropology, by Cheikh Anta Diop, 1981.

Early America Revisited, by Ivan Van Sertima, Transaction Publishers, 1998.

Heaven's Mirror: Quest for the Lost Civilization, by Graham Hancock & Santha Faiia, Three Rivers Press, 1998.

The Illustrated Encyclopedia of Native American Mounds & Earthworks, by Gregory Little, Eagle Wing Books, 2009.

Iron Age America Before Columbus, by William D. Conner, Coachwhip Publications, 2009.

Lost America: The Story of Iron-Age Civilization Prior to Columbus, by Arlington H. Mallery, The Overlook Company, 1951.

Lost Cities of North & Central America, by David H. Childress, Adventures Unlimited, 1992.

Maps of the Ancient Sea Kings: Evidence of Advanced Civilization in the Ice Age, by Charles Hapgood, Adventures Unlimited, 1997.

Missing Connections: Challenging the Consensus, edited by J. Douglas Kenyon, from Atlantis Rising Anthology Library, 2016.

Mound Builders: Edgar Cayce's Forgotten Record of Ancient America by Little, Gregory L., Little, Lora H., Auken, John Van, Eagle Wing Books Inc., 2001.

Nile Valley Civilizations, by Ivan Van Sertima, Journal of African Civilizations, 1985.

The Origin Map: Discovery of a Prehistoric, Megalithic, Astrophysical Map and Sculpture of the Universe, by Thomas G. Brophy, Writers Club Press, 2002.

The Origin of Civilization: The Case of Egypt and Mesopotamia from Several Disciplines, by David C. Jones, Union Institute & University, 2007.

Origin of the Ancient Egyptians, by Cheikh Anta Diop, cited in *Great African Thinkers*, Ivan Van Sertima (ed.), Transaction Publishers, 1986.

Philosophy Podium Vol. I, by Naba L. Morondenibig, Firefly Productions, 2008.

Predynastic Egypt: An African-Centric view, by James Brunson, Illinois, Published by James Brunson II, 1991.

The Red Record, by David McCutchen, Avery Publishing Group, 1995.

The Shadow of Atlantis, by Alexander Braghine, Kessinger Publishing, 1940.

The Star of Deep Beginnings, Charles Finch, Khenti Press, 1998.

They Came Before Columbus, Ivan Van Sertima, Random House, 1975.

Research Papers & Presentations

African Origins of America, by Ra Nu, *Black Today*/Wordpress, 2013.

Algonquin Indian Genealogy, from the *Handbook of American Indians North of Mexico*, by Frederick W. Hodge, House of Representatives 59th Congress, 1st session. House Document No. 926, part 1, (Serial Set 5001), Washington, DC: Government Printing Office, 1906.

Ancient African Writing Systems and Knowledge, by Clyde Winters, online blog post, 2008.

Ancient America: Hohokam Ball Courts, Ojibwa Indians, from *Daily Kos*, Feb 2014.

Ancient Pemaquid and the Skeleton in Armor, by W. Med Stapler, *NEARA Journal*, Volume XXXII, No. 1, Summer 1998.

Atlantis in Mexico: The Mande Discovery of America, by Clyde Winters, 2013.

The Ball Game of Mesoamerica, by Mark Cartwright, from the *Ancient History Encyclopedia*, 2013.

BETWEEN THE LINES: Reading the Nazca Markings as Rituals Writ Large, by Anthony F. Aveni and Helaine Silverman, *The Sciences*, 31: 36–42, Aug. 1991.

The Discovery of the Old World by Native Americans, by Steven Sora, *Atlantis Rising* #80, March/April 2010.

Gran Vilaya, by PH Fawcett, *The Great Web of Percy Harrison Fawcett*, 1999.

The Hohokam: Who were the Hohokam? from the Tempe History Museum Online.

Hopi Tribe, from the Inter Tribal Council of Arizona. ITCA Online, 2011.

Lost Histories: The Story of New England's Stone Chambers, by Benjamin Lord, *Northern Woodlands Magazine* Online, Winter 2013.

Malians in Ancient America, by Clyde Winters 2015.

The Most Well Known Image of the Olmecs are the Olmec Heads, from the Olmec Heads Slide Show Presentation, Dr. Clyde Winters, Governors State University, 2017.

The Mound Matrix Mystery, by Ronald J. Pastore, *Atlantis Rising* #28, July/August 2001.

Native Americans in the Old World, by Steven Sora, *Atlantis Rising* #80, March/April 2010.

Precolumbian Muslims in the Americas, by Youssef Mroueh, Preparatory Committee for International Festivals to celebrate the millennium of the Muslims arrival to the Americas, 1996.

Pyramids and Temple Mounds: Mesoamerican Ceremonial Architecture in Eastern North America, by Charles R. Wicke, *American Antiquity* Vol. 30 No. 4, April 1965.

Race and Identity: Ancient Relations between Africans and Mexicans, by Clyde Winters, Governors State University College of Education.

A Revised Chronology of the Lowest Occupation Layer of the Pedra Furada Rock Shelter, Piaui, Brazil: The Pleistocene People of the Americas, by G. M. Santos et al. *Quaternary Science Reviews* Vol. 22, Issues 21-22 Nov-Dec 2003.

The Top-50 Megaliths, from The Ancient Wisdom Foundation online research facility.

Underwater Stone Formation at Bimini, Bahamas Reveals Its Secrets: Ancient Maritime Culture in Bahamas Confirmed, by Greg Little, from *Alternative Perceptions Magazine* Issue #100, April 2003.

About David Imhotep, Ph.D.

Dr. David Imhotep became interested in history with a special interest in the Black foundation of the civilizations of the world while completing his undergraduate studies at the University of Maryland. He was convinced that only by re-evaluating and restoring Africa's place in the history of the world could the physical and mental shackles and vice grip of colonialism be lifted from Africa and the United States.

Today, David Imhotep is an author, lecturer, researcher, anthrophotojournalist and the first person in the United states to hold a Ph.D. With specialization in ancient African history. His doctoral dissertation, "The Origin of Civilization: The Case of Egypt and Mesopotamia from Several Disciplines," was accepted in 2007 and will be updated and published in 2021. He has appeared in numerous television, radio, magazine, and newspaper interviews. His slide/lecture presentations contain cutting-edge data and has been described as both informative and entertaining.

He has traveled the world for the last forty years searching for information relating to the cultural heritage of Africa and the African diaspora. He has lectured widely throughout the United States, Africa, the Caribbean, South America, Central America, and Europe, and has also been cited and quoted voluminously.

For lectures, interviews, documentaries, etc., write to david.imhotep@ gmail.com.

Dr. Imhotep snorkeling above the megalithic blocks of the Bimini Road in the Bahamas. *Photography by Teresa Gray-Jones.*

Index

310, 315, 321, 322–323, 329–330, 332–334. *See also* Nubia and Nubians

Egyptian Museum, Cairo, 184, 242

Ekchuah, 187–188, 207

England. *See* British Isles

Ephorus, 178

Epigraphy (writing on stones), 118, 177

Epipaleolithic period, 291

Erikson, Leif, 285–286, 288, 312

Erik the Red, 285

Eskimo/Esquimos/Esquimau people, 58, 72, 75, 82–83, 85, 95, 145, 148–149, 169, 287, 297–298

Ethiopia and Ethiopians, 26–27, 130, 134, 247, 310, 334. *See also* Cush and Cushites

Ethiopic Ocean, 134, 333

Ethnicity or race. *See* Race or ethnicity

Etruscans, 289, 311, 331

Europe and Europeans, 1–6, 12–16, 17–18, 19, 22–23, 26–28, 31–32, 38, 41–42, 45, 59, 61, 66, 72, 73, 80–81, 83, 85, 87–88, 90–93, 95–96, 99, 100, 105, 112, 114, 122, 124, 134, 137–138, 142, 149, 151, 157, 158, 159, 160–161, 166, 172, 173, 175–179, 202, 220, 225–226, 227–230, 234, 238–240, 242–243, 244, 262, 284–293, 298, 300–303, 304–305, 309–312, 329. *See also* Vikings

Evans, Sir Arthur, 298

F

Family. *See* Human family; Languages and linguistic connections

Farming by ancient peoples in Americas, 157–162, 300

Fawcett, Col. P. H., 156

Feathered serpent, 213, 214

Fell, B., 75, 99–100, 116–117, 169, 176, 177, 220, 229–230, 239

Female Pharaoh, 125, 335

Fiji, 37

Filed teeth, 21–23

Finch, C. S., 85, 87

Finns, 86–87, 88, 89

Firestone, R., 47, 255, 261, 267, 272, 273, 281–282

Fish Fin, 189

Flint arrowheads, 241–242

Flood, post-Ice Age, xxi–xxii, xxv, xxvii, 29, 56, 68–69, 113, 193, 202, 209, 251, 254, 256, 257, 258–261, 268, 272–273, 274, 284, 307, 335

Folsom & Folsom, archaeologists, 180

Fountain of Youth, 315

Fox, 44

Fuegians, 6–7, 32–33, 73, 85–86, 88, 89–90, 149

G

Gallina River, 97, 98

Garamantes, 290

Garvey, M. M., 338

Gauls, 178, 179

Proctor, S., 276

Proctor's Road, 316, 318

Prognathic facial features, 70, 139, 240

Proto-Americans, 43, 45, 46, 56, 58–59, 61, 66, 69, 84, 86, 97–99, 118, 134–135, 147–149, 162–163

Proto-Mandings/Mandingoes, 110–111, 127, 130, 140, 144, 149, 226, 242–244, 295, 299

Proto-Saharans, 74, 110–111, 149. *See also* Proto-Mandings/Mandingoes

Proto-Viking ships, 93

Pueblos, 55, 73–74, 97–98, 115, 146–149, 163, 242–244, 326–327, 328

Pygmies, 15, 61, 75, 81, 82, 83, 87, 89, 99–100, 286

Pyramid builders, 113, 187

Pyramid of the Magician, 87–88

Pyramids, xxiii–xxvii, 18–19, 87–88, 97, 113, 118, 132, 149–151, 161, 166, 172, 183–184, 187, 189–196, 198, 199–207, 210–212, 213, 215, 217, 221, 223, 227, 232, 242, 246, 248–255, 279–280, 298–299, 311, 315, 321, 334–335, 337

Q

Qafzeh, 291

Quetzalcoatl, 187–189, 206, 213–214

Quirigua Izabel, 189

Qustul. *See* Ta-Seti

R

Ra, 118, 120

Race or ethnicity, xxvii–xxix, xxxii–xxxiii, 5, 14, 17, 23, 24, 27, 33, 49, 55, 83, 85, 86–90, 99, 112–113, 115, 126, 128–129, 134, 141, 142, 144, 146–149, 153, 167, 168, 171, 206, 236, 238, 241, 294, 296, 298, 299, 310, 312. *See also* individual races, ethnicities or cultural groups by name

Ramses, 53–54, 121, 217, 222, 322–323

Rebikoff, D., 278

Red Record (Walam Olum), 43, 44, 45–46, 58–61, 123, 168, 325

Reed boats, 12, 205, 245–246, 247–248

Reservations, Native American, 33, 43, 48

Rhacotis, Egyptian harbor of, 330

Rhesus system, 206

River craft, 127

River systems, ancient, 127, 130–131

Roanoke River Valley, 233

Rock formations, 120, 122, 123, 209, 255, 264, 267, 268, 276–278, 306–307, 317–318, 319, 330, 332

Rome and Romans, 80, 92–93, 96, 126, 142, 151, 289, 311, 331

Round skull, 57, 75, 78, 79, 99, 145

Round vs. flat Earth, 24–25

Rubber, 132, 133, 163, 198–199, 321–322

Runnels, C., 229

S

Sacsayhuaman, 221

Sahara, 26, 126–131, 202, 246, 292, 312, 314

Upcoming Titles

"Ali & Me"

Life after the Greatest Show on Earth

In the later years of Muhammad's career, many professionals were interviewed to become Mr. Ali's nutritionist. Dr. Imhotep Ph.D. had just finished an advanced degree in nutrition and was also a former athlete—a football starter at Collage Park's University of Maryland, an NCAA Division I program. After interviewing several candidates, Dr. Imhotep was chosen because he was found to be the best person qualified for the position.

In a "sneak peek" at this "Ali & Me" book is a collection of photos and wonderful experiences the author had while being employed by Mr. Ali. A long list of colorful experiences, (*very* colorful experiences if you knew this man) fills this story of being part of Mr. Ali's "entourage," working and traveling with "The Greatest" for his last six fights.

Many herbs, as well as fruit and vegetable juice recipes are included that Dr. Imhotep squeezed for Muhammad with his "Norwalk Hydraulic Press-Juice Extractor," to give him more energy, stamina, and weight loss. David also sparred with members of "The Muhammad Ali Boxing Team."

What an experience with one of the "Greatest Human Beings I ever met!"

This book is also about:

Ali's entourage, "The *Terrible* 10" he called us:

Howard Bingham "Ali's Best Friend"

Angelo Dundee "Trainer"

Drew Bundini Brown "The Motivator"

Dr. Ferdie Pachecio M.D. "The Fight Doctor"

Lana Shabazz "The Great Cook"

Gene Kilroy "The Facilitator"

Howard "Pat" Patterson "Security"

James Anderson "Security"

Louis Sarria "Masseur"

Dr. David Imhotep Ph.D. "Nutritionist"

David sparring with "The Muhammad Ali Boxing Team." *Photo taken at the "World Famous 5ᵗʰ Street Gym in Miami" by Teresa Gray-Jones.*

#5 David returning a kickoff for the University of Maryland Terrapins, College Park, Md. in 2001. *Photo taken by Teresa Gray-Jones.*

"The Origin of Civilization"

Highlights of Ancient African History: The Greatest Story NEVER Told

Dr. Imhotep's Dissertation

The definition of "Power": The ability to define and shape reality and have others accept your definition of reality as if it were their own. (Author unknown)

The definition of "History": History is important, for those who do not know their history are doomed to repeat the mistakes of the past. (Quoted by Winston Churchill, and before him, by George Santayana.)

In this historic story, the popular media declares that Mesopotamia was the "Cradle of Civilization." In this study the author investigates the primacy of civilization—was it Mesopotamia or Egypt? The answer shall clearly arise after reading this interdisciplinary study, done from the following disciplines: Anthropology, Archaeology, Astronomy, Cartography, Epigraphy, Linguistics, Mathematics, and Watercraft were used in this intensive investigation.

Through the use of these disciplines, the cultural history of Egypt and Mesopotamia was studied, compared, and contrasted. The evidence that was found uncovered exclusively, that Egypt's power reigned supreme.

I wish to make it known, that I take no credit for this information. It comes, first from the Creator, to whom I give thanks for giving me the ability, the desire, and the drive to go after the information presented in this book.

I also wish to make it known that this material is not meant to give fuel to the fire of Black prejudice, for prejudice, no matter who the perpetrator is, is negative, damaging, selfish, and psychologically harmful. I was always taught, "All White folks are not prejudiced, and not all Black folks are good."

One of the perspectives this information will shift is that it will help balance out the Caucasians who think they are superior, and the people of African descent who think they are inferior.

Studying the work of several knowledgeable people who conducted research for many years has allowed the author to have a better view. This does not mean however, that the author is superior to any of the others. It just allows the author to see far more, and clearer than those without such a view.

In attempting to make this work precise, the author has not been able to go into any great detail. Therefore the author urges the reader to read the books that have been the best sources to possibly use. Hopefully, you, the reader, will begin to stock your bookshelves at home and use these great books as a guide and reference for:

1. Your own knowledge
2. To teach your family
3. To share with your relatives and friends
4. To make sure that world history includes ancient Black history

Made in the USA
Columbia, SC
21 January 2025

52196815R00222